MS. PRIME MINISTER

Gender, Media, and Leadership

Ms. Prime Minister offers both solace and words of caution for women politicians. After closely analysing the media coverage of four former prime ministers – Kim Campbell of Canada, Jenny Shipley and Helen Clark of New Zealand, and Julia Gillard of Australia – Linda Trimble concludes that reporting both reinforces and contests unfair gender norms. News about women leaders gives undue attention to their gender identities, bodies, and family lives. Men in equivalent positions, however, are also treated to evaluations of their gendered personas. Moreover, Trimble finds, some media accounts expose sexism and authenticate women's performances of leadership.

    Ms. Prime Minister provides important insight into the news frameworks that work to deny or confer political legitimacy. It concludes with advice designed to inform the gender strategies of women who aspire to political leadership roles and the reporting techniques of the journalists who cover them.

LINDA TRIMBLE is a professor in the Department of Political Science at the University of Alberta.

Ms. Prime Minister

Gender, Media, and Leadership

LINDA TRIMBLE

UNIVERSITY OF TORONTO PRESS
Toronto Buffalo London

© University of Toronto Press 2017
Toronto Buffalo London
www.utorontopress.com
Printed in Canada

ISBN 978-1-4426-4550-9 (cloth)   ISBN 978-1-4426-1363-8 (paper)

♾ Printed on acid-free, 100% post-consumer recycled paper with
vegetable-based inks.

Library and Archives Canada Cataloguing in Publication

Trimble, Linda, 1959–, author
Ms. Prime Minister : gender, media, and leadership / Linda Trimble.

Includes bibliographical references and index.
ISBN 978-1-4426-4550-9 (cloth). – ISBN 978-1-4426-1363-8 (paper)

1. Women politicians – Press coverage.   2. Press and politics.   3. Mass
media – Political aspects.   4. Political leadership.   5. Sexism in political
culture.   I. Title.

HQ1236.T75 2017   320.082   C2017-906089-9

This book has been published with the help of a grant from the Federation
for the Humanities and Social Sciences, through the Awards to Scholarly
Publications Program, using funds provided by the Social Sciences and
Humanities Research Council of Canada.

University of Toronto Press acknowledges the financial assistance to its
publishing program of the Canada Council for the Arts and the Ontario
Arts Council, an agency of the Government of Ontario.

Canada Council   Conseil des Arts
for the Arts   du Canada

ONTARIO ARTS COUNCIL
CONSEIL DES ARTS DE L'ONTARIO
an Ontario government agency
un organisme du gouvernement de l'Ontario

Funded by the   Financé par le
Government   gouvernement
of Canada   du Canada

Canadä

I could not have completed this manuscript without my husband, Robert's, love and encouragement. In addition to being incredibly understanding when I locked myself in my office for hours – or days – on end, especially during the final writing marathon, he always listened carefully while I tested some of the more outrageous propositions on him. Robert never gave my arguments an easy pass, and his ardent and sometimes relentless interrogations helped considerably more than I let on at the time. Honey, this one's for you.

Ms. Prime Minister is also dedicated to the courageous women who governed Canada, New Zealand, and Australia with such intelligence and aplomb. Because of the strength and perseverance of Kim Campbell, Jenny Shipley, Helen Clark, and Julia Gillard, it will be easier for all the women who will, one day, follow in their footsteps.

Contents

Tables

Acknowledgments

This book took a very long time to come to fruition. I am profoundly grateful for the support of the University of Toronto Press's acquisitions editor, Daniel Quinlan, who championed the manuscript from the beginning and expressed unwavering confidence in my ability to get it done. By keeping in touch, asking to read sections as they were drafted, and offering encouraging comments as the chapters dribbled in, Daniel gently pushed me towards the metaphorical finish line. Working with the promotion and production teams at the Press as they steered *Ms. Prime Minister* through the various stages of the publication process was an absolute pleasure. I especially want to thank associate managing editor Wayne Herrington, marketing coordinator Breanna Muir, and ace copy editor Stephanie Stone.

Funding from the Social Sciences and Humanities Research Council of Canada, and additional support from the University of Alberta's Faculty of Arts and McCalla Professorships program, made this project feasible. Thanks to generous financial assistance, I had the opportunity to work with a bevvy of enthusiastic, and exceptionally diligent, graduate students. Natasja Treiberg served as the lead research assistant for four years, taking charge of the New Zealand component of the project and orchestrating the work of the University of Alberta team members. I could not have completed the research without Natasja's exemplary organizational skills, keen intelligence, and generosity of time and spirit. Sue Girard did a stellar job of gathering and coding the Canadian media coverage, Bailey Gerrits deftly compiled qualitative and qualitative data from the Australian news reports, and Elizabeth Macve helped with content analysis of the 2008 New Zealand election stories. Sara Daniels spent a fruitful summer researching the biographies of

Campbell, Clark, and Shipley, and Gabrielle Betts patiently worked the interlibrary loan system and the microfilm reader to retrieve articles not yet available on news databases. Liz Moore, a student at Victoria University in Wellington, New Zealand, went to the National Library to dig up news stories that could only be accessed there.

Many colleagues at the University of Alberta and scholars from around the globe generously offered their wisdom and expertise as I presented various bits and pieces of this volume at invited lectures, research colloquia, and scholarly conferences in Canada, Australia, New Zealand, the United States, England, and Japan. Thanks to a visit arranged by Marian Sawer and the Australian National University's Gender Institute, I had the pleasure of testing chapter 5, Body Politics, on an Australian audience. The two anonymous reviewers recruited by the Press to assess the manuscript went well beyond the call of duty, furnishing many thoughtful insights and helpful suggestions for revision. This book is infinitely better because of their interventions.

I am also especially appreciative of New Zealand colleague Jennifer Curtin's friendship and sage advice. Jennifer kindly included me in her department's speakers' series and two of the research symposia she organized at the University of Auckland, and she introduced me to the Chapman Archives, where I was able to view television coverage of Shipley's and Clark's leadership "coups." Tim Gordon, the Chapman's archivist, patiently helped me find the materials and navigate the rather arcane video equipment.

Sharing one's angst and dreams is invaluable when wrestling with a big writing project. Shannon Sampert, Kalowatie Deonandan, Judy Garber, Lori Thorlakson, Angelia Wagner, Daisy Raphael, Mary MacDonald, Anna Yeatman, and Debby Waldman always listened patiently, with kindness and encouragement. And Jennifer Hsu bolstered my spirits whenever I agonized about the length of time I was taking to complete the manuscript; cocktails at the Hotel MacDonald with Jennifer bear considerable responsibility for the realization of this book. Finally, I owe a very special and heartfelt thank you to Robert and Rob, Colleen and Kathy Trimble, and the Crompton clan, who gave the precious gift of time spent with loving family members.

MS. PRIME MINISTER

Gender, Media, and Leadership

Chapter One

Introduction: Gender, Media, and Leadership

I want to say just a few remarks about being the first woman to serve [as prime minister of Australia]. There's been a lot of analysis about the so-called gender wars, and me playing the so-called gender card, because heavens knows no one noticed I was a woman until I raised it. But against that background, I do want to say about all of these issues, *the reaction to being the first female prime minister does not explain everything about my prime ministership, nor does it explain nothing about my prime ministership ... it explains some things*, and it is for the nation to think in a sophisticated way about those shades of grey.[1]

Julia Gillard's reflections on the role played by gender in shaping public perceptions of her term in office neatly capture the big point of this book, which analyses news coverage of women prime ministers in Australia, Canada, and New Zealand. Gender matters. The stories told about women leaders by the news media reflect widely circulated gender norms and assumptions. Reporting about Gillard's tumultuous term in office used her gender identity as a reference point when relaying how she unseated incumbent Prime Minister Kevin Rudd in 2010, quickly called an election, and led a minority Labor government for three years before Rudd staged a dramatic comeback. Gillard's status as the first woman prime minister of Australia was frequently marked in newspaper stories about her entry and exit from the prime minister's post, and her physical appearance and marital situation garnered considerable attention over the course of her time in office. Most strikingly, when Gillard dared to speak out in Parliament about the hostile and often pornographic representations directed at her by opponents, she was accused of unfairly playing the gender card and waging a destructive gender war. For the Australian press, gender mattered greatly when a woman was in the prime minister's office.

News coverage of Gillard's rise highlighted her gender identity, despite the fact that she was by no means the first woman to become prime minister of a Westminster-style democracy,[2] nor was she the first to secure office through a general election win. Sri Lanka's Sirimavo Bandaranaike assumed the post in 1960, followed by India's Indira Gandhi in 1966, and the United Kingdom's Margaret Thatcher in 1979. In fact, Gillard trod in the footsteps of a small but growing list of electorally successful women prime ministers, including Thatcher, who governed for eleven years; Gandhi, who boasted almost fifteen years in office; and Helen Clark, who served as New Zealand's prime minister for nine successive years. While Gillard's rise was a first for Australia, by 2010 it was no longer unthinkable for a Westminster parliament to be led by a woman.

Indeed, Australia lagged both Canada and New Zealand in this regard. In Canada, Kim Campbell won the leadership of the governing Progressive Conservative (PC) Party in 1993, briefly assuming the prime minister's role before calling, and losing, a general election. Her term in office was short, at just over four months. Jenny Shipley became the first woman prime minister of New Zealand in 1997 when she replaced the leader of the governing National Party, and she held the post for two years before losing the 1999 election to Helen Clark. Clark is the lone woman in this group who did not step into the prime minister's office when she became party leader. She successfully challenged an incumbent for the Labour Party leadership in 1993, when the party formed the Official Opposition (most competitive second party). Despite a narrow loss in the 1996 election, Clark led her party into four additional campaigns, winning three of them and serving as New Zealand's prime minister from 1999 until 2008. Clark stands out as the most successful of the four women included in my study and, indeed, as one of the longest-serving women elected to govern a Western, industrialized, democratic nation. Each of these women was represented as a norm-breaker in news reporting about their careers. Each embodied the news value of unusualness, as the first women to occupy, or be elected to, the prime minister's office in Canada, New Zealand, and Australia.

Unfortunately, women party and government leaders cannot yet anticipate news-mediated normalization of their candidacies, career paths, and achievements. *News-mediated normalization* means that the perceived ordinariness of a woman in power is communicated by news accounts of her leadership. Normalization happens when a phenomenon is no longer seen as extraordinary, but women's leadership is far from commonplace. The rise of a woman to the prime minister's role continues to be heralded for its unusualness. In eleven advanced parliamentary democracies with stable party systems, including Australia, Canada, and New Zealand, only 14 per cent of the national party leaders selected between 1965 and 2013 were women (O'Brien 2015, 1024). Equally uncommon are women presidents and prime ministers (Jalalzai 2010). At the time of writing, there are only eighteen women serving as heads of government for almost 200 nations.[3] On November 8, 2016, the world was poised to witness Hillary Clinton break the ultimate glass ceiling, but her hopes of attaining the presidency of the United States were shattered. Most countries have never had female leaders, and when women do succeed, they typically serve in the role for less than four years.[4]

Although women's representation in elected political institutions has grown, in all but a few nations most legislators and government leaders are men. Based on current trends, the majority of elected officials in Australia, Canada, and New Zealand will continue to be men for decades to come. Presently, women hold 26.0 per cent of the seats in Canada's House of Commons, 26.7 per cent in Australia's lower house, and 31.4 per cent in New Zealand's House of Representatives.[5] These levels of representation are better than the global average of 22 per cent, but nowhere near gender parity. As a result, the mere fact of a woman prime minister's gender remains a significant point of discussion. That opponents, journalists, and voters alike talk about gender when a woman holds the highest political office is unsurprising.

Why should political scientists, activists, partisans, and aspiring politicians be concerned about media representations of political leadership? Simply put, most of what the public knows about politics and politicians is gleaned from the media. As Taras maintains, denying the considerable power of the media is "the equivalent of arguing that the Earth is flat" (1990, 3). The media serve as a crucial intermediary "between the citizenry, on the one hand, and the institutions involved in government, electoral processes, or, more generally, opinion formation on the other" (Strömbäck 2008, 230). Consequently, the news media play a significant role in introducing, describing, and evaluating political leaders; circulating norms of effective leadership; and constructing leadership prototypes (Kahn and Goldenberg 1991, 181). Mediated descriptions of women's political ambitions and fortunes provide a crucial backdrop against which emerging candidates make decisions about whether to seek leadership roles. The intrusive, critical, and even degrading ways in which some women leaders are represented in mainstream and social media can serve as a deterrent for politically ambitious women (see Anderson 2011; Johnson 2015). On the other hand, reporting about the sexist derision levelled at those who seek the highest political positions may encourage women's candidacies. Hillary Clinton's bid for the White House in 2016 sparked an intensely misogynistic backlash, prompting scholars who study women's political representation to worry about its impact on women's political ambitions.[6] Yet organizations devoted to persuading women to run for office in the United States have reported a surge in interest, with thousands of women signing up for training programs since Clinton's defeat.[7] When high-profile women politicians are in the news, ideologies of gender are on display, for better or worse.

Ms. Prime Minister provides longitudinal, comparative, and holistic accounts of media representations of four women prime ministers: Campbell, Shipley, Clark, and Gillard. Because my goal is to map the diverse and complex ways in which gender is invoked and politicized in news stories about them, I examined reporting about these women throughout their tenures as party leader. News stories were gathered at four crucial junctures: winning the party leadership role, contesting election campaign(s), governing, and departing from the prime minister's office. In Gillard's case, I included coverage of the so-called sexism and misogyny speech she delivered in Parliament because, in their responses, members of the Australian press corps frequently and overtly referenced gender through the use of playing-the-gender-card and gender war(s) metaphors. Newspaper articles about the men who challenged three of the women prime ministers[8] for the top job during election campaigns offered useful comparisons and challenged some of the conventional wisdom about media coverage of men leaders. Using both quantitative and qualitative methods, I analysed 2,550 news items, 1,797 of which gave substantive attention to the four women prime ministers and 753 written about the six men who were in serious contention to defeat Campbell, Clark, and Gillard during federal election campaigns. Despite differences in their partisan affiliations, political contexts, pathways to office, and electoral longevity, culturally and politically constructed understandings about gender and political leadership were expressed in news coverage of each of these women prime ministers.

As a departure from much of the literature on news reporting about women politicians, I argue that media attention to gender does not invariably perpetuate and reinforce "masculinist assumptions about politics and politicians" (Kaneva and Ibroscheva 2015, 226). By highlighting the unusualness of women in political office, news coverage draws attention to women's political under-representation, exposing gendered power hierarchies and questioning the fairness of democratic processes and institutions. Moreover, women's everyday exercise of power makes observable the deeply entrenched association of leadership with men and norms of hegemonic masculinity. By winning office and enacting legitimate government authority, women prime ministers present the site, and sight, of woman as leader (Clare 2002). This, in and of itself, unsettles conventional understandings about gender roles, attributes, and competencies. Reporting about men politicians similarly unmasks gendered norms informing political leadership. As Judith Butler emphasizes, in *Undoing Gender*, gender "is the mechanism by which notions of masculine and feminine are produced and naturalized, but gender might very well be the apparatus by which such terms are deconstructed and denaturalized" (2004, 42). Indeed, the four women prime ministers whose media coverage is assessed in this book were, to varying degrees, represented as powerful, commanding, and convincing in their performances of political leadership. Although their ability to exercise power in an authentic and comprehensible manner was questioned because of their gender, news coverage occasionally challenged the association of political leadership with normative understandings of men and masculinity.

Ms. Prime Minister contributes to the burgeoning literature on gendered mediation by paying close attention to the narratives used to describe women prime ministers throughout their terms in office, comparing reporting about women and equivalent men leaders, and observing the ways in which stories about leadership both shore up *and* disrupt gender-based norms and conventions. By studying news coverage of women prime ministers from three nations across their entire political careers, I advance the scholarship about mediated politics and draw out its relevance to the real world of politics. Identifying the lessons to be learned from media representations of women who pursue the top jobs, regardless of the outcome, will expand the study of gendered mediation. In the conclusion of this volume, I present a series of recommendations based on the findings gleaned from my study. That section is designed to help would-be leaders develop gender strategies for political communications and to serve as a guide for journalists who aim to cover all candidates fairly.

Gendered Mediation

One of the primary goals of this book is to complicate and nuance the concept of *gendered mediation* in ways that are theoretically and empirically valuable. To this end, I offer some new ways of thinking about, observing, and analysing "the manner in which the mediated presentation of politics is gendered" (Sreberny-Mohammadi and Ross 1996, 103). The concept *gender* captures "any social construction having to do with the male/female distinction, including those constructions that separate 'female' bodies from 'male' bodies" (Nicholson 1994, 79). Butler refers to this as the two-sex/gender binary (1993, 30–2), arguing that distinctions between male and female, and homosexual and heterosexual, are symbolic, discursive paradigms. Yet they regulate our everyday lives in powerful ways through "constellations of meaning that are politically contextualized and constructed" (Beckwith 2005, 130–1). The alleged differences between bodies are enacted, thus exaggerated, through the performance of gender, creating an illusion of their own stability. We understand gender through the "regularized and constrained repetition of norms" (Butler 1993, 95), These norms, called "gender regulations" (Butler 2004, 40–3), reflect the principles of social organization operative in a given time and place. But as Butler takes care to note, "gender is not always constituted coherently or consistently in different historical contexts," and "gender intersects with racial, class, ethnic, sexual and regional modalities of discursively constituted identities" (Butler 2006, 4). In other words, the norms guiding expression and comprehension of gender identities are shaped by context, place-based specificities, and the impact of other socially and culturally resonant identities. White, able-bodied professional women who identify as heterosexual experience their gender differently than do racial minority women, poor women, disabled women, and those who express alternative sexualities.

Mediation is a complex process involving the selection, production, and consumption of media products (Allen 2004, 4). Self-presentation, the "instrumental use of mass media by political actors," is a key form of mediation (Sampert and Trimble 2010, 2). So too is audience reception of the stories told by journalists – that is, how people react to, digest, and perhaps even change their thinking and behaviour in response to the news. But both have a recursive relationship with gendered media content, such as news stories. *Gendered news* – which I define as news reports that explicitly or implicitly invoke gender regulations – informs audience perceptions of and attitudes towards politicians (Aalberg and Jenssen 2007; Dolan 2014; Kahn 1992). Also, candidates' articulations of their personas and ideas are reflected in news presentations of gender and leadership (Beail and Longworth 2013; Goodyear-Grant 2009, 2013; Tolley 2016). For example, US vice-presidential nominee Sarah Palin emphasized her status as a mother, coining the phrase "mama grizzly" to foreground her alignment with the patriarchal family form, while at the same time highlighting strength and determination (Loke, Harp, and Bachmann 2011, 213). These themes were reflected in media coverage and resonated with conservative elements of the American public.

Politicians' attempts to control the message are not always successful. The news media do not by any means report every incident, nor do journalists and editors simply act as a conveyor belt for information. In this sense, mediation refers to the techniques used by mainstream news media to transform events and issues into attention-grabbing accounts (Sampert and Trimble 2010, 1–4). Through selection, filtering, framing, and evaluation, happenings "out there" are narrated for the public. Stories are chosen for their newsworthiness, condensed to fit a tight news format (a few hundred words or a few minutes of broadcast time), framed to emphasize certain meanings and to ensure that readers capture the gist of an event or issue, and assessed in a manner often designed to convey judgments about the characters and actions of politicians. *Framing* is a deliberate process of selection and emphasis that "determines what is included and excluded, what is salient and what is unimportant" (Cappella and Jamieson 1997, 38). Frames organize and simplify information, thereby fitting complex and novel events or issues into familiar categories or stereotypes, and cueing cultural norms and social assumptions (Entman 1993, 53). The choice of frame shapes how readers interpret the text (Tolley 2016, 17–18). As a result, news content – the "discursive form of the message" – "has a privileged position in the communicative exchange" (Hall 1980, 118).

The concept of *gendered mediation* captures the ways in which processes and products of news-making reflect gender norms, binaries, and power relations. Gendered mediation represents the intersection of gender regulations, performance of gender, and media practices. So it is important to emphasize that while sexual identities have multiplied and the rigid boundaries around gender have been ruptured by gender fluidity and by transgender, intersex, queer, multiple, and non-binary identities (Monro 2005, 12–15), gender continues to be comprehended and enacted according to relatively fixed dualities. Bodies, traits, skills, and roles are perceived as male or female, feminine or masculine. Few elected politicians challenge the parameters of sex/gender divides, and even when they do, alternative performances of sexuality and/or gender "are often recuperated back into a two-sex/gender schema for the purpose of 'making sense' of these performances" (Holland 2006, 27). For example, popular accounts of trans identities reinforce the two-sex/gender binary with phrases such as "trapped in the wrong body" (Engdahl 2014). By insisting that we understand people as either male or female, variant body experiences are dismissed as invalid or incomprehensible.

Women's participation in politics is still comprehended through the lens of gender binaries. Although women are now represented in elected political office, the public man/private woman binary continues to configure how individuals think about and engage in political life (Siltanen and Stanworth 1984). This form of dualistic thinking associates men and the performance of masculinity with the formal political realm and agentic traits like rationality, aggression, detachment, and independence. In contrast, women and allegedly feminine, communal qualities such as emotionality, nurturance, passivity, and dependency are tied to the domestic world of family, care, and intimacy (Brescoll 2016; Cirksena and Cuklanz 1992; Hoyt and Murphy 2016). Because the public man/private woman binary informs gender regulations and performances, women politicians are perceived to be "stronger on 'compassion' traits and issues while men politicians are favourably associated with being tough, assertive, decisive, and strong on issues such as the economy and foreign policy" (Murray 2010b, 19). When social and political life is conceptualized in this manner, the very real politicization of domestic spaces and routines is ignored, along with personalization of political spaces and the everyday interdependence of these allegedly separate realms.

The *gendered mediation thesis* posits that news consistently upholds the public man/private woman binary by situating women as anomalous outsiders to politics (Ross and Comrie 2012, 971). This argument rests on three propositions. First, "the news media reflect the culture in which they are situated," and this culture is imbued with patriarchal norms and assumptions (Goodyear-Grant 2013, 5–6). Gender regulations will therefore be expressed in news stories, opinion pieces, and editorials. Second, because men are over-represented in formal political spaces and roles, political news adopts a distinctly masculine narrative, accepting men politicians as the norm and scripting politics as a masculine playing field or battleground (Gidengil and Everitt 1999; Rakow and Kranich 1991; Sreberny and van Zoonen 2000). Third, and following directly from the first two propositions, "women politicians are presented differently than their male colleagues as a function of the fact that they are women" (Goodyear-Grant 2013, 4). Even when explicit stereotypes or overtly sexist impositions are absent, gendered forms of news selection, framing, and evaluation instantiate men's dominance of political life (Gidengil and Everitt 1999, 49).

A considerable amount of this now flourishing body of work on gendered mediation is reviewed in this volume, so here I offer but a few examples of the ways in which women politicians are depicted differently from men in news accounts of their identities and political performances. All but the most competitive, novel, or high-profile women politicians are typically found to be less visible in the news (Bystrom, Brown, and Fiddelke 2013; Hooghe, Jacobs, and Claes 2015; Vos 2013; for an exception, see Jalalzai 2006). Women politicians tend to be evaluated more harshly than equivalent men politicians (Bystrom and Dimitrova 2014) and presented as less likely to win office and as less competent, experienced, and suitable for the top political jobs (Byerly and Ross 2006; Gidengil and Everitt 2000; Kahn 1996; Lawrence and Rose 2010). Framing of women situates gender identity as an important aspect of their political personas (Falk 2010; Heldman, Carroll, and Olson 2005; Sreberny-Mohammadi and Ross 1996) and reflects distinctly gendered tropes, such as sex object, beauty queen, mother, and Iron Maiden (Alexander-Floyd 2008; Anderson and Sheeler 2005; Goodyear-Grant 2013).

While I accept each of these propositions as valid and provide quite a lot of evidence to support them in the chapters to follow, I argue that because gender dualisms are artificial and unstable social constructs, they can be exposed as such through news mediation of political life. Gender regulations are socially and discursively produced, so words and deeds can unsettle the lines of demarcation between woman/ man, public/private, and feminine/masculine. It is crucial to avoid reifying hegemonic gender schemas when theorizing and observing gendered mediation, thereby "reestablishing the gender order" being criticized (Lünenborg and Maier 2015, 183). For instance, measuring how often news stories associate women politicians with "feminine" and men politicians with "masculine" characteristics, behaviours, and policy issues tends to mask the ways in which certain performances and ideas cannot be slotted into either category because they trouble, or transgress, the boundaries of two-sex/gender schemas. As Butler argues, "to the extent that gender norms are reproduced, they are invoked and cited by bodily practices that also have the capacity to alter norms in the course of their citation" (2004, 52). One of the most consequential conduits for the citation and evaluation of gender norms is the mass media. Thus, while "gendering continues to be a constitutive aspect of political reporting" (Lünenborg and Maier 2015, 192), it has the potential to expose and even transgress gender binaries. Studies of gendered mediation should allow for the possibility of resistance and change through the enactment of political leadership and through news accounts of these performances.

Often overlooked in the gendered mediation literature's mapping of "normative journalistic practices that rely on social and cultural norms of feminine and masculine roles to tell stories" (Harp, Loke, and Bachmann 2017, 229) is how some of the professional practices and processes of news making, especially qualities associated with the "unlovable press," might work to expose and upset normative understandings of gender and politics. For instance, the sensationalism evident in the tabloid press, and the shift towards "politainment" and celebritization in broadsheets and on television, are widely criticized for "dumbing down" the news by personalizing and trivializing politics (van Zoonen 2005, 1–15). But as I show in the chapters to follow, the willingness of journalists to emphasize the emotive, sensational, and dramatic aspects of events; revel in conflict; "afflict the powerful"; and challenge conventional opinions and interpretations (Schudson 2005) can disrupt power hierarchies and taken-for-granted assumptions. Bringing emotions and drama into stories about political leadership implies that individualism, detachment, and cool rationality, qualities typically associated with men and norms of hegemonic masculinity, are not the only qualities required for success. Nurturing political relationships and making emotional connections with voters require different skills, often falsely aligned with women and hegemonic performances of femininity, and these qualities may be brought into view when women leaders enter the picture. The media's obsession with conflict, and predilection for reifying and glorying in the spectacle of gladiatorial combat, is argued to cast women as outsiders to the competition. But by placing leaders on a metaphorical battlefield where they (rhetorically) fight to the death for electoral supremacy, the war metaphors so widely used in election news coverage associate women with strategic thinking, assertiveness, and heroism. Finally, journalists' cynicism about the motivations of politicians, coupled with the professional practice of offering more than one version of events, can have the effect of challenging gendered forms of conventional wisdom, especially when sexism is exposed. When gender becomes the story, as is often the case with women prime ministers, journalists have an opportunity to interrogate the parameters of gender, politics, and leadership.

Feminist critical discourse analysis provides the theoretical foundation for my analysis because it attends to the discursive (re)production of gendered power relations (Lazar 2005, 11). *Discourses* are sets of "meanings, metaphors, representations, images, stories, statements and so on that in some way together produce a particular version of events" (Burr 1995, 48). Since socially and politically consequential ideas are produced "in and through discourse" (Hall 1980, 121), critical discourse analysis identifies themes, rhetorical devices, lexical choices, linguistic structures, and value claims reflected in and created by discourses (Trimble and Treiberg 2015, 228). This approach is particularly attentive to the ways in which discourses reproduce understandings about power and dominance (Fairclough 2001; van Dijk 1991, 1993, 2008). Because power relations are often expressed through metaphors (Carver and Pikalo 2008, 4), and my study examined several persistent and politically resonant metaphors, I blended critical metaphor analysis with critical discourse analysis to explore how metaphoric language works to "reproduce or transform relations of power as well as relations of meaning" (Mottier 2008, 189). I also wanted to extend the gendered mediation thesis by remaining open to the subversive potential of news discourses: in Butler's terms, to acknowledge that gender regulations can be "undone" (2004) or, at the very least, exposed as political impositions (Hall 1980, 124–5). Feminist approaches to performing critical discourse identify "the complex, subtle, and sometimes not so subtle, ways in which frequently taken-for-granted gendered assumptions and hegemonic power relations are discursively produced, sustained, negotiated, *and challenged* in different contexts and communities" (Lazar 2007, 142; emphasis mine). Adopting this theoretical framework helps reveal the ways in which representations of political leadership may both sustain and rupture gender binaries, and reinforce or critique gendered power imbalances.

Situating discourses within their relevant settings is a key feature of critical discourse analysis because socially and culturally produced meanings are embedded in, and reflect, these contexts. I wanted to see whether important parallels and variations in the political pathways and experiences of the women prime ministers of Canada, New Zealand, and Australia shaped the discourses about their identities and their capacity to enact authoritative leadership. The next section explains and justifies the case studies, describing each of the four prime ministers' pathways to power and identifying important similarities and differences in their personal lives, political environments, and degrees of success. These contextual factors, I argue, shaped the mediated representations of Campbell, Shipley, Clark, and Gillard in important ways.

Ms. Prime Minister: The Leaders and Their Contexts

Case Studies

I chose to analyse the news coverage of those who followed in the footsteps of the first woman prime minister of an English-speaking parliamentary system, the legendary Margaret Thatcher, who governed the United Kingdom for eleven years. Canada, Australia, and New Zealand offered fruitful case studies. Shortly after Thatcher's departure from the premiership in 1990, Kim Campbell became Canada's first woman prime minister for a short time in 1993. Two women rose to the top in New Zealand, with Jenny Shipley governing the country from 1997 to 1999 and Helen Clark holding three terms in office: 1999 to 2008. In 2010, Julia Gillard ascended to the prime minister's post in Australia, serving for three years. Canada and Australia are among the nations with one woman making the history books, while New Zealand stands out for its two successive female prime ministers. Unfortunately, this manuscript was drafted before Theresa May, who secured the Conservative Party leadership left open by Prime Minister David Cameron's post-Brexit resignation, was sworn in as Britain's second woman prime minister, and the book was about to go to press when Labour leader Jacinda Ardern became the third woman to enter the Prime Minister's Office in New Zealand. It will be interesting to see whether May's and Ardern's experiences with the press are less centred on their gender, looks, and family lives than was the case for Campbell, Shipley, Clark, and Gillard. Somehow I doubt it, not least because of the intense focus on Ardern's relative youth and likelihood of bearing a child while in office, and a long-standing media fetish for May's footwear. For example, early reports about May featured headlines like this one: "Theresa shows her steel: Metal toe-capped shoe-wearing PM stamps her authority on the Tories."[9]

Reporting about Thatcher was not included in this study because she stands apart as an extreme case, a first of firsts, a leader who "acquired an iconic status" because of her gender identity (Nunn 2002, 15). Neither Thatcher's circumstances nor her approach to gender politics has been replicated. She won the leadership of the British Conservative Party in 1975, nearly two decades before Kim Campbell followed suit in Canada. Unique because she secured the helm of a right-wing party at a time when women politicians were an extremely rare breed and women government leaders almost unheard of, Thatcher had to "struggle against many of the sexist prejudices of her day to achieve her political ambitions" (Purvis 2013, 1014). Sexism persists, but Campbell, Shipley, Clark, and Gillard – and now May – became prime minister at a time when women's presence in legislatures was growing and women in leadership roles were no longer strikingly anomalous. And while Thatcher steadfastly refused to promote gender equality measures or to advance women within the party and government (Campbell 2015, 47), the women who have followed her reflect new sensibilities about gender equality. The four women in my sample did not hesitate to stand as role models for women and support women's political participation. Similarly, Britain's May has been spotted wearing a T-shirt declaring, "This is what a feminist looks like."[10]

Heather Nunn argues that Thatcher's "ambivalent placing as woman and as masterful masculine political leader crystallized the gendered demarcations that underpin social being" (2002, 18). In other words, Thatcher both consolidated and reshaped notions of gender and political power. She signified and epitomized the power-holding woman, but her ideology and governing style stood out as decidedly antithetical to women's social, economic, and political advancement. Arguably Thatcher's most discursively potent legacy is the "Iron Lady" epithet with which she was branded (Laher 2014, 108). As a result, powerful women politicians are framed as "Iron Maidens" when they act assertively and decisively, or violate codes of exaggerated femininity (Goodyear-Grant 2013, 65). Each of the four women prime ministers discussed in this volume was equated with Thatcher, notwithstanding obvious ideological differences in the cases of Clark and Gillard, who led centre-left parties.

Unsurprisingly, mentions of her notorious predecessor peppered coverage of Britain's second woman in the top job. "The Tory Party may have found another Iron Lady in Theresa May," exclaimed the *Daily Telegraph*.[11] So while Thatcher is not formally part of this study, her iconic image and its mediated resonances are evident in reporting about women who lead national governments, regardless of their partisan stripe.

This study takes a comparative case study approach to analysing news coverage of Canada's, Australia's, and New Zealand's women prime ministers (Bahry 1991; George and Bennett 2006). There is a strong "family resemblance" among the three nations (Sawer, Tremblay, and Trimble 2006, 2). As former British colonies, each features a modified version of the Westminster-style parliamentary system. All are constitutional monarchies, with appointed governors general acting as the Queen's representative and formal head of state, and prime ministers exercising executive authority. Their political institutions reflect the Westminster inheritance of representative democracy, responsible parliamentary government, and strong party discipline. Other similarities include an elected lower house, in which executive power is located, and legacies of settler colonialism, which shape political institutions, relationships, debates, and policies. There are notable political differences among these nations, however. Reflecting vast differences in geography and population size,[12] New Zealand is a unitary state, while Canada and Australia adopted federal systems of government. New Zealand abolished its upper house in 1951 and now has a unicameral Parliament. Australia and Canada are bicameral systems, with Australia electing and Canada appointing senators. In addition, variations in the nature of party and electoral systems shape political-opportunity structures for women as well as media narratives about electoral politics.

All three nations now feature multi-party systems, but in practice only two parties compete for power, while the rest achieve varying degrees of representation in the lower house, styled the House of Commons in Canada and the House of Representatives in Australia and New Zealand. In Canada, the (Progressive) Conservative[13] and Liberal parties have alternated in office. In New Zealand, the Labour Party has competed with the National Party, and in Australia power shifts back and forth between the Labor Party and the Liberal-National Coalition (hereafter referred to as the Coalition). As a result, pathways to executive office at the national level have been restricted to two political parties in each country. The party winning the plurality of the seats is invited to form the government, and the leader of that party, by convention, becomes prime minister. As Beckwith emphasizes, for "parliamentary systems, the major path to prime minister is through the gateway of party leader" (2015, 722).

Until very recently, most Australian and New Zealand parties chose their leaders by a simple majority vote of members of the parliamentary caucus (Cross and Blais 2012a; Miller 2005, 130).[14] Shipley, Clark, and Gillard unseated incumbent party leaders by requesting a leadership vote, and these leadership transitions were enacted within a matter of days. In this situation, the route to party leadership seems expeditious and relatively obstacle-free, but challenging incumbents often comes with high political costs, especially when leadership turnovers are widely labelled "coups" by party members and media commentators. In chapter 2, I show how damaging the spectre of a coup can be for women who dare to unseat male leaders. In Canada, women who want the job do not have to face these perils as party leaders typically depart from the role voluntarily, through resignation or retirement. A party then schedules a leadership convention, and party members choose their next leader through a nationwide electoral competition, which is similar in some respects to American primaries (Courtney 1995). Campbell competed to replace a retiring leader, winning the job by securing votes from delegates elected by party members to participate in a leadership convention. As documented in chapter 2, differences in Campbell's, Shipley's, Clark's, and Gillard's pathways to the party leadership role shaped news coverage of their ascension stories, in turn introducing particular understandings about their characters and abilities that persisted throughout their political careers.

Election campaigns are routinely narrated with a particular news frame, called the *game frame* or *strategy frame*. Frames are devices used by journalists to simplify complex political events, and the conceptual framework of the game offers a valuable interpretive schema (Scheufele and Tewksbury 2007, 12). Because audiences understand the spectacle of the horse race or boxing match, the game frame makes elections comprehensible and interesting. As a result, this frame dominates election news coverage and arguably serves as a meta-narrative for journalists (Cappella and Jamieson 1997, 37–57; Patterson 1994, 53–93; Trimble and Sampert 2004). By focusing on the leaders of the parties in contention to win; highlighting their campaign tactics, gaffes, and errors; and continually reciting polling data at the expense of reflections on policy stances and ideological differences among the parties, game framing focuses on strategy over substance (Farnsworth et al. 2007). This frame is replete with aggressive metaphors and is by nature rather caustic, with evaluations becoming particularly harsh when a candidate is losing ground (Lawrence and Rose 2010, 181–3).

That said, the specific rules of the game shape how the story is told as an election unfolds, and Australia, Canada, and New Zealand have different electoral formulae. Canada continues to elect members of its House of Commons based on the Westminster model, the single-member plurality electoral system, which (fairly) regularly produces majority governments because the winning party is over-represented relative to its vote share. In minority government situations, the party with the plurality of seats governs with informal support, on a vote-by-vote basis, from another party or parties. Australia uses a majority preferential process to elect its House of Representatives, but because of the strength of the de facto two-party system, the party that wins usually gains a majority. Indeed, the 2010 election was rare in producing the first hung Parliament (i.e., a tie) since 1940 (Costar 2012, 357). New Zealand implemented a mixed-member proportional (MMP) system, used for the first time in its 1996 election. As a result, minority or coalition governments are now commonplace, and political parties must negotiate governing relationships. Chapter 6 shows how the coalition-building processes that occur both during and after election campaigns inflect media discourses about parties and their leaders with themes of romance.

A final factor to consider is women's political representation as the presence of a "critical mass" of women in legislatures and executive positions helps normalize women's political ambitions. The four women at the heart of my study won party leadership roles at times when women were under-represented in elected political roles, but signs of progress were evident. Although women held only 13 per cent of the seats in Canada's House of Commons when Kim Campbell became leader of the then-governing party, 1993 was a high-water mark for women in party and executive leadership. Including Campbell, there were ten women party leaders across Canada, two at the national and eight at the sub-national level, plus three women premiers (Trimble and Arscott 2003, 72–5). When Helen Clark assumed the leadership of the Opposition Labour Party in 1993, women held 21.2 per cent of the seats in New Zealand's House of Representatives (McLeay 2006a, 72). Activism within the Labour Party and the introduction of the MMP electoral system boosted women's representation even further, to 29 per cent of the seats in 1996, the year before Jenny Shipley became New Zealand's first woman prime minister (Curtin 2008, 493–4). New Zealanders were guaranteed a woman prime minister when Clark and Shipley faced off electorally in 1999, and women's presence in Parliament increased slightly, to 31 per cent. The numbers ebbed and flowed during Clark's time in office, reaching a peak of 33 per cent in 2008, her final election campaign. Finally, in Australia, women's electoral progress had stalled in the decade before Gillard's term in office, hovering around 25 per cent of the seats in the House of Representatives (Sawer 2012, 261). The 2010 election was no different, returning women to 24.7 per cent of the seats in the House of Representatives, but the number of women in the elected Senate rose to a record level of 39.5 per cent (Sawer, 2012, 263). Although Gillard remains the only woman to have led a major party and helmed the government at the national level in Australia, during her term in the prime minister's office (2010–13), four women served as premier of a state or chief minister of a territory.

In addition to the institutional factors shaping the fortunes of party leaders in each country, I expected similarities and differences in the personal lives, political contexts, leadership trajectories, and levels of electoral success of the four women prime ministers to factor into their media representations. After all, success at the polls is greeted with more adulatory reviews than is defeat. And surely the "first woman" trope grows stale when a woman prime minister wins her third election campaign, as did Helen Clark in 2005. After sketching the political biographies of Campbell, Shipley, Clark, and Gillard, I summarize the ways in which their identities and career paths aligned and diverged.

Canada: Kim Campbell

Kim Campbell began her political career in the province of British Columbia by serving as a Vancouver school board trustee from 1980 to 1984, when she was in her early thirties. Recruited to run provincially for the governing Social Credit Party, Campbell was defeated in her first attempt, in 1983, then rather boldly went after the party leadership in 1986 to raise her profile and gain experience at the provincial level (Campbell 1996, 68). Although unsuccessful in her leadership bid, Social Credit was returned to office in 1986, and Campbell won a seat. She served as a member of the BC Legislative Assembly for two years before resigning to run for the PC Party in the 1988 federal election. The party won re-election, and a victorious Campbell was appointed to Cabinet, where she served in three ministries, including the high-profile portfolios of Justice and Defence, gaining experience and growing support from caucus and party members for a leadership bid when long-serving Prime Minister Brian Mulroney retired. Despite warnings that she would be a "sacrificial lamb" because of the government's unpopularity, and concern that only a "miracle worker could stop the Tories' slide into oblivion," Campbell entered the party leadership contest (Trimble and Arscott 2003, 83). It was not the coronation many predicted, requiring a second ballot, but Campbell won handily nonetheless. A brief "honeymoon" phase bumped Campbell's approval ratings, but failed to improve the fortunes of her party, which experienced a historic defeat on October 25, 1993, reducing it to a mere two seats. As such, Campbell's time in the prime minister's office was brief, lasting from June 25 to November 3, 1993. Under pressure from her party, Campbell resigned as party leader in December 1993.

New Zealand: Jenny Shipley

Jenny Shipley joined New Zealand's National Party at a young age, and she was active in the organization before standing for office and winning election in 1987, when she was in her mid-thirties and the party was in Opposition. The 1990 election brought National to office, and Shipley secured a Cabinet post, serving in numerous portfolios, including Social Welfare, Health, Transport, and Women's Affairs. National was returned to office in 1993 and continued to hold power, although it failed to win a majority in the 1996 election, the nation's first to be contested under the MMP electoral system. As a result, National formed a governing coalition with the New Zealand First Party, but unpopular policies and dissatisfaction with Prime Minister Jim Bolger's administration prompted a leadership challenge, led by Shipley, who had the support of caucus members. Rather than face a confidence vote, Bolger resigned, and Shipley was elected unopposed in November 1997 and sworn in as the nation's first woman prime minister on December 8. However, New Zealand First leader Winston Peters's unhappiness with the change in leadership created considerable instability in the coalition arrangement, and it ultimately collapsed in 1998 (McLeay 2006b, 96). Shipley retained the confidence of Parliament through two confidence votes by securing support from former members of New Zealand First and other opposition members. Her efforts to rebrand and revitalize the party ultimately proved unsuccessful as National was defeated by

Labour in the 1999 election. Shipley served as leader of the Opposition until late 2001, when she was ousted through a leadership challenge mounted by Bill English, and she retired from politics in 2002.

New Zealand: Helen Clark

Having joined the Labour Party in 1971 while she was in university (Pond Eyley and Salmon 2015, 24), Helen Clark ran for national office unsuccessfully in 1975, at age twenty-five, and chose not to stand for election in 1978. First elected as a member of the New Zealand House of Representatives in 1981, when Labour was in Opposition, Clark found herself isolated within the parliamentary party (Edwards 2001, 160), and she was overlooked for a Cabinet post when Labour formed the government in 1984. Although she criticized members of Labour's leadership team for sexist attitudes and behaviours (Curtin 2008, 496), Clark advanced in the government, winning a place in Cabinet in 1987. She presided over three ministries, Conservation, Housing, and Health, and was promoted to deputy prime minister late in 1989. But by then, mounting unhappiness with the free market cost-cutting, deregulation, and privatization reforms introduced by the Labour government between 1984 and 1990, labelled "Rogernomics" because they were championed by Finance Minister Roger Douglas, precipitated Labour's defeat in the 1990 election.

The party's 1993 loss under the leadership of Mike Moore prompted caucus members to seek a new leader. Clark, who was then serving as deputy leader of the Opposition, led the challenge by asking for a leadership vote, which she won. But vitriol delivered by Moore and his supporters both during and after the "coup," along with continual attempts by Moore to unseat Clark as leader and disastrously low ratings in opinion polls, made Clark's term as Opposition leader extraordinarily difficult (Edwards 2001, 234–47; Pond Eyley and Salmon 2015, 97–114). Despite these formidable obstacles, Clark came very close to securing office during her first election campaign as party leader, held in 1996. Labour was just seven seats shy of National, and, had the party holding the balance of power after the 1996 election chosen Labour as its coalition partner, Clark would have become New Zealand's first woman prime minister. However, as noted above, the National Party formed a coalition with New Zealand First. Clark prevailed in the 1999 election, a historic occasion because, with women leading the two major parties, the country was guaranteed a woman government leader. With her victory, Clark became the first woman to be elected to the prime minister's post in New Zealand. She won three consecutive elections, with success in 2002 and 2005 securing her reputation as a strong competitor and adept campaigner. While Clark remained popular going into the 2008 campaign, the electorate was in the mood for a change of government. Immediately after the election loss, Clark resigned the leader's post, having served fifteen years as party leader and nine years as prime minister. She resigned her House of Representatives seat in April 2009.

Australia: Julia Gillard

Julia Gillard entered politics in her mid-thirties, as the chief of staff for the state of Victoria's Labor Opposition leader in 1996. Two years later, she was preselected for the Australian Labor Party and won the federal seat of Lalor when the party was in Opposition. By 2003, Gillard was serving in the shadow Cabinet. Widely regarded as a popular and highly skilful parliamentarian, Gillard was appointed deputy leader in 2006. Labor, under the leadership of Kevin Rudd, defeated the long-serving Coalition government in 2007, and Rudd selected Gillard as his deputy prime minister. Three years later, with the Labor Party increasingly dissatisfied with Rudd's leadership style and more and more worried about its re-election prospects, moves were made to unseat him (Gillard 2014, 19–20). Although Rudd said he would contest the challenge, he withdrew his name from the ballot, and on June 24, 2010, Gillard was elected unopposed.

Replacing a first-term prime minister during an election year is highly unusual, so while Gillard's victory was hailed as a "staggering and historic day" in Australian politics and celebrated as a major breakthrough for women (Trimble 2014, 672), Gillard herself was accused of disloyalty and treachery for overthrowing a sitting prime minister (Hall and Donaghue 2013, 638). The new prime minister quickly called an election for late August 2010, hoping to consolidate her leadership with an election win. Instead, the vote produced a tie between Gillard's Labor Party and the Opposition Coalition. Gillard deftly negotiated the support of the Green Party and three Independents, and was able to form a minority government, but she was dogged by controversies over unpopular policies. She was also continuously confronted with challenges to her leadership from the man she had deposed, widely reported (or rumoured) in news coverage (Curtin 2015, 194);

as documented by Australian journalist Kerry-Anne Walsh (2013), the Rudd forces made many clandestine attempts to undermine Gillard, two of which came to the fore, in February 2012 and March 2013. Eventually, with Labor's polling numbers dropping and an election looming, Rudd mobilized enough support to defeat Gillard in a leadership ballot held on June 26, 2013.

Similarities and Differences

Personal lives matter in politics, especially for women (Braden 1996; Ross and Sreberny-Mohammadi 1997; Trimble et al. 2013). As is typical of elite politicians, Campbell, Shipley, Clark, and Gillard are uniformly cisgender,[15] heterosexual, and white, and they enjoy the socio-economic privileges accorded these identities. However, they have different family situations. Shipley stands out among the four women because of her conventional family. She was married and had two children, who were in their late teens by the time she assumed the party leader's role. During the time periods included in this study, Clark was married to husband Peter Davis; Gillard was in a common-law relationship with her partner, Tim Mathieson; and Campbell was single, having divorced twice. Like many women political leaders, Campbell, Clark, and Gillard did not have children.

I chose to focus on these cases because of politically salient similarities and differences in their career trajectories. All four prime ministers expressed interest in electoral politics fairly early in their lives – in their twenties and thirties – and all had an atypical level of political success, winning national office on their first or second try and attaining recognition for their leadership skills by serving in Cabinet. Both Clark and Gillard were appointed deputy prime minister, a high-status position. Each of the women secured the leadership of a competitive political party, achieving the position when her party was governing (Campbell, Shipley, Gillard) or in contention to form the next government (Clark). This particular career path is unusual for women, who are more likely to be selected by minor parties or opposition parties with slim chances of winning office (O'Brien 2015).

Gillard stands apart because she took the party leadership from a first-term prime minister, something that many in the Labor Party and public judged unfair. In contrast, Campbell replaced a retiring leader who had led the government for two terms, and Jim Bolger was in his third term as New Zealand's prime minister when Shipley unseated him. Campbell and Shipley followed the trend of women leaders by emerging in parties with unfavourable electoral trajectories (Bashevkin 2009; O'Brien 2015); as a result, their stints in the prime minister's office were short-lived, just four months for Campbell and two years for Shipley. Gillard assumed the leadership of a governing party, albeit amid concerns about Labor's standing in the polls in the lead-up to the 2010 election, and she governed for nearly a full term before she was deposed from the leadership role in 2013. Clark was clearly the most electorally successful of the four. Although she became Labour leader when the party was in Opposition, and low in the polls, she led the party to a strong showing in 1986; won office in 1999, 2002, and 2005; and served as prime minister of New Zealand for nine years.

Reporting Ms. Prime Minister: Texts and Methods

This study examines news coverage of the women prime ministers at four crucial stages in their political careers, each of which drew considerable media attention to their personas and performances as leaders: selection as party leader, governance, election(s), and departure from the leader's role. The first, and highly formative, stage is their quest for the party leadership role, either through a so-called coup (Clark, Shipley, and Gillard) or a campaign to win support of party members (Campbell). Be it a formal and public leadership contest stretching over a period of several weeks or a more subterranean and speedy leadership challenge, any party leadership transition is reported in considerable depth, especially when the party forms the government or is highly competitive. I was interested in whether gendered mediation is as prolific in news coverage of women once they begin performing the role of prime minister, so I included one month of reporting about each woman while they were governing. For Campbell, Shipley, and Gillard, who became prime minister immediately after their leadership ascension, the governance phase directly followed the leadership win. Because Helen Clark won office three times, I gathered news coverage of three distinct periods of governance for the month after each of her electoral victories.

The third career phase is electoral competitions. By concentrating media attention on the personalities, leadership styles, and campaign performances of major party leaders, election campaigns "are the crucial moment in the image building of a political candidate" (Enli 2015, 110). Campbell, Shipley, and Gillard each contested one election during her tenure as party leader; Clark led her party through five campaigns. Finally, news coverage of the women's departures from the party leadership role was analysed. Campbell and Clark resigned immediately after election defeats, while Shipley and Gillard were removed through leadership challenges. During this phase, the media coverage comes in a short burst, emphasizing the leader's contributions to political life and governance, summarizing her achievements and failures, and often passing judgment on her character. In Gillard's case, I also gathered articles published over the course of her term in office that featured the gender card or gender wars metaphors. While most of these texts fell outside the four career phases included in this study, they clearly performed a powerful form of gendered mediation.

Comparing women and men leaders is not my primary goal as such comparisons run the risk of situating men as "norm" and women as anomalous outsiders, but a comprehensive approach to studying gendered mediation recognizes that every political actor is a gendered subject, whose identity and performance of leadership are mediated by the processes of news making. In the chapters to follow, I show how women and men leaders' gender identities were represented in their coverage. Because I wanted to test some of the propositions about gendered news coverage invariably treating men and women leaders differently, I adopted a paired sample design to identify equivalent men who sought the same office through a general election campaign (Falk 2010, 7). Fortuitously, all but one of the seven campaigns featured a women and a man as the primary competitors – that is, as leader of the governing party and the party comprising the Official Opposition. Although it was not possible to match Shipley with an equivalent man because she contested the 1999 New Zealand election against Clark, that campaign offered a unique glimpse into the media framing of an election guaranteeing victory for a woman. Kim Campbell's electoral opponent in the 1993 Canadian election was Liberal leader Jean Chrétien. Helen Clark faced five different leaders during her fifteen-year stretch as New Zealand's Labour Party leader, running against incumbent prime ministers Jim Bolger in 1996 and Jenny Shipley in 1999 before facing Opposition leaders Bill English in 2002, Don Brash in 2005, and John Key in 2008. All Clark's opponents were leaders of the National Party. Labor leader Julia Gillard contested the 2010 Australian election against Liberal leader Tony Abbott, who led the Coalition.

To determine how the party leaders were represented by domestic news sources, I chose three major daily newspapers for each nation based on their circulation rates, geographic reach, and agenda-setting roles in each country's media environment (see the Appendix for more details). Thanks to direct access to television reporting about the New Zealand and Australian leadership "coups," this coverage is analysed in chapter 2, which explores the ways in which news organizations narrated each of the women prime ministers' rise to the party leadership role. I chose traditional news sources because most social media platforms played an insignificant role in political communications until the mid- to late 2000s (Taras 2015, 7). By then, all but one of the women prime ministers whose reportage is analysed in this study had departed from office. Even more importantly, television and the online editions of established news media organizations continue to dominate the news information cycle, providing key entry points into political debate (Nielsen, Kleis, and Schroder 2014, 473–4). Since the bulk of the news items circulating on social media originate from mainstream media organizations, "political leaders and parties still need to get their messages through the crucible of the traditional media to reach the public" (Taras 2015, 275). That said, in chapters 5 and 7, I discuss the role played by social and online media in circulating demeaning and misogynistic materials about Gillard during her time in office because these texts were discussed in mainstream media accounts of Australian political life.

Considerably more information about source selection, sampling dates, and criteria is provided in the Appendix. In a nutshell, all news stories, including regular news, features, opinion pieces, guest columns, and editorials over 250 words in length, that named a woman leader or her electoral competitor in the headline or lead paragraph and gave substantive attention to that leader were included in the analysis. Table 1.1 summarizes the number and type of news stories per career phase for each of the four women leaders at the heart of this study. Since I offer a comparative analysis of key aspects of news reporting about the women and comparable men leaders during election campaigns, table 1.2 documents the number of newspaper articles analysed for each of these campaigns. In total, 2,550 news items were analysed, 1,797 about the four women prime ministers at key points in their political careers and 753 about the six men party leaders.

Offering a holistic and nuanced account of the ways in which party and government leaders are gendered in news accounts of their performances requires a diversity of methods, not limited to quantitatively enumerating the presence of certain preoccupations, frames, or tropes. Both quantitative and qualitative approaches were employed. Content analysis, a systematic approach to identifying the message

Table 1.1 Number of News Stories Analysed, by Woman Leader and Career Phase

Woman leader	Party leadership		Governance	Election(s)	Defeat or resignation	Other[a]	Total
	Newspaper stories	TV news items	Newspaper stories	Newspaper stories	Newspaper stories	Newspaper stories	
Kim Campbell	141	–	98	78	13	–	330
Helen Clark	76	29	104	495[b]	21	–	725
Jenny Shipley	140[c]	23	32	70	27	–	300
Julia Gillard	105	22	76	123	28	88	442
Total							1,797

[a]Captures the stories about Gillard featuring the gender card or gender war(s) metaphors.
[b]Clark contested five election campaigns, hence the higher number of news stories for her than for Campbell, Shipley, or Gillard, who led their parties through one campaign.
[c]Because Shipley won the party leadership in November 1997 but was not sworn in as prime minister until December 8, we assigned stories published before she officially assumed the prime minister's role to the leadership phase of her career. The governance phase spanned the Christmas holiday, and relatively few stories published during this phase met the search criteria.

characteristics in a text (Budd, Thorp, and Donohew 1967; Neuendorft 2002; Neuman 2000, 2007), was used to quantify the number of news stories about each leader mentioning their gender identity, physical appearance, racial identity, marital situation, and children or childlessness (see the Appendix for details about the coding scheme and coder reliability). Whenever these aspects of a leader's persona were described and/or evaluated in a news story, they were recorded in a qualitative database, including what exactly was said, who said it, and the context in which it was said. Qualitative textual analysis proved to be the most effective approach to identifying and analysing patterns of gendered mediation. The intensity of certain representations – for instance, the level of concentration on a leader's family life – became evident by analysing the qualitative data, and it also allowed me to determine whether the depictions resulted from self-presentation (for instance, leaders' deliberate mentions of children or spouses) or were the opinions of opponents, journalists, or other news sources. I also documented how certain gender-resonant metaphors were deployed in the news stories, detailing allegories of war and romance as they were applied to the women and men leaders. The gender card and gender war(s) metaphors evident in the coverage of Gillard were analysed as significant forms of gendered mediation, but they did not appear in reporting about any of the other prime ministers.

Table 1.2 Number of Election News Stories Analysed, by Country, Leader, and Election Campaign

Country	Election date	Party leader				Total
		Name	N	Name	N	
Canada	1993	Kim Campbell	78	Jean Chrétien	57	135[a]
New Zealand	1996	Helen Clark	84	Jim Bolger	81	165
	1999	Helen Clark	88	Jenny Shipley	78	166
	2002	Helen Clark	103	Bill English	70	173
	2005	Helen Clark	114	Don Brash	133	247
	2008	Helen Clark	127	John Key	198	325
Australia	2010	Julia Gillard	123	Tony Abbott	136	259
Totals			717		753	1,470

[a]There are fewer stories for the 1993 Canadian election than for elections in New Zealand and Australia because, as discussed in the Appendix, Canadian news stories were substantially longer, often over 1,000 words, compared to between 300 and 800 words for stories in the other countries.

These quantitative and qualitative databases, while immensely valuable, did not always capture how the subtleties of gendered news coverage were embedded in particular narrative approaches. When aspects of reporting are disaggregated – for instance, by focusing on references to family life or physical appearance – the analysis cannot paint a comprehensive picture of the ways in which gender permeates assessments of political legitimacy and authenticity. For instance, journalists' evaluations of Campbell's speaking style became apparent through a more holistic reading of her coverage over time. To ensure a complete and nuanced interpretation of the meanings produced by gendered descriptions and evaluations, the news texts were analysed through a three-stage qualitative data analysis process (Bryman, Teevan, and Bell 2009, 259). I began by reading each news story before taking detailed notes to document both explicit and latent forms of gendered mediation and identify intersecting or conflicting meanings. A second read-through of these notes highlighted mini-narratives reflecting gendered understandings of power, such as the fictional genres used to script each woman's rise to the party leadership role. This phase also identified patterns that persisted over time for each of the women prime ministers and across jurisdictions. In the third stage, the notes (and sometimes the original articles) were carefully re-examined to ensure that the analysis was complete and any incongruities were noted and explained.

Overview of the Book

Ms. Prime Minister expands the gendered mediation thesis by acknowledging and observing the disruptive potential of news reporting about political leaders. I argue that news mediation of politics is gendered when its processes and products reinforce, or *trouble* (i.e., question, unsettle, or even defy), gender norms and binaries. An example of a newspaper report that both replicates and questions gender stereotypes is a *New York Times* piece describing the fuss made in the United Kingdom about Prime Minister Theresa May's $1,250 pair of leather trousers.[16] The first half of the article focuses on "Trousergate," quoting a series of critics who charged May with displaying flagrant elitism in a time of (government-imposed) austerity. Only at the end of the piece did commentators identify the sexist double standard inherent in fixating on a woman prime minister's expensive outfit, while ignoring men leaders' high-priced bespoke suits. As this example shows, gendered news can validate or delegitimize women's political aspirations and accomplishments.

Throughout this book, I assess the extent to which the four women prime ministers of Canada, New Zealand, and Australia experienced *mediated legitimacy*, defined as media reporting that accepts a lawful political actor's right to seek, hold, and exercise a political leadership role. Mediated legitimacy does not mean unwaveringly positive or affirmative coverage. News reporting can be critical of politicians' ideas or actions without challenging their right to think or act in certain ways because of ascribed characteristics such as gender. Understanding the ways in which news coverage conveys or denies legitimacy on the basis of gendered identities is key to mapping the nature and nuances of gendered mediation.

Chapter 2, "Ascension Stories," starts at the beginning by analysing how news outlets scripted Campbell's, Shipley's, Clark's, and Gillard's leadership challenges. Stories about a politician's rise to the top matter greatly to mediated legitimacy because they introduce newly selected political leaders to the public, framing and evaluating their leadership styles at a crucial point in their political careers. As I show, these first impressions shaped subsequent representations of each prime minister's persona, competency, and authenticity in a political leadership role. This chapter takes a qualitative approach to analysing newspaper reporting about Campbell's quest for the PC Party's leadership contest and television news coverage about Clark's, Shipley's, and Gillard's so-called leadership coups. Techniques, genres, and plots associated with fictional chronicles were obvious and compelling elements of these narratives, with the fable of the tortoise and the hare structuring newspaper coverage of Campbell's leadership bid and features of melodramatic storytelling infusing televised accounts of the New Zealand and Australian leadership "coups." After reviewing the literature on the role of fiction in news, which shows how commonly referenced storylines, myths, and morals are used to organize and dramatize news stories, I describe how the moral reasoning evident in these "real fictions" reflected key features of the hegemonic gender order, shaping interpretations of each woman's rise to the top party job. While coverage of all four women was influenced by contextual factors, each of these narratives made gender regulations visible, both reinforcing and questioning dominant archetypes of political power and understandings of authoritative leadership.

Ascension stories placed gender at the forefront of mediated accounts of the prime ministers' political careers, a theme that is investigated further in chapter 3, "First Women and the X Factor," which documents the prevalence of and meanings communicated by gender markers. Gender markers, or labels, explicitly identify the gender of a political actor with phrases like "first woman prime minister" or "the right man for the job." By inferring that the gender of the actor is relevant to evaluations of their political capabilities and achievements, these deliberate lexical choices politicize gender. This chapter tests two assertions from the gendered mediation literature: first, women politicians' gender identities are invariably at the forefront of their news coverage, considered essential to understanding their performance of leadership; and second, men politicians are portrayed as gender-free, their gender identities unmarked. I analysed the percentage of news stories containing at least one explicit gender signifier for each of the women prime ministers at key points in their careers and for each of the men leaders during election campaigns, producing some surprising findings. Qualitative discourse analysis of the labels unveiled complicated and sometimes contradictory perceptions of the role of gender in elite politics, reflecting both unease with and celebration of women's political achievements.

The next two chapters offer new ways of investigating widely studied forms of gendered mediation: representations of politicians' family lives and physical appearance. That news stories personalize women politicians is now conventional wisdom. Indeed, the media's laser-like focus on appearance and families is referred to as the "lipstick watch" (Heith 2003, 123) and the "hair, hemlines and husbands" problem (Lawrence and Rose 2010, 63). In addition to comparing the number of news stories mentioning the looks and family situations of women and equivalent men leaders, I use discourse analysis to examine Campbell's, Shipley's, Clark's, and Gillard's coverage holistically and longitudinally, identifying themes, lexical strategies, and narrative tropes that persisted, or changed, over time. Chapter 4, "First Men and the Family Strategy," uses both quantitative and qualitative methods to explore the "intimization" of politics through reporting about familial relationships (Stanyer 2013). I begin with depictions of the "first men," or lack thereof in Campbell's case, showing how hetero-normative versions of masculinity are embedded in assessments of prime ministers' marital partners. I also theorize the nature and impact of the *family strategy*, which I define as the deliberate politicization of family life to gain media attention and public support for a candidate. As this analysis indicates, this strategy is commonly mobilized against women leaders, but it can be named and resisted. Moreover, the politicization of intimate relationships reveals the socially and discursively constituted boundaries between public and private.

Chapter 5, "Body Politics," offers an inclusive approach to documenting mediated representations of politicians' bodies. I argue that because the body is the site on which socially and discursively constructed meanings about gender (and race) are inscribed, and party leaders' bodies are increasingly assessed for their ability to personify the party brand and embody the myths and dreams of the nation, the performance of leadership cannot be disentangled from the body of the leader. That I searched in vain for any mediation of race demonstrates the extent to which whiteness is normalized in media accounts of political leadership. Using content analysis, this chapter tests the argument that the media pay more attention to the physical appearance of women politicians than to the looks and style choices of their male counterparts or competitors. By developing a comprehensive operational definition of the concept *physical appearance*, my analysis captured the many ways in which reporting references the look, demeanour, and styling of women's *and* men's bodies. Using feminist discourse analysis techniques, I assessed the proposition that men are described as personifying political leadership, while women's looks are highlighted and used as a discursive strategy for communicating their visual dissonance from the prototypical body of the (white, male, heterosexual) leader. Finally, chapter 5 details the ways in which three of the women leaders were intrusively sexualized by news coverage of their bodies and sexual identities, adding an important dimension to analysis of the embodied performance of leadership.

Metaphors are important sites of investigation because of their ubiquity in media discourses, their powerful persuasive role, and their ability to reflect, reinforce, or challenge gendered relations of power. Indeed, the language of battle is so conventionalized in mediated accounts of political competitions that we understand politics as a form of (discursive) warfare. Chapter 6, "Love and War," broadens the focus to include the metaphorical language of love, exploring the complexly gendered connotations communicated by both battle and romance metaphors. My goal is to critically examine a central contention of the gendered mediation thesis: the "masculine" vocabularies and metaphors used to describe political life are so deeply rooted in patriarchal traditions and power relations that they invariably situate men politicians as the norm and women as anomalous outsiders to elite political competitions. Combining critical metaphor and critical discourse analysis techniques, I explain how love and war metaphors alike work to both reinforce and subvert the socially and discursively constructed boundaries between man and woman, public and private. While there seems to be a discursive collision between the "masculine" world of warfare and the "feminine" domain of love and romance, these seemingly discordant interpretations highlight the emotional and relational aspects of political life. Scripting political leadership as a form of romance may seem trivializing, but love metaphors affirm the importance of political friendships, especially relationships between leaders and followers.

Bonds of political affection are easily ruptured when a leader's approach to political speech is questioned or condemned. Chapter 7, "Speech and Shame," demonstrates how Kim Campbell and Julia Gillard were chastened for their public speeches: Campbell for how she spoke politically when competing for party and government leadership roles, and Gillard for what she said in Parliament from her position as prime minister. I review the literature on women and public speech, which argues that since public forms of powerful speech have been associated with men and masculinity, women's speech provokes unease, especially when it violates the speaking rules governing political institutions or challenges dominant cultural myths. Feminist critical discourse analysis of newspaper reporting about Campbell's speaking style and Gillard's willingness to speak about sexism and misogyny confirms the role played by the news media in silencing or containing certain forms of speech. That Hillary Clinton's presidential candidacy sparked such a virulently sexist backlash in 2016 highlights the importance of investigating discursive silencing. Even when the condemnation originates with opponents – for instance, the "Lock her up" chant initiated by the Trump campaign to undermine Clinton's legitimacy – it is afforded wider audiences and trustworthiness when circulated by mainstream news outlets.

The concluding chapter, "Dealing (with) the Gender Card," develops the concept of mediated legitimacy and assesses the extent to which gendered news coverage negotiated political legitimacy for Campbell, Shipley, Clark, and Gillard. As I show, culturally and politically constructed understandings about gender and political leadership were evident across the four cases. The second section of the chapter builds on the evidence presented in chapters 2 to 7 to offer a series of lessons learned from the study. This advice is designed to inform both the gender strategies of aspiring women prime ministers and the techniques used by journalists when reflecting on the "gender factor." After highlighting my theoretical and empirical contributions to the gendered mediation literature, I make a number of suggestions for further research. While *Ms. Prime Minister* answers many questions about gender, media, and leadership, much more work needs to be done to understand how news coverage can work to address and redress the discursive barriers to elite political office – not just for privileged women, but for all women.

Chapter Two

Ascension Stories[1]

Introduction

> The Labour Party is heading for a brutal leadership contest, with a bitter Mr. Moore vowing to fight to the end for his job. The coup leaders backing his deputy, the Rt. Hon. Helen Clark, will give notice of a challenge when the caucus convenes on Wednesday. ... [Moore] lashed out against Helen Clark, painting himself as the champion of the Labour tradition.[2]

Political ascension stories are of great interest to the news media, as the example of Helen Clark's leadership bid illustrates. The quest for party leadership presents a captivating tale featuring conflict, clashing personalities, heroes, villains, winners, losers, and emotional upheaval. These dramatic and engaging stories matter to political careers because they introduce freshly minted political leaders to the public. Political actors may not be well known before seeking the leadership of a major political party, and even those who are familiar to citizens will be reintroduced by the press as aspiring government leaders, interpreted for their ability to perform in that role. By presenting information and entertaining anecdotes about politicians' personal lives, personalities, ideologies, and political styles, the media have the potential to shape audiences' perceptions of leaders at a crucial moment in their political ascents. First impressions of rising political leaders have an effect on subsequent representations by the media, and perhaps even on opinion formation by audiences (Harp, Loke, and Bachmann 2010, 292–3). As I show throughout this book, the descriptive tropes and evaluative frameworks used by the media to characterize the four women prime ministers during this crucial formative phase reverberated throughout their political careers.

In this chapter, I argue that the news media used elements of fiction to script stories about the leadership contests waged by Campbell, Clark, Shipley, and Gillard. I begin by explaining why news coverage of politics uses the plot lines and techniques associated with fictional storytelling and by relating how the norms and myths associated with fictional renditions of political events highlight ideologies of gender. The news-mediated narratives about each of the prime ministers are then presented in the order in which the women contested the party leader's position, beginning with Campbell (March to June 1993) before turning to Clark (December 1993), Shipley (November 1997), and Gillard (June 2010). For Campbell, the analytical focus was on newspaper reporting about her quest for the party and government leader's post, but the availability of television news broadcasts[3] allowed me to examine television news coverage of the leadership challenges in Australia and New Zealand. Despite the difference in media genre, each of the four ascension stories was narrated with fictional storylines and genres, revealing gendered assumptions about the performance of political leadership. By adapting a fable to relay Campbell's rise to the top and by scripting Clark's, Shipley's, and Gillard's victories as melodramas, the news coverage created what Nimmo and Combs (1982, 56) call "dramatic pseudo-realities." As discourse analysis of these texts demonstrates, the values, myths, and plots associated with fiction were used as devices to evaluate the women leaders' desire for, and ability to effectively wield, political power.

News Storytelling and "Real Fictions"

The media play a significant role in constructing leadership and imbuing it with meanings. When telling stories about politics, the news media report "facts" – who did what, when, where, and how. But particular details are selected, emphasized, scrutinized, and presented as frames for comprehending the story and its cast of characters. Through this mediation process, news creates "real fictions" by offering "rhetorical compositions that select and organize data in an intentional unity that might not otherwise exist" (Nimmo and Combs 1982, 46). In other words, the events themselves are considerably more complex and disorganized than news stories can reasonably portray. By imposing a narrative structure on the inevitable messiness of politics, news can be made more comprehensible and more entertaining (Weldon 2008, 17–18). Political happenings such as leadership challenges are mediated by the organizational needs and conventions of news reporting, which require excitement and immediacy to hold the attention of readers and viewers. Thus, news is produced as a "dramatic pseudo-reality created from the ongoing flow of events 'out there' but transformed into an entertaining real-fiction that conforms to the logic of the medium while assisting people to relate those events to their everyday lives" (ibid.). By selecting, filtering, organizing, and framing political events and issues for production and consumption as news stories, the news writer is generating meanings and thereby playing a central role in the construction of political reality.

News is a form of storytelling, so it is not surprising that it borrows attributes of fiction in an effort to relay a compelling, audience-grabbing tale. As Reuven Frank, a former executive producer of the NBC television news, famously wrote in a memo to staff, "Every news story should, without any sacrifice of probity or responsibility, display the attributes of fiction, of drama" (quoted in Johnson-Cartee 2005, 139). Relating politics to commonly referenced plots, myths, and morals helps a journalist convey a point efficiently; thus, facts are "embedded in a frame or story line that organizes them and gives them coherence" (Gamson 1989, 157). Journalists, like fiction writers, produce narratives complete with "characters, scene descriptions, conflict(s), actions with motives, and, ultimately, resolutions" (Pan and Kosicki 1993, 60). White (1987, 84) argues that news stories feature attributes of novel- or play-writing. Indeed, the reporting process has been likened to "a literary act, a continuous search for 'story lines' that goes so far as to incorporate the metaphors and plots of novels, folk traditions, and myths" (Nimmo and Combs 1982, 46).

Because of their reliance on words, print journalists reflect this literary tradition by drawing on evocative metaphors, commonly shared stories such as fables, or the characters and lexicon featured in popular entertainment programming. The plots commonly used in literature, especially those involving conflict between individuals, are prevalent in newspaper reports (McCartney 1987, 170). For instance, Barr (2012, 22) describes how science fiction idioms and motifs permeated the *New York Times'* coverage of US presidential politics. Television news, on the other hand, needs to tell stories with fewer words but more visuals, thus tends to borrow attributes of films, soap operas, and prime-time dramas (Bennett 1998, 40; Nimmo and Combs 1982, 45; van Zoonen 2005, 20). As a result, the social and political issues reported by television news are sometimes presented as melodramas (Milburn and

McGrail 1992, 618). Notable examples include coverage of the Anita Hill–Clarence Thomas sexual harassment hearings, which presented Hill's accusations against US Supreme Court nominee Thomas as a psychodrama (Lipari 1994), and the sensationalization of the Three Mile Island nuclear power plant accident (Nimmo and Combs 1982).

Fictional storytelling tropes are imbued with morality tales. The most appealing and deeply resonant news stories embrace the shared narratives widely circulated in any given society as audiences need to identify with the structure and moral of the story. These commonly referenced narratives "establish commonalities, promote goodness and discourage wickedness," providing societies with a framework for moral reasoning (Johnson-Cartee 2005, 149). The Bill Clinton and Monica Lewinsky affair, for instance, was relayed as a soap opera, prompting strong moral judgments (van Zoonen 2005, 20). That melodramatic framing of political news makes sharp distinctions between good and evil was evidenced by the signification of the United States as a "morally powerful victim" of the September 11 terrorist attacks, thus justified in seeking heroic retribution (Anker 2005). Similarly, the structure of the fable is designed to persuade readers to "accept socially defined moral positions" expressed as an "explicitly stated moral point" (Hanauer and Waksman 2000, 108).

Moral reasoning is deeply gendered. Ideas about valour, wickedness, goodness, justice, and human nature are imbued with gender stereotypes. For instance, norms of heroism reflect an understanding of heroes as embodying warrior masculinity and aggressively masterful leadership styles (Nunn 2002, 13). What is considered "good" or justified behaviour for a man – for instance, displaying ruthlessness or ambition – may be viewed as wrong and even despicable for a woman. Popular myths of femininity as enigmatic and threatening, nurturing and caring, and as practised in and through the body rather than the mind, are invoked in morality tales (van Zoonen 2005, 93). As such, the characters, archetypes, and plot trajectories of dominant news narratives reflect gendered understandings of the social and political order. However, as argued in chapter 1, news mediation can disrupt gender regulations. In retelling old stories or borrowing elements of fiction, gender norms may be revealed and contested. For instance, van Zoonen (2005, 23) contends that because the genre of soap opera is associated with women, the private sphere, and femininity, conventional understandings of politics as exclusively masculine territory are interrupted when the media use the narrative of the soap. News storytelling can reproduce or challenge the dominant political culture, and it may also reify or unsettle the gender order.

In my analysis of the four prime ministers' ascension stories, I show how the storytelling techniques associated with fiction reflect gendered understandings of political leadership. These understandings are politically consequential because fictionalized features of news stories become "real" through telling and retelling. For instance, news coverage of American presidential campaigns features a "master narrative," which is used to interpret "highly publicized moments ... as incidents that reveal the underlying character of the candidate" (Lawrence and Rose 2010, 52). Since the mass media are the primary source of information about political actors, the symbolic material created by the media helps create impressions of politicians' identities, motivations, and actions. S.R. Lichter and R.E. Noyes, in their 1995 book, *Good Intentions Make Bad News: Why Americans Hate Campaign Journalism*, said that, in this way, "journalists have at least as much control over the public images of national leaders as the politicians have themselves" (quoted in Johnson-Cartee 2005, 147). "Real fictions" resonate throughout politicians' political careers, branding their identities for the media and the voting public.

The particular trajectory of a narrative also shapes the news story, so their different pathways to party leadership played an important role in the media characterizations of the political ascensions of Campbell, Clark, Shipley, and Gillard. In Australia and New Zealand, the major parties choose their leaders by means of a simple majority vote by members of the parliamentary caucus (Cross and Blais 2012a, 18–19; 2012b, 133; Miller 2005, 130). While sitting leaders sometimes step down willingly, prompting an open competition for the job, Clark, Shipley, and Gillard challenged the incumbents, forcing a caucus vote to decide between the incumbent leader and the contender. This approach to seeking the party leadership is invariably rather stealthy as potential candidates must secure sufficient support before making a move (Miller 2005, 130), and it is speedy, often taking place over a twenty-four-hour period. That such leadership challenges are widely referred to as "coups" or "spills" reflects their dramatic nature and their association with acts of violence and revolution. In all three cases, the media presented these women's so-called leadership coups as spectacles by employing elements of the melodramatic genre of fictional storytelling.

Campbell's leadership challenge was also presented as a remarkable political event because it elected the Progressive Conservative (PC)

Party's first woman leader, and, as head of the governing party, Campbell automatically assumed the role of Canada's prime minister. But the path to party leadership takes quite a different trajectory in Canada than in Australia or New Zealand because of the involvement of the extra-parliamentary party in the process. While leadership "coups" are completed in a matter of hours or days, Canadian leadership contests are lengthy processes, requiring leadership candidates to gather support from party members across the country (Courtney 1995, 129). For the 1993 PC leadership campaign, delegates were chosen in each electoral district to vote for the candidate of their choice at the party leadership convention held in mid-June. During the three-month-long competition for the leadership of her party, Campbell raised money for campaign expenses, garnered support from party members, participated in televised leadership debates before and during the convention, and appealed to other candidates for support on the convention floor as voting took place (Campbell 1996, chap. 13). While this race lacked the intrinsic sensationalism of the Australian and New Zealand leadership "coups," not least because Campbell was the clear frontrunner, the media coverage dramatized the event by adopting the fable of the tortoise and the hare as a narrative strategy.

A Fable

Fables have two features: a mutually supportive plot and an overtly identified moral point. The explicit moral of the story is designed to "make sure that the reader understands the socially defined interpretation of the specific events and actions described in the narrative" (Hanauer and Waksman 2000, 108). Fables are used as narrative devices in the works of classical philosophers, poets, and politicians, and, because they are both pithy and memorable, their basic storylines and messages are commonly referenced in everyday life (Clayton 2005, 2). Aesop's fables are still widely consumed, and even those who have never read the parables of the tortoise and the hare, or the mouse and the lion, have been introduced to their plots and messages through everyday oral storytelling and popular-culture renditions of these tales. Because fables are simplistic, entertaining, and pedagogical in tone and narrative, they are ideal for news storytelling.

Clayton (2005, 8) argues that fables can be given political meaning when brought into political discourses. When applied in a specific political context, such as a party leadership contest, the fable works to inform the audience about the lessons it should learn from the story. Characters in fables are overtly chastised, or rewarded, for their behaviour, and parables often serve as cautionary tales. In the well-known Aesop fable of *The Tortoise and the Hare*, a boastful hare mocks a turtle for its slow pace and challenges it to a race. Tired of the hare's taunting, the tortoise agrees, and a course is set. After the hare gets off to a speedy start, quickly outpacing the tortoise, it decides to take a nap, bragging that it will have no trouble winning the race despite such a flagrant display of indolence. But the hare sleeps too long, awakening just as the tortoise is approaching the finish line. Despite its speed, the hare does not have enough time to remedy this mistake, and the tortoise emerges victorious. The most widely cited moral of the story is "slow and steady wins the race," suggesting that hard work and determination will be rewarded in the end, as it was for the tortoise. But there is another moral, this one about the hare, whose arrogance and overconfidence caused it to lose a competition it should have easily won. That this fable was adopted by the news media in its narration of the PC Party's 1993 leadership contest reflects the popularity of the *quest*, "the typical story of heroic pursuit against all odds" (van Zoonen 2005, 106). The choice of parable also revealed discomfort with the idea of a woman leading the pursuit for the highest political prize.

The Hare and the Tortoise in the 1993 PC Leadership Race

Kim Campbell was a high-profile cabinet minister in the PC government of Brian Mulroney when the prime minister announced his retirement on February 24, 1993, and she formally entered the contest to replace him a month later. Identified as the clear front-runner even before the campaign was officially launched (Courtney 1995, 117), Campbell "had an enormous head-start, hyped by the media as the heir apparent and backed from the outset by party heavyweights and almost two-thirds of the Tory caucus."[4] The press referred to the contest as a Campbell coronation,[5] but she did not, as initially predicted by the media, win on the first ballot. It took a second round of voting for Campbell to prevail over her closest competitor, Jean Charest (Courtney 1995, 123).

The Canadian newspapers in my sample mediated this particular leadership contest by directly adopting the plot and morals of *The Tortoise and the Hare*. Very early on in the leadership contest, a headline in the *Globe and Mail* declared, "Tortoise chases the hare," positioning Charest as the plodding turtle to Kim Campbell's sprinting hare.[6]

A month later, the newspaper noted that the "turtle" was gaining on Campbell,[7] although it warned that "Charest's late momentum" was "not enough to carry the tortoise past the hare."[8] When Campbell won the race, the *Globe* explained that the tortoise had run "out of time and luck."[9] Frequently invoked by Canadian news coverage, the fable became the mantra for the Charest campaign as well as the motif for a *New York Times* story about the outcome.[10] Even when the parable was not explicitly mobilized in news reports, the two morals of the story were evident in representations of Campbell and Charest. The press used the fable to elevate Charest's candidacy and produce the illusion of a close race, thus heightening the news value of the competition. But the parable was also invoked to discipline Campbell for her unabashed self-confidence and desire for political power.

A *Vancouver Sun* story printed after the leadership convention noted that the "trouble with fables is that they're make believe. In real life, hares outrun tortoises every time."[11] But the news reports represented the fictional ending of the fable as an entirely possible "reality" for this particular campaign because it fit with the dominant news frame for political competitions: the game frame. Central to this frame is one question: who is winning? The Canadian news media embrace the metaphor of the horse race when describing party leadership contests by focusing on who is winning the most delegate support, who is behind, and what they are doing to catch up or stay ahead of the pack (Courtney 1995, 93). Given the prevalence of this frame, there is nothing less enticing than a one-horse race, as was the case in the 1993 PC leadership competition. With one candidate far in the lead from the outset, the excitement and urgency fuelling news storytelling seemed remarkably absent. As the *Globe and Mail* pronounced, "Without having even declared her candidacy, or submitted to extensive public scrutiny, Kim Campbell has run away with the Conservative leadership."[12] This phenomenon, dubbed "Campbellmania,"[13] quickly became a media buzzword, but it could not sustain three months of news storytelling. After the sensation of a woman in the lead for the top job quickly waned, a news vacuum was created, one that had to be filled. In lieu of an alluringly close competition, the press turned to Campbell, scrutinizing the candidate and her campaign for any signs of trouble, reporting minor difficulties as major "stumbles,"[14] circulating revelations about the candidate's "sense of self-importance and arrogance,"[15] and calling her large campaign team "unwieldy and disorganized."[16]

Questions about Campbell's character emerged, shifting the storyline in a manner that mirrored one of the morals of the tortoise and the hare story – that the hare's unfounded sense of superiority and foolish overconfidence caused it to lose the race. News reports described Campbell as arrogant, haughty, boastful, and elitist. "Snippets of evidence about the Campbell sense of self-importance and arrogance have been given wide circulation in recent weeks, as her stature in the Conservative race galloped ahead," said a report published in the *Globe and Mail*.[17] Quotations from a magazine profile of Campbell written by a leading Canadian journalist were frequently recycled in newspaper reports, offered as "proof" of her haughty and elitist nature.[18] The word "arrogant" appeared throughout the campaign coverage. For instance, a *Vancouver Sun* story quoted critics who said that Campbell was "arrogant" and "abrasive," with one labelling her an "arrogant, egotistical snob."[19] Campbell was called "dismissive" and "conceited" in another article.[20] At issue were the candidate's desire for power and affinity for self-promotion.[21] Indeed, Campbell was described as "an immature boastful bimbo"[22] who exhibited "mighty, even politically fatal, self-esteem."[23] Campbell, like the hare in the fable, was regarded as too confident and too overtly aspirational. Such accounts disciplined Campbell, delegitimizing her quest for power. That she was characterized as a "bimbo" punctuates the gender norms underlying these evaluations. Women's political ambition and professional advancement is commonly evaluated as unseemly, selfish, unfeminine, inappropriate, and unprincipled (Lawrence and Rose 2010, 93; Ross 1995, 502). A feminist academic quoted in a news story headlined, "Is media focus on Campbell sexist?" observed the gendered nature of such evaluations of Campbell. "I think there's very much the uppity woman syndrome at work here – that self-promotion is unbecoming of a female politician."[24]

Having situated Campbell as the self-important and boastful hare, journalists subsequently created a "real fiction" by suggesting that her campaign was in trouble and positioning Charest as a serious challenger. Just three weeks after Campbell declared her candidacy, headlines such as "Is Kim Campbell's star beginning to dim?"[25] and "Campbellmania fizzles"[26] began to appear. News writers asked whether Campbell could "restart a campaign that is apparently stalled."[27] Columnist Jeffrey Simpson said Campbell "turned what should have been a cakewalk into a contest."[28] News organizations then turned their attention to Campbell's closest competitor, Jean Charest, who was at that point in a rather distant second place. By flocking to his campaign[29] and drawing a comparison between Charest and the tortoise in the widely known fable, the media suggested that the fictional ending of that tale was, in fact, possible. In an article published just a few weeks after Campbell officially entered the campaign, a *Globe* columnist wrote, "In Tory Leadership Campaign '93, Environment Minister Jean Charest is the tortoise to Defence Minister Kim Campbell's hare, trying to show that 'slow and steady wins the race.'"[30] Indeed, the Charest team embraced the image of the plucky, hard-working tortoise by adopting it as the catchphrase for the campaign. Charest's campaign workers wore "Turtle Power" buttons, supporters showered the candidate with turtle paraphernalia,[31] and Charest "boasted ... that his campaign is being driven by turtle power, implying that he will eventually cross the finish line first."[32]

The fable offered a compelling plot line, one that reinvigorated interest in the campaign by creating the illusion of a close race. "What began as a runaway campaign by Ms. Campbell for the leadership of the party and the prime minister's mantle 14 weeks ago is coming down to a classic race," said one report.[33] Newspaper stories emphasized growing support for Charest by labelling it "Turtlemania,"[34] and the media were clearly captivated by the tale of the valiant underdog. As a writer for the *Vancouver Sun* maintained,

> If there were no fable about a tortoise and a hare, Jean Charest would have had to invent one for his relentless pursuit of Kim Campbell. There was always something improbable about Charest's pursuit of the swift-running defence minister who seemed to have the race won before it began. But late last week, near the wind-up of the campaign's delegate-selection process, Charest was still standing, and still inching along.[35]

While journalists were careful to relay the "facts" of the story by noting that delegate tracking showed Campbell consistently in the lead, and even in sight of a win on the first ballot,[36] many refused to rule out the possibility of a Charest victory.[37] One reporter opined that "the tortoise Charest could stick his long neck out just far enough to get his snout over the finish line" if supported by another candidate's delegates.[38] The myth that Charest could overcome his competitor was fuelled by his doggedness and determination to keep running despite long odds. But by relaying this myth, the media reflected an underlying dynamic in the parable: a desire to see the tortoise succeed because of its plucky character.

Like the hare, Campbell was seen as too erratic, unpredictable, and egotistical to be worthy of party or public support. Her occasional verbal gaffes were read as indicators of both flightiness and off-putting haughtiness. For instance, a columnist asserted that Campbell had "lost control of the agenda," in part because of a "tongue too directly connected to a mind that tends towards arrogance."[39] Moreover, and as fully documented in chapter 4, newspapers widely reported the Charest campaign's attempts to present Campbell's two divorces and childlessness as evidence of emotional instability. In contrast, Charest was portrayed as the quintessentially trustworthy and stable family man. News coverage stressed Charest's image as the ordinary guy and contrasted his "likeability" with Campbell's allegedly aloof, combative, and arrogant personality.[40] While Campbell left party members cold, Charest won "the hearts of the party's grassroots," argued a *Vancouver Sun* writer.[41] Campbell "increasingly came to be portrayed in the media as ambitious, unstable, arrogant: in short, as a 'loose cannon'" (Courtney 1995, 121). In contrast, Charest's putatively greater appeal was the focus of several stories, citing polling data to demonstrate his growing popularity among party members and the voting public.[42] One article declared, "The Tories face electoral disaster" under Campbell's leadership,[43] and a *Globe and Mail* editorial called Campbell "the politically riskier choice" of the two candidates.[44]

Even after Campbell had prevailed at the convention, thereby upsetting the fictionalized ending of the fable, journalists continued to invoke the parable. "Tortoise runs out of time and luck," declared the headline of a *Globe and Mail* story offering in-depth analysis of the leadership contest, suggesting that Charest *could* have won if only given a few more days or weeks to win the hearts of more delegates.[45] *Globe* reporters wrote, "This time the hare finished first … but her margin of victory was slim."[46] Moreover, the coverage implied that Charest, like the tortoise, *deserved* to win because of his hard work and good character.[47]

> Mr. Charest almost never put a foot wrong. … He emphasized his status as an underdog, the tortoise who, in Aesop's fable, showed that "slow and steady wins the race." … He also transmitted a more *modest, approachable and comfortable image* than his adversary.[48]

Charest's success in nearly catching Campbell was depicted as "real," his appeal genuine, his hard work commendable. In contrast, Campbell's victory was characterized as a product of "strength fed in the early stages as much by *myth, telegenic image and media hype* as by reality."[49] Here we see the media implicating themselves as a lead author of this particular tale. Indeed, the critical role of the press in changing the direction of this story was observed by Courtney (1995, 121). "Even though delegate polls consistently showed her as having a commanding lead in delegate support, newspaper coverage quickly turned on Campbell and her campaign was damaged by negative media coverage of her performance."

However, a few members of the press offered pointed counter-narratives. Lysiane Gagnon questioned the critique of Campbell's political ambition in a *Globe and Mail* column titled "Why isn't Campbell judged by the same yardstick as male politicians?"[50] and articles published in the *Vancouver Sun* suggested that media coverage of Campbell was sexist.[51] Columnists highlighted the tendency of Campbell's opponents to question her character by engaging in a "whispering campaign" about her two divorces and childlessness.[52] Jeffrey Simpson identified "reverberations of sexism" during the campaign, including the references to Campbell's marital status.[53] According to Simpson, questions about whether Campbell was the right woman implied a double standard. Gagnon argued that it is next to impossible for any woman candidate to be judged adequate. About Campbell, Gagnon observed,

> She is too much of a "liberated" woman for the average PC activist – and radical feminists see her as a sellout. This is a problem male politicians never have to worry about. Mr. Charest is not expected to represent all men or be an advocate for any segment of the male population; nor is he expected to embody maleness. Just like any other male politician, he is judged as an individual.[54]

In addition, a few media voices celebrated Campbell's achievement as a historic first for women.[55] *Globe* columnist Margaret Wente wrote, rather optimistically, that "women have at last arrived, not as tokens, or as rare faces around the cabinet table, but as equal players in national political life."[56] Indeed, a few of the overtly celebratory stories argued that Campbell's victory ushered in a new and more welcoming era for women – for example,

> The election of Ms. Campbell as Tory leader and prime minister–designate goes far beyond modest change, in terms of gender politics. The party that notoriously betrayed a serious female contender – Flora MacDonald, in

1976 – moved smartly in proving that gender is no longer as great a disadvantage for women politicians.[57]

Disciplining the Hare: Gendered Mediation by Fable

News coverage of the 1993 PC leadership contest was shaped by the particular trajectory of the event itself, coupled with the organizational demands of the media. Newspapers could not simply declare, "Kim Campbell will win the race" as there was nothing in that particular rendition of the story to keep audiences interested or entertained. And the other obvious storyline, "a woman will win the top job for the first time in Canadian history," neither fit the classic horse race frame for party leadership coverage nor provided the kind of saga capable of sustaining months of reporting. The fable of the tortoise and the hare, on the other hand, dovetailed with the horse race motif by scripting the possibility of a different, more compelling, ending to the story. While one writer thought that Campbell had authored her own fate with a disappointing performance,[58] others argued that the media deliberately constructed the tale to chastise Campbell and favour Charest. As *Globe* columnist Jeffrey Simpson declared, by "falling for" the tortoise and the hare saga, the media closely scrutinized Campbell's "declarations, comportment, record and family history," while blithely giving Charest a "free ride."[59]

By evoking the morals associated with the parable of the tortoise and the hare, the press reflected and reinforced gendered assumptions about the performance of political leadership. Campbell was cast as the arrogant hare, consistently boastful despite her putative ineptitude, thus deserving of being bested by her stalwart opponent. Thus, this particular fiction presented Campbell as the undeserving frontrunner who deserved a dramatic comeuppance at the hands of the heroic Charest. As a peg for the narrative, the tortoise and hare story prompted readers to embrace the myth that the underdog can, if he is steady, courageous, determined, and honourable, prevail. The trope of the uppity woman dominated the storyline, with Campbell presented as unpalatably brash and calculating.[60] In sum, although a few columnists applauded Campbell's historic achievement for women and gender equality, the moral of the story was that the inappropriate aspirations of a woman can, and should, be contained and constrained by the heroic performance by a man.

Prime Time Melodramas

Clark's, Shipley's, and Gillard's leadership transitions were deemed to be "coups" by party members and pundits alike, and each was scripted as a melodrama by television news coverage. Anker defines melodrama as "a mode of popular culture narrative that employs emotionality to provide an unambiguous distinction between good and evil through clear designations of victimization, heroism, and villainy" (2005, 23). Melodrama is, therefore, "not merely a type of film or literary genre, but a pervasive cultural mode that structures the presentation of political discourse" (ibid.).

Four features of the melodramatic genre are relevant to gendered news representations of political events such as leadership challenges. The first, *sensationalism*, is fuelled by spectacle. Political conflict is often intrinsically sensational, especially when it features brutal attacks and equally violent acts of retribution. These elements foster tension and a sense of urgency, drawing the audience into the story (Singer 2001, 48). Emphasis on conflict highlights socially accepted and often taken-for-granted patterns of domination and exploitation (Connor 1997, 959), such as violent behaviour that runs counter to traditional gender-role expectations. As Gidengil and Everitt (1999, 2003a, 2003b) document in their analysis of reporting about Canadian election debates, television news coverage greatly exaggerates female leaders' aggressive behaviours because of the sheer novelty of a woman duking it out in the metaphorical boxing ring. In this context, characterizing women in "negatively charged and aggressive tones" suggests that they are inappropriately engaged in political combat (Gidengil and Everitt 1999, 50–1).

The second trademark of melodrama is *emotion*, and events are positioned as incidental triggers to the personality clashes and poignant conflicts that prompt audience identification with the characters (Joyrich 1988, 138; Lipari 1994, 302). By putting human emotions on display, melodrama brings the gender regulations associated with the public/private binary into stark relief. Women are conventionally regarded as passive, submissive, and emotionally overwrought, while men are viewed as active, dominant, and coolly rational. When the real-life characters in a melodramatic rendering of a political event fail to conform to type, a focus on emotionality is likely to heighten the disjuncture between the performance itself and hegemonic gender expectations (Singer 2001, 253).

Heightened emotions underpin the third feature of melodrama, *pathos*, represented as pity for an undeserving victim (Anker 2005, 23–34). This plot device also underscores gendered power relationships as women are culturally more likely to be understood as helpless and submissive victims, in need of rescue by a gallant male. When men are victimized, they are rarely regarded as completely passive or power-less; indeed, male victims invariably fight back. That characters are por-trayed starkly as virtuous or wicked demonstrates the final key element of melodramatic storytelling, *moral polarization*: simplistic and absolut-ist identifications of characters as villains, victims, or heroes (Lipari 1994, 302; Roth 2004, 51).

Melodramatic news thereby frames events according to culturally resonant and familiar myths (Milburn and McGrail 1992, 617). In poli-tics, as van Zoonen observes, the hero is central to mythical narratives, and heroism is invariably typed masculine (2005, 76). Gender regula-tions associate femininity with the domestic, the emotional, sexual-ity, and the body. Yet dominant metaphors of political power feature hyper-masculine men heroically facing their enemies in battle (Parpart 1998, 202), consolidating the "conventional association of public politi-cal power and strong leadership with masculinity" (Nunn 2002, 13–14). There are few historical models of women as fighters, revolutionaries, or saviours (Motion 1999, 64). As a result, the discursive positioning of leadership challenges as "coups" invokes deeply rooted patriarchal myths, including tropes of heroic warrior masculinity and subjugated femininity. Consider the synonyms for *coup*: revolt, insurgency, revolu-tion, rebellion. The lexicon of the coup is militaristic and violent, and it shapes descriptions and evaluations of those who dare to topple sit-ting party leaders, regardless of the gender of the challenger. That said, when women perform the roles traditionally reserved for men, as in the cases of the Clark, Shipley, and Gillard "coups," clichés and stereotypes about women and political power are evoked (Lipari 1994, 299).

Melodrama's narrative conventions, particularly its tendency to dramatize and oversimplify events, render ideologies of gender both "visible and watchable" (Lloyd and Johnson 2003, 11). Joyrich argues that melodramatic narratives are likely to articulate the "the threat of the feminine" by exploring issues of female subjectivity (1988, 139), and Roth maintains that melodrama is unable to fundamentally chal-lenge patriarchal power structures because it "ultimately remains trapped within dominant ideology" (2004, 61). In contrast, I argue that this approach to storytelling has the potential to disrupt social constructions of gender. In summary, melodramatic television news coverage of women's ascension to political positions typically held by men can reveal the deeply gendered underpinnings of mythical constructions of political leadership.

The leadership ascensions of Helen Clark, Jenny Shipley, and Julia Gillard were mediated by television news reporting through the conventions of the melodramatic genre. However, crucial differences among these events shaped the nature of storytelling by the news media. Shipley and Gillard were sworn in as prime minister as a result of their leadership challenges, while Helen Clark served as leader of the Opposition before winning office. Moreover, the men whom Shipley and Gillard challenged removed their names from the ballot before the vote could take place, while Clark's opponent refused to step down, and five days of media coverage passed before the caucus vote was held. Clark's challenge, therefore, was the most sensational of the three "coups."

Helen Clark: "Come Helen High Water"

Helen Clark sought the leadership of the New Zealand Labour Party in the immediate aftermath of the 1993 election. She was well positioned to go after the top job, having served as an MP[61] since 1981, as a Cabinet minister from 1987 to 1989, and as deputy prime minister for a few months before the Labour government's defeat in 1990 (Trimble and Treiberg 2010, 127). By 1993, Clark and her supporters were unhappy with the party's second electoral defeat in a row and were concerned that Labour would not perform well in the 1996 election. On November 26, 1993, television news stations reported that Clark had requested a leadership ballot. Labour leader Mike Moore was loath to relinquish the job, and he engaged in a media-fuelled campaign to swing support his way over the course of several days before a vote was held and Clark emerged victorious.

> Leading the news tonight: *the conspiracy to topple* Mike Moore. The deputy who would be leader: Helen Clark and her supporters keep a low profile as they *plot a leadership coup.*"[62]

This was the teaser for a story about the Clark challenge, broadcast on November 26, 1993, the night the story broke. Violent coup discourses abounded throughout the coverage. Sensationalized descriptors included the words *threat, conspiracy, battle, power play, simmering revolt, betrayal*, and *takeover*. Occasionally less brutal lexical choices, such as *challenge, roll*, and *spill*, were deployed in the television news stories, but more typically, the language was forceful and warlike. The "coup" was depicted as an ugly business: nasty, bitter, and intensely bloody. In deploying all the elements of melodramatic storytelling – sensationalism, emotion, pathos, and moral polarization – television news coverage of Clark's ascension to the leader's role invoked deeply held gender norms, especially the fear of women who exercise power in the public realm.

As with any melodrama, which makes clear distinctions between good and evil, no doubt was expressed about the victim of this real-life television production, which was presented as a tragedy for Mike Moore. When the story broke, Moore was described as "the embattled leader" who was "clinging on for dear life against Helen Clark."[63] "Come Helen High Water," read the deliberately provocative on-screen title for the lead story broadcast the night before the caucus vote.[64] According to this script, Clark's ambitions represented Mike Moore's hell. Moore made very public emotional appeals to supporters through the media, while Clark refused to speak to the press about the challenge until three days after the story had been revealed, allowing Moore to build sympathy for his plight. In interview after interview, Moore maintained that he had been unjustly challenged and was "not going down without a fight."[65] That Moore was willing to battle to the bitter end shored up ideals of aggressive masculinity. But it was not a fair fight, according to the besieged leader, as the "ringleaders of the coup" refused to come out of hiding and address the issue "face to face."[66] Journalists echoed this narrative, showing images of Clark meeting with constituents and going about her everyday business, while declaring that she was "maintaining silence" and "refusing Moore's offer of a peace conference."[67] In contrast, television news broadcasts emphasized that Moore was well liked in the electorate, "a man in touch with his people,"[68] and announcers and interviewers alike expressed incredulity that Moore was "fighting for his political life" at this juncture.[69] Thus, much of the coverage suggested that Clark was plotting a stealthy, mean-spirited, and unjustified challenge to a legitimate and highly popular leader.

Television reporting further cast Clark as the undisputed villain by asserting that she deliberately and calculatedly knifed her opponent in the back. For example, Clark's post-victory television interview was introduced with this teaser: "Next, in the studio with *Mike Moore's blood still fresh on her hands,* the new leader of the Labour Party, Helen Clark."[70] The very first question posed to Clark in this interview reiterated the accusation of treachery. "Helen Clark, I can't see any blood on your hands, but what's it like to knife a leader in the back like that?"[71] Moore was represented as the undeserving victim of Clark's unruly political ambitions. Pathos and moral polarization drove the storyline. After Clark's victory in the caucus vote, news stories sustained sympathy for Moore, while communicating contempt for Clark. Moore's accusation of personal betrayal was reinforced with images of his loyalists declaring their shock, disgust, and dismay with the result of the leadership challenge and voicing their anger towards the Labour Party.[72] Person-on-the street interviews expressed indignation with the party's behaviour towards the former leader, and Clark was called a "double-crosser."[73] An interviewer described Clark's win as "a victory for the politics of conspiracy and betrayal."[74] She was accused of plotting to wrest the leadership from Moore as early as 1990 and certainly as scheming during the 1993 election campaign. "You used Mike Moore during the campaign, knowing that you would dump him immediately afterwards."[75] Given the "circumstances of this leadership coup," this interviewer demanded, "how can we trust you?"[76] The trope of the unruly woman, who makes a spectacle of herself by dominating men and disrupting expectations of feminine behaviour (Anderson and Sheeler 2005, 28), was clearly evident in these representations of Clark.

Clark's gender was marked both directly and indirectly by the television coverage. An announcer's observation that "the other woman in Mike Moore's life proved his undoing," suggested that female duplicity is mobilized from the private realm, in the manner of a mistress seeking revenge.[77] By saying that Clark had "dumped" Moore, broadcasters invoked images of a personal relationship gone sour. The coverage was gendered in its evaluations of Clark as well. TV3 explicitly drew attention to the consternation prompted by a woman in a leadership position by proclaiming that *"her gender is causing problems* for the party's Maori MPs."[78] Even more prevalent, and destructive, were depictions of Clark as callous and emotionally detached, thus fundamentally unwomanly. Television interviewers circulated this theme repeatedly. For example, "I don't mean to be cruel ... [but] the perception of you by the public polling methods that are done is that you are cold, you are an intellectual; you are not a warm person, you are not the kind of person who attracts public support as a leader."[79] TVNZ's interviewer said, "You have a rather cold and remote image. Now, you're also seen to have blood on your hands. That is surely going to deepen public hostility."[80] That Clark was consistently represented as aloof and emotionally out of touch, "neither liked nor loved,"[81] shows the discomfort she provoked by transgressing the boundaries of normatively feminine behaviour. Melodramatic storytelling constructed Clark as villainous, cruel, heartless, and power-hungry, a sufficient threat to the dominant social and political order to be criticized and even reviled for her actions.

Jenny Shipley: "Jim's Gone and Jenny's In"[82]

New Zealand MP and Cabinet minister Jenny Shipley was identified as a strong candidate for party leadership, but she kept her plans to unseat long-serving National Party leader and Prime Minister Jim Bolger firmly under wraps until the evening before the challenge was mounted.[83] According to a newspaper report, Bolger's "lacklustre" campaign against Clark in the 1996 election had prompted Shipley and her supporters to make their move.[84] After he returned from an overseas journey, advisors told the prime minister that Shipley had mobilized enough support from caucus to easily defeat him. Bolger stepped aside before a vote could be held, although he continued in the role for a month after the "coup." Shipley was sworn in as prime minister of New Zealand on December 8, 1997.

If New Zealand broadcasters were hoping that the governing National Party's leadership transition would provide another sensational, prolonged, and bloody "battle," they were surely disappointed as the challenge was played out quickly and surreptitiously. Shipley's plan to contest the party leadership was reported on November 3, 1997, and Bolger's resignation and the simultaneous ascension of Shipley to the leadership took place the next day. Attempts to hype the leadership upset by focusing on classic coup themes of acrimony and duplicity included this breathless opener: "Bitterness in the beehive, Bolger's betrayed, and Shipley says, 'Shift out, I'm leader.'"[85] But the outcome was never in doubt. Any chance of a lengthy and bloody contest evaporated when Prime Minister Bolger, presented with irrefutable evidence that he would lose the vote, agreed to gracefully depart from the leader's office.

While it was called a coup, a shake-up, and a takeover, there was little opportunity to evoke pathos for the vanquished government leader. Even though television news broadcasts stressed Bolger's emotional reactions – for instance, by describing him as "close to tears"[86] – newscasters were hard pressed to portray him as a deeply wounded victim. Bolger was widely acknowledged to be gracious in defeat. Moreover, the woman who had "caused his downfall" offered a heartfelt tribute to the former prime minister, praising him for being a "wonderful leader of this country in the last ten years."[87] Television news reports never accused Shipley of plunging a metaphorical dagger into her opponent's back. For instance, TV3's John Campbell, who is generally much more acerbic, said that Shipley was "being seen almost as a meanie."[88] As a result, Shipley was portrayed as commanding but kind, nurturing in her ability to effect a smooth leadership transition.

Although Shipley was not cast as a ruthless villain, television reporting certainly dramatized and sensationalized the event in ways that revealed gendered norms and assumptions. The reports played up the uniqueness of a woman in the top job. "A world first and *a coup for women*: that's how political analysts are describing National's leadership shake-up," said an announcer.[89] This first woman framing, admiring in its tone, highlighted the novelty of a woman in power. For example, images of Shipley in action were interspersed with adulatory quotes from politicians and regular folk, narrated to the tune of Helen Reddy's feminist anthem, "I Am Woman."

Moreover, a spectacle was created, and melodrama's need for conflict was met, by redrawing the battle lines. Television news coverage declared that Shipley's fight was not with the man she had replaced; instead, it was with another woman, Labour leader Helen Clark. When news of the coup leaked the night before the official announcement, the announcer said that Shipley's victory would "wreck Helen Clark's dream."[90] Another rather gleefully echoed the view that Clark was the real casualty of Shipley's victory. "Helen Clark's tutu has been crushed quite severely by this because that great prize of being the first woman prime minister in New Zealand has actually been taken quite swiftly away from her."[91] These representations feminized and infantilized Clark by characterizing her as a young child whose dreams of political power were akin to those of a girl imagining herself as a prima ballerina. Clark's hopes were thus metaphorically crushed by Shipley's rise to power. Even more titillating to the press was the prospect of two women going head to head in an election "battle." As a political reporter declared, "You could sell tickets to this. It's sort of like going from the male boxing to the female boxing. It's *sort of a spectacle*."[92] Indeed, the New Zealand press characterized the resulting electoral contest between Jenny Shipley and Helen Clark as a "catfight" between two "Xena princesses" (Fountaine and McGregor 2003, 4); this is discussed further in chapter 6.

Jenny Shipley's leadership challenge was also gendered in the conventional manner experienced by women politicians, through attention to her domestic roles and intimate relationships. Because Shipley stepped into the exalted role of prime minister, television news featured a coronation theme in much of the reporting about both her "coup" and the swearing-in ceremony held a month later. Coronations evoke pride in a nation's cultural heritage, "provide reassurance of social and cultural continuity," and invite admiration for the person accepting the crown (Dayan and Katz 1992, 37), and in this instance, cultural stability was maintained by presenting the new prime minister as a mother and housewife. Several stories featured images of Shipley's husband and children.[93] An interviewer even asked Shipley about her husband, Burton's, role in the new regime,[94] inscribing cultural norms of femininity, which situate powerful women as extensions of their husbands (Anderson and Sheeler 2005, 16). The emphasis on Shipley's motherhood and traditional family life branded her political persona as maternal and thus fundamentally unthreatening (Roth 2004, 57).

Further, Shipley's gendered identity was positioned as an impediment to her effective and authoritative performance as New Zealand's head of government. Although the new prime minister was described in television reports as strong, capable, and tough – indeed, as "New Zealand's Iron Lady of politics"[95] – her capacity to govern was questioned because of her gender. For example, TV3's political reporter, Jane Young, noted, "Some in the party *say they don't want to be led by a farmer's wife*."[96] Shipley further attenuated the threat she posed to dominant power structures by expressing a lack of confidence in her own abilities, confessing that she was "a bit overwhelmed" by her new position.[97] A more subtle, although no less delegitimizing, message was conveyed by playing the song "Dreams Are Ten A Penny" as the musical backdrop to Shipley's scenes in a video montage of the new prime minister.

Jenny, Jenny, dreams are ten a penny
Leave them in the lost and found
Jenny, Jenny, dreams are ten a penny
Get your feet back on the ground.[98]

The lyrics suggested that Shipley's dream of holding the prime minister's post was merely a flight of fancy. Although some of the reporting was celebratory, heralding the rise of the nation's first woman prime minister, the melodramatic scripting positioned Shipley's gender identity as unthreatening but antithetical to an authoritative performance of political leadership and any enduring claim on the levers of power.

Julia Gillard: "Factional Puppet"

As did Shipley, Julia Gillard replaced a sitting prime minister. Gillard had championed Kevin Rudd's quest for the Australian Labor Party's leadership in 2006, and she was appointed deputy prime minister when the party was elected in 2007. While her political ambitions were clear, Gillard was noted for her unswerving loyalty to Rudd.[99] By June 2010, his popularity had plummeted, and he was perceived to have bungled key issues such as climate change and mining taxes. After a long meeting with the prime minister late into the evening of June 23, 2010, Gillard told the press that she would be a candidate for the party leadership in a ballot to be held the next morning. Rudd announced that he would contest the ballot, but ultimately withdrew his name before the vote. Gillard was elected leader and sworn in as the country's first woman prime minister on June 24, 2010.

Julia Gillard's last-minute challenge to Kevin Rudd's leadership of the Australian Labor Party caught the media off guard due to the speed with which it developed and the surprise element of Gillard's move. "Leadership rumblings" were announced on June 23, 2010, but even as late as the 7:30 p.m. news, the "Labor leadership spill update" was inconclusive, with the Australian Broadcasting Corporation (ABC) unable to confirm that Gillard was planning to contest the party leadership.[100] By the 10:00 p.m. broadcast, ABC was remarking on the "extraordinary night" that was unfolding, with "right-wing factional bosses" plotting against Rudd, planning to unseat him with or without Gillard's candidacy.[101] Therefore, Gillard was, from the beginning, positioned as a "puppet" of these factional bosses, an instrument of their power and control over the Labor Party. At 10:22 p.m., Kevin Rudd held a brief press conference. A vote would be held the next morning, Rudd announced, and he would be contesting the leadership.[102] However, he ultimately withdrew his name from the ballot, and Gillard was "elected unopposed."[103] Gillard was sworn in as prime minister in the early afternoon of June 24, and the entire transition was done and dusted in well under twenty-four hours.

The media were agog. "What a moment in Australian political history," said the lead-in to one of the stories broadcast at the end of what ABC called "a staggering and historic day" in Australian politics.[104] Gillard's ascension was viewed as an extraordinary turn of events. In a story titled "First Female PM," the announcer declared, "The Gillard ascendancy is remarkable in so many ways. But the achievement of becoming the nation's first female prime minister is what's resonated here and across the country."[105] As with Shipley, the first woman frame underscored the novelty of a woman climbing to a position of power. Moreover, Gillard's feminine identity was placed firmly in the spotlight by showing the new prime minister embracing her partner, with the narration describing "Australia's new first bloke" as "a hairdresser turned real estate salesman."[106] This story went on to remind viewers that Gillard had been judged unsuitable for high political office because she was "deliberately barren."[107] But for television news coverage, the spectacle was more than merely the anomaly of an unmarried, childless woman in the top job. This had all the hallmarks of a melodramatic political event. As a news announcer put it, "No one here's seen anything like it. A first-term prime minister dumped, a female prime minister sworn in, all after a political mugging that was ruthless, swift, and effective."[108] Although the word *coup* was rarely used, vivid and indeed violent language was strewn throughout ABC's commentary. Rudd was toppled, brought down, dumped, overthrown, and vanquished. The manoeuvre was deemed a challenge, plot, crisis, overthrow, spill, political mugging, and swift and ruthless dispatch, and Opposition leader Tony Abbott described it alternately as a scalping and a political execution.[109] One report even called it the "Gillard revolution."[110]

Melodrama's need for high emotion was also met by this particular "coup." Kevin Rudd performed the poignant scenes well beyond media expectations when he paused several times, teary-eyed, in an effort to gain control during his post-defeat news conference. Moreover, he drew attention to his own tears. "What I'm less proud of is that I have now blubbered."[111] These scenes were replayed in each of ABC's stories about Rudd's reaction, often in close-up, and narrated with repeated references to the high emotional stakes.[112] ABC's political editor, Heather Hewitt, judged these tearful moments "excruciating to watch,"[113] underscoring widely held social discomfort with men exhibiting behaviours stereotyped as feminine. Rudd's public weeping violated norms of hegemonic masculinity. However, close-ups of his tears and references to the "sheer brutality" of his dispatch from office[114] did not entirely serve to represent the former prime minister as an undeserving victim, a core requirement of pathos. The bulk of the television coverage described Rudd as the author of much of his own misfortune. According to ABC coverage, the "writing was on the wall" for Kevin Rudd.[115] Labor's poor standing in the polls was highlighted in several stories, as were his policy missteps and off-putting leadership style.[116] Rudd's culpability was punctuated with this assessment: "It's not difficult to work out how the groundswell of caucus support for Julia Gillard grew yesterday. There's been a genuine fear Labor could lose the election and concern that public perception of Kevin Rudd was the real problem."[117]

There was no disguising the fact that Kevin Rudd went unwillingly. His removal from the party leader's post was called a ruthless and brutal betrayal and a "spectacular fall from grace."[118] But the Labor Party was represented as the primary villain, not Julia Gillard. She was called the coup leader in only one report.[119] More importantly, the "stabbing your colleague in the back" metaphor was mobilized just once, and even then very feebly. In a lengthy interview broadcast on the ABC's 7:30 report, Gillard was asked how hard it was to "plant the knife," but the interviewer quickly dropped this line of questioning.[120] Instead, Gillard was consistently described as a faithful deputy and a reluctant challenger, unwilling to push Rudd out of the post. "She remained loyal to Kevin Rudd right up until yesterday, repeatedly dismissing speculation about a threat to his leadership."[121] In short, the party was blamed for Rudd's removal from office; he was, according to one interviewer, "shafted by his own party."[122]

Even better for Gillard, ABC's coverage presented her as a heroic figure for women and for the country as a whole. Long touted as a prime minister in the making, her ascent seen as inevitable, Gillard's "rise to the top" was celebrated in several stories, with lingering shots of the swearing-in ceremony, interviews with proud family members and pleased constituents, and adulatory summaries of her successful political career.[123] But this was more than a coronation; as one report asserted, "She marched to glory and into leadership."[124] "She's made it," said another.[125] However, these images of Gillard as the valiant redeemer did not successfully reconfigure the norm of heroic warrior masculinity because she was described as "brought to glory" not by her own initiative and fortitude, but rather by the factional leaders within the

Labor Party. ABC news maintained that a wave of pressure from the party's "right-wing factional bosses" had carried Gillard into power.[126] Indeed, it was this "cabal of factional warlords" who "helped destroy" Kevin Rudd's career and deliver the prize to Julia Gillard.[127] Although this narrative served to (temporarily) exonerate Gillard in the "midnight assassination" of Kevin Rudd,[128] it also situated these "factional bosses," all of whom were identified as men, as the real power behind the throne. One news story described Gillard as a "factional *puppet*" and asserted that "even senior Labor insiders share some concerns about the circumstances of her rise."[129] Puppets do not rule on their own authority; instead, they dutifully submit to the exercise of power by men (Anderson and Sheeler 2005, 19). The implication was that Gillard, as a woman, could serve merely as the standard-bearer for the party, holding power at the behest of the back room boys. The assumption of male domination and female subservience thus undercut the seemingly heroic characterization of Gillard.

Melodrama and Gendered Mediation

The challenge posed by Helen Clark to Mike Moore in 1993 was truly a made-for-TV melodrama. Dramatic intensity was sustained throughout the event, pathos was elicited when Moore took to the airwaves to fight for his job, and moral polarization rendered Clark the villain, brutally and single-mindedly pursuing her political aspirations by knifing Moore in the back. That this was treachery, not heroism, was amplified by the assertion that a "normal" woman would not so ruthlessly and unfeelingly dispatch her opponent. Television news fashioned the spectre of a disloyal, scheming political operator willing to kill her colleague's political career to advance her own unruly ambitions. By casting Clark's challenge as cruel and destructive, the television coverage situated women's claims to power as threatening and dangerous.

In contrast, while coverage of the Shipley and Gillard challenges was certainly melodramatic, with considerable sensationalism and emotionality, neither woman was presented as a villain. A key factor underlying the more adulatory depictions of Shipley and Gillard was that their ascensions vaulted them into the illustrious and dignified role of prime minister. Not surprisingly, a coronation theme echoed through the television coverage, particularly of their swearing-in ceremonies. Yet the novelty value of the first woman to soar to the prime minister's post was highlighted in television news stories, and the first woman frame so frequently applied to both Shipley and Gillard marked their presence in the political field as anomalous. As well, neither Shipley nor Gillard was written into the melodramatic script as an authoritative political leader. Even though Shipley was described as tough, determined, and strong, her traditional performance of femininity was highlighted by the coverage to articulate doubts about her ability to successfully hold the reins of power. Melodramatic renditions of Julia Gillard's rise to power reinforced norms of male dominance and female subjugation, even while it seemingly celebrated her heroism. Gillard was portrayed as the loyal deputy to the man she had deposed, thus as a reluctant queen. But it was the queen-makers, the men who held the power behind the throne, who were accused of installing Gillard as their "puppet." ABC news reporting of the "Gillard revolution" in Australia thereby invoked tropes of female subjugation by pronouncing Gillard's victory a result of behind-the scenes manoeuvrings by the "factional warlords" in the Labor Party. Underlying the adulatory reports of Gillard's remarkable political achievements was a cautionary tale: women's presence in political leadership roles is enjoyed at the bequest of powerful men.

Conclusions

As many studies confirm, a "cultural fear of feminine strength" becomes visible when women gain power in the public realm (Anderson and Sheeler 2005, 17). Media characterizations of women's desire to rule as unseemly and even dangerous evince profound uneasiness with women in powerful political positions (Anderson and Sheeler 2005, 11–34; Bashevkin 2009, 2; Lawrence and Rose 2010, 200; Trimble and Treiberg 2010, 129). As I have shown in this chapter, discomfort was evident in media characterizations of the rise of Campbell, Clark, Shipley, and Gillard to top political leadership positions. While coverage of all four women was shaped by contextual factors, each of these narratives highlighted and reinforced dominant archetypes of political power and authoritative leadership. By adopting, and adapting, the fable of the tortoise and the hare, newspaper reports presented Campbell as undeserving because of her desire for power, her putative superiority and arrogance, and her alleged inability to manage her private life or her "unwieldy" campaign team. The trope of the uppity woman was central to this particular storyline, emphasized by the newspapers' fixation on the heroic performance of the underdog challenger, Jean Charest, whose gender was read as evidence of stability and competence.

Similarly, by scripting the Clark, Shipley, and Gillard leadership challenges as melodramas, particular "facts" were selected, organized, framed, and emphasized to create compelling storylines. For all three women, the use of melodramatic and often violent coup discourses by television news heightened the drama and made gender both visible and constitutive of the very nature of the "battle." Even though Clark, Shipley, and Gillard succeeded in vanquishing men, discourses of rebellion and conquest, villain and victim, revolts and plotters evoked a masculine battlefield on which women's very presence was anomalous, thus disruptive.

However, counter-narratives contested these associations of political power with men and masculinity and worked to expose gendered power relations. Columnists pointed out the sexism underpinning the evaluations of Campbell, drew attention to women's political under-representation in Canadian politics, and situated her victory in the leadership contest as a remarkable achievement for women. Television stories offered celebratory and congratulatory accounts of Shipley's and Gillard's ascensions to the prime minister's role. By broadcasting the swearing-in ceremonies and lingering on smiling faces of family members and delighted citizens, news reports hailed these historic achievements with words and images. In contrast, because she took over the leadership of an opposition party, Clark did not benefit from this coronation theme.

That ascension stories shape subsequent media representations of political leaders is amply revealed by the characterizations of the four women prime ministers throughout their political careers. As detailed in chapter 6, depictions of Clark as cruel and domineering continued to circulate through news coverage of her leadership, with epithets like "political dominatrix" and "Helengrad" underscoring negative evaluations of her political persona and governance style (Ross and Comrie 2012, 974–5; Trimble and Treiberg 2010, 129). Echoing news coverage broadcast during her leadership "coup," Shipley's hetero-normative family life was emphasized in news coverage of her first, and only, electoral competition as prime minister by fore-grounding her husband and children and contrasting her domestic "normality" with Helen Clark's childlessness (Fountaine 2002, 14–16; Trimble and Treiberg 2010, 125). The family strategy employed by Shipley is assessed in chapter 4, which also examines how Campbell's opponents' portrayals of her two failed marriages as evidence of emotional (and political) instability gained traction in press accounts of the leadership contest. The ways in which first impressions echo and reverberate is shown by descriptions of Campbell as arrogant, shamelessly overconfident, and, as explored in chapter 7, verbally maladroit. Gendered understandings of Gillard similarly cycled through subsequent news interpretations of her persona and performance. Gillard's political authority was undermined during the 2010 election by what Marian Sawer (2012, 257) calls an "extraordinary level of scrutiny" of the prime minister's private life, which I document in chapter 4. Also, as discussed in chapter 7, when a surfeit of sexist comments and accusations impelled Gillard to give a fifteen-minute speech to Parliament decrying sexism and misogyny in political and media discourses, she was accused of inciting a "gender war."

Chapter 3 further demonstrates the importance of gendered identities to mediated accounts of political leadership as it examines the practice of labelling political actors as women or men, female or male. By comparing attention to the gender labels employed in newspaper representations of the four women prime ministers and the men against whom they competed in federal elections, I assess the argument that a woman's gender is invariably at the forefront of her news coverage, while the gender of men leaders is assumed and thus unstated. Examining the meanings underpinning the application of gender markers reveals the extent to which they work to delegitimize women's performance of political leadership, while normalizing the presence of men in leadership roles. As well, I explore the possibility that demarking gender can expose gendered power imbalances and subtly challenge the gender order.

Chapter Three

First Women and the X Factor

Introduction

"Tories ready – finally – to accept a woman leader."[1]

"Woman of steely resolve in good times and bad."[2]

"Mixed reaction to first woman PM."[3]

"She's right on tax, and a woman too."[4]

As these headlines about Campbell, Clark, Shipley, and Gillard show, the news media are inclined to foreground the novelty of a woman prime minister. Even though the fact of her gender identity is obvious to even the least politically aware observer, it is pointed out nonetheless and is sometimes signalled by the headline as being integral to the news story. According to Sreberny-Mohammadi and Ross (1996, 109), a "woman politician is always described as such, her gender always the primary descriptor." But is a woman prime minister's gender identity invariably at the forefront of her media coverage? If so, what sorts of meanings are produced by these representations? Does referencing gender confer or deny legitimacy in the leadership role?

In this chapter, I gauge the extent to which gender-based identifiers were woven into news coverage of the women prime ministers at key points in their careers, and I compare the amount of explicit attention to gender for the equivalent men leaders during election campaigns. To do so, I examine the presence of, and meanings conveyed by, gender markers. *Gender markers* (or *labels*; I use the two terms interchangeably throughout this chapter) are deliberate lexical choices made by journalists and editors. They explicitly identify and often emphasize the gender of political actors in accounts of their personas and performances. Although the practice of noticing gender may seem perfectly innocent and inconsequential, these words and phrases are far from neutral in their underlying assumptions and the meanings they convey. "The right man for the job" communicates something very different from "first woman prime minister." By prefacing nouns like *candidate, leader*, and *prime minister* with gender identifiers such as *woman, female, mother*, and *lady*, news coverage highlights gender distinctions and suggests that they are politically meaningful and important for making judgments about a leader's authenticity and legitimacy. For example, the phrases *female prime minister* and *ladylike speech* tie a woman's gender identity to her political persona. When labelled a "woman leader" or "the female prime minister," women are described as performing leadership *as women*, rather than being depicted as political actors who are performing leadership.

I begin with a discussion of gender labelling, summarizing the literature on the subject and outlining my approach to measuring and analysing these indicators of gendered mediation. Quantitative findings are presented in the second section, beginning with data on the presence of gender markers in news stories about the women leaders at key points in their political careers. After offering a numerical comparison of the amount of attention to the gender of the women and the men against whom they competed in general elections, the third part of the chapter delves into the qualitative analysis by examining the meanings conveyed by explicit gender notations for both the women and the men leaders. As the findings illustrate, gender is highlighted and revealed as a socially constructed category in news reporting about political leaders. Representations of gender in descriptions of the leaders' ideas, personas, speeches, and campaign strategies assume that the performance of political leadership is itself gendered. Yet by observing the gender of a political leader, media coverage may expose power imbalances and gendered assumptions about who should exercise political leadership. Competing and contradictory meanings often coincide in news accounts of leaders' political careers and activities. The argument that explicitly gendered language delegitimizes women's political ambitions and marks them as "deviant" in formal political spaces is both supported and contested by qualitative analysis of the gender markers applied to Campbell, Clark, Shipley, and Gillard. Overall, the news coverage reveals considerable confusion about what a woman prime minister's gender means for her own ambitions and for political life more generally.

What's in a Label? Politicizing Gender

Gender marking is the practice of explicitly signifying the gender of an individual in news reports, and the gendered mediation literature argues that it politicizes gender in four distinct but related ways. First, gender labels reinforce the public man/private woman binary by situating women as "others" in the political sphere. As Sreberny-Mohammadi and Ross (1996, 109) put it, she is "not simply a politician (male as norm), but a special kind of deviant professional, a woman politician." By identifying women politicians as women in overt and obvious ways, news coverage confirms that because most inhabitants of elite political positions are men, women's presence in leadership roles is unique and unusual (Meeks 2012, 179). The emergence of women as elite political actors is viewed as remarkable, worthy of special attention and elaboration of the meanings and implications associated with their presence in leadership positions.

Second, gender markers reveal "the unspoken cultural understanding that politicians, senators and candidates must be men" (Falk 2010, 93). For instance, by asking newly sworn-in New Zealand prime minister Jenny Shipley whether it would be difficult to be a woman in the prime minister's post, journalists suggested that her gender would affect her performance. Posing such pointed questions to women signals that they are not up to the job *because* they are women. Moreover, there is no effective response. Shipley replied, "Walking over television cords in high heels is, I suspect, more difficult than for my male colleagues."[5] She was trying to meet a ridiculous question with good humour, but Shipley's response punctuated her (alleged) gender-based difference from the men who usually occupy the prime minister's office. A "man candidate would not be asked how as a 'man president' he would handle world leaders" (Falk 2010, 86). By *not* asking men how their gendered social locations affect their ability to lead, media coverage implies that men's gender is irrelevant to assessments of their viability or performance. They are good or bad, successful or unsuccessful, notwithstanding the gender category under which they are classified.

Third, gender distinctions are considered worthy of mention "precisely because the culture contains the belief that men and women are different in important ways (relevant to politics)" (Falk 2010, 94). Gender marking essentializes politicians' gendered identities by drawing a link between women and biology. A woman's capabilities and aspirations are thus understood and discursively constructed as being limited by her body and its reproductive capacities (Nicholson 1994, 81). Gender distinctions therefore work to reinforce the public man/private woman binary, associating women and men with different skills and areas of competence. As a result, gender markers signal to news audiences that the attributes and skills of the political actor being described should be read through the lens of gendered understandings about how they might be perceived by the voting public. During the 2008 Democratic presidential nomination process, for instance, Hillary Clinton's electability was much more frequently questioned in newspaper stories that explicitly denoted her gender, thereby inferring that a "woman may not be electable to the highest office in the United States because of the fact of her gender" (Miller, Peake, and Boulton 2010, 178).

Fourth, the playing-the-gender-card metaphor politicizes gender quite overtly by asserting that women politicians inappropriately deploy their gender identity for political gain. Falk shows how the "gender card" metaphor is mobilized in mediated accounts to argue that a self-conscious use of gender identity by women candidates gives them a strategic and unethical advantage in the competition (Falk 2013, 196). During her bid for the Democratic presidential nomination in 2008, Hillary Clinton's seemingly inconsequential observation that women face discrimination in political competitions was represented as dishonourable and unfair campaign tactics (Falk 2013, 202–3). While the playing-the-gender-card metaphor did not surface very often for Clinton in 2008, a similar gender marker exploded on both mainstream and social media in late April 2016, during the American presidential primaries. Republican candidate Donald Trump accused Clinton, again seeking the Democratic nomination, of playing the "women's card" to win her bid for the presidency.[6] The only thing Clinton had going for her was her gender, Trump insisted. "If Hillary Clinton were a man, I don't think she would get five percent of the vote."[7] Trump's controversial comments reflected the proposition that women achieve positions they do not deserve, and have not earned, merely on the basis of their gender.

Throughout this book, I argue that gendered mediation has the potential to both reinforce and challenge the assumptions underlying socially and discursively constructed gender regulations and dualisms.

Gender markers provide an excellent example of the contradictions embedded in mediated political discourses. On the one hand, applying gender labels suggests that men and women will perform political leadership differently because of their gender identities (Falk 2010, 96). On the other hand, since the political man/private woman binary is socially, politically, and discursively constructed, gender markers can play a role in the *reconstruction* of politics as a realm suitable for, and indeed welcoming to, women. Gender identifiers may "other" women, but they also make visible the assumption that politics is a male preserve. For example, women's history of exclusion from political leadership roles is communicated by acknowledging their status as "firsts." By highlighting the first woman party leader or first woman prime minister, news coverage draws attention to the previous *absence* of women from these roles. Reporting, however, may suggest that gender equality has been achieved, which is far from the truth.

As another example, when the presence of women in political leadership positions is the big point of a story, audiences might be informed about women's ability to carry out these roles (Falk 2010, 95). Positive evaluations of a woman leader's performance can expose, challenge, and perhaps even change culturally embedded notions about who has the "right stuff" for political leadership. Yet, these success stories are about a particular type of woman, one who is white, able-bodied, middle to upper class, and heterosexual, suggesting that only certain women have the necessary qualities to succeed.

Finally, certain gender markers prompt a discursively productive response in mainstream and/or on social media. In reaction to Republican candidate Donald Trump's insistence that Hillary Clinton was playing the "woman card," the hashtag #womancard quickly trended on Twitter, with observers pointing out the many ways in which being a woman is far from an advantage in social, economic, or political life.[8] These reactions exposed the power relations inherent in the woman card metaphor, which serves as a particularly pointed and powerful form of gender marking. As the wave of misogyny and sexism expressed towards Clinton during the 2016 presidential election campaign indicates, mediated representations of gender on social media can be both hateful and harmful to women's political ambitions.

Because I am interested in the *politicization* of gendered personas, I operationalize the concept of the gender marker as the explicit and unequivocal identification of a politician's gender with deliberate lexical choices such as *woman, female, lady, sister, daughter,* and *princess;* or *man, male, guy, son, brother,* and *prince.* Overt gender categorization – for example, labelling Kim Campbell a "member of the other founding gender" – is also included as a form of gender marking. While gender identity is unavoidably signified by pronouns or prefixes such as *he, she, her,* and *his,* as well as honorifics like *Mrs., Mr., Miss,* and *Ms.,* these lexical choices were not classified as gender markers for the objectives of this analysis. I am interested in the purposeful selections made by reporters and columnists to signal the gender identity of political actors. Reporters, who are following newspaper style, use gendered pronouns (*he* and *she*) and honorifics (*Mr.* and *Ms.*) as a matter of convention. In all three countries, the women leaders were typically referred to either by their surname or as "prime minister" or its abbreviation ("PM"). Less frequently, journalists and editors included first and last names in the text of a story or used the prefix "Ms." In New Zealand, the choice of honorific signalled marital status as Shipley was, by choice, called "Mrs. Shipley," and Clark was occasionally deemed "Miss Clark," despite the fact that she was married. The meanings of these references for understanding marital situations and family lives are explored in chapter 4, "First Men and the Family Strategy."

In the pages that follow, I examine the application of gender markers in newspaper coverage of Campbell, Clark, Shipley, and Gillard at four discrete stages of their political careers: winning the party leadership role, governance, election(s), and defeat or resignation from political office. The use of the gender card metaphor to describe Gillard's post-election strategies is analysed as well, along with gender marking of the men with whom Campbell, Clark, and Gillard competed during election campaigns. Both quantitative and qualitative methods were used to analyse the gender labels. Content analysis determined the percentage of news stories that employed gender markers for each of the leaders. If a news story about a leader used any of the gender-specific terms itemized above, it was coded as containing a gender marker. As well, each explicit reference to gender was recorded and compiled into a qualitative database, a corpus of all words and phrases used to communicate the gender of these political actors, as were notations about who employed the label (a reporter, the leader, a colleague, or an opponent) and the context in which the marker was used. Content analysis of this inventory allowed me to compare the number of gender labels applied to the women prime ministers and their male competitors. To tease out the meanings communicated by gender markers, I turned to qualitative analysis of this corpus. When performing discourse analysis of the words or phrases denoting gender identity, I looked for the politicization of gender through links between gender markers and understandings of power and political leadership.

Gender Marking Women's Political Careers

Women are often considered novelties in elite political spaces, their bodies noticed and "othered" by explicit references to their unusualness in the male-dominated world of elite politics. Unsurprisingly, therefore, women who seek high political office are likely to have their gender referenced in news coverage of their leadership or election bids. Falk (2010, 86) found that the nine women who had sought the US presidency from 1872 to 2008 were consistently branded by their gender. Indeed, early women presidential candidates often had their gender specified in news headlines, which represents a particularly prominent, thus emphatic, form of gender marking (Falk 2010, 91). German Chancellor Angela Merkel is also explicitly marked as female in both news and entertainment coverage (Lünenborg and Maier 2015, 185–6). This trend is not unique to media coverage of politics. Internet news stories from US media outlets feature a "preponderance of unnecessarily gendered language," such as "Chairman" and "spokeswoman" (Burke and Mazzarella 2008, 409). Television commentary about women's and men's collegiate basketball tournaments and tennis matches in the United States consistently reminds viewers that women are the players, that these are "women's games"; but male athletes and their games are rarely described as such (Messner, Duncan, and Jensen 1993, 126).

Using content analysis, I determined the percentage of news stories about each woman leader that featured at least one gender marker. The results shown in table 3.1 confirm the application of gender-specific representations of the women leaders at key points in their political careers. Differences among the four women in the proportion of gender markers at different career stages are explained by the intersection of contextual factors with particular news values. Explicit gender descriptors were especially prevalent during the leadership ascension phase, which includes coverage of their rise to the prime minister's role or, in Helen Clark's case, to the position of leader of the Official Opposition. This is not surprising as they were the first women to claim these positions and the fact of their gender was a unique element of the story, one with immense news value. Both Campbell and Clark had their gender

Table 3.1 Percentage of News Stories Containing Gender Markers, by Country, Leader, and Career Phase

Country	Leader	Leadership, %	Governance, %	Election		Resignation or defeat, %
				Date	%	
Canada	Kim Campbell	33	28	1993	27	54
New Zealand	Jenny Shipley	23	34	1999	17	22
	Helen Clark	33	6	1996	13	19
				1999	24	
				2002	9	
				2005	13	
				2008	10	
Australia	Julia Gillard	55	15	2010	20	54

observed in a third of the stories about their climb to the metaphorical top of the political ladder. For Gillard, a whopping 55 per cent of the newspaper articles printed about her leadership challenge denoted her gender. Clearly, the novelty of a woman prime minister had not waned by the time Australians celebrated this historic first. In contrast, Jenny Shipley's gender was signalled in under a quarter of the newspaper articles about her leadership challenge. During the month-long stretch between her "coup" and her swearing-in as prime minister, many news articles about Shipley focused their attention on her government's high-stakes negotiations with its coalition partner, and her status as the first woman prime minister took a back seat to discussions about whether the government would survive.

Table 3.1 shows considerable variation in the number of articles applying gender markers to these four women during the governance phase of their careers, reflecting the different trajectories that they took to the prime minister's office. After she officially assumed the duties of prime minister, Shipley's status as the first woman to lead the country was a source of much commentary by the New Zealand press corps as over a third of the articles mentioned it during her governance phase. Similarly, Campbell began serving as Canadian government leader immediately after her ascension to party leadership, and the novelty of a "first woman" in the prime minister's office was reflected in newspaper coverage of her governance phase, with 28 per cent of the news stories marking her gender identity in some way. This was not the case for Gillard, whose stint as prime minister also followed right on the heels of her ascent to the party leader's role. Although her gender was still considered notable, as it was pronounced in 15 per cent of the stories, the attention of the press shifted to a range of urgent policy matters that the new prime minister was eager to address before she called an election. Gender markers were infrequently applied to Clark during the governance phases of her career. She won the prime minister's post more than five years after claiming the title of Labour Party leader, and by then, her status as a "first woman" had lost its news salience. Moreover, Clark succeeded New Zealand's first woman prime minister, so she was not the first woman to claim the position. That her gender was rarely noted when Clark was governing the country may indicate acceptance, at least in that context, of women in political leadership roles. After she won the 1999 election and won re-election in 2002 and 2005, Clark was written into news stories as the prime minister, not as the woman prime minister.

The gender identities of the women leaders were woven into news articles published during their election campaigns, with the highest proportion of gender marking during an election evidenced during the 1993 Canadian election. Campbell had her gender overtly referenced in 27 per cent of the stories written about her during the campaign. Similarly, a great deal of attention was paid to the gender of the leading contenders during the 1999 New Zealand election, which featured "a battle between two women"[9] and guaranteed the election of a woman prime minister. During this election, Clark's gender was discussed in almost a quarter of the articles focused on her, while for Shipley, close to a fifth of the stories contained some sort of gender reference. The New Zealand newspapers did not hesitate to comment on the unusualness of two women fighting for the top job, even calling it a "spectacle."[10] But as table 3.1 shows, Clark's gender was of considerably less interest to the press after she won office in 1999 and competed in subsequent elections. Finally, in Australia, while the first flush of attention to Gillard's status as the first woman prime minister had waned by the time she called the 2010 election, a fifth of the election campaign stories explicitly observed her gender.

Gender came to the fore when the women leaders resigned after an election loss (Campbell and Clark) or were defeated in a leadership "coup" (Shipley and Gillard). Over half the stories referenced Campbell's and Gillard's gendered identities in the wake of their exits. For Campbell, this was likely because her stunning electoral defeat came so closely on the heels of her historic victory in the leadership campaign. That a woman rose and fell so quickly was a key element of the story.[11] In Gillard's case, gender became a locus of political discussion in the weeks and months before her demise because of her parliamentary speech on sexism and misogyny and other speech acts, which prompted the news media to accuse her of "playing the gender card" (discussed later in this chapter) and "inciting a gender war" (detailed in chapter 7). In comparison, the New Zealand prime ministers attracted less attention to their gender when they were defeated, perhaps because of the relatively long time they had spent in party leadership roles. Shipley served as National's leader for four years and as prime minister for two years. Clark was Labour leader for fifteen years and prime minister for nine. When she stepped down from the party leader's role after losing the 2008 election, Clark's status as a "first woman" was mentioned only in passing, while journalists presented the highlights of her lengthy and distinguished political career.

Sreberny-Mohammadi and Ross's (1996, 109) assertion that gender is "always the primary descriptor" for women politicians can be assessed with the data presented in table 3.1. The novelty of a woman in a political leadership role was indeed highlighted in a large percentage of articles about each of the four women prime ministers. But when it ceased to be unusual, as was the case when Helen Clark held the Labour Party leadership for fifteen years and the prime minister's post for nine, gender was not as frequently mentioned. That longevity mitigates the unusualness of a woman performing an elite political role suggests that the presence of women in high political office may be discursively normalized as more women are elected and re-elected.

Gender Signposts on the Campaign Trail

Many studies have found that women leaders are much more likely than equivalent men leaders to be marked by their gender in campaign news coverage. Reporting about candidates in primary races held for the position of US senator or governor in 2000 noted the gender of women candidates in 12.7 per cent of the newspaper articles predominantly about them, but the gender of the men candidates was never mentioned in any of the articles focused on them (Bystrom, Robertson, and Banwart 2001). A more expansive analysis of newspaper coverage of campaigns for US senate seats and the position of state governor held in 1998, 2000, and 2002 determined that candidate gender was noted in 7 to 10 per cent of the news stories for the women contenders and only 1 per cent of stories about the men seeking these positions

(Bystrom et al. 2004, 179). Falk's examination of the press coverage of the women and comparable men who sought the US presidency discovered that while women candidates were consistently branded by their gender, men candidates were rarely labelled with explicit gender markers (2010, 86). Individual case studies of women who sought the US presidency, such as Geraldine Ferraro, Elizabeth Dole, and Hillary Clinton, produced similar findings. These leaders were significantly more likely than the men they opposed to have their gender identified in media accounts of their campaigns (Heldman, Carroll, and Olson 2005, 315; Meeks 2012, 184; Miller, Peake, and Boulton 2010, 178). Similarly, when Angela Merkel sought the German chancellorship in the 2005 Bundestag election, newspaper and television reporting more frequently emphasized the role her gender played in the campaign than was the case in stories about her opponent, incumbent Chancellor Gerhard Schröder (Semetko and Boomgaarden 2007, 166).

When a woman leader's gender is explicitly manifested in news stories while a male competitor's gender goes unobserved, the implication is that a woman's gendered persona is considered essential to understanding and assessing the event or issue, while a man's is assumed to be entirely unrelated to the story (Falk 2010, 86). As Falk puts it, "women are portrayed as hampered by their gender, whereas men are portrayed as gender-free" (ibid.). The argument that gender labels cast women politicians as anomalous outsiders, while conventionalizing the presence of men in leadership and governance roles, hinges on confirming that men's gendered social locations are rarely, if ever, recorded or discussed in news coverage. So what does it mean when men are as likely as women to have their gender highlighted by press coverage of their campaigns, as was the case when the women in my sample competed with men in election campaigns? My analysis paints a very different picture than does much of the literature. Table 3.2 compares the percentage of election news stories featuring gender markers for the women leaders and their male opponents. In four of the six elections featuring a contest between a woman and a man – Campbell's 1993 campaign against Liberal leader Jean Chrétien and Clark's three campaigns as the incumbent prime minister of New Zealand – a slightly larger percentage of newspaper articles indicated the gender of the *men* leaders than that of the women. In only two of these six elections were women signified by their gender in a higher percentage of stories than the men against whom they competed for votes: Clark's first campaign in 1996 and Gillard's 2010 election contest.

Table 3.2 Percentage of News Stories Containing Gender Markers, by Country, Election Date, and Candidate

Country	Election date	Woman leader	Stories, %	Man leader	Stories, %
Canada	1993	Kim Campbell	27	Jean Chrétien	28
New Zealand	1996	Helen Clark	13	Jim Bolger	4
	1999	Helen Clark	24	n/a	n/a
		Jenny Shipley	19	n/a	n/a
	2002	Helen Clark	9	Bill English	13
	2005	Helen Clark	13	Don Brash	19
	2008	Helen Clark	10	John Key	13
Australia	2010	Julia Gillard	20	Tony Abbott	13

This is a surprising finding, and it demands explanation. Since the content analysis simply captured the percentage of news stories making at least one mention of a leader's gender identity, I wondered whether there were fewer discrete gender notations per story for the men than for the women. But this was not the case. As the qualitative inventory of gender markers applied to each candidate revealed, in four of the six elections in which women competed against men, the gender of the men leaders was mentioned more frequently than was the case for the women leaders (see table 3.3). In some instances, the differences were slight. For example, twenty-seven discrete gender markers were applied to Jean Chrétien in the newspaper articles in my sample compared to twenty-five for Kim Campbell. Helen Clark's gender was frequently mentioned during the 1999 campaign featuring female opponent Jenny Shipley, but after she became prime minister, her male opponents were reported with a higher number of gender markers in stories written about them. In these cases, differences were acute. News coverage of Bill English in 2002 said something about his gender more than twice as often as for Clark in the reporting about her campaign. In the 2005 election coverage, Brash had forty-five gender-specific descriptors compared to only twenty-five for Clark. Only in two instances – Clark's first election performance, in 1996, and Gillard's quest for a mandate in Australia in 2010 – were the women leaders' gendered identities marked more frequently than was the case for their male opponents.

This puzzling result stands in stark contrast with the findings of much of the literature and requires further exploration. Perhaps gender labels convey different meanings when applied to women and men

Table 3.3 Number of Gender Markers, by Candidate and Election Campaign

Country	Election date	Gender markers			
		Woman leader	N	Man leader	N
Canada	1993	Kim Campbell	25	Jean Chrétien	27
New Zealand	1996	Helen Clark	22	Jim Bolger	7
	1999	Helen Clark	48	n/a	n/a
		Jenny Shipley	22	n/a	n/a
	2002	Helen Clark	10	Bill English	22
	2005	Helen Clark	25	Don Brash	45
	2008	Helen Clark	25	John Key	31
Australia	2010	Julia Gillard	44	Tony Abbott	21

leaders – for instance, by regularizing men as political leaders, while situating women as atypical or extraordinary actors in elite leadership roles. To explore this possibility, I turned to feminist critical discourse analysis of the gender markers. The next section examines the gender labels applied to the male party leaders when they campaigned for office, illustrating the extent to which hegemonic forms of masculinity are taken for granted in representations of political leadership. I then turn to a detailed examination of how gender markers discursively constructed the women leaders' political interventions as emanating from their gendered identities.

Good Guys and Family Men

For the women leaders, an adjective or noun connoting gender was consistently employed to qualify political nouns or actions (Falk 2010, 93). Falk terms this lexical strategy "gendering nouns" (2010, 95). Campbell, Clark, Shipley, and Gillard were frequently labelled the "female prime minister" or "the first woman to take the leadership" or "the only woman leader." In stark contrast to this trend, none of the articles referred to the "male party leader" or "male candidate." These leaders were assumed to be men. So when their gender was explicitly indicated in newspaper coverage, it was often to merely call them "men," without elaboration, or to describe the *type of men* they were perceived to be.

Gender markers for the men leaders typically noted their gender classification in passing. During the 1993 Canadian election, Liberal leader Jean Chrétien's self-styled identity as the "little guy from Shawinigan"[12] was regularly cited in newspaper articles about him.[13] A columnist's assertion that supporters of Don Brash, Helen Clark's opponent in 2005, "knew their man"[14] and an observation that John Key, who defeated Clark in 2008, was "the man current polls indicate may run this country"[15] provide typical examples of this trend. Similarly, Tony Abbott, who contested the 2010 Australian election against Gillard, was "a guy" who stood up to a truculent reporter.[16] The word *guy* communicates ordinariness, and its use presented some of the men leaders as being in tune with, or at one with, the electorate. However, John Key was regularly called a "boy" – for instance, "the political new boy"[17] – as a way of contrasting his newness and relative youth with Clark's experience and longevity in the prime minister's job.[18] This tag arguably trivialized Key's political persona by connoting extreme youthfulness.

Journalists applied gender markers to men when reflecting on their characters or personal qualities, revealing the ubiquity of gendered assumptions about personality traits and leadership skills. Canada's Chrétien was a "Teflon Man," a "man of experience," a "man of action," a "practical man," and, less flattering, "yesterday's man."[19] Helen Clark's first electoral opponent, Jim Bolger, was deemed a "great helmsman."[20] Bill English, who lost to Clark in 2002, was frequently called a "family man,"[21] and he was also cast as a "nice guy"[22] and a "man of incredibility ability and integrity."[23] Clark's final opponent, John Key, was presented as an "affable guy" and an "honest guy"[24] as well as a "man who pulled himself up by his bootstraps."[25] Australia's Tony Abbott was labelled "rugby union man"[26] and "the marathon man,"[27] nods to his penchant for intensive fitness activities. Abbott's gendered descriptors, particularly "action man" and "primal man,"[28] evoked hegemonic ideals of rugged masculinity (Johnson 2013, 20). One columnist went so far as to contrast Abbott's manly man persona with the "nerdy" and "fussy" demeanour of Gillard's predecessor, Kevin Rudd.[29] Self-presentations and media evaluations of the men's characters linked their gender to their leadership in subtle ways, thereby presenting male leaders as populists, go-getters, experienced and capable politicians, and trustworthy characters. Hegemonic masculinity was reinforced through the family man and action man tropes (Connell and Messerschmidt 2005). By gendering men, these markers implicitly conveyed understandings about how leadership ought to be enacted. Importantly, qualities like ordinariness, trustworthiness, experience, and loyalty to family were presented as characteristics of men leaders.

While, in general, the political behaviours of the men were not explicitly interpreted as gendered, one notable exception to this pattern brought unspoken understandings about social constructions of masculinity and political leadership to the fore. During the 2005 New Zealand election campaign, a widely quoted comment by National leader Don Brash attracted a flurry of attention to gender politics on the campaign trail (Devere and Davies 2006), thus explaining the relatively high number of gender markers for Brash in newspaper coverage of this election (see table 3.2 and table 3.3). Widely criticized for a rather lifeless and ineffective performance in a televised party leaders' debate, Brash told the news media that he "went easy on Prime Minister Helen Clark" because he felt it "not entirely appropriate for a man to aggressively attack a woman."[30] He was simply being a *gentleman*, Brash explained, thereby articulating an assumption that women, as the "weaker sex," need to be protected by men. In this instance, Brash chose to present his gender as relevant to assessments of his capacity to enact political leadership. The reaction of the New Zealand press corps was sceptical. Most commentators concurred with Clark, who asserted that Brash emphasized his gentlemanly persona merely as an excuse for losing the debate.[31] "Dr. Brash should have been concentrating on rebutting Helen Clark's arguments, not on her gender," argued a columnist.[32] In fact, Clark was described as tougher, stronger, and indeed more manly than Brash. "Clark doesn't share Brash's gentlemanly reluctance to go for the jugular," another columnist declared, and news stories about the debate admiringly called her a "superior debater" and a "tough, hardened political operator."[33] As the commentary confirmed, women and men leaders alike are expected to act authoritatively, even aggressively, in their pursuit of political power.

With Brash as the notable exception, the gender labels applied to men leaders during the election campaigns conveyed an impression of ordinariness. They were "just men" or "this kind of man." The labels were often perfunctory and unelaborated. Men's performance of masculinity was rarely the overt feature of these markers, although nods to hegemonic masculinity appeared, especially through family man and action man tropes. The male leaders' gender markers presented information about their characters, not about their ability to perform politically *as men*. The fact that they were men occupying positions of political leadership and authority was not interrogated. In contrast, the gendered social and political locations of the women leaders was underscored and elaborated by gender markers. As the following sections detail, when they were not being labelled "first women," Campbell, Clark, Shipley, and Gillard were assessed based on their performances *as women* on the political stage. In particular, the lexical strategy of gendering nouns shaped impressions of these women's historic political achievements.

First Women

An unsurprising difference in the treatment of men and women is the use of gender as a heuristic device to underscore the unusualness of women in political leadership roles. As Meeks (2012, 184) discovered, women who seek executive office in the United States attract significantly more uniqueness labels (e.g., "first," "lone," and "pioneer") than do the men competing against them. In fact, 13 per cent of the articles about Sarah Palin's 2008 campaign for vice-president featured uniqueness references, but Barak Obama did not receive a single notation of his distinctiveness as the first African American to seek the presidency (Meeks 2012, 186). Similarly, I found that while the "first woman" label punctuated the unusualness of women in leadership roles, the men who ran against them in elections were never branded as "first men" because, of course, they were *not* the first men to occupy these roles. Each of the men in my sample of political leaders was merely one in a long list of men who had come before him. In contrast, the first woman trope is an obvious hook for news stories about women who achieve the top political job.

Falk observed the pervasiveness of the "first woman" descriptor in newspaper coverage of the most prominent women who had sought the US presidency between 1872 and 2008, noting that many of them had been treated to this label, even those who were not, in fact, the first woman to seek this position (2010, 35–6). Almost half the in-depth newspaper articles about Elizabeth Dole's bid for the US Republican presidential nomination in 1999 employed a first woman reference despite the fact that she was far from the first to campaign for the presidency (Heldman, Carroll, and Olson 2005, 325). Unsurprisingly, the media have a "fetish for firsts" (Trimble and Arscott 2003, 23) because "firsts" have the news value of unusualness. This was evident in the media's use of the first woman label to characterize the women who served as prime minister of Australia, Canada, and New Zealand. I measured the prevalence of "first woman" phrasing to represent Campbell, Clark, Shipley, and Gillard throughout their careers by counting its appearance in the corpus of gender markers about each of the women. This descriptor was liberally applied by the press to all four women, appearing most frequently during their ascendance to party leadership and governance roles and in the coverage of their defeats or resignations from office. However, some notable differences among the women appeared. The first woman trope dominated the gender marking of Shipley and Gillard as 39 per cent of Shipley's and 40 per cent of Gillard's gender markers used the word "first" to highlight their achievements. In contrast, the first woman label constituted 30 per cent of Campbell's gender markers and only 22 per cent of Clark's.

As was the case with differences among the women in the prevalence of news stories featuring gender markers, these data reflect the women's particular career trajectories and the newsworthiness of the first woman motif in their particular political contexts. New Zealand's first woman prime minister, Jenny Shipley, was frequently described in this manner throughout her career because she was, in fact, the first. Similarly, the novelty of the nation's first woman in the top job captivated the Australian press, as illustrated by the persistent use of the label in Gillard's case. The nature of party leadership competitions in Canada likely explains why a lower percentage of references to Campbell as a first woman appeared in the coverage. Campbell was not represented as the first woman prime minister until after the votes had been counted and a victor declared in the party's leadership contest. Thus, while Campbell was often marked as a woman during the lengthy leadership campaign, she was not labelled a "first woman" until she won.

Clark's case illustrates how the news value of the first woman trope shapes its application by the press. Although she was not the first woman prime minister of New Zealand, as that distinction went to Shipley, when she won the 1999 election a large number of the overt gender references called her a "first" of some kind – for example, by noting that she was the first woman *elected* to the role. This shows the tendency of the news media to highlight the novelty of a woman in an elite political leadership position. The fact that Clark was not labelled a "first woman" during her governance phases and subsequent election campaigns punctuates this point. The first woman frame lost currency after Clark was elected to serve as the second woman prime minister, and it certainly had little salience when she was re-elected. However, the notation was resurrected when Clark resigned from the party leader's position after the 2008 election defeat, and it was used to remind New Zealanders of their long-serving prime minister's historic contributions to political life and as a pioneer for women.

Is the lexical choice of *first woman* a mere descriptor, or is it a framing device? There is a qualitative difference between mentioning a candidate's gender in passing and using it as an interpretive manoeuvre to situate particular events in their social or political context (Heldman, Carroll, and Olson 2005, 325). To qualify as a frame, the first woman label must appear consistently and serve as a peg for a storyline (Norris 1997a, 6). As shown above, the repetition of the term served to constantly remind news audiences of the novelty of a woman in the top job. Even though the label was often represented as a mere fact about the women, the ubiquity of the phrases "first woman prime minister" and "first female prime minister" rendered them a dominant feature of news coverage. The words "first woman" (or "first female") were written into between 22 and 40 per cent of the news articles about the four prime ministers, often gratuitously sprinkled into news reports even when it was irrelevant to the topic of the story. For example, "Australian investors have thrown their support behind Australia's first female prime minister, Julia Gillard, but warn that any delays to a compromise deal with the miners over the resource rent tax would cause an investor revolt."[34] Journalists' fetish for firsts worked to foreground the unusualness of these women's ascension to, and performance of, the prime minister's role, as illustrated by a New Zealand news story declaring, "The first woman leader of the parliamentary Labour Party, the Rt Hon Helen Clark moved immediately to heal the wounds created in the leadership battle."[35] Novelty was the central framing device, even when the fact of the leader's gender was tangential to the main point of the story.

According to Tolley, the language of "firsts" articulates women as political anomalies "who do not necessarily belong in electoral institutions" (2016, 41). However, I found evidence of a "first woman breakthrough" frame positioning the political ascensions of Campbell, Shipley, Clark, and Gillard as "an important and positive breakthrough for all women" (Norris 1997b, 164). Words like "historic" and "revolutionary" appeared in news reports of the women's victories, celebrating their rise to power. An article titled "You go, girls: Gillard's rise to top hailed as inspiration" called Australia's first female prime minister a role model for girls and a hero for women.[36] Campbell's leadership win was represented as a "sweet moment of gender triumph,"[37] and Campbell herself observed that she would be seen as a role model for [Canadian] women.[38] Similarly, Shipley said that she "felt proud for women in New Zealand" when she rose to the top.[39] Clark was described as having "regularized the role of women in powerful positions" because she was the first elected woman prime minister of New Zealand.[40]

As these examples illustrate, the characterization of women as "firsts" acts simultaneously as a hegemonic and as a counter-hegemonic narrative. By celebrating women's accomplishments, it exposes the previous exclusion of women from political leadership roles, revealing the extent to which a man is thereby seen as a natural inhabitant of the political realm while a woman is regarded as an interloper. On the other hand, the "fetish for firsts" singles women out as "exceptional individuals acquiring positions usually held by men" (Trimble and Arscott 2003, 23). As such, it sets them apart from the usual inhabitants of these roles and, indeed, from "ordinary" women.

These sorts of discursive contradictions were also evident in other characterizations of the women prime ministers' gender. All four women were trivialized or infantilized by gender markers. But at the same time, and sometimes in the same news story, their gender identities were expressly linked to a strong and powerful performance of political leadership, thereby interrupting the association of political leadership with men and norms of hegemonic masculinity.

Girls, Iron Ladies, and Powerful Political Women

The idea that women's chromosomal differences render them members of a unique group linked by their gender-specific traits and qualities was communicated by stories likening Campbell, Clark, Shipley, and Gillard to Margaret Thatcher, whose iconic status as one of the first women prime ministers elected in a Westminster parliamentary system seems to prompt journalists to compare every newly minted woman leader to the quintessential "Iron Lady" of British politics (Sheeler and Anderson 2014, 490). Clark was seen to be executing "Maggie Thatcher–style ruthlessness" in her firm and effective response to an attempted leadership "coup" by the man she had deposed.[41] Similarly, Gillard was deemed to be "as tough as Margaret Thatcher," although this pundit also pointed out that the Australian prime minister's "beliefs are far distant from the Iron Lady."[42] As leaders of conservative parties, both Shipley and Campbell were characterized as Thatcher-like in their approach to governance.[43] By equating the prime ministers of Canada, Australia, and New Zealand to Thatcher, the media asserted that women leaders should be viewed as a group with shared characteristics. This assumption irked Campbell. In response to a reporter's suggestion that she might well be another Thatcher, Campbell retorted that all women are not of a kind. "I am not Mrs. Thatcher, nor Golda

Meir, nor Benazir Bhutto nor Indira Gandhi. ... I am me."[44] Campbell
wanted newsmakers to judge her as her own woman. Implied in her
rebuke was the proposition that women do not embrace particular ideologies or perform leadership in particular ways merely because they
are women.

A few of the gender markers expressed essentialist thinking, which
links differences between women and men to bodily characteristics and
positions biology as the site of character formation (Nicholson 1994, 80).
For instance, describing Gillard as "Australia's next prime minister and
its first with ... two X chromosomes"[45] situates gender as a product of
one's DNA, not as a series of socially constructed rules and codes. Similarly, biological determinism underpinned characterizations of Shipley
as a leader who would provide "a feminine touch"[46] and a "very female
and inclusive approach"[47] to carrying out her new role.

References to the women leaders as ladies and girls highlighted
their bodies and trivialized their power and authority as party and
government leaders. When Campbell won the Progressive Conservative Party of Canada leadership in 1993, she was called "First
Lady."[48] Similarly, during the 1999 New Zealand election, Shipley
and Clark were referred to as the "First Ladies." This label delegitimized their political status and aspirations by likening them to the
American First Lady, a ceremonial role widely understood as the
homemaker and helpmate of the president (Anderson and Sheeler
2005, 23). Also, Clark was deemed the "Lady of the house," and a
political observer wondered whether Gillard would be relegated to
the status of a "political cleaning lady."[49] In these texts, the lexical
choice of *lady* evokes an image of compliant and demure behaviour,
historically constituted as more appropriate to domestic tasks than
to governing the nation. Campbell, Clark, Shipley, and Gillard were
all referred to as "girls" or had their public performances labelled
"girlish" or "girlie." "Now the girl from Gore is set to become the
country's first woman Prime Minister," said a report about Shipley's
rise.[50] More pointedly, Clark's visit with a constituent was described
as a "girlish prime minister taking tea and almond cakes with a
happy Government-sponsored home owner."[51] According to a columnist who was writing about Campbell's love life, the prime minister "aches like a woman, but she breaks just like a little girl."[52] A news
writer observed about Gillard, "the Prime Minister was reduced to
girlie giggles."[53] Arguably, representing the act of political leadership
as being undertaken by a "girl" or characterizing it as a "girlish"

performance demeans both the role itself and the woman enacting it (Messner, Duncan, and Jensen 1993, 129).

Intriguingly, some of the descriptions of women political leaders as girlish or ladylike were simultaneously contradicted or disputed in the news story, sometimes in the same sentence. About Campbell, a colleague declared, "This lady's going to march to her own drum," thus emphasizing Campbell's fortitude and independence.[54] Similarly, when she was referred to as "the girl most likely" (to succeed), the article admired her skills and ambitions, which had been evident from childhood.[55] In other instances, journalists drew attention to ways in which the prime ministers disrupted normative conventions of femininity. Clark "didn't get to the top of the Labour Party and hold her position within the party by being ladylike," pronounced a columnist.[56] In other words, Clark's political performance defied the norms of ladylike behaviour. Some commentators saw no disjuncture in a "womanly" woman enacting power and authority. A photographer who snapped photos of Gillard for a women's magazine "found the nation's first female killing machine 'quite vulnerable as a woman.'"[57] Moreover, the women leaders' gender identities were more often discursively linked to their strength and competence in the political realm than to childish or demure qualities. They were frequently described as strong and tough, traits typically associated with men and the performance of political leadership than with women and the nurturing roles socially assigned to the "private" realm. Clark, who was frequently assessed as tough and authoritative, was, for instance, described as a "purpose-driven woman with a steely determination to succeed against all odds"[58] and an "iron-willed woman."[59] Shipley and Campbell were labelled powerful and strong women.[60] Gillard was dubbed a "highly intelligent, competent woman,"[61] one who has "shown she has what it takes to rise to the top job."[62]

Tough talk by New Zealand's women leaders prompted the press to, on occasion, refer to them as men. Shipley was "the only man in cabinet,"[63] and Clark was "da man" and "a man in charge."[64] According to one newspaper report, both women were "accused of becoming more male than the men around them in their efforts to master the hostile environment of politics."[65] Here we see both the association of political leadership with hegemonic masculinity and the uncoupling of masculinity from men's bodies. That the women leaders were characterized as childlike, submissive, and decorous, yet at the same time represented as tough, strong, ambitious, capable, and determined, illustrates

how media discourses can both reinforce and contest gender regulations. This form of discursive imposition is more thoroughly discussed
in chapter 6, which analyses how love and war metaphors structure
descriptions and interpretations of political leadership.

The X Factor

The gendered identities of Campbell, Clark, Shipley, and Gillard were
also interpreted as a crucial X factor propelling their careers. As with
the television series of the same name,[66] in which performers seen to
possess the necessary charisma and star power to capture the attention of world audiences are sought and celebrated, these four leaders
were judged for their ability to translate their (gendered) personas into
political success on the national stage.

Reflecting the game frame for election coverage, and its emphasis on
strategies and outcomes, news commentators mused about the ability
of women leaders to win votes from women. In Canada, the question
of whether Campbell's gender would be an influential dynamic in the
1993 election campaign appeared frequently in the coverage, and careful attention was paid to gender gaps in polling data and their possible impact on the election outcome.[67] News stories published in New
Zealand and Australia also stressed the gender factor on the campaign
trail by maintaining that Clark, Shipley, and Gillard planned to deploy
their gender to appeal to voters. An account of Clark's initial electoral
contest in 1996 declared, "Labour leader Helen Clark is pushing gender
as a campaign issue in a move aimed at cementing Labour's strong
support about women voters."[68] "Political strategists expect National to
market Mrs. Shipley as the archetypal mainstream New Zealand family
woman," announced a news commentator in the lead-up to Shipley's
electoral contest against Clark.[69] Similarly, an article about Gillard's
strategy for the 2010 election campaign asserted, "Ads are likely to play
up her intelligence and, yes, her feminine charms" to win votes.[70] A
headline opined, "Gillard can count on the XX factor."[71] Even though
Gillard was careful not to raise her gender as a campaign issue, a few
columnists introduced the gender card trope. As one asserted, Australia's prime minister was so adept at playing the game of political
opportunism that "she can even play the gender card by announcing
she's not playing the gender card."[72] In contrast, none of the men leaders were described as using their gender to appeal to men voters. News
coverage thereby conveyed a rather crude proposition about voting

behaviour – women will vote for women because of innate gender solidarity.

However, gender binaries and regulations were unsettled by debates about whether gender mattered to political competition and whether it *should* matter. It is "Australia's turn to ask what it means – if anything – to be led by a woman," said a report in the *Sydney Morning Herald*.[73] Media commentators were undecided about the role and impact of gender as an identity or as a political variable. Some journalists declared the gender of the leader beside the point or irrelevant to political success. For instance, "Mrs. Shipley has gained her position not because she is a woman but because of her undoubted political skills."[74] Similarly, Gillard had secured the Labor Party leadership because "she was considered such an effective politician, not because she was a woman."[75] In contrast, Campbell's gendered identity was seen as the primary reason for her success in the party leadership contest. The party had chosen Campbell because she was "from the right founding gender," insisted an editorial.[76] Media commentators said that the party wanted to appeal to women voters and put a fresh face on a tired government, and, as "a young, female Defence Minister from the West Coast," Campbell "appeared a fresh contrast to the tattered and distrusted Brian Mulroney."[77]

Confusion about whether the X factor counted, and if so, how, illustrates the consternation created when gendered expectations are defied by the selection of women for elite political leadership roles. The 1999 New Zealand election, which guaranteed a woman "at the top," was considered such a breakthrough for women that it rendered the gender factor passé, according to one newspaper article. "The most remarkable element in this election is the unremarkability that the choice of Prime Minister is between two women ... in the media there is no gee-whizz about this extremely rare factor. It seems the country has become used to it."[78] However, as the prevalence of gender markers in the coverage of Clark and Shipley during this election campaign suggests, the press regarded the gender of the party leaders as remarkable indeed, a matter of sufficient concern to be highlighted by the heavy-handed application of the first woman trope and the frequent invocation of the many ways in which these women's gender mattered to politics. Similar to Hvenegard-Lassen's findings with regard to Denmark's first woman prime minister, here we see a paradoxical representation of the gender identities of women leaders as simultaneously unimportant *and* consequential (2013, 154–5).

A particularly destructive form of gender labelling, the gender card metaphor, appeared only four times during the 2010 election campaign, but it was regularly employed in newspaper reports about Gillard's final eight months as prime minister of Australia. As mentioned in chapter 1, and as documented much more fully in chapter 7, the gender card and gender war(s) metaphors were mobilized in response to Julia Gillard's attempts to decry the sexism and misogyny she had experienced while serving as prime minister. The phrase "gender card" appeared forty-nine times in thirty-eight newspaper articles[79] published after Gillard's so-called "sexism and misogyny" speech, during which she documented numerous gender-based attacks on her character, some of them levelled by Opposition leader Tony Abbott. Opponents and critics, some of them news columnists, used this particular gender label to criticize Gillard for drawing attention to her gender, arguing that it was a crass political move designed to deflect critiques of her policies and leadership style.[80] "Gender card hides failures," read the headline of a column asserting that the "government's focus this week on playing the gender card is no more than an attempt to divert attention from its policy and personnel failures."[81] Moreover, discussing gender was read as a "sign of desperation,"[82] showing that Gillard considered her gender more important than her qualifications or achievements.[83] The metaphor likened raising issues of gender inequality and sexism to a card game, wherein "waving" or playing the card conferred unfair advantage.[84] The gender card was also described as a weapon Gillard deployed against her opponents in an effort to cling to the party leadership.[85] Most Australian accounts condemned Gillard for "playing the gender card"; however, a few commentators commended the prime minister for speaking out about the sexism prevalent in Australian society and political life.[86] Others noted the gendered discourses inherent in the backlash directed at Gillard. "Like nagging or bitching, playing the gender card becomes a useful silencing term, through which female grievance can be reduced to phatic noise."[87] The irony of Gillard being criticized for "noticing" her own gender when, in fact, her gender identity had been mobilized against her as a form of demonization was rarely mentioned in the Australian news coverage, as Johnson observes (2015, 304).[88]

Conclusions

Gender marking reinforces the man/woman binary. As my study demonstrates, gender labels and gendering nouns are regularly used to distinguish between women and men political leaders. The fact that Campbell, Clark, Shipley, and Gillard are women inspired a great deal of commentary, particularly in press coverage of their leadership victories. While I did not find that women prime ministers were always, or invariably, characterized through the lens of their gender, it was certainly a dominant theme in the news coverage of them throughout their service as party and government leaders, with the first woman trope particularly evident in news reports of ascensions to leadership roles. A woman prime minister's gender "difference" was considered interesting and important enough to be politicized through lexical choices punctuating her unusualness.

Surprisingly, and in contrast to findings in much of the gendered mediation literature, I discovered that the gender of men party leaders was marked as frequently, and sometimes more frequently, than that of the women against whom they were competing during election campaigns. These markers typically served to normalize men and reinforce the public man/private woman dualism and the two sex/gender binary. As I have demonstrated through discourse analysis of the gender labels, while male leaders' gender is often signalled in news stories, it is invariably used to communicate comfort with their appearance in elite political roles. Less frequently, but importantly, the gendered identities of the men in my sample were emphasized when they illustrated their conformity to or lack of compliance with hegemonic norms and ideals of masculine identities and leadership styles. In other words, that they were men was taken for granted or assumed, except when they displayed behaviour or characteristics antithetical to the gender norms regulating the performance of masculinity. In contrast, a close reading of the gender markers shows how they identified the four women leaders as a notable departure from the "norm" of male leadership. Yet at the same time, some of the marking worked to disrupt dualistic and essentialist understandings of gender.

My analysis reveals intriguing counter-narratives. While Campbell, Clark, Shipley, and Gillard were branded as unusual, even aberrant, through the frequent application of gender markers, these representations served to expose gendered assumptions about political leadership. Media attention to their status as "firsts" through the frequent use of phrases like "first woman prime minister" underscored the under-representation of women in positions of political power. The first-woman-breakthrough frame was evident in these accounts, offering a celebratory tone proposing that women should be welcomed into elite governance roles, not least because they were laying a path for the women who would follow them into political office. Moreover, while some gender markers trivialized and delegitimized the women prime ministers' political ambitions, others emphasized their strength and resolve as well as their willingness to perform authoritative styles of leadership, a topic explored more fully in chapter 6.

This research suggests a typology of gender markers based on what these labels communicate about a political actor's legitimacy in a party or government leadership role. *Delegitimizing* references include infantilizing nouns such as *boy* or *girl, princess* or *prince. Differentiating* labels draw gender distinctions. Gendering nouns fall into this category (*woman prime minister*), as do *type of man* or *type of woman* references, which replicate assumptions underpinning the public man/private woman binary. *Disrupting* markers expose or contest the gender order by identifying power imbalances (by noting the absence or under-representation of women in the role) or celebrating women's political accomplishments (e.g., with the first woman breakthrough frame). *Regularizing* labels communicate acceptance of a politician's presence in the leadership position or performance in the role – for instance, by calling a woman "the right person for the job" or refraining from "gendering" her performance of leadership. By pressing the Delete key on gendering nouns and using gender-neutral prefixes and descriptors, such as *they, person,* and *individual,* news writers could help normalize the presence of women in politics.

Journalists and the commentators they quoted in news stories could not agree on the political salience of the X factor. Does a woman's gender identity help or hurt her at the polls? While this question was posed for Campbell, Shipley, Clark, and Gillard alike, the answers differed. Some accounts asserted that the mere fact of their gender would win support from women voters or that their performance of femininity might boost overall approval. But as other news stories insisted, gender did not and should not matter because qualifications, experience, and competence are the primary determinants of political success. Thus, when a woman suggests that her gender is relevant to politics, as did Gillard in her parliamentary speech about the sexism and misogyny she had experienced while serving as prime minister, it is considered an unfair political manoeuvre. The playing-the-gender-card metaphor prevents women leaders from drawing attention to the ways in which gendered hierarchies of power disadvantage women. Commentators are allowed to notice gender, but it is considered deeply inappropriate and even offensive for the women whose gender identities are mediated in news accounts, or mobilized by opponents to critique their personas and performances of political leadership, to raise these issues in public political spaces.

Gendered assumptions and assertions are communicated not merely by explicit gender markers but also by the descriptions and evaluations of leaders' identities and behaviours. In the chapters that follow, I explore the different ways in which gender was mediated in the news coverage of the women and men leaders, analysing the impact of these discursive gestures for the women prime ministers' experience of mediated legitimacy. Beginning with discourses about marital arrangements and family life in chapter 4, bodies in chapter 5, electoral performances in chapter 6, and speech acts in chapter 7, I show how the four women prime ministers were evaluated for their performance as women, their political roles and actions frequently assessed through the prism of their gender.

Chapter Four

First Men and the Family Strategy

Introduction

The personal lives of politicians have long been a source of fascination for the news media. Pierre Elliott Trudeau, who served as Canada's prime minister from the late 1960s until the mid-1980s, enjoyed a very public bachelorhood in his first few years on the job, and his liaisons with a succession of famous women, from chanteuse Barbra Streisand to Margot Kidder of *Superman* movie fame, were detailed in photographs and gossip columns.[1] Later, stories about Trudeau's ill-fated marriage and tumultuous divorce were followed by poignant images of the single dad playing with his young sons.[2] Similar examples of reporting about the intimate lives of previous government leaders, from John F. Kennedy to Tony Blair, are easily mustered. Communications scholars argue that the phenomenon of personalization has intensified in the contemporary media environment, which features twenty-four hour news reporting, talk radio, online news sources, and the proliferation of digital and social media. As Stanyer writes in his book *Intimate Politics*, the "zone of privacy which once surrounded politicians and those in public life seems to be slowly disappearing with and without politicians' consent" (2013, 6–7). With the rise of the permanent campaign and political strategists' increasing awareness of the market imperatives of news making, politicians' families are incorporated into campaign optics. Justin Trudeau exhibited his beautiful wife and three young children for the cameras during the 2015 Canadian federal election and continues the practice as prime minister.[3]

Media practices and campaign branding strategies align to present politicians as "intimate strangers." Citizens do not know them personally, but they learn all about their families, relationships, and lifestyles (Campus 2010, 223). The personal lives of Canada's, New Zealand's, and Australia's women prime ministers were certainly placed under the media microscope, with newspaper stories detailing failed marriages, happy relationships, physical intimacy, and deeply personal decisions about whether to have children. Kim Campbell's marital history was highlighted in news reports about her leadership bid, her two divorces cited as evidence of emotional and political instability. In New Zealand, Jenny Shipley's hetero-normative performance of family life was contrasted with opponent Helen Clark's childlessness, and news stories about Clark's subsequent election campaigns interrogated the authenticity of her marriage and questioned her ability to relate to the needs of "ordinary" New Zealand families. In Australia, a senator labelled Julia Gillard "deliberately barren," thus unfit for political office, and other observers criticized her for "shacking up" with her partner. In fact, opponents of Campbell, Clark, and Gillard mobilized appeals to gender stereotypes and patriarchal family forms, a technique I refer to as the *family strategy*.

This chapter identifies the gender work performed by media attention to the family lives of political leaders. I begin with a discussion of the politicization of intimacy and the gender-specific implications of mediatized attention to politicians' family lives. This trend is illustrated in the second part of the chapter by measuring the level of focus on the women prime ministers' marital situations and children – or, for Campbell, Clark, and Gillard, their childlessness – at all four career phases. Discourse analysis shows how the media fixated on the presence – or absence, in Campbell's case – of a "first man" and reported a "mommy problem" for all but Shipley, the only leader in my sample who had borne children. In the third section, I compare the amount of consideration given during election campaigns to the families of the women prime ministers and their male opponents, and I report an intriguing finding: overall, the wives and children of the men were referenced in a higher percentage of the news stories about their campaigns than was the case for the women leaders. This result is explained in large part by the family strategy, a technique mobilized by leaders or aspiring leaders with traditional families. By engaging in this tactic, leaders situate themselves as caring and in tune with the policy needs of voters, while at the same time drawing attention to the allegedly atypical family lives of their female opponents. My exploration of the family strategy suggests that while it is a more successful technique for men than for women, it does not go uncontested by the media. The politicization of spouses and children thereby creates avenues for disrupting the social construction of political personas and performances as being somehow separate from family and intimate relationships.

Politicizing Intimacy

Industrialized democracies are witnessing an "intimization" of politics as personal lives and familial relationships are brought into public discourse through journalistic norms and practices (Hirdman, Kleberg, and Widestedt 2005, 110; Stanyer and Wring 2004, 1, 6). Intimization is the process whereby journalism pays attention to the activities and relationships associated with personal lives, including familial relationships and romantic involvements (Hirdman, Kleberg, and Widestedt 2005, 109; Stanyer 2013, 11; van Zoonen 1991, 223). While there is as yet little evidence that the media are now more consumed with personal matters than ever before (see Karvonen 2009; Trimble et al. 2013), the personal lives of politicians are invariably of interest to the press. Journalists peer into political leaders' families to entertain the public, so the media gaze now encapsulates the personalized, celebritized, and fetishized politician (Van Aelst, Sheafer, and Stanyer 2012, 205; van Zoonen 2005, 69). Politicians are often complicit in this trend, offering their families and aspects of their domestic lives to the public through the media. In fact, many political leaders view both the personal and the private elements of their lives as a resource to be exploited as they construct a political identity for themselves and the political parties they represent. As Langer (2010, 61–2) writes, since party leaders "embody the party brand, their personal lives can personify the party's wishes and policies, [and] symbolize people's aspirations." Not surprisingly, the media reference family life as an indicator of a leader's identity and character.

Once subjected to publicity and public scrutiny and thus rendered matters of public discussion, personal topics like marriage and children are politicized (Stanyer 2013, 14). Politicization of personal lives is a form of gendered mediation because "the private" has different meanings for women and men. While men are understood as seamlessly cohabiting the public and domestic realms, women's lives are more typically defined by their roles, and duties, as wives and mothers. Many high-profile men politicians willingly parade their families for the media as a way of demonstrating their virility, humanizing their political personas, establishing emotional connections with voters, and consolidating the party brand (Langer 2010, 63; van Zoonen 2005, 76). In contrast, women politicians, especially those in the brightest media spotlight, often refuse to discuss their personal lives with journalists because media narratives about a woman politician's marital relationships and/or child-bearing and child-rearing roles and practices can position their political ambition as unnatural and raise doubts about their devotion to family life (Garcia-Blanco and Wahl-Jorgenson, 2012, 433; Halevi 2012, 200; Muir 2005b, 78; van Zoonen 2006, 295).

Intense scrutiny of the marital relationships and reproductive choices of women in political leadership roles makes it difficult for those individuals who do not want their personal lives exposed in this manner to succeed in politics (Langer 2010, 73). "Intimization" may, therefore, narrow the range of people who are considered suitable for political leadership (Bashevkin 2009, 88–94). Politicians who are not in heterosexual relationships, or who are divorced, separated, single, or childless, draw the most scrutiny because of their deviation from the hetero-normative patriarchal family form. For women with political aspirations, both the presence and the absence of a conventional family life are regarded as problematic. The families of women politicians are seen to suffer because of their ambition, but women without prototypical nuclear families are judged to be aberrant and lacking in "femininity" and maternal instincts (Muir 2005b, 86). As such, media attention to politicians' intimate relationships and family lives tends to reinforce gender dualisms and regulations, especially the public man/private woman binary and the association of women with domestic labour and nurturing qualities. But revelling in the details of politicians' family lives presents an opportunity for counter-narratives that can work to challenge the assumptions underlying the division of public and private worlds along gender lines. The artificial bifurcation of politics as a field of rationality and coolly objective judgment, and the domestic realm as guided by emotionality and intimate commitments, is unmasked when political actors are portrayed, at one and the same time, as political decision-makers *and* family members.

Love, Marriage, and the Baby Carriage

Women politicians, especially those in leadership roles, are typically single and childless, and rarely do they have young children (van Zoonen 2006, 293). The women prime ministers from Canada, New Zealand,

and Australia certainly reflect this pattern as Campbell was divorced and childless, Clark married and childless, and Gillard in a common-law relationship and childless when they ascended to political leadership roles. Shipley was a wife and mother when she became prime minister, although her children were in their late teens and attending university at that point. In contrast, all the men leaders against whom the women competed for party leadership and governance roles were legally married, all but one had children, and a few had young children.

My analysis of the newspaper reporting about Campbell, Clark, Shipley, and Gillard illustrates how difficult it is for women party and government leaders to negotiate media attention to their intimate lives. I investigated the extent to which such coverage focused on family life, using content analysis to determine the percentage of the newspaper articles discussing each woman's marital situation and children. Any reference to Shipley's children was included, as were mentions of Campbell's, Clark's, and Gillard's childlessness and/or decision not to have children. Marital situation was measured as an overt identification of marital status (e.g., descriptions of Campbell as "twice divorced") or explicit identification of a spouse or partner (e.g., "Helen Clark's husband"). However, honorifics like *Ms.* or *Mrs.* were not counted as communicating marital status because the results for the New Zealand women would have been confounded by the different choices made by the two women prime ministers. Shipley chose to be called "Mrs. Shipley" and was referred to in this fashion consistently throughout her career. Clark told the press after her election to Parliament that she wanted to be referred to by her name alone, no "Miss or Mrs."[4] But despite her wishes, news reports published from 1993 to 2008 frequently called her "Miss Clark," suggesting that she was single. Campbell, who was unmarried, and Gillard, in a common-law relationship with her partner, were both referred to by their first and/or last names or as "Ms."

Table 4.1 indicates the level of interest in these women's marital relationships, especially during their ascents to the party leadership role. Campbell's, Clark's, and Gillard's marital partnerships were highlighted in newspaper coverage of their leadership contests, discussed significantly more frequently than their childlessness. Shipley stands out as attracting a fairly constant amount of attention to her marriage *and* children throughout her term as party leader, reflecting her traditional family life, the public visibility of her husband, and her willingness to play the "mum" card during the 1999 New Zealand election.

Table 4.1 Percentage of News Stories Mentioning Marital Situation and Children (or Childlessness), by Country, Leader, and Career Phase

Country	Leader	Leadership, %		Governance, %		Date	Election, %		Resignation or defeat, %	
		Marital situation	Children	Marital situation	Children		Marital situation	Children	Marital situation	Children
Canada	Kim Campbell	15	7	9	1	1993	4	0	8	0
New Zealand	Jenny Shipley	10	9	9	9	1999	6	5	11	11
	Helen Clark	16	4	3	1	1996	0	0	10	5
	Helen Clark					1999	8	5		
						2002	6	2		
						2005	7	1		
						2008	2	2		
Australia	Julia Gillard	21	13	13	3	2010	7	5	14	4

Shipley's marriage was mentioned in a lower percentage of articles during her leadership "coup" than were the relationships of the other women leaders, arguably because the press had already become familiar with her spouse during her high-profile role as a Cabinet minister. The leader most likely to have her marital status and childlessness discussed in newspaper coverage during the leadership phase was the most recently elected prime minister, Julia Gillard, illustrating the high level of intimization in the contemporary media environment. While media interest in Gillard's partner and childlessness waned slightly during the 2010 Australian election, it was revitalized when she left the party leadership role. As table 4.1 also shows, newspapers also returned to the topic of family life in descriptions of Campbell's, Clark's, and Shipley's career denouements.

A significant difference among the women shown in table 4.1 is in the amount of attention to marriage and children during the governance and election phases of their careers; this was particularly evident with Clark. This result is explained by Clark's slower path to the prime minister's office. Campbell, Shipley, and Gillard entered their governance phases immediately after securing the party leadership role, and newspapers commented on the absence or presence of a "first man" and children in the prime minister's residence. In contrast, Clark's personal life had been so thoroughly hashed out during her rise to the party leader's role and during the 1999 election, when Shipley had juxtaposed her traditional marriage against Clark's less conventional marital relationship and childlessness, that there was little traction left in the topic when Clark began serving as prime minister.

Discourse analysis of the references to marital situation and children, or childlessness, revealed two broad topics of discussion and evaluation, each of which worked to reinforce gender regulations. First, the presence (or absence) of a "first man" sparked consternation in the press. News writers did not know how to report on a prime minister's husband or partner or, for that matter, the lack of a husband. As a result, they resorted to evaluating the men's compliance with norms of hegemonic masculinity and familial patriarchy. Second, childlessness was viewed as a problem for women prime ministers. For Shipley, the presence of children was normalized, while for Campbell, Clark, and Gillard, their absence was highlighted, assessed as culturally anomalous, and linked to the woman leader's personal character and her capacity to make decisions in the interests of families. On the other hand, these gender stereotypes were occasionally contested in media accounts.

First Men

The news media are familiar with first ladies thanks in no small part to the global popularity and prominence of a succession of US presidents' wives, from Jackie Kennedy to Michelle Obama (Burrell, Elder, and Frederick 2011). The American-style tradition of an exalted and highly visible role for the wife of the president is not emulated in Canada, New Zealand, or Australia, and many prime ministers' wives choose to stay out of the media spotlight. This does not seem to be an option when the prime minister is, for the first time in a nation's history, a woman and her spouse is a man. Journalists did not have a script for reporting the presence, or absence, of a "first man" or for establishing and evaluating his role. What should the "first husband" be called? What if there is no man in the picture, as was the case for Campbell? What if, as in Gillard's case, the prime minister has not officially "tied the knot"?

Kim Campbell's marriages and ex-husbands were discussed in exhaustive detail during her campaign for the party leadership role, with several profile pieces saying more about her "failed" relationships than about her political ideas and career path.[5] In response to questions about prospects for a new romance and possible third marriage, Campbell herself was remarkably uninhibited, referring "openly to the lack of a man, a relationship, or sex."[6] When she was sworn in as prime minister, Canadian newspapers pondered the implications of the absence of a marital partner, with one columnist noting that Campbell would arrive at the prime minister's residence "alone, without a husband or young family" and would have no one to "help pick out curtains" or coordinate her busy social schedule.[7] This writer was more concerned with public perceptions of the prime minister's residence as a symbol of the patriarchal family than with the loneliness of its tenant. With a "single woman as its sole occupant," 24 Sussex Drive [the prime minister's residence] "wouldn't be the family home that the Mulroneys made it into, nor would it be the idyllic single man's retreat that Pierre Trudeau enjoyed before or after his troubled marriage."[8] In other words, the prime minister's official home is imagined as a place for a man to enjoy his private life, however he chooses to live it. That there was no "first man" to share the big house with Campbell was, however, of less interest to commentators than her two divorces. Indeed, as discussed below, her opponent in the leadership race deployed a family strategy to undermine Campbell's credibility and enhance his own appeal with voters.

In Australia, the fact that Julia Gillard was not legally married sparked a great deal of commentary when she became prime minister. Deemed the "first unmarried PM," Gillard was called a single woman despite having lived with her partner, Tim Mathieson, for five years.[9] An entire article was devoted to the question of whether Gillard and Mathieson would be wed.[10] Another questioned whether Mathieson was "actually living with the PM" and wondered whether he would move into the prime minister's residence, called the Lodge.[11] Their cohabitation was cast as a game – "If Gillard chooses to *play house* with Tim Mathieson in the Lodge"[12] – and as an affront to common decency – "Shacking up is hard to do."[13] Australian journalists looked around for people willing to criticize Gillard's relationship, asking voters whether the new prime minister's marital status would "affect her ability to do her job."[14] When family groups refused to bite, a news writer managed to find a preacher who "savaged Julia Gillard as being unfit to be Prime Minister because, if elected, she would live out of wedlock" with her partner.[15] This was a minority opinion, however, and the tone of the "first man" coverage was often light-hearted. For instance, Australian news commentators were at a loss about what to call Mathieson.

> No one quite knows what to call the new Prime Minister's partner. Husband? Not accurate. Consort? A little antique. The wits around Canberra, thus, have settled on 'first dude.'"[16]

Some news reports, in true Aussie vernacular, labelled Mathieson the "first bloke."[17]

Implicit in the coverage of the "first men" was a set of standards for evaluating them, set by the press (and, by extension, the public). They were assessed for their devotion to and support of their wife or partner, their likeability, and their conformance with key features of hegemonic masculinity. In New Zealand, the presence of a prime ministerial husband was regularized for Shipley, whose traditional marriage was central to her political brand. She married at age twenty-one, raised two children while helping husband Burton run a family farm, and, when she was elected as an MP, "her husband ran the household."[18] With her supportive husband and adult children, Shipley was the archetypal married career woman. News coverage emphasized the happiness of the Shipley marriage and described Burton as "the ultimate political accessory."[19] An article titled "Burton's up to the job" gushed about

New Zealand's new "first man," calling him a "supportive husband, a top-line dad, generally all round good guy and balanced being" and evaluating him as eminently suitable for the role of prime ministerial husband.[20] His appeal was based in part on his performance of hegemonic masculinity, as emphasized by depictions of him as a manly man doing manly things. Burton was described as a farmer, a "keen sportsman," and a "big bear of a man," and he was quoted as admitting that he was less inclined than his wife to perform certain domestic tasks such as cleaning the toilet.[21]

In contrast, Clark's relationship with husband Peter Davis was represented as a departure from the marital "norm" in two key respects. Questions about the verisimilitude of her marital relationship circulated throughout much of Clark's career. News articles published during her leadership challenge noted that the couple had lived together for five years before marrying in 1981, when Clark was seeking a seat in Parliament.[22] As Clark informed the press, she chose to marry at that point because she "was tired about the innuendo" about the couple's relationship and rumours that she was a lesbian.[23] When Clark won the leadership of the Labour Party, a party spokesperson responded to the accusation that the "coup" was a "lesbian plot" by insisting that Clark and Davis had a "very genuine" and a "very loving" relationship.[24] Similarly, newspapers ran photos of the couple kissing, emphasizing physical intimacy between them. One image, labelled "Leadership Passion," showed Clark leaning back into Davis's arms to receive a kiss, eyes partly closed, as if to initiate an intimate sexual act.[25] The photo in the *New Zealand Herald* was more circumspect as it portrayed Davis kissing a smiling Clark on the cheek, with the caption "Partners in Triumph."[26] Arguably, however, the images accompanying Clark's leadership win demonstrated the impulse of both newspapers to hetero-normalize her marriage. The trend persisted. During the 2005 election campaign, a program host asked a series of intensely personal questions during a televised interview with Clark and Davis, sparking commentary in the newspapers about the physical nature of the relationship.[27] It was not until Clark lost her final election campaign in 2008 that she was described as "happily married to her husband Peter for 25 years."[28]

News coverage also highlighted the fact that Clark and Davis led relatively independent lives and that he did not accompany his wife on the campaign trail. "She lets me live my life and I let her lead hers," Davis was quoted as saying.[29] Davis "has taken a mostly low-profile role in Miss Clark's political life," noted an article published during the 1999 New Zealand election campaign.[30] Another, printed during the 2002 election, said that Clark was "married to a man she sees irregularly and whom many New Zealanders would not recognize if he was holding her hand."[31] Clark attempted to challenge the assumption that women leaders should present their husbands to the public as a form of political partnership. For example, when asked by a bystander at a rally, "Are you here today with your husband?" Clark retorted, "No, actually I'm allowed to go out on my own everyday."[32] However, Clark's husband's low-profile role in her political career, coupled with persistent rumours about Clark's sexual identity and intimations that the marriage was merely for show, unsettled the New Zealand news media. While Davis was described as supportive of Clark, and proud of her accomplishments as party leader and prime minister,[33] he was never depicted as a political asset.

Julia Gillard's partner, Tim Mathieson, was similarly scrutinized, with mixed opinions about his ability to boost the new prime minister's political appeal. Stories discussing his career choices, likeability, and suitability for what one article deemed a "significant public role" put the spotlight on their intimate relationship.[34] Described as unfailingly supportive of Gillard's political career and proud of her success,[35] a "great guy,"[36] and a kindly neighbour,[37] Mathieson was also lauded for his promotion of politically innocuous causes such as men's health.[38] A television morning show host was quoted as saying, "Julia needs to wheel you out a bit more often" because of Mathieson's demeanour and likeability.[39] On the other hand, the author of the book *Media Tarts* wrote a column (presciently) warning Gillard to expect "endless chatter about … the marvelous convenience of having a hairdresser for a partner."[40] Indeed, news articles continually reminded readers of Mathieson's former job as a hairstylist,[41] a profession not typically associated with the hetero-normative performance of masculinity. Several stories emasculated Mathieson by inferring that his new career as a property developer had resulted from his relationship with Gillard, not his experience and qualifications.[42]

Contradictory representations were evidenced by consternation about Mathieson's compliance with gender regulations. At first, he was seen as a romantic figure, with reporters asking when he and Gillard would be legally married ("what about wedding bells?").[43] News reports highlighted the couple's "love story" by relaying tidbits from a spread published in a widely circulated Australian women's magazine, including teasers like "How I won Julia's heart" and revelations about their domestic life.[44] As one news pundit gleaned from an enquiry into the couple's domestic routines, "Mathieson, it was revealed, likes cooking 'fresh veggie soups and pastas,' which they eat in front of the TV."[45] Most outrageously, a radio host interrogated Gillard about the sexual identify of her partner. "Tim's gay," he declared, continuing, "He must be gay, he's a hairdresser."[46] As with Clark's husband, Gillard's partner was judged to be inadequate for the job of prime minister's spouse because of his putatively atypical performance of masculinity.

From these portrayals of the prime ministers' marital partners, we see a mixing of gender scripts. The "first man" is expected to epitomize patriarchal and hetero-normative ideals of masculine behaviour. He should be "man" enough to insist on a traditional, legal marriage. He should be his own man, with a long-established career independent of his partner's political role, in the manner of Burton Shipley, who managed the family farm. On the other hand, archetypes culled from the performances of prime ministers' wives were evident in the evaluations of the "first men." Journalists looked for evidence of Shipley's, Davis's, and Mathieson's respective willingness to actively and wholeheartedly support their partner's political career in the public and domestic realms. Burton Shipley was cited as an exemplar of the role because of his readiness to perform child-rearing duties and cheerfully accompany his wife on the campaign trail and at public functions. In contrast, the emotional independence demonstrated by Clark and her husband, Peter Davis, was evaluated as unusual, and even suspect, behaviour in a marital relationship. While Mathieson's partnership with Gillard was at first celebrated for its romantic storybook qualities, his former career as a hairdresser and alleged reliance on Gillard for a new job prompted commentators to describe him as dependent and unduly focused on domestic routines and to raise questions about his sexual identity. The double bind confronting the prime minister's spouse is obvious, and it was certainly foreshadowed by media treatment of Dennis Thatcher when Margaret Thatcher served as Britain's government leader from 1979 to 1990. Widely recognized as a "dignified consort and an invaluable support to his wife," Thatcher was regularly emasculated in satirical accounts.[47]

The Mommy Problem

Public fatherhood is invariably regarded as a sign of normalcy for men politicians (Langer 2010). Public motherhood is considerably trickier, as the literature shows, although it is less of an issue for women politicians whose children are grown (Loke, Harp, and Bachmann 2011, 208; Murray 2010a, 239). Newspaper coverage of Jenny Shipley never accused her of dereliction of parental duty as her children were adults attending university when she assumed the prime minister's role.[48] Childlessness was, on the other hand, presented as a problem for Campbell, Clark, and Gillard as it was interpreted as signifying both character flaws and lack of suitability for political leadership. In Canada, New Zealand, and Australia, childlessness was regarded as evidence of selfishness, unseemly ambition, and inability to relate to "ordinary people" or represent the needs of families.

Campbell, Clark, and Gillard found themselves justifying their life choices to the press. An article profiling Clark's marriage said that the couple "by choice have no children."[49] Australia's newly elected prime minister had simply let the biological clock wind down, suggested one columnist,[50] while another declared that, at the young age of 16, Gillard had told her mother she never wanted children.[51] Campbell "has had to explain why she has no kids," said the author of a news story, who also relayed the explanation – "She tried, but no luck."[52] Journalists were careful to steer clear of a sensitive issue as only one article posed the issue of infertility. Perhaps Campbell's disclosure that she had tried to have children was sufficient to reassure the media of her nurturing instincts as she was never explicitly criticized for her childlessness. In contrast, Clark and Gillard were openly censured for making this particular choice about their family and personal lives.

Fountaine (2002, 14) argues that Helen Clark's childlessness was a constant reference point for the media during her political career. While the issue was not raised frequently in the news stories in my sample, it did indeed circulate throughout the coverage of Clark, and it was offered as evidence of her single-minded careerism and political ambition.[53] As Campus observes, if women leaders are unmarried and "career oriented, they are pictured as deviant and perhaps cynical workaholics" (2013, 97). According to news reports, Clark's decision not to have children led New Zealanders to view her as emotionally distant and unduly reserved.[54] Journalists asked Clark's husband why they had made this choice, inferring that it was viewed as evidence of their "unusual" marriage.[55] Most damagingly, political opponents and pundits represented Clark as unqualified to represent New Zealand families because she had not raised children herself. "Was Helen Clark, childless, able to understand the concerns of parents?" queried a columnist.[56] Clark's childlessness was "counted against her by some who feel she is out of touch with 'ordinary' Kiwi families," said another journalist.[57]

Gillard's childlessness was similarly represented as both "unnatural" and problematic. As a columnist put it, the country was being "led by a woman who has eschewed marriage and children."[58] Prominent in the coverage was an Australian senator's characterization of Gillard as "deliberately barren." Offered in 2007, the attack was dusted off and recirculated by the media after she had ascended to the prime minister's role.[59] "The contest between the 'deliberately barren' Gillard and the 'mad monk' Tony Abbott is going to be a fiery and fascinating one,"[60] breathlessly announced a journalist in a seemingly deliberate non sequitur. One writer responded with a humorous anecdote relayed by Gillard herself. "After Senator Bill Heffernan attacked her for being 'deliberately barren,' people would roll down their windows at stop lights … and yell at her, 'You can borrow my kids if you like, love.'"[61] However, as was the case with Clark, Gillard's childlessness was explained as a side effect of political ambition, her decision not to have children assumed by some to reveal a lack of putatively "natural" maternal instincts. "Most women want to have children – Gillard is an exception," said a columnist.[62] "Until you have your own kids you have no idea what it's like to be a family," opined a voter.[63] But in Gillard's case, the proposition that a politician could neither understand nor represent those whose life experiences she did not share was contested in a few of the news reports, with journalists and their sources situating this assumption as insulting or absurd. Gillard's father offered a pointed rebuttal. "Women are not breeding machines, you know."[64] A former premier observed that negative commentary about Gillard's childlessness "offends not only many women but also many men."[65] In response to the assertion that Gillard's childlessness was an impediment to winning votes, a columnist asked, "Would the same logic apply to male politicians with low sperm counts?"[66] Also, when a former Labor Party leader turned television presenter declared, "Gillard ain't no soccer mom so there might be a failure to connect there," the intrepid reporters covering the story sought the views of several moms.[67] All but one dismissed the idea that they could not relate to a childless woman as prime minister. "I focus on who she is rather than whether she has children," said one of the women interviewed for the story.[68]

Childlessness was raised as a campaign issue for Campbell, Clark, and .Gillard, forcing them to respond to accusations about their ability to understand family issues and needs. Both Clark and Gillard reminded journalists, and voters, that they did indeed have families. Clark often referenced her extended family – for instance, by delivering "a powerful homily on her own family relationships" during the 1999 campaign.[69] Gillard did likewise. "Ms. Gillard, who is unmarried and without children, used the experiences of her own upbringing to assure families that she understood their concerns."[70] But when the Gillard team offered a series of baby-laden photo ops and encounters with young children during the 2010 Australian election, news reports reminded readers of Gillard's childlessness, proposing that the attention to children was a campaign ploy.[71]

Campbell took a different tack, articulating her family situation as a political advantage, freeing her to spend time with Canadians. "In a sense I can make the whole country my family," she told her hometown newspaper.[72] This approach gained little traction with the press as only one article reported the statement. Yet German Chancellor Angela Merkel was able to brand her childlessness as a virtue, a form of "motherless motherhood," thereby allowing her to serve as the "mother of them all" for the nation (Cantrell and Bachmann 2008, 438; Wiliarty 2010, 152). Perhaps Campbell's self-declared desire to perform a form of metaphorical motherhood was dismissed by the Canadian media because opponents had already cited her literal childlessness as evidence of unsuitability for political leadership. During the party leadership contest, Campbell's childlessness was represented as part and parcel of her "unstable" family life as "a twice-divorced childless woman."[73] As the next section of the chapter demonstrates, the family strategy – a campaign tactic sometimes used to subtly question the character or undermine the leadership abilities of childless women – was widely reported but only occasionally criticized in media accounts.

The Family Strategy

That the family lives of women politicians are subjected to a higher level of media scrutiny than are the marriages and children of men politicians has become accepted wisdom. According to Campus, "Information on marital status and number of children is made available in most cases for female candidates, while the private life of equally prominent male politicians is ignored unless they choose to shape their public image in that direction" (2013, 94). To be sure, a considerable amount of quantitative evidence supports this observation. Women candidates for senator and governor in the United States were found to be more likely than equivalent men candidates to have their spouses and children discussed by the press (Bystrom et al. 2004, 178–9; Bystrom, Robertson, and Banwart 2001, 2005–6; Devitt 1999, 17). Likewise, the children and marital partners of women seeking the US presidency were mentioned more often than were men's in newspaper coverage of their candidacies (Falk 2010, 185). However, in some cases – for example, Elizabeth Dole and Hillary Clinton – this was partially explained by their husbands' high-profile political careers (Heldman, Carroll, and Olson 2005, 324; Lawrence and Rose 2010, 165, 167).

The pattern has been observed in other countries as well. A study of newspaper coverage of pioneering women politicians in Australian states and territories found that it paid persistent attention to their spouses and made little mention of political wives (Jenkins 1999, 79). As Jenkins (2006, 55) observes, from the "time the first women set foot in any Australian parliament in 1921 until the present, the expectation has been that female politicians should be wives and mothers." In Canada, the marital arrangements of women candidates for the leadership of national political parties were more likely to be mentioned than the spouses of men candidates (Trimble et al. 2013, 469). However, the men candidates' children were commented on more frequently, perhaps because many of the women were childless or had adult children when they sought these party leadership roles (Trimble et al. 2013, 474).

My study produced divergent findings from much of the literature. A comparison of the percentage of news stories mentioning marital status and children for each of the women leaders with the men they had opposed during the election campaigns revealed that there were *more* articles referencing the men's family lives (see tables 4.2 and 4.3). In fact, as table 4.2 demonstrates, men's marriages were mentioned more frequently in all cases except for the 2005 New Zealand election, when the same percentage of news stories discussed Labor leader Helen Clark's spouse as they did National leader Don Brash's wife. Similarly, marital status was referenced in an equal percentage of stories for Gillard and Abbott during the 2010 Australian election. In other words, the women leaders' marital situations were *never* more likely than those of the men to be discussed during election campaigns. Moreover, the men's children were *always* more likely to be discussed in the newspaper coverage than was the childlessness of the women they opposed (see table 4.3). Overall, the family lives of the men leaders were discussed in twice as many stories as were those of the women leaders.

Table 4.2 Percentage of News Stories Mentioning Marital Situation, by Country, Leader, and Election

Country	Election date	Marital situation mentioned			
		Woman leader	%	Man leader	%
Canada	1993	Kim Campbell	4	Jean Chrétien	16
New Zealand	1996	Helen Clark	0	Jim Bolger	6
	1999	Helen Clark	8	n/a	n/a
		Jenny Shipley	6	n/a	n/a
	2002	Helen Clark	6	Bill English	14
	2005	Helen Clark	7	Don Brash	7
	2008	Helen Clark	2	John Key	10
Australia	2010	Julia Gillard	7	Tony Abbott	7

These data support Cross and Henderson's (2004, 152) contention that the "figure of the male politician as family man routinely features in [New Zealand] election campaigns." The numbers also punctuate the pervasiveness of the family man trope in Canada and Australia. I argue that these quantitative findings reflect the deliberate mobilization of a family strategy by certain parties and leaders during election campaigns. As discourse analysis of mediated conversations about family lives illustrates, men politicians are more inclined to brand themselves by and through their family lives. All but one of the leaders who deployed a family strategy was a man.

I define *family strategy* as the deliberate politicization of family life to gain media attention and public support for a candidate. During election campaigns, the traditional, hetero-normative nuclear family provides a visual backdrop during campaign events and serves as a discursive manoeuvre in interviews with the news media. Displaying and discussing their families is a strategy of normalization often deployed by men to win or hold onto political leadership roles (Langer 2010; van Zoonen 2006). By surrounding themselves with the trappings of intimate family life, politicians try to signal qualities and values such as trustworthiness, reliability, kindness, and devotion. Families also provide a form of moral capital, evoking responsibility, capability, and strength (Adams 2011, 223). The presence of spouses and children helps depict political leaders as "complete human beings combining caring and working responsibilities" (van Zoonen 2006, 298). Personal and emotional connections with voters can also be established through the family strategy. By sharing details about their everyday family lives,

Table 4.3 Percentage of News Stories Mentioning Children (or Childlessness), by Country, Leader, and Election

Country	Election date	Children (or childlessness) mentioned			
		Woman leader	%	Man leader	%
Canada	1993	Kim Campbell	0	Jean Chrétien	5
New Zealand	1996	Helen Clark	0	Jim Bolger	1
	1999	Helen Clark	5	n/a	n/a
		Jenny Shipley	5	n/a	n/a
	2002	Helen Clark	2	Bill English	9
	2005	Helen Clark	1	Don Brash	4
	2008	Helen Clark	2	John Key	9
Australia	2010	Julia Gillard	5	Tony Abbott	9

leaders "display a degree of vulnerability and emotional reflexivity, which are key to appearing personable and in touch" (Langer 2010, 66). As well, elite politicians draw on their own experiences as spouses or parents to "personify political values and authenticate policy positions" on issues affecting family life, such as childcare and education (ibid.).

This political tactic is most useful to party leaders with traditional marriages and, ideally, offspring. I argue that the family strategy is best suited to men's political campaigns because of the cultural persistence of the public man/private woman binary. For men, public and private spheres are understood to be distinct but inherently compatible (van Zoonen et al. 2007). Men are assumed to enjoy a realm of personal comfort and support in the private realm, provided by the unpaid labour of their wives or family members, or the paid labour of domestic workers. As a result, men politicians are typically portrayed by the press as "living in an integrated world of public and private duties" (van Zoonen 2005, 91). Public displays of marital fidelity and fatherhood allow them to demonstrate the caring qualities and empathetic postures associated with the private realm of home and family without undermining the authoritativeness necessary for a successful display of political leadership (Adams 2011, 224; Burnette and Fox 2012, 91). Moreover, public fatherhood signals virility and youthfulness (Langer 2010, 66). For men whose marital lives have not been marked by infidelity or divorce, foregrounding spouses and children is a useful campaign tactic.

For women leaders who are divorced, in common-law relationships, or childless, the family strategy can be mobilized against them, both to highlight their difference from the "norm" of political leadership and to question their ability to connect with or even understand the experiences and policy needs of people with families. But even those who are married with children do not necessarily benefit from media scrutiny of their intimate family lives because women are culturally associated with the duties and virtues of domesticity and conjugal loyalty. Stressing motherhood and faithfulness may be insufficient to deflect rumours of adultery in the case of women politicians, for instance (Mukda-anan, Kusakabe, and Komolsevin 2006, 158). As well, public roles, especially high-profile and enormously time-consuming jobs like party leader or prime minister, are considered to be a threat to the stability and health of the family and especially to the productive upbringing of children. Women politicians, like French presidential candidate Ségolène Royal, are still asked who is minding their children (Campus 2013, 96), but this question is rarely posed to men politicians. Moreover, while men's childlessness is neither noticed nor evaluated, childlessness for women is perceived as a dereliction of womanly duty, evidence of unruly and unseemly ambitions and "unnatural" desires (van Zoonen 2005, 91).

Even those exceptional women who demonstrate that they can "do it all" by blending paid work with family roles are judged to be anomalous because of their political ambition. Adams's (2011) examination of *Commander in Chief*, the dramatic television series depicting a female president of the United States, illustrates how association with the family undermines rather than enhances the moral-capital worthiness of female government leaders because of the persistence of gender role stereotypes and tropes of "good" motherhood. As van Zoonen (2006, 299) observes, family life "is a potential site of trouble for women politicians ... because it is a continuous reminder of women's odd choice of public mission instead of private fulfillment." Women, therefore, are in a classic double bind. The family is, at one and the same time, a symbol of their "normalcy" and of their unusualness.

Discourse analysis of statements about the leaders' marital situations and children, or childlessness, shows that the family strategy was mobilized against Campbell, Clark, and Gillard. Shipley, the only one in this group of four women prime ministers with a traditional family arrangement, attempted to deploy the tactic in her competition with Clark. Newspaper coverage of their campaigns reflected, and thereby consolidated, the normative assumptions underlying the family strategy. Yet some of the reportage contested these assumptions. Occasionally, the press exposed the family strategy as a campaign tactic, and some commentators decried its intrinsic gendered double standard. Also, the approach was named and resisted by the women leaders themselves, albeit infrequently and not without risk.

Kim Campbell was confronted with the family strategy during her bid for the leadership of the Progressive Conservative Party of Canada in 1993. The novelty of a woman in the running for the prime minister's job, coupled with Campbell's strong and well-funded campaign and her status as the front-runner, prompted media scrutiny of every aspect of her personal life and political career, especially her "unhappy family life and failed marriages."[74] Campbell had been married and divorced twice before entering the leadership contest, and while she had step-children as a result of her first marriage, she had not given birth to children. In contrast, her primary opponent during the leadership contest, Jean Charest, had a traditional family life and did not hesitate to include his wife and very young children in campaign photos and public events. Charest "posed for a photograph with his wife giving him a warm embrace on the cover of this week's *Maclean's* magazine," observed a *Globe and Mail* article.[75] Campbell's strategists quickly identified "favourable media coverage of the Charest family" as a problem for their candidate.[76] As a leaked memo revealed, the team believed that images of the Charest family would be used to draw unflattering attention to Campbell's "marital and family history."[77] Columnists concurred, writing about a "whispering campaign" coming from the Charest camp, designed to boost its candidate's credibility, while raising questions about Campbell's character and leadership qualities.[78] The media complied, reporting that Campbell was deemed unsuitable for the role of party and government leader because of her two divorces.[79] In fact, Campbell's "two failed marriages" were described in intimate detail, with some feature stories giving Campbell's marital history as much attention as her career trajectory.[80]

In Campbell's case, newspaper coverage played an important role in articulating the assumptions underlying the successful deployment of the family strategy – the traditional family as a symbol of normalcy, good character, and likeability – by directly quoting Charest supporters. The "fact that Mr. Charest has a 'beautiful wife and children' gives him an advantage with voters," said an admirer.[81] Convention delegates told newspaper writers "that they relate better to the married father-of-three than they do to the twice-divorced Campbell."[82] The family tactic went beyond the issue of electability as it was also linked to party values and candidate integrity. Charest was represented as stable and level-headed because of his family relationships, while Campbell's childlessness and divorces were mustered as evidence of instability and unreliability.[83] For example, according to Charest supporters, public opinion poll results purportedly demonstrated that almost "two-thirds of Canadians think Kim is unpredictable."[84]

However, the Charest team's family strategy did not go unmediated. Because it fit neatly into the game frame, it was exposed as a campaign device, a way to spin the story. For instance, a columnist described the gender-based biases she had witnessed on the convention floor during the voting, among them the propensity of Charest supporters to deploy family man and family values tropes while invoking "the code word 'stability.'"[85] She wrote,

> I suggested that some of this talk about stability, and emphasis on Mr. Charest's family, was a bit underhanded. "Look, why shouldn't we emphasize our candidate's attractions?" the Charest worker replied. "And anyway, we can't get two divorces before Sunday just to be politically correct."[86]

Another columnist drew attention to the stealth and subtlety of the strategy. Charest and his supporters "will never be caught publicly mentioning the status of ... Kim Campbell as a twice-divorced woman," but would instead "invite comparisons to the family background of Mr. Charest," he critiqued.[87] Other columns portrayed the focus on family life as evidence of a gendered double standard.[88] "Would you ask why a man didn't have children? Would you question how two failed marriages would affect his politics?"[89] asked one news commentator, while another asserted that "repeated references by Charest supporters of Mr. Charest as stable and unflappable were seen as code words aimed at those still harbouring sexist tendencies."[90]

Campbell herself seemed reluctant to directly counter this strategy, despite her team's identification of the tactic as a problem for her campaign. Perhaps she believed the media critique, outlined above, was sufficient to undermine the potency of the strategy, or maybe she feared that any response would only serve to legitimize the derisory observations about her character. As one news report proposed, Campbell was reluctant to drag family members into the limelight. "When her failed marriages and childlessness became character issues, her image makers had to pry her teeth apart with a crowbar for a single mention of [her first husband] Nathan Divinsky's three daughters, because Campbell did not want to demean her loving relationship with her stepchildren," a writer opined in a feature article.[91] Urged to reference the stepchildren from her first marriage to establish her credibility with Canadian families, Campbell reluctantly mentioned them once during the leadership convention, when she expressed her sympathy for young people, like her stepchildren, who faced peer pressure.[92]

The family issue dogged Campbell during her brief governance phase, with news articles reminding readers of the controversy. For instance, "Campbell survived suggestions that because she is divorced and has no children she was unsuitable for 24 Sussex Drive."[93] This statement is also telling: "Ms. Campbell's handlers are sensitive to the whispered criticisms by some of her fellow Tories during the recent leadership campaign about her status as a twice-divorced single woman."[94] However, journalists had apparently exhausted the news value of the subject (or their interest in it) by the time the election was called as Campbell's "two failed marriages" were mentioned only once in the coverage of her campaign.[95] The family strategy was marshalled once again, this time by Liberal Party leader Jean Chrétien, who spoke about his wife frequently with the media. Yet while newspaper reports commented on the presence of Chrétien's wife, children, and grandchildren at campaign events,[96] his marriage was never directly contrasted with Campbell's single status, and Campbell's childlessness was not discussed in the newspaper articles focused on her campaign.

By contrast, stories about the 2010 Australian election juxtaposed Gillard's childlessness and common-law marital relationship against Liberal Party leader Tony Abbott's traditional nuclear family, further revealing the normative assumptions about the function of the family for political leaders, especially on the campaign trail. An article titled "Family ties or in a bind? Abbott welcomes his wife as Gillard goes it alone,"[97] communicated the understanding that spouses and children are invaluable helpmates and champions, providing emotional support during the rigours of an election campaign. The article focused on the absence of Gillard's partner, Tim Mathieson, from campaign events. Since he had not "been sighted on the hustings since the campaign began more than a week ago," Gillard "confronted the fact that she would be alone on the trail."[98] After observing that Gillard was not legally married, the article emphasized the presence of Tony Abbott's wife, Margie, at his campaign events. The Opposition leader, readers were reassured, did not have to "go it alone."[99] Abbott also "used his family status as a point of differentiation" from Gillard during a televised party leaders' debate, pronouncing, "My wife and I know what it's like to raise a family."[100] Reporters asked Gillard whether she "felt threatened by the tactic," and while she said no,[101] her approach seemed to shift in response to the family strategy deployed by Abbott. Initially, Gillard insisted that her partner would not be joining her on the campaign trail as he was neither a Labor Party official nor a candidate.[102] However, as a story published later in the campaign observed, Gillard "visited two shopping centres with her partner Tim Mathieson, receiving a largely positive reception."[103]

Abbott also employed the family strategy to communicate a loving and empathetic persona and pitch his party's policy platform. His wife and two of his three daughters accompanied him to numerous campaign events, watching him kick a ball at a football match and glad-hand at a small business, for instance. Widely reported was their frequent presence, as well as Abbott's praise for his wife and daughters.[104] Journalists seemed to accept without question or challenge the image of the family man aided by his proud spouse and children, and the presence of his wife as a campaign prop. Abbott also used his family relationships to underscore his commitment to family-friendly policy. "I'm particularly pleased Margie has been able to join me on the campaign trail today,"[105] he enthused, citing his wife's experience as a community-based care provider as he pledged more funding for occasional care.[106] Abbott's displays of familial love and support, and the conscription of his wife and daughters to appeal to women voters, were also documented in coverage of his campaign. "Margie stands by her man as Abbott woos women,"[107] said a headline. Another article reported that "21-year-old daughter Louise [was] on hand to soften her dad's image."[108] For Abbott, the family strategy seemed designed to convince the public of his kindness and humanity, while at the same time communicating moral conservatism through carefully deployed traditional family tableaux. Johnson (2013, 22) argues that Abbott's family strategy was designed to evoke "forms of protective masculinity" as a patriarchal model of "the responsible, caring, protective father who plays the key role in providing for families."

During her election campaigns as Labour leader in New Zealand, Helen Clark also faced variations on the family strategy. Clark's marriage and decision not to have children were never discussed in the newspaper articles about the 1996 election, her first as Labour Party leader. Her opponent, Jim Bolger, talked about his wife, but neither he nor the journalists covering the campaign drew attention to Clark's domestic life, perhaps because questions about her marriage and sexual orientation had been such a prominent element of the newspaper coverage of her leadership "coup" in 1993. In contrast, during the 1999 election, incumbent Prime Minister Jenny Shipley played the "mom" card as a matter of credibility and experience and as a way of distinguishing her character and approach to policymaking from Clark's. Fountaine argues that Shipley "deliberately highlighted her status as a mother, in an attempt to influence the media framing of her and Clark's leadership styles" (2002, 13). Indeed, Shipley was widely expected to do so. As one article declared, "Political strategists expect National to market Mrs. Shipley as the archetypal mainstream New Zealand family woman, and to try and contrast her in the public mind with the childless and academic Ms. Clark."[109] Shipley took pains to distinguish between her experience as a mother and Clark's childlessness and bring them to the attention of the media. For instance, the National Party ran a campaign advertisement stressing Shipley's mothering role. In addition, Shipley gave this pointed statement, widely reported: "I'm a politician, but I am a mum as well. I have the same hopes and concerns for my children as other parents do."[110]

Shipley's public declaration of motherhood seemed to have some traction as Clark's childlessness was mentioned in 5 per cent of the articles about her during this campaign, typically framed as evidence of her aloofness and inability to comprehend the concerns of parents and families.[111] As a result, "the motherhood theme was closely linked to the women's (Clark in particular) perceived ability to lead the country" (Fountaine and McGregor 2003, 4; also see Cross and Henderson 2004, 155). But, as was the case when Jean Charest deployed the family strategy against Kim Campbell, some media commentators criticized Shipley's willingness to highlight her child-bearing and -rearing roles. A columnist said this was merely campaign spin.

> Mrs. Shipley, stern school-marm, has been airbrushed into Jenny, sweet, smiling mumsie-pie. ... The message is that this is middle New Zealand running your country, your sort of folk. ... They've begotten families and they pick flowers and drive farm bikes in working clobber.[112]

The reporting of Shipley's attempt to deploy the family strategy ranged in tone from bemused to derisory. In addition to calling her strategy disingenuous, newspaper articles highlighted Clark's critique of this campaign tactic, quoting the Labour leader at length. "What the public wants to know is, what direction will these two women take us in? What are their policies? That's what they are interested in – not our family circumstances," Clark argued.[113] Clark's assertion that the National Party had "misjudged the public by focusing on Prime Minister Jenny Shipley's attributes as a mother" was also cited.[114] As a result, Clark's counter-narrative – a leader's family life is irrelevant to voters' policy concerns – was profiled in the coverage of Shipley's public declarations of motherhood, allowing Clark to directly challenge the underlying assumptions.

Two of the men Clark competed against in subsequent elections also positioned their families for political advantage – Bill English in 2002 and Don Brash in 2005. Both displayed their wives and wove fatherhood into narratives about caring and compassionate leadership. The coverage of English's campaign foregrounded his large family and praised his wife, Mary, "mother-of-six," as poised, immaculate, accomplished – indeed, as "the perfect politician's wife."[115] "Mr. English is leaning on his image as a family man," said a news report about the 2002 election.

> He refers regularly to his wife Mary, who is always there in the background. And on issues such as education and crime, he assures voters that, as a father of six, he cares greatly about such issues. It is no accident that he reminds us – without actually having to say it – that Miss Clark is childless and married to a man she sees irregularly.[116]

In response, journalists recycled rumours about Clark's marriage and quoted her husband, Peter Davis, who explained that the couple "have been too busy working to have children."[117]

For Don Brash, National Party leader during the 2005 election, the family strategy was a risky manoeuvre because of his divorce and the frisson of scandal surrounding his relationship with his second wife. Because his infidelity was public knowledge, Brash spoke frankly with the media about it. He had fallen in love with Je Lan "at first sight," he revealed, and they had established a relationship despite the fact that she was married at the time.[118] He stressed their mutual devotion and told journalists about their twelve-year-old son,[119] perhaps to symbolize his virility and vitality, and assuage concerns about his age. Described as a "gentle old bank manager,"[120] Brash turned sixty-five during the campaign. The National leader was also keen to note his wife's Chinese heritage, offering "the marriage as proof of his multicultural credentials."[121] Finally, Brash sought credibility with women voters by crediting daughter Ruth for opening his eyes to gender equality and equal rights issues. "It wasn't until I saw the world through my daughter's eyes that I realized the world was not equal," he admitted.[122] By emphasizing his family, Brash may have been able to rebrand his own persona and establish trust and credibility with voters concerned by his relationship history. During this campaign, Clark's childlessness was noted once, in a comment she made to the press about being called a "no-kids lesbo" by opposition supporters at a leaders' debate.[123] Also, as noted in the "First Men" section of this chapter, Clark's relationship with her husband was probed when a television interviewer asked pointed questions about their physical intimacy.

National leader John Key decided not to deploy his family for electoral advantage during the 2008 New Zealand election campaign. As a profile about the newly elected prime minister explained, although "the fact he was a parent was a point of difference for Mr. Key over Helen Clark, he said he had decided before the campaign that he did not want to be seen using them."[124] A lengthy profile of Key's wife, Bronagh,[125] failed to slake journalists' desire for information about the children. News reports noted that Key's offspring had been "kept out of the limelight since Key's rapid rise to the National Party leadership."[126] Starved for details about the soon-to-be "first family," news writers responded by lavishing attention on the subject during a lengthy interview with the newly elected prime minister after the campaign was over.[127] While several articles drew attention to Key's affluence and opulent lifestyle, he was seen as "an everyman" with "a nice house in Parnell and a loving wife and children."[128] New Zealand's rich new prime minister was just a regular guy, after all.

This qualitative analysis of mediated discourses about the family prompts two observations about the utility of invoking intimate familial relationships as part of a campaign communications strategy. First, family status is linked to traits like warmth and empathy, leadership qualities such as compassion and decency, and the capacity to understand the needs, and make governing decisions in the best interests, of "ordinary" families. Men leaders with supportive wives and traditional families were able to pitch their personas and policies by campaigning alongside, or talking about, close family members. Wives and children were seen as assets, as evidence of virility, steadfastness, and stability. This approach also seemed to have some currency for Shipley, the lone woman leader with a conventional nuclear family. The press called husband Burton the ideal "first man" and did not ask New Zealand's first woman prime minister who was taking care of the children. But Shipley's profiling of her "mom" status as a way of contrasting her family life with Clark's childlessness was directly challenged in several news articles, punctuating the second observation: public fatherhood is easier to comprehend than public motherhood. The family is a deeply gendered institution, both in practice and in its idealization. Myths about the family invariably reinforce patriarchal norms and the gendered division of familial labour.

Conclusions

Family matters in politics, especially for party leaders. A sound marital relationship, complete with healthy, happy children, is assumed to signify loyalty, dedication, kindness, evidence of good character, and sound domestic management. Families are increasingly marketed to voters as being integral to a leader's brand, but the trend towards foregrounding spouse and children to project a caring image and approachable personality relies on deeply inscribed cultural norms about intimate family life. Despite the fact that the archetypal nuclear family – the dad as breadwinner, mom taking care of two and a half children – is on the extinction list, many men politicians do inhabit this family form and can stand at its helm as exemplars of virility, ordinariness, stability, and virtue. So it is no surprise that many of the male leaders in my sample employed the family strategy to forge allegiances with voters. Even the divorced and adulterous Brash was able to peddle his newly constituted second family, complete with young child, as a political asset. In contrast, the divorced single woman (Campbell); the independent, career-oriented childless couple (Clark and Davis); the political mom (Shipley); and the childless, not legally wed woman (Gillard) were discursively marked as unusual because of their family arrangements, thus unable to glean much of a profit from them. Shipley, the lone woman prime minister with the closest possible facsimile of the prototypical family, was criticized for her attempt to link mothering to her political identity. To summarize the argument, family is a sign of ordinariness for men politicians, but for women, it is an indicator of difference.

My analysis of the news reporting about the four women prime ministers found that it paid considerable attention to their marital arrangements, especially at the moment when they entered the top echelons of electoral politics as party or government leader. Interest in the topic dropped slightly as they carried out the tasks associated with governing the nation, or competed in election campaigns, but journalists were keen to remind news audiences of these women's marital situations when they left the prime minister's office. In all cases, a higher or equal percentage of news stories mentioned the women leaders' marriages (or divorces, in the case of Campbell) than was the case for the men against whom they contested elections. As discourse analysis of these references revealed, there was considerable consternation about how to frame the presence, or absence, of the "first man" or understand his function. Yet the wives paraded on the campaign trail by their political husbands were accepted in the role of the passive, decorative helpmate (Higgins and Smith 2013, 199). Shipley's husband, Burton, also made sense to the press as she had raised the children while he ran the family farm, and she did not gain the prime minister's post until the children were adults. And while Burton was content to be profiled as the ultimate political accessory, the press also presented him as a manly man. But Gillard's partner, Tim Mathieson, was quite another matter given his career as a hairdresser and reliance on Gillard for an employment makeover. He was constructed as being economically and romantically dependent on Gillard, his sexuality questioned as a result. Finally, that Helen Clark's husband, Peter Davis, had an independent life and career, and did not traipse along beside her on the campaign trail, was seen to symbolize a lack of intimacy in their relationship. Norms of hegemonic masculinity were expressed in reporting about the "first men."

The issue of children was less often raised for the women leaders than for the men they competed with for electoral victory. As I have argued, the greater levels of attention paid to the men leaders' children resulted from two factors. First, many of the men deployed a family strategy, profiling and praising their wives and children as a campaign tactic. That this works, and journalists cannot seem to resist the lure of a politician's children, was illustrated by the commentary on Tony Abbott's daughters during the 2010 Australian election and the onslaught of writing about John Key's teenagers when the newly elected New Zealand prime minister finally lifted the media embargo on access to information about them. Second, the fact that three of the four women prime ministers were childless when they assumed the top job likely dampened the amount of attention the media paid to this aspect of their family lives. The absence of children is a sensitive subject. That said, even though Campbell's, Clark's, and Gillard's childlessness was mentioned infrequently in news articles, journalists certainly did not hesitate to enquire into the reasons for the absence of biological offspring. This manoeuvre suggested that an explanation for childlessness was both demanded by the public and essential to voters' assessments. As I have shown, childlessness was represented as a failing or cited as evidence of unsuitability for political leadership roles. Yet counter-narratives were offered by observers, columnists, and occasionally the women leaders themselves. The idea that only those who have borne and raised children can understand the experiences and policy needs of the "ordinary" family was directly contested in some of the news articles about Clark and Gillard. Overall, however, the family strategy prompted deeply hurtful and politically damaging epithets and evaluations, such as representations of Gillard as "deliberately barren," Campbell as unstable, and Clark as emotionally distant and out of touch with "ordinary" families.

The politicization of intimacy is a double-edged sword for women political leaders. On the one hand, politics and family life are still regarded as a zero-sum game for a woman. If she's considered ambitious, family life is thought to suffer, and if she is regarded as too emotionally and physically devoted to caring for family members, she is seen as lacking the drive and singular focus necessary for political success. The continued association of women with domestic tasks and nurturing qualities renders the subject of the family a dangerous topic for elite women politicians, regardless of the form their family lives take. On the other hand, when tales of familial intimacy are written into news coverage of political leaders, the artificial boundaries between the public and the private realms are exposed. Coverage of the family, whatever its configuration, helps ordinary citizens see politicians as "real" people who make profound emotional commitments, display kindness and affection, and (more mundanely) make dinner or pick up the dry-cleaning. After all, political leaders cannot leave their jobs at the office, and their home lives shape their political achievements.

Reading about politicians' family lives thereby disrupts the socially constructed myth of separate, and rigidly separated, political and domestic realms. In this respect, the politicization of intimacy by the press creates discursive space for challenging the patriarchal family order. Similarly, when positioned as a site of political commentary and evaluation, politicians' bodies reflect and reproduce gender regulations and norms of political leadership. Chapter 5 investigates media attention to the bodies of the women prime ministers and the men they opposed during the election campaigns, paying particular attention to the ways in which the press drew associations between physical appearance and the performance of political leadership. Bodies are central to the process of news-mediated legitimacy, I argue, as the corporeal presence of a political actor is interpreted for its congruence with gendered expectations about how a leader should look.

Chapter Five

Body Politics

Introduction

> There he was, in a tight T-shirt and red boxing gloves on the BBC: Canada's new prime-minister-designate. There he was again – shirtless and flexing this time – on the homepage of Britain's The Independent newspaper. Justin Trudeau was even more ubiquitous on social media, where Twitter and Facebook users traded links to pictures of him showcasing his, um, leadership skills. "The votes are in and Canada has come out of its election with a super hot new leader" was how the Australian news website news.com.au put it.[1]

This example of reactions to the election of Canada's newest Prime Minister Trudeau illustrates how, in a mediatized, celebrity-focused, and intimized public sphere, the elite politician's body is brought into view. A steady flow of images, fostered in part by an increasingly voyeuristic pop culture, ensures that the physical appearance of politicians is no longer "private." Indeed, political leaders are subjected to considerable scrutiny and evaluation by the media (Stanyer 2013, 14–15), profiled and assessed for their ability to personify the images and goals of their parties and for their symbolic resonance with the myths, dreams, and values of the public (Coulomb-Gully 2009, 208). Managing the image of a party leader is now key to selling the party's brand and its policies (Marland 2012, 216). As a result, bodies matter in political life. The bodies of political leaders are regarded both as objects to be marketed to voters and as subjects of political interpretation for the politically relevant messages they convey.

As both objects of the external gaze and subjects of popular discourse, bodies are sites on which gender is inscribed (Leder 1990, 6). Depictions of bodies in television programs, movies, magazines, advertisements, and other popular-culture texts reveal the socially constructed nature of gender identities (Ross 2010, 41–63). However, as Clare (2002, 1) notes, "Little has been done to address the interrelationship of body, gender, and aesthetics which produces the spectacle of women performing as leaders in the political and public domain." News stories provide a useful site of investigation because they reflect the gender regulations circulating in any given society, mirroring "society's cultural preconceptions about what women [and men] should look like, talk like and act like in public life" (McGregor 1996, 187). News coverage of women and men political leaders reveals how discourses about bodies reproduce gendered assumptions about who should hold political power and how they ought to look while enacting leadership roles (Duerst-Lahti and Kelly 1995). As I show in this chapter, mediated representations of politicians tend to delegitimize women's bodies as sites of political authority, while reading men's bodies as personifying leadership. Discourses about the personas and performances of political leadership thus reflect and reinforce norms of hegemonic masculinity such as virility, imposing physical stature, strength, whiteness, and hetero-normativity. But when women (or men) are noticed primarily for their physical difference from the masculine form, the socially constructed association of hegemonic forms of masculinity with authentic representations of political power is exposed and may be contested. Media texts explicitly or implicitly associating women's physical appearance with strength, vigour, agency, and authority may unsettle the gender order as they contest the socially constructed boundaries between femininity and masculinity.

The first section of the chapter assesses an argument widely articulated by women politicians and the scholars who study them: the media pay more attention to the physical appearance of women politicians than to the looks and style choices of their male counterparts or competitors. Using content analysis, I compare the amount of attention given by newspaper stories to the looks of the four women prime ministers and the men they competed with in general elections. Discourse analysis of descriptions and evaluations of leaders' physical appearance reveals how these representations differ in emphasis and implication. Because my focus is on the ways in which mediated representations of looks and sexuality *politicize* the body by bringing it into discourses about political leadership, the second part of the chapter examines how descriptions of leaders' bodies are used to communicate evaluations of their political performances. Who is said to "look like a leader" (or not) and why? I ask how features of the body, such as its size, comportment, adornment, and physical attractiveness are mobilized as symbols of political authenticity or inauthenticity in media accounts. In the third section, I extend this analysis to the most successful leader in my study, Helen Clark, examining the implications of the "makeover" metaphor, which was applied to Clark throughout her lengthy political career. The fourth and final section investigates the politicization of the body through sexualizing news discourses, illustrating a disconcerting level of attention to sexuality for women leaders who do not conform to hetero-patriarchal norms of feminine behaviour.

The Leadership Style Watch

Women politicians from around the world decry media attention to their hair, clothing, and make-up, arguing that journalists rarely comment on such superficial matters for men politicians (Jenkins 1999, 78; Ross 2002, 89; Sreberny-Mohammadi and Ross 1996, 108; Walsh 2015, 1029). While men and women alike must "surrender to inappropriate sartorial scrutiny," the physical objectification of men politicians is thought to be infrequent, while for women politicians it is the rule, according to Ross and Sreberny-Mohammadi (1997, 104). Comparisons of news coverage of women and men candidates for elite political office lend credence to these concerns, as reporting tends to accord more attention to women's looks than to those of equivalent men politicians (Bystrom et al. 2004, 178–9; Devitt 1999, 17; Falk 2010, 184; Heldman, Carroll, and Olson 2005, 323–4; Miller, Peake, and Boulton 2010, 177; Trimble 2007, 984–5; Trimble and Everitt 2010, 65; Trimble et al. 2013, 469). Notably, Falk's (2010, 87) examination of newspaper coverage of prominent women and comparably competitive men who ran for the US presidency between 1872 and 2008 discovered that the physical appearance of the women presidential candidates was mentioned significantly more often than was the case for the men.

Yet as the example presented at the beginning of this chapter showed, men who seek or hold high political office do not escape scrutiny of their physiques and sartorial choices. In an era of intensely personalized politics and the allure of the celebrity politician, the news media are increasingly likely to notice and comment on the looks of men politicians (Langer 2010, 65; van Zoonen 2006, 297). For instance, Barak Obama was the subject of just as much discussion of his appearance as was Hillary Clinton in news reporting about the 2008 US Democratic presidential nomination contest (Falk 2010, 184; Lawrence and Rose 2010, 165, 167). Similarly, as research from the United States, Germany, Canada, and New Zealand has found, roughly equal levels of attention were paid to the physical appearance of women and men party leaders during election campaigns, and in some cases, a higher percentage of news stories mentioned the looks of the men (Bystrom, Robertson, and Banwart 2001, 2008; Semetko and Boomgaarden 2007, 166; Trimble and Treiberg 2010, 124). In their qualitative analysis of news and entertainment coverage, Lünenborg and Maier (2015, 187–8) discovered more intense media interest in the appearance of Germany's vice-chancellor, Frank-Walter Steinmeier, than in the grooming and styling of the nation's chancellor, Angela Merkel.

These seemingly contradictory findings point to the need for consistency in quantitative measurement. It is not always clear which aspects of the body and its public presentation researchers count as references to "appearance." Because men's bodies are often noticed for different features than are women's, research that does not include stature, comportment, and facial expressions as indicators of looks will likely under-represent attention to men politicians' physical attributes. For instance, although there was a similar amount of media attention to Clinton's and Obama's looks during the 2008 Democratic presidential nomination campaign, the focus of Obama's descriptions was his skin colour, youth, and size, whereas for Clinton, it was the shape of her body (notably her cleavage) and attire (Falk 2010, 158). Similarly, as Falk's (2010, 88–90) analysis of nine women and comparable men who sought the US presidency revealed, while much of this coverage of the women focused on their style and wardrobe choices, for men the spotlight was on their age, health, and facial expressions.

My study emulated Falk's (2010) approach to studying media reporting about politicians' bodies by adopting a comprehensive operational definition of the concept *appearance*.[2] Each news story about a particular leader was coded for whether it mentioned aspects of the appearance, or "look," of the body. In addition to coding for literal mentions of looks (e.g., "looks like," "appeared") and evaluations of a leader's physical appearance (e.g., as glamorous, beautiful, youthful, fit or unkempt, unattractive, or aging), I took account of all references to any aspect

Table 5.1 Percentage of News Stories Mentioning Appearance, by Country, Leader, and Career Phase

Country	Leader	Leadership, %	Governance, %	Election Date	Election %	Resignation or defeat, %
Canada	Kim Campbell	12	15	1993	13	15
New Zealand	Jenny Shipley	8	13	1999	12	11
	Helen Clark	7	7	1996	11	5
				1999	9	
				2002	8	
				2005	9	
				2008	9	
Australia	Julia Gillard	22	8	2010	12	21

of the body, from its parts (eyes, lips, shoulders, hair), stature (height, weight, strength), adornment (with clothing, accessories, hairstyles and make-up), and deportment (gestures, body language, facial expressions). I also searched for attention to the racial(ized) identities of the leaders' bodies, but found that this was an area of complete discursive silence. That all the women prime ministers and the men against whom they competed in federal elections were white was never mentioned or discussed as a matter relevant to their ability to represent the body politic. Sexualization of leaders was analysed as a separate category and is discussed later in this chapter.

Table 5.1 shows a consistently high level of media attention to appearance, reported as the percentage of news stories describing any aspect of the body or its "look" for each of the women prime ministers throughout their careers. Roughly a tenth of the articles, and sometimes more, contained at least one remark about the material features or exhibition of their bodies. Helen Clark was least likely to be described physically, with between 5 and 11 per cent of articles mentioning some aspect of her appearance. In contrast, between 12 and 15 per cent of stories about Kim Campbell discussed her looks. For Jenny Shipley, the range was 8 to 13 per cent. The pattern was similar for Julia Gillard during her governance and election phases, with 8 to 12 per cent of stories saying something about her body's deportment, adornment, shape, or styling. However, depictions of Gillard's physical appearance occurred in a much higher percentage of news articles during her ascent to the prime minister's office through a leadership challenge (22 per cent) and again in her defeat three years later by a counter-challenge (21 per cent). That over a fifth of the newspaper stories printed about Gillard at the

Table 5.2 Percentage of News Stories Mentioning Appearance, by Country, Leader and Election

Country	Election date	Woman leader		Man leader	
Canada	1993	Kim Campbell	13	Jean Chrétien	8
New Zealand	1996	Helen Clark	11	Jim Bolger	1
	1999	Helen Clark	9	n/a	n/a
		Jenny Shipley	12	n/a	n/a
	2002	Helen Clark	8	Bill English	4
	2005	Helen Clark	9	Don Brash	14
	2008	Helen Clark	9	John Key	10
Australia	2010	Julia Gillard	12	Tony Abbott	8

beginning and end of her tenure as prime minister referenced her looks in some way illustrates a high level of personalization, with its attendant focus on image and aesthetics (Street 2004, 444).

Women politicians observe that they receive more attention to their body and its embellishment than do equivalent men politicians. This perception is supported by comparisons between the women prime ministers and the men they opposed during election campaigns. As table 5.2 illustrates, with the exception of Clark's final two election campaigns, the looks of the women leaders were discussed in a higher percentage of election stories than was the physical appearance of the men leaders. Between 9 and 13 per cent of reports about the women's campaigns said something about their bodies, while for men, the coverage ranged from negligible (1 per cent of articles about Jim Bolger during the 1996 New Zealand campaign) to fulsome (14 per cent of the stories about Don Brash during the 2005 New Zealand election). Notably, in the 2005 and 2008 New Zealand elections, the looks of the male leaders were mentioned in a higher percentage of stories than was the case for their opponent, Helen Clark. That said, in the 2008 campaign the difference was slight, just 1 percentage point. These data are intriguing because they show that men's bodies are, in fact, brought into view by news coverage of their candidacies. But using the story as a unit of analysis obscures the level of detail about appearance contained in any given news report. These data merely reflect the percentage of news stories making at least one mention, however brief, of a leader's looks. As a result, an article noting the colour of a man's tie is given as much weight as an in-depth profile of a woman's wardrobe, hairstyle, grooming practices, and physical attractiveness. It is therefore necessary to perform a qualitative analysis of each of the representations and determine the extent of attention to the look, styling, and deportment of particular leaders' bodies.

Discourse analysis revealed considerably more in-depth and expansive discussions of the physical appearance of the women leaders than was the case for the men leaders. In fact, revelations about the women prime ministers' looks were at times excessive, comprising lengthy sentences, paragraphs – indeed, entire stories – and featuring lavish descriptions of physical features, make-up, or clothing, as is detailed below. For the men, comments about their appearance were usually incidental to a story and offered in a few words or at most a short phrase. As examples, Canadian Liberal Party leader Jean Chrétien wore his "trademark blue-denim shirt,"[3] and New Zealand National Party leader Bill English purchased a new "blue silk tie,"[4] during their election campaigns. Australia's Tony Abbott presented a "poker face."[5] Rarely were full sentences devoted to these superficial elements of men's candidacies, and never a complete news story.

Most of the descriptions of how the men looked were literal, conveyed with words and phrases such as "looked like" or "appeared." Helen Clark's first opponent, Jim Bolger, "generally appeared cool and unrattled,"[6] and the second man she competed against, Bill English, "looked a little pale and perhaps a touch shellshocked."[7] Descriptions of Don Brash looking "shifty," "stodgy," "flustered," "red-faced," "bumbling," "unprepared and uncomfortable," and "rattled by heckling"[8] constituted the majority of comments about his physical appearance during the 2005 New Zealand election campaign, and they explain why a higher percentage of stories about him referenced his looks than was the case for Clark. In the Canadian context, there would have been little discussion of Jean Chrétien's appearance during the 1993 election campaign had the governing Progressive Conservative (PC) Party not broadcast an attack ad highlighting his partial facial paralysis. In response, journalists said Chrétien's "crooked mouth" gave him a "raffish look,"[9] and Chrétien was quoted as "joking about" his "lopsided look."[10] As these examples illustrate, representations of the way male leaders looked tended to describe their demeanour and performances as political actors rather than their grooming or the fit of their suits.

While Campbell, Clark, Shipley, and Gillard were regularly evaluated for their aesthetic choices, including hairstyles, wardrobes, and grooming practices, men leaders' bodies, haircuts, and wardrobes were so taken for granted that they were not seen as deserving of substantive commentary by the press. As a noteworthy example, the hair of the male leaders was so rarely discussed during their election campaigns that only the most discerning and dedicated reader of the election news coverage would have noticed it at all. I found just two references to hair in the entire corpus of 753 articles about the six male leaders, both of which hinted at the importance of a youthful image. A news story about Chrétien recorded "suspicion" that he was dyeing his hair in an effort to look younger.[11] Brash was described as having "wispy grey hair."[12]

The men's clothing was occasionally examined and evaluated, but was most likely to be noticed when it deviated from the standard political uniform of dark suit and tie. Only in New Zealand, where news reporting occasionally reads like an episode of the American reality television series *Project Runway*, did commentators scrutinize the wardrobes of all party leaders, men and women alike, in an effort to judge who was "best dressed" for the election campaign.[13] Even then, for the men leaders the focus was on the wardrobe choice as a political strategy rather than as a way of looking physically attractive. Chrétien's casual blue-denim shirt, worn often in the 1993 Canadian election campaign, was, in the words of one news commentator, designed to reinforce his "little guy from Shawinigan image" as an ordinary, working man.[14] Brash, who ran against Clark in 2005, shed his "red tie this time for a sober powder blue," a choice judged more suitable for his party's conservative brand.[15] John Key, who defeated Clark in 2008, wore "special cufflinks – one shaped like the North Island, the other like the South Island"[16] to appeal to voters from across New Zealand. Tony Abbott's Lycra cycling gear, donned during the 2010 Australian campaign for early morning bike rides, was interpreted as personifying his fit and energetic persona.[17] Rather than fixating on these men's bodies as objects for the public gaze, this sort of coverage "interpreted the deeper 'political meanings' of their sartorial choices and the impact these might have had on the public's perception of them" (Langer 2010, 65). The men leaders were thus constituted as empowered subjects, actively constructing their political identities through their wardrobe and style selections. They certainly did not have to develop strategies for dealing with undue media attention to their apparel and grooming during elections.

In contrast, hair and hemlines coverage dogged all four women while they were on the campaign trail and was abundant in newspaper stories throughout their political careers. As Duerst-Lahti argues, by directing attention to women's bodies and styling, news reporting presents them as novelties, subtly questioning their political legitimacy (2006, 37). Each of the women prime ministers' hair was discussed, but the unusualness of Gillard's hair colour caught the attention of news commentators. Coverage of her swearing-in ceremony as prime minister said that television screens "were occupied with the visage of the red-headed woman,"[18] as were the news writers and their sources. That no one with that particular hue had previously occupied the prime minister's post fuelled Australian media commentary, and Gillard herself joked about it, calling her first day on the job a "good day for redheads."[19] She was variously labelled a "Ranga" (slang for *redhead*), "Red Maggie," and "a smart red mare."[20] The media indulged in snide interpositions about her partner, a former hairstylist, "tending her red locks."[21] As these examples illustrate, Gillard's hair colour was not merely recorded; it was highlighted for its novelty and used as a device for questioning her intimate relationship with her partner. In Canada, Campbell's blondness was brought into the coverage just as gratuitously as was Gillard's red hair, but it was also used to convey harsh evaluations of her political persona. Calling her a "blond phenom"[22] suggested that Campbell's political celebrity status reflected her physical novelty, not her political substance. Assessments of her as "a straight right-winger with fluffy blond hair"[23] and a "glassy eyed, tense, blonded doll"[24] cued (dumb) blonde jokes and denigrated her accomplishments and ambition (Hole 2003, 321).

New Zealand journalists also commented on the hairstyles of both of their country's women prime ministers. Shipley's "short, cropped" style was regarded as the "traditional" look for a woman of her political stature,[25] but New Zealand's first woman prime minister was urged to adopt a more traditionally feminine style by a personal development consultant, who suggested that it ought to "be grown longer at the back and more softly styled."[26] A strong pattern of media focus on Clark's changing hairstyle was observed throughout her career, from her ascent to the party leadership role in 1993[27] to her final election campaign in 2008.[28] Her willingness to have her hair professionally styled during election campaigns was emphasized in news reports. "You know an election is coming when she ... gets regular blow-dries and her gold-brown hair suddenly turns glossy."[29] Attention to the prime ministerial hairdo reflected the view that the nation's top political leaders should be appropriately styled for the public, and media, gaze.

Cosmetics were mentioned only in New Zealand, stressed during the 1999 election, when two women were competing for the prime minister's post. The media foregrounded make-up to symbolize what journalists viewed as an atypical display of femininity during this campaign. A columnist pronounced, "It's not all policies and promises this election – there's plenty of interest *in the makeup* and frocks ... this campaign has a strong feminine feel."[30] Incumbent Prime Minister Shipley's pink lipstick was judged "strictly traditional,"[31] her campaign bus dubbed "Lipstick One."[32] Both women leaders were expected to adorn themselves with cosmetics, thereby associating the performance of femininity, on whatever field, with glamour and artifice. However, the idea that applying cosmetics is akin to preparing for battle was evident in descriptions of Clark's grooming practices in subsequent campaigns. An article published during the 2005 election said, "Miss Clark, decked in red with matching lipstick, was aggressive,"[33] thereby linking her look with her political demeanour. During the 2008 campaign, two articles characterized Clark's "make-up regime" as "professionally applied war paint."[34] Here we see a discursive disjuncture because Clark was viewed as complying with norms of exaggerated femininity *and* warrior masculinity. Perhaps this rhetorical assertion helped journalists resolve the cognitive dissonance of a woman performing political leadership in a confident and capable manner.

Pundits, style gurus, and political opponents were quoted, sometimes at length, on the subject of the women leaders' clothing. This commentary was far from perfunctorily descriptive, as was the case for the men leaders. Instead, it was evaluative, suggesting that clothing choices were a reflection of their authenticity and authority. For instance, a journalist assessed Gillard as "dressing appropriately"[35] for her new position when, shortly after being sworn in as prime minister, she donned a dark pin-striped pantsuit for a photo shoot with a leading Australian women's magazine.[36] But just before her removal from office, Gillard was pilloried for looking "soft and feminine" when she posed in a loose-fitting dress, knitting in hand, for another magazine photo spread.[37] "Shot not at the Lodge but in a photographer's studio complete with wind machine to give her that elegantly tousled look, it was such an excruciating fake that it dismayed many of her admirers and exposed her to ridicule everywhere else," pronounced a columnist.[38] Similarly, when Campbell tried to fit in with western Canadian cowboy culture by getting "decked out in jeans, cowboy boots and a buckskin shirt with fringes and feathered tassels," she was accused of trying too hard to project a populist image.[39] Both women were described as using clothing as a masquerade to simulate a persona that they were judged unable to authentically embody.

In New Zealand, the hue of the women prime ministers' clothing was interpreted as being politically meaningful. During the 1999 election campaign, "Miss Clark was drab in olive,"[40] while Shipley was "resplendent in National royal blue."[41] Apparently, sporting the party colour was an appropriate choice for the National leader, but Labour red was construed as going too far for Clark. In the 2002 campaign, she took "a few knocks for her clothes sense," "including a bright red number ... which some commentators compared to a walking Labour billboard."[42] Because of the length of time Clark spent as party leader, her clothing attracted the most prolific commentary of all four of the women prime ministers. She was variously described as wearing a "dowdy dress"[43] and as looking "cool and calm in a pale green pant suit."[44] Regardless of the tone of the evaluation, the fit, style, and colour of Clark's suits, dresses, and jackets were brought into the political discourse during election campaigns in a manner never experienced by the men who opposed her.

Most significantly, entire news stories were devoted to the subject of each woman prime minister's body and its ornamentation, with hairstylists, fashion designers, and image consultants passing judgment on the physical appearance of the woman holding power. A column titled "A few fashion pointers for the neophyte prime minister" offered Kim Campbell advice about clothing, jewellery, hair colour, weight, and posing for photo ops.[45] Jenny Shipley endured the same sort of treatment with a story called "Image gurus say it won't take a lot to get Shipley shipshape."[46] Helen Clark's wardrobe and grooming practices were dissected in full-length articles throughout her career.[47] Signalled with the headline "Clark's mouth 'really is hers,'" one news item focused entirely on "Ms. Clark's swept-up glamorous image."[48] Finally, Julia Gillard's "dazzling red bob," "shimmering necklaces," and "sophisticated attire" were detailed in an article called "Gillard's challenge – leadership style."[49] In these stories, designers, hairstylists, and image consultants were considered the "experts" capable of judging a woman leader's "look."

News coverage emphatically communicated an expectation that women prime ministers will attempt a level of physical grooming and fashion styling typical of female celebrities, reflecting the "hyper-femininity of current celebrity culture and post-feminism, with fashion, sexuality, glamour and consumption as core ingredients" (van Zoonen 2006, 298). However, the press criticized any styling that it perceived as leaning too far in the direction of exaggerated femininity. For instance, a commentator admonished Campbell, "You don't need to look like a female impersonator to stand out in Parliament."[50] Similarly, Gillard was condemned for looking too glamorous in a cover shot for an Australian women's magazine. "Our first female Prime Minister looked more like a supermodel than a cabinet minister."[51] In this respect, beauty discourses were narrated alongside, and sometimes collided with, evaluations of political competency and authenticity.

In the leadership style watch, the *mien* of the male leaders' bodies was given little attention in media discourses about election campaigns. That they were white men with close-cropped hair wearing dark suits was simply taken for granted and rarely interrogated. In contrast, discussion of the women leaders' clothing, hair, and make-up implied that women's bodies were unusual in elite political spaces. There is no commonly agreed-upon uniform for a woman prime minister, no consensus on proper attire or adornment, as shown by the prolific news discussion of wardrobe and styling choices. Even when a woman adopts the power-suit costume of the elite politician, her performance of leadership may be read as counterfeit. After all, the suit remains "the globalized dress code and symbol for politics and masculinity" (Flicker 2013, 210). In the next section, I show how the discursive disjuncture evident in discussions about a woman politician's physique, wardrobe, hairstyle, or make-up was exposed by media musings about who looked the part of the authoritative government leader.

Looking Like a Leader

Many scholars argue that attention to bodies and their visual appearance is more politically consequential for women politicians than for men because of the long-standing separation of "women, bodies, sex, emotions and intimate relationships" from the political world (Holmes 2000, 305). Gender binaries associate women with the body and men with the mind (Butler 2006, 17); thus, descriptions of their bodies and the ways in which they are styled convey negative evaluations of women's fitness for political office (Mandziuk 2008, 314; Ross and Sreberny-Mohammadi 1997, 104; Trimble and Treiberg 2010, 124–6). Depictions of women politicians' looks may underscore their visual appeal, while detracting from their ideas and accomplishments. For instance, in 2004,

Conservative Party leadership contender Belinda Stronach was judged to be fundamentally unsuitable for the role of Canada's prime minister in newspaper coverage that consistently foregrounded her blonde hair and designer wardrobe (Trimble and Everitt 2010, 66). Democratic presidential candidate Hillary Clinton's pantsuits, weight, and wrinkles were cited as reasons in 2008 why voters should reject her (Carlin and Winfrey 2009, 332). When she was premier of the Australian state of Victoria, Joan Kirner was subjected to merciless criticism for her body shape and clothing choices. Coined by her opponents, appellations such as "Miss Piggy" and "Mother Russia" were widely disseminated by news commentators (Hurst 1993, 128–30; Jenkins 1999, 84). The Australian press fixated on Australian Democrats leader Natasha Stott Despoja because she was "young, single, blonde, petite and attractive," simultaneously accusing her of embracing "style over substance" (Muir 2005a, 61). As these examples illustrate, bodies "are not merely static sites on which truth is represented; they are instruments of representation used in ways that must be interpreted" (Holmes 2000, 308).

Since media discourses reflect culturally inscribed norms and assumptions, newspaper commentaries about party and government leaders' physical appearance are likely to reveal assessments of what the quintessential leader should (and should not) look like. As discourse analysis of these texts demonstrates, gendered assumptions about the qualities and skills that a leader should project through their physical presence circulated through the newspaper coverage. Overall, references to wardrobes and grooming habits reinforced ease with men in positions of power and revealed discomfort with women as leaders of parties and governments. Only the men were explicitly pronounced to look like government leaders. During the 1993 Canadian election campaign, Jean Chrétien was described as "looking very prime ministerial in a grey suit and white shirt."[52] In other words, he had the right outfit (and body) for the job. John Key, who defeated Clark in 2008, was also thought to look like a government leader expressly because of his gender. "John Key looks like a prime minister in the same safe, competent, pinstriped, clean-cut way that Kevin Rudd of Australia or Stephen Harper of Canada look like prime ministers."[53] Another article quoted a voter as saying that Key "looks the part" because "a clean-cut guy is what's needed" for the country.[54] More subtly, but with the same message, a columnist declared Australia's Kevin Rudd to be "the very model of the conventional leader" when he was restored to the prime minister's office after his successful challenge to Gillard.[55] In all three countries, media coverage of elections emphasized that white, able-bodied, heterosexual men looked the part of the political leader. This is not surprising; they mirrored all the men who had come before them, and thus their physical appearance symbolized sameness, stability, and assurance.

None of the women was said to look like a prime minister. In fact, news stories emphasized their physical difference from the norm of the male leader. Campbell was designated as being among those "few politicians who, visually at least, represent such an *extreme change* from the middle-aged men in dark suits who have always run Quebec and Canada."[56] Similar comments were made about Gillard – for instance, "The Australian Labor Party wanted to present a very different face on a very unappealing body, and it's hard to get a much more *different look* to Rudd than a female redhead."[57] Even when they avoided directly contrasting women and men prime ministers, news writers' observations about the archetypal female body and its gendered modes of adornment highlighted the visual dissonance created by the presence of a woman in the top job. "Our Prime Minister chooses a necklace in the morning and not a tie," exclaimed an Australian pundit,[58] and another commentator said he caught an enticing glimpse of "the prime ministerial cleavage."[59] In New Zealand, an "image guru" urged Shipley to choose outfits that de-emphasized "the size of her bust."[60] Clark, "a gal who once didn't wear lipstick,"[61] was said to have "recognized cosmetics as a girl's best friend."[62] Commentators may just as well have announced, "The prime minister's a woman! She has breasts! She wears jewellery and lipstick!" These sorts of observations reminded newspaper readers that, as one journalist put it, a "blouse [was] in the prime minister's chair,"[63] and she looked quite different from the usual occupants of the position.

In addition to situating women prime ministers as novel and visually distinct from the "norm" of the male leader, newspaper articles exposed the assumptions linking physical appearance with assessments of leadership style and performance. Depictions of Kim Campbell and Don Brash, both of whom were represented by the press as decidedly un-leader-like in their appearance, demonstrated the politicization of bodies through gendered mediation. Brash, who lost the 2005 New Zealand election to Clark, was termed awkward, geeky, red-faced, and flustered[64] – in other words, as anything but brash. Descriptions of his physical demeanour served as a proxy for negative evaluations of his leadership style and persona. Labelled unflashy, bland, old, bespectacled, thin, hunched, drawn, pale, and uncomfort-able,[65] his awkwardness was contrasted with Helen Clark's poise and confidence[66] on the campaign trail. Brash was seen to be physically unappealing because of his age, size, and bearing. "He is 64, thin and wears glasses," a columnist noted. "He is what young people might call a geek."[67] "He just didn't look good," said another commentator.[68] Such observations and evaluations of Brash's physical appearance sug-gested that he did not fit the mould of the strong, commanding, and in-control political leader. These negative assessments reflected culturally inscribed expectations of political leadership: leaders should be confi-dent, self-assured, forceful, and in command. If they are not literally young, they should be energetic enough to portray a youthful image. If their body is small, thus not physically powerful, they must project an imposing personality.

These expectations were manifest in depictions of Campbell, whose capacity to lead was also viewed through the lens of her body. News coverage of the PC party leadership campaign described her as physically unconvincing in the role because of her size and demean-our. For instance, Campbell "did not look like the front-runner for the most powerful public office in the land," declared a columnist.[69] As constant references to her "diminutive" body[70] implied, she lacked the physical stature perceived to be necessary for a top leadership role. Height is equated with power, and it acts as a specific form of agency (Sanghvi and Hodges 2015, 1683). Because Campbell is short, she was seen as lacking in authority. The trope of exaggerated femi-ninity further punctuated the point about her physical difference from the standard embodied by male leaders. For instance, according to a *Globe and Mail* columnist, Campbell had once projected an image of a "broad with balls," but had been repackaged as a "glassy-eyed, tense, blonded doll."[71] Indeed, news stories about the leadership cam-paign drew attention to the "soft white shoulders,"[72] "bare-shoulder pose,"[73] and overt "femininity"[74] displayed in a photograph of an "apparently topless" Campbell. By depicting her as a small, bottle-blonde woman willing to bare her body for the camera, news reports questioned Campbell's judgment and highlighted her departure from the culturally inscribed standard of the physically imposing, buttoned-up, conservatively attired political leader. Only one opinion writer offered a counter-narrative, challenging the gendered assump-tions underlying the physical judgments of Campbell. "Next time you see Kim Campbell on television, listen to her. Recognize that because she wears lipstick, the words coming out of her mouth are perceived differently."[75]

Further, by dissecting the look Campbell projected through her facial expressions, news writers suggested that she lacked the controlled neutrality and intrinsic pleasantness necessary to convey the leadership qualities of likeability, empathy, and charm. Instead, according to journalists, she frowned, sulked, and even displayed rabid surliness.[76] "In a happy encounter ... she has a sisterly exuberance, a sparkle in her eyes, and a captivating smile," asserted a columnist.[77] "But in any challenging situation her facial muscles tighten, the frown appears, her look becomes icy blue, her mouth fluctuates between ironic smiles and icy sneers, and she attacks with the alarming frenzy of a rabid fox."[78] To counter the negative image fostered by her putatively grim countenance, Campbell was advised to "put on a happy face"[79] and "smile and flash your eyes" when talking about policy issues during the election campaign.[80] As this particular news discourse illustrates, an effervescent personality is seen as an appropriate mode of feminine behaviour, while a stern countenance is judged to be inappropriately aggressive for a woman politician.

In summary, the bodies and visual performances of Campbell and Brash were said to lack stature and gravitas. Brash was described as thin and geeky, Campbell as small and womanly. What was even more damaging, journalists latched onto their physical features as symbols of their allegedly inadequate and inauthentic performance of political leadership. Brash was scripted as being awkward and uncomfortable, Campbell as unable to convincingly mimic the controlled demeanour of a successful political actor. In both cases, news mediation of their bodies, wardrobes, hairstyles, and deportment was intensely gendered. Reporting relied on sex stereotypes and tropes of masculinity and femininity, such as the manly man and the beauty queen, to delegitimize their claims to high political office.

If a man's body can be used as a metaphor for his inadequate performance of political leadership, can a woman who performs the role successfully for years challenge gendered assumptions about how an authoritative leader should look? Given that Helen Clark was Labour Party leader for fifteen years, contested five elections, won three of them, and served as prime minister for nine years, it is not unreasonable to expect that the New Zealand press corps grew accustomed to the appearance of a woman in an influential political role. In the next section, I argue that despite the persistence of the "lipstick watch" throughout her political career, Clark was often presented as both commanding and convincing.

Helen Clark's Extreme Makeovers

As discussed in chapter 2, Clark emerged from her leadership "coup" with an image problem. She was widely portrayed as ruthless and relentlessly ambitious, even unlikeable. Yet over the course of her fifteen-year stint as party leader, media perceptions of Clark changed dramatically, in part because she was reported to change her "look" in ways that were interpreted positively. I argue that the media coverage narrated the evolutions of Clark's physical appearance as a series of "extreme makeovers." As with the reality television program *Extreme Makeover*,[81] noticeable changes to Clark's physical image were effected under the guidance of paid experts and media marketers. Each of these political image makeovers was met with approval by the press.

Superficial changes to her physical appearance were interpreted as signalling a visual "softening" of Clark's public persona immediately after she won the Labour Party leadership in 1993. "Ms. Clark is perceived as cold and hard, though a change of hairstyle and makeup during the election warmed appearances slightly," said a newspaper story.[82] The focus was on Clark's "new hairdo."[83] According to MacGregor, the "New Zealand Herald ran 20 paragraphs breathlessly quoting both an 'image-maker' and a university psychologist on Helen Clark's 'new hairstyle'"(1996, 183). While Clark's first makeover was far from extreme – as Clark herself described it, she merely "had a fringe cut"[84] – it was interpreted as having a significant effect on her political persona. This very modest style shift sparked some initial thawing in media perceptions, and assessments, of Clark's political appeal.

During the 1996 election, Clark's first campaign as Labour leader, New Zealand newspapers described how she honed her media skills to present a confident and likeable public image. "Clark changes from ugly duckling to canny swan," announced a headline for an article describing her newly acquired "poise and smoothness."[85] This makeover paralleled elements of *Extreme Makeover*, which promises fairy-tale scenarios in the form of complete transformations guided by a veritable team of experts. Clark's image renovation was deemed a "Cinderella-like transformation" in her televised performances, "aided by the fairy-godmother-touch of her media trainers."[86] Despite the gendered references to the well-known fairy tale, news coverage made it clear that this makeover was a transformation of Clark's performance of leadership for the television cameras, not an overhaul of her body or its styling. The makeover provided by media coaching helped the press see Clark as a persuasive, and even appealing, political actor. News report after news report said that Clark was "looking and acting like a winner"[87] due to her "growing confidence" on television, "new look," and noticeable changes in her presentation style.[88] For instance, Clark "looked relaxed and unrattled" during a party leaders' debate.[89] Another article said, "The debate showcased Ms. Clark's developing campaign style, in which brittleness has given way to a smooth, authoritative performance."[90]

The following quotation best summarizes the pundits' perspective on the restyling of Clark as a media-savvy politician: "Ms. Clark's rise in the past few weeks of the campaign has been spectacular and has been based – as much as she hates it – on smartening up her television image. … For so long the victim of television she is – for the first time – its master."[91] When the 2002 election campaign rolled around, Clark's transformation "from ugly duckling to media darling" was said to be complete, and completely convincing. "The severe, aloof figure of yesteryear has been replaced by a confident, polished politician,"[92] who "looked comfortable as she took the microphone"[93] and "looked good in the debates."[94] Clark, in other words, was seen to offer a persuasive, and indeed commanding, performance of political leadership.

The third makeover, frequently mentioned and often praised by the press, reflected Clark's willingness to submit to quintessentially feminine rituals of grooming while campaigning for votes. As Clark herself acknowledged in an interview,

> Left to myself I would dress as I see fit for the occasion. I think that what's increasingly become apparent to me with respect to television is that the whole meaning of television is a performance. How you look, tragically, is probably more important than anything you say. (McGregor 1996, 183)

That Clark agreed to focus attention on tailoring and hairstyle choices while on the campaign trail was evident in the news coverage of her campaigns from 1999 to 2008. As one commentator put it, "Miss Clark has had more image makeovers than Madonna," but they occurred "roughly once every three-year election cycle."[95] Clark's attention to styling was purely for the sake of political marketing, journalists asserted – for example,

> The real-life Miss Clark is a handsome woman who works out regularly, but one gets the feeling that she is not the sort who has the time or inclination to devote to the frivolities of makeup and hairdo. Glam is not her natural style, but glam is how she will be marketed.[96]

The image makeover as a political marketing strategy was particularly evident during the 1999 election, when newspaper coverage noted digital alterations to Clark's face for her party's campaign billboards, posters, and brochures. Journalists wondered what kind of technological magic had been used to convert Clark into what a political opponent called an "airbrushed vision of loveliness" for the Labour Party's campaign materials.[97] One article listed the various ways in which the image had been photoshopped to render Clark's face more attractive and arresting.[98] Transfixed by the visual transformation, the columnist asked, "Is that really Helen? Who's her hairdresser and when can I get an appointment? When did she get her teeth done?"[99] While the image "had definitely been worked on," a Labour spokesperson admitted, he asserted that this was "normal" for politicians.[100] Moreover, a political scientist approved of the party's effort to put a gloss on its leader's image, arguing that the public expected "politicians to have their posters look good."[101] A column titled "Trying to look the part" concurred, judging Labour's decision to "bombard" voters with Clark's "tantalizing new image" to be the correct strategy for the woman seeking the prime minister's job.[102]

Style makeovers seem to be the duty of the successful woman political leader. Mary Robinson, the first woman to serve as Ireland's president, took a colleague's directive to "get yourself a makeover" seriously enough to do just that (Walsh 2015, 1029). A Bulgarian MP, ridiculed in the press for her lack of beauty and style, undertook a "dramatic make-over" (Ibroscheva and Raicheva-Stover 2009, 119). Van Zoonen notes that German Chancellor Angela Merkel, who "does not care much about her appearance and style," was forced by her position into a "complete makeover," including hair, clothing, and make-up (2006, 295). "The style change was part of a larger attempt to temper Merkel's image as a rational, cold, non-compromising politician" (van Zoonen 2006, 296). Two of Clark's makeovers were similarly interpreted as being techniques for communicating a personable public persona by embodying conventional norms and practices of femininity.

Longitudinal analysis of references to Clark's makeovers confirms the gendered mediation literature's suspicion that the style watch plagues women throughout their political careers. Yet instead of trivializing Clark's performance, reporting about the New Zealand prime minister's make-up, wardrobe, and grooming often conveyed laudatory evaluations of her leadership persona. For instance, Clark was described as "confident," "polished," and "elegantly tailored" during the 2002 election campaign[103] and as looking "authoritative in a smart-casual grey jacket and black top" for a televised leaders' debate.[104] When read cumulatively, accounts of Clark's body and its adornment suggest that she engaged in a highly strategic, comprehensive, and largely successful overhaul of her political image. Clark's style makeovers were viewed, and accepted, as political marketing practices necessary for a commanding performance of leadership and electoral success. Did applause for Clark's makeovers merely reflect her willingness to play the game and comply with socially agreed-upon standards of feminine attractiveness? Or did it signal admiration for Clark's performance of leadership? The answer is both. As much approval was expressed for the prime minister's communication style as for her hairstyle, and Clark's makeovers were read as a willingness to embody both authority and likeability. However, other aspects of Clark's body were not read as positively. As the next section illustrates, her claim to power was delegitimized by intense and persistent sexualization of her leadership persona.

"Pornifying" the Prime Minister

News accounts of a political leader's sexuality and sexual allure serve to "intimize" the politician and politicize the body (Hirdman, Kleberg, and Widestedt 2005, 109; Stanyer 2013, 14). While men's virility and sexual prowess is seen to accord with power and agency, the female body is culturally inscribed as an eroticized object, a "conduit and mirror of desire" designed to be commodified and fetishized (Gundle and Castelli 2006, 11). By emphasizing women's sexual desirability and intimate relationships, news coverage tends to undermine a woman's political and electoral legitimacy (Anderson 2011, 337; Trimble and Everitt 2010, 65; Wasburn and Wasburn 2011, 1038). For example, Elizabeth Dole was sexualized in editorial cartoons about her 1999 campaign for the Republican presidential nomination; she was depicted as the "object of her husband's sexual revitalization by Viagra, the erectile dysfunction drug" (Gilmartin 2001, 51). Political cartoonists drew the former leader of the Australian Democrats, Cheryl Kernot, in bed with male politicians (Van Acker 1999, 154). Reporting about Belinda Stronach during the Conservative Party of Canada's 2004 leadership contest emphasized the desirability of her body as she was considered to be "better than Viagra" for a party in need of an electoral boost (Trimble 2007, 985; Trimble and Everitt 2010, 65). Metaphors of pornography marked the media coverage of Hillary Clinton's campaign for the Democratic presidential nomination and Sarah Palin's campaign for vice president (Anderson 2011, 333).[105] By aggressively sexualizing Palin – for instance, by framing her as a "MILF" (Perks and Johnson 2014), news reporting cast her as an object of desire to be consumed by news audiences (Carlin and Winfrey 2009, 330–1).

As a discursive gesture, sexualization ties the performance of leadership to the body. Gibson (2009, 53) defines sexualization as "a focus on personal appearance and descriptors of women that relate to their sexual attractiveness and desirability from the perspective of the male gaze." By positioning women leaders as sexual objects, news coverage suggests that their bodies are both desirable and undesired in political spaces. In the public realm, the "beautiful woman can never be trusted for she will arouse the passions, not the intellect, of those around her" (Anderson and Sheeler 2005, 23). News coverage of women politicians' sexual attractiveness often positions them as objects designed for the pleasure of the male observer or consumer, thus as "frivolous, coquettish and – worst of all – loose" (van Zoonen 2006, 202). In some cases, they are described as sexual predators and situated as active subjects. When expressed in a certain manner in the political realm, women's sexuality may be interpreted as voracious and dangerous. Hillary Clinton was portrayed as an "antiseductress" (Carlin and Winfrey 2009, 331), whose political ambition posed a threat to existing power relationships and male dominance of the political sphere (Lawrence and Rose 2010, 200). Either way, the sexualization of women politicians in the news acts as a form of discipline because it undermines their agency and legitimacy as political actors.

Sexualized attention to the body can take the form of revelations or speculations about a politician's sexual identity, sex life, or sexual attractiveness. Discourse analysis of references to the women and men leaders' sexual identities determined that these forms of sexualization were only once applied to a male leader, but were glaringly evident in the coverage of Campbell, Clark, and Gillard. Indeed, to use Anderson's term, these three prime ministers were "pornified" by news reporting (2011, 328). As Anderson explains, "Pornification highlights sexuality in contexts that otherwise are not normally sexualized and, through the use of crude humor or gender-based parody, disciplines individuals who do not conform to traditional gender norms" (2011, 335). While some of these representations – for instance, calling a leader "sexy" or highlighting her physical desirability – may seem innocuous or even complimentary, they often appear without the woman's consent or participation and work to "reinstantiate women citizens and leaders as vixens, sex objects and/or nymphomaniacs" (Anderson 2011, 336).

With the exception of Don Brash, whose adulterous affair with and sexual attraction to his second wife were profiled in newspaper stories,[106] in large part because Brash himself spoke directly about these topics with the media, none of the men leaders included in this study had their sexuality investigated, described, or evaluated in newspaper articles. Even those deemed handsome (John Key)[107] or physically fit (Tony Abbott)[108] were not described as sexually attractive. Reporters and news commentators did not see these men's bodies as sites of sexual objectification. This was also the case for Jenny Shipley, perhaps because of her firmly articulated identity as a wife and mother. She was consistently referred to as "Mrs. Shipley" and chose to foreground her husband and children as a central element of her political persona. Shipley's sexuality was regarded as a private matter, contained within the sanctity of the hetero-normative marital relationship, not to be pried into by the news media. Yet the sex lives and sexual allure of Campbell, Clark, and Gillard were considered fair game for the press. Campbell was portrayed as sexy, verbally incontinent about her lack of a sex life, and sexually available. Gillard was represented as flirtatious and sexually appealing, and she was victimized by obscene images circulated online and reported in the mainstream media. Clark's sexual orientation was questioned in news accounts of her leadership, and she was judged to be sexually ambiguous and therefore politically dangerous.

Canadian news coverage overtly sexualized Kim Campbell by saying that she "presented a seductive persona"[109] and describing her as "not actually beautiful but certainly sexy,"[110] "interesting and sexy,"[111] "filled with sexual energy,"[112] and "brain power and sexual appeal all rolled into one neat little female."[113] Some commentators linked her sexual allure to her proximity to power. "She was as sexy as Madonna, or would be once power had endowed her with its aphrodisiacal magic."[114] Others were inspired by the publication of Campbell's infamous bare-shouldered photograph, calling the photo "sexy"[115] and noting that she appeared "apparently topless on a Saturday front page"[116] in the manner of a centrefold. The pornification of Campbell is further evinced by intrusive reports about her sex life, including a news story reporting "personal jokes about secret photographs from ex-husband Nathan Divinsky."[117] Another story quoted Divinksy as claiming he would "get an I Screwed the Prime Minister bumper sticker" if Campbell emerged victorious from the leadership campaign.[118]

One news writer argued that Campbell was responsible for her own pornification because her tendency to make ribald jokes propelled her sexuality to the fore in news reports.[119] For instance, she "was able to inject sex into the story, telling a gathering of Scots that the Highland fling is the only fling she has time for these days."[120] Similarly, in response to a question posed during a television interview about whether she could "enjoy as exciting a love life as former prime minister Pierre Trudeau had when he was a bachelor," Campbell replied, "I think there's a double standard for men and women. And besides, I don't have the time. I check my agenda every day for hanky-panky, but there's nothing like that there."[121] Campbell's "hanky-panky" comment was repeated (*sans* observation about the sexual double standard) in a column titled "Sex and the single leader."[122] While Campbell may have been trying to use humour to deflect media attention from her sex life, she likely did not mean for these quips to be deployed in a manner that cast her as sexually available. Yet media observers did not hesitate to use lexical choices that characterized her as a seductress. One declared, "Ms. Campbell has evidently discovered political foreplay and is enjoying it."[123] Canada's first woman prime minister undertook a "summertime seduction of the Canadian electorate," another wrote.[124] Candidate self-presentation was not, in this instance, responsible for the pornification of Campbell in mediated accounts of her leadership.

Similarly, news writers labelled Australia's first woman prime minister an object of sexual fantasy, calling Julia Gillard "damned sexy" and "even sexier than she was two days ago" because of her rise to the leadership role.[125] Allegedly, her proximity to power rendered Gillard "the kind of babe that made conservative men quiver."[126] Even more pornographically, a news story described the various Facebook groups that popped up after Gillard had entered the prime minister's office. "A cursory glance reveals the unique passions stirred up by our new

Prime Minister, with groups such as … Julia Gillard IS Slightly Hot … Julia Gillard is the hottest 'fanta-pants' in Australia … [and] Is she, or is she not, the hottest ranga you ever saw?"[127] Gillard's sexual desirability was also emphasized during the 2010 election campaign. A columnist led an article with a Shakespearean quote about women's breasts before bragging about having given Gillard "a bear hug and a slurpy kiss on the cheek."[128]

Moreover, Gillard was regularly stereotyped as a sexual temptress, strategically deploying her charms to win support. With Gillard in power, said a columnist, "there is the added frisson of sexual politics. … Gillard flirts and charms to deflect criticism."[129] During the 2010 election campaign, she was described as flirting shamelessly with journalists, spectators, and football players alike. Here is one example of many. Gillard "seems to have a particular affection for *The Australian*'s political correspondent Matthew Franklin, repeatedly touching his arm and smiling in his direction, gently rebuking and teasing."[130] A television reporter (and former Labour Party leader) went so far as to accuse Gillard of a rhetorical form of sexual harassment, declaring that he had "got from Ms. Gillard 'the patronizing, condescending stroke down the front. I haven't been stroked down the front from a woman other than my wife for some time actually.'"[131]

After the election was over, the prime minister's sex life was considered so interesting to Australians that the Australian Broadcasting Corporation parodied and dissected Gillard's intimate relationship with her partner, Tim Mathieson, in a four-part television comedy series titled *At Home with Julia*.[132] In the third episode, actors Amanda Bishop (as Gillard) and Phil Lloyd (as Mathieson) spice up their sex lives by having sex in the prime minister's office. Viewers saw the pair sharing a post-coital cuddle, their modesty preserved by the Australian flag. The series was marked by the overt personalization, and explicit sexualization, of Gillard (Stevenson 2013, 53–4). As one news columnist observed, "Only now that there's a female prime minister has the gender and sexuality of the office holder become central to political discussion."[133]

Indeed, Gillard's sexual persona continued to be a site of political satire until her defeat in a leadership challenge brought by Kevin Rudd on June 26, 2013 (Stevenson 2013, 56). While much of it originated on the "parallel universe"[134] of Internet blogs and social media, some of the more virulent commentary was reported by mainstream news organizations. Newspaper articles described pornographic and derisory online and social media commentary, including cartoons of Gillard "strapping on a dildo as she prepared to meet Greens leader Bob Brown"[135] and viral email images of her face photoshopped onto a buxom nude body.[136] Newspapers covered Gillard's interrogation by a radio interviewer, who quizzed her about the sexual orientation of her partner, Tim Mathieson, demanding to know whether she really was in a heterosexual relationship.[137] Two weeks before Gillard lost the prime minister's post to Rudd, newspapers reported on a "joke" menu for a Liberal Party political fundraiser; it included a dish described as "'Julia Gillard Kentucky Fried Quail – Small Breasts, Huge Thighs & [another offensive remark].'"[138] Only at the end of Gillard's term as prime minister did columnists acknowledge the degrading treatment she had received. A columnist for the *Sydney Morning Herald* wrote that Gillard "has been sexualized in a way no previous prime minister has been sexualized," confronting "sexism and misogyny that was, at times, quite literally obscene."[139] These representations mirror the forms of pornification evident in the treatment of Clinton and Palin in 2008, which Anderson (2011, 333) argues reflected misogynistic elements of US political culture.

In contrast to the portrayals of Campbell and Gillard as objects of sexual desire and pornographic fantasy, Helen Clark was never deemed to be sexually attractive or seductive. Instead, news coverage questioned her performance of hetero-normativity by transmitting rumours that she was a lesbian. As observed in chapter 4, this trope surfaced during Clark's bid for the Labour Party leadership in 1993, when the newspaper coverage characterized her challenge as a "lesbian plot."[140] One commentator noted the sexist double standard at play. "She is married but has no children. So is Mike Moore – but it is Ms. Clark who has had her sexuality questioned."[141] Yet the news media did not hesitate to report suggestions that Clark had married to mask her sexual identity. For instance,

> In 1981 she entered Parliament as the MP for Mt. Albert, overcoming accusations that she was a lesbian and a radical. She subsequently married Auckland doctor Peter Davis, who she had been living with for five years, saying the only reason was she was tired of the personal innuendo.[142]

This journalist's lexical choices – words like "accusations" and "innuendo" – associate homosexuality with deviance, underscoring the two-sex/gender heterosexual schema policing gender boundaries

(Butler 2006, 30–2). These rumours were recirculated in the coverage of Clark's election campaigns. In 2002, she "faced questions about her private life, including her marriage to Peter Davis and a 'whispering campaign' that she was a lesbian."[143] During the 2005 election, Clark reported that members of the audience for a party leaders' debate had called her a "no-kids lesbo."[144] As well, a television interviewer indirectly, if indelicately, approached the subject by accusing Clark and Davis of having an "ambiguous marriage" and asking for proof of physical intimacy – for instance, by asking whether they touched each other.[145] By challenging Clark's self-declared heterosexuality, news coverage represented her performance of femininity as unconvincing.

After she became prime minister, appellations like "black widow," "dominatrix," and "Helengrad" represented Clark's sexuality as rapacious and threatening. During the 2002 election campaign, New Zealand First leader Winston Peters likened Helen Clark to a black widow spider who stings, then eats her potential coalition mates,[146] and this label was embraced by the New Zealand press, repeated in four articles and featured in two headlines.[147] Sexual cannibalism of this sort is understood as being lethal to men, as illustrated by the tagline for the 1987 Hollywood film, *Black Widow*. "She mates and she kills. No man can resist her."[148] The implication is that when held by women, political power is both irresistible and perilous. During the 2005 campaign, Clark was referred to as a "political dominatrix – whose regime has been termed Helengrad."[149] A dominatrix is a woman who takes a dominant role in bondage, submission, and discipline, and "Helengrad" was a term coined and used frequently by pundits in 2000 to describe Clark as a "control freak" and parliamentary disciplinarian (Ross and Comrie 2012, 974). As Ross and Comrie argue, the "continuing, although irregular use of 'Helengrad' since 2000, reveals an underlying ambivalence about the appropriateness of strong female leadership" (2012, 975). By associating Clark's political power with her allegedly aberrant sexuality, the news coverage framed her as a ruthless and maleficent leader.

Campbell and Gillard were trivialized by sexualizing depictions, rendered as objects of male fantasy and desire. Their sexual allure was seen to be enhanced by their proximity to power, and these representations discredited their political ambitions by evoking stereotypes about women as always being sexually available to men. In contrast, Clark was regarded as dangerous because of her putatively ambivalent performance of heterosexuality and her authoritative demeanour. Anderson (2011, 345) argues that techniques of pornification serve to discipline women candidates for seeking and wielding political power. Media discourses reify and reinforce hetero-normative gender regulations by sexualizing, and denigrating, women who disrupt conventional ideas about gender roles and sexual behaviour. That Shipley exemplified the role of traditional housewife in all but her political aspirations protected her from this form of mediated discipline. In contrast, the invasive and politically destructive media incursions into the sexual identities and behaviours of Campbell and Gillard invited the public to look on these women as sexual objects and Clark as a sexual predator. Their bodies, therefore, were brought into political discourses in a manner that objectified and fetishized their personas and undermined their political legitimacy.

Conclusions

The performance of leadership cannot be disentangled from the body of a leader. The media do not see leaders' bodies as neutral signifiers for whatever traits and ideas a politician wishes to project to the public. Instead, leaders' bodies are interpreted for their compliance with or dissonance from gendered norms of political leadership. Ross's (2010, 42) assertion that media coverage provides "stereotypical renditions of what women and men should *look* like, if not *be* like" was supported by my study. I found that the news coverage noticed the women leaders' bodies to a greater extent than the bodies of the men against whom they contested elections. Campbell's, Clark's, Shipley's, and Gillard's physical appearance was regularly and fulsomely profiled in the news coverage of the campaigns and, indeed, throughout their political careers. In contrast, the attention paid to male leaders' bodies was perfunctory and often unelaborated. The bodies of all but one of the male leaders in my sample were assumed to be normative, taken for granted, and not questioned with the same level of interest and scrutiny as the bodies of the women prime ministers. While the women's bodies were described as being unusual, anomalous in elite political spaces, depictions of the men conveyed comfort with their visual compliance with norms and patterns of political leadership – unless, as in the case of Don Brash, they departed from the prototype of hegemonic masculinity. The lone male leader who was seen as deviating from the archetype of the robust, energetic, and physically imposing male form was cast as inept and ineffective, his body referenced as a discursive strategy for criticizing his performance.

Mediation largely reinforced gender stereotypes, reflecting the culturally embedded expectation that women politicians' bodies ought to be presented to the public in a manner exemplifying hegemonic femininity – well coiffed, styled, and made up, and physically attractive. In the cases of Campbell and Gillard, tropes of emphasized femininity and pornification performed ideological work by positioning them as passive objects rather than as an active subjects, thereby undermining their agency and legitimacy as political actors. By communicating comfort with the stereotypical and hetero-normative performances enacted by Shipley and the men leaders, news coverage reinforced the gender norms identified by Judith Butler in *Gender Trouble* – "ideal dimorphism, heterosexual complementarity of bodies, [and] ideals and rules of proper and improper masculinity and femininity" (2006, xxiv–xxv). Despite the fact that most of the physical descriptions reinforced gendered assumptions about who should hold power and how they should look while enacting leadership roles, reporting about Helen Clark's "extreme makeovers" suggested that a woman's body is capable of embodying power. Conformity with the gendered expectations surrounding the performance of leadership – being confident, commanding, and strong – can be read as convincing and authoritative when conducted in a skirt, heels, and red lipstick, as was evident in newspaper reporting about Clark. Yet the simultaneous questioning of her performance of femininity through sexualizing discourses undercut confidence in her body as an appropriate site of political leadership.

Why does it matter that women leaders' bodies are gazed upon more frequently and voraciously than men's? Referencing Neil Postman's work in *Amusing Ourselves to Death*, Street (2004, 439) suggests that it is no longer "arguments that decide whether voters will support one candidate rather than another, but 'style'; that is, 'how they looked, fixed their gaze, smiled and delivered one-liners.'" In other words, the celebritization of politics reifies the trivial and superficial aspects of politicians' identities by profiling appearance and image. As a result, the "performative, aesthetic dimension of the representational relationship" cannot really be separated from the ideational, ideological dimension (Street 2004, 444). Indeed, details of appearance and image have become central strategies for political marketing (Sanghvi and Hodges 2015). While men are also intimized and even pornified by the press, as evidenced by the sexualization of then German vice-chancellor and now President Frank-Walter Steinmeier (Lünenborg and Maier 2015, 187) and not infrequent references to the "hotness" of Canadian Prime Minister Justin Trudeau,[150] these invocations tend to inscribe political power on the male body. As we have seen in this chapter, the aesthetic aspect of the media gaze tends to situate women leaders as novelties and objects rather than as subjects capable of enacting political authority and legitimacy.

Despite the overwhelming evidence of the delegitimation and pornification of women leaders' bodies presented in this chapter, I want to end on a more positive note. Media depictions of women's bodies as the site (and sight) of political leadership may work to disrupt binary understandings about gender roles. Even when women's bodies are noticed mostly for their difference, and portrayed as uncommon and even aberrant in political spaces, these representations expose the historical and ideological associations of men and hegemonic masculinity with political power. Media texts explicitly or implicitly describing women leaders as exhibiting strength, vigour, agency, and authority, as was the case for Clark, identify women's bodies as being capable of an authentic performance of political leadership.

Although I did not find many examples of such representations in the descriptions of the bodies of the four women prime ministers, it is important to note their potential to both reveal and disrupt the socially and discursively constructed boundaries between femininity and masculinity. Over time these disruptions, along with contestations of the figure of a leader as inevitably white, cisgender, able-bodied, and heterosexual, may enable the mediated legitimacy of political aspirants whose bodies do not emulate the archetypal leader. By changing the language used to describe and evaluate party and government leaders, journalists can broaden the perceptions of who looks, and acts, the part. Metaphors are discursively powerful linguistic choices, so paying attention to metaphors is critical to gendered re-mediation, as chapter 6 demonstrates. Allegories help journalists tell compelling stories, and the metaphorical language of love and war both reinforces and challenges gendered assumptions about power and leadership.

Chapter Six

Love and War[1]

Introduction

> Helen Clark and John Key are now locked in a fight to the political death in which there can only be one winner.[2]

> The final head-to-head televised debate between Helen Clark and John Key was so filled with sugar and spice, it was in danger of ending in a group hug.[3]

Media coverage of electoral politics is replete with war metaphors. News articles relate how parties storm to the campaign front line, where they fight for electoral territory and exchange explosive rhetorical ripostes. Much less frequently, but no less poignantly, politics is described as a love affair, with political alliances equated to the emotionally charged relationships enjoyed by family members and intimate partners. During the 2002 New Zealand election, news stories characterized Labour's relationship with the Green Party as so fraught with "simmering tensions" that it eventually erupted into "open warfare."[4] Then, in a seemingly stunning reversal, the potential political alliance was cast as a romance, as the two parties eventually "made up."[5] Similarly, an article musing about the possibility of a grand coalition between New Zealand's two major parties employed the language of dating and courtship, but ultimately concluded that Prime Minister Helen Clark was "not about to put aside a half-century of trench warfare" to make a deal with her party's long-standing political foe.[6] These competing allegories seem to reflect a discursive contradiction: how can a competition between political parties be characterized as both a violent battle and an intimate romance?

Linking these seemingly incompatible representations is an under-standing of politics as intensely and ardently relational. Love and war metaphors highlight the importance of relationships among political parties, their leaders, and the electorate. Moreover, the metaphorical language of love and war brings emotions to the fore, characterizing politics as both passionate and deeply impactful. The vivid, emo-tive language of combat and romance suggests that political events are something citizens should think, and care, about very deeply. But what does scripting political competitions and relationships as wars and love affairs mean for women who hold party or government lead-ership positions? This chapter explores the complexly gendered con-notations embedded in the language of love and war. I examine the ways in which battle and romance metaphors were used to portray the leadership performances of Campbell, Clark, Shipley, and Gillard. In particular, I test the argument that the allegorical language(s) of politics invariably write women out of the competition.

The gendered mediation literature asserts that war metaphors invariably masculinize politics, thus bracketing out women and their embodied performances, while love and romance metaphors sexualize, privatize, and trivialize the ambitions of women leaders. In my view, because the lexicon of love and war brings gender dualisms, hetero-normativity, and the public/private dichotomy into stark relief, election news discourses have the potential to destabilize and possibly subvert prevailing gender regulations. In this chapter, I show how violent com-bat metaphors and allegories of romance implicate both women and men party leaders in their quest for political power. Women and men leaders alike are depicted as fighting pitched battles for voter loyalties, occupying electoral territory, falling in love with political fellow trav-ellers or opponents, and inspiring devotion from citizens. Such char-acterizations can redefine political spaces by drawing attention to the emotional and relational elements of political life, in the process upset-ting gender binaries.

I begin with a discussion of the political salience of metaphors, argu-ing that the metaphors employed by the press both reflect and shape political understandings. I summarize the key contentions of the gen-dered mediation thesis, which maintains that love and war metaphors support gender binaries and regulations. However, both hegemonic and counter-hegemonic narratives are evident in news coverage of Campbell, Shipley, Clark, and Gillard, as detailed in the second and third sections of the chapter, which discuss the application of war and love metaphors, respectively. As I argue, and demonstrate, women's claim to political leadership is both delegitimized *and* authenticated by metaphors situating them on the battlefield or in the bedroom. By associating the "private" world of intimate relationships with the "public" world of politics, and by illustrating the prevalence of emotion in political discourses, romance and combat allegories expose and disrupt gendered assumptions about political leadership.

Metaphors and Gendered Mediation

Metaphors are important sites of investigation because of their ubiquity in political and media discourses, their powerful persuasive role, and their ability to reflect, reinforce, or challenge gendered power relations. A *metaphor* is a seemingly straightforward rhetorical device functioning "principally as a way of conceiving of one thing in terms of another" (Lakoff and Johnson 1980, 36). Understandings are shaped when two seemingly disparate items, events, or ideas are linked in "cognitive and emotional association" (O'Malley and Tynan 1999, 590). For instance, when political leaders employ journey metaphors, they are characterizing political action as movement towards a desirable destination (Charteris-Black 2009; 2011). In addition to evoking positive images of progress and greener pastures, the expedition allegory renders complex political goals and strategies intelligible by linking them to the tangible concept of travel. A key function of metaphor is to facilitate comprehension (Lakoff and Johnson 1980, 36). Because metaphors draw on taken-for-granted and seemingly common sense understandings of everyday concepts, they "simplify abstract issues by activating pre-existing knowledge" (Charteris-Black 2011, 34). When a politician is described as landing a "knockout punch" on an opponent during a televised election debate, for instance, the audience is invited to understand the act of debating as a violent form of political pugnaciousness.

The metaphorical language of politics is largely communicated in and through the mass media. Castells (1996, 311) maintains that the media extensively control the space in which politics happens. Despite the increased use of social media, television and the online editions of established news media organizations dominate the news information cycle, providing key entry points into political debate (Nielsen, Kleis, and Schroder 2014, 473–4). Moreover, audiences tend to see the news as an objective source of "reality" (Falk 2013, 194). But what audiences are receiving is a heavily mediated version of events, and metaphors are a common feature of this mediation process. Metaphors make stories about politics more vivid, dramatic, and entertaining (Gidengil and Everitt 1999, 51). As well, they act as a form of shorthand for journalists, helping to communicate abstract and complex ideas by presenting them in a simplified and accessible manner. Metaphors are not simply stylistic devices or mere descriptions; they are powerful tools of persuasion (Koller and Semino 2009, 12; O'Malley and Tynan 1999, 591). Allegorical language is regularly deployed to punctuate political arguments and assert certain positions, while delegitimizing others (Cammaerts 2012, 245). In fact, the primary use of metaphors in political rhetoric is to "frame how we view or understand political issues by eliminating alternative points of view" (Charteris-Black 2011, 32). When used as ideological strategies, metaphors privilege and naturalize certain accounts by focusing attention on one aspect of an issue or event, while diverting audiences from aspects that are inconsistent with the point being made (Lakoff and Johnson 1980, 10). As the media's persistent use of the "knockout punch" to describe success in a party leaders' debate illustrates, a non-violent exchange of political ideas and information is associated with the pugilistic goals and practices of a boxing match. By casting a political debate as an oratorical boxing ring in which fighters throw verbal punches at each other, the ideational, collaborative, and reflexive aspects of argumentation are concealed.

Metaphors serve as "mini-narratives which are not fully explicated – the spelling out of the story is done by the audience which draws upon their tacit knowledge of the historical, social or political context to do so" (Mottier 2008, 191). Because they tap into social myths and popular understandings, metaphors reveal the cultural values resonant in the society within which media texts are produced and consumed (Falk 2013, 193; Gidengil and Everitt 1999, 51). For example, even seemingly benign metaphorical source domains, such as gaming, may be ideologically laden. As revealed in Falk's (2013, 192–3) analysis of the US news media's use of the playing-the-gender-card metaphor in reports about Hillary Clinton's 2008 bid for the Democratic presidential nomination, the metaphor was used to "silence the idea that traditional sex roles affect who has access to power" (Falk 2013, 203). This form of silencing reinforced the myth of equal opportunity in American society. By implying that gender becomes a factor in politics only when women themselves raise it, the gender card metaphor occluded the reality of sexism and the unequal representation of women in political life (Falk 2013, 198).

Feminist analysis shows how metaphorical language reinforces certain spaces, characteristics, and activities as "male" and others as "female," thus consolidating the socially constructed dividing line between gender categories. The gendered mediation literature maintains that commonly used metaphors position politics as male-dominant by valorizing the activities and characteristics associated with men and hegemonic masculinity and delegitimizing the traits and spheres linked to women and stereotypical versions of femininity (Ahrens 2009; Anderson and Sheeler 2005; Falk 2013; Johnson 2013; Lim 2009; van Zoonen 2005). As a result, the discursive terrain of election campaigns is regarded as tricky for women political leaders to negotiate. The language of war and violence is alleged to support the idea of politics as exclusively masculine territory (Koller 2002; O'Malley and Tynan 1999; Shaw 2011). Gidengil and Everitt (1999, 51) argue that the "masculine narrative" dominating the news coverage of elections inadvertently conveys "the message that women do not really belong in politics because they lack the requisite attributes to participate" (ibid.). While love metaphors are rarely analysed, perhaps because the language of romance is significantly less prevalent than battle words in media depictions of political competition, scholars assert that they are equally treacherous for women leaders because romance metaphors represent an intensely sexualizing and privatizing form of discourse. Love is constituted as emotional and irrational, the domain of women and children, and indeed as antithetical to rationality and reason, commonly understood as the domain of politics (Anderson 2011; Borisoff and Hahn 1993; Đurović and Silaški 2010; Koller 2002).

The gendered mediation literature stresses the importance of assessing the gender-specific meanings communicated by love and war metaphors. As Lim observes, "gendered metaphors of power are not merely stylistic devices but foundational to the making and our understanding of political identities and realities" (2009, 258). In the sections that follow, I investigate the ways in which love and war metaphors reinforce gender regulations and power hierarchies, and also challenge them. At the same time, the analysis is sensitive to the specific political contexts in which the four women prime ministers engaged in electoral "warfare" and formed intimate political alliances.

Electoral Battlefields

Electoral politics is continually framed by the news media as a strategic game, with intense focus on campaign strategies and tactics

(Aalberg, Strömbäck, and de Vreese 2012). That the media narrate electoral tactics as brutal and vicious contests among competing factions is widely documented in the political communication literature. Blankenship's (1996) inventory of the metaphors used to describe the 1972 US Democratic Party nomination demonstrates how extensively words associated with violence, warfare, and highly competitive sports dominated the news coverage of this event. In his analysis of political reporting in US newspapers and periodicals from 1980 to 1985, Howe (1988) found that the most commonly used metaphors were derived from the language of sports and war (e.g., "team player" and "guerrilla warfare"). Similarly, the 1984 US presidential and vice-presidential debates, and the party leaders' debates televised during the 2000 Canadian federal election, were cast as war zones, the contenders described as "ambushing," "firing at," and "outflanking" each other (Blankenship and Kang 1991, 308–9; Gidengil and Everitt 1999, 59). Gidengil and Everitt's content analysis of television reporting about the Canadian party leaders' debates confirms the ubiquity of militaristic language. These scholars found that "one metaphor in three (34 percent) used the language of the battlefield" (Gidengil and Everitt 1999, 58). In this form of "political warfare," the "weapons" are words. When they were not engaged in rhetorical warfare, the leaders were described as committing acts of violence ("fought, hammered, ganged up"), with 13 per cent of the metaphors falling into this category (ibid.).

As these studies illustrate, news accounts routinely script party leaders as "generals" leading their troops into battle, "shooting," "sniping," and "bombing" in an attempt to mortally wound their opponents and gain control over the disputed territory. The conflation of war and politics is now so commonplace, party campaign strategists themselves embrace battle language. They hunker down in "war rooms," where they strategize for the "phoney war" waged during the first few weeks of a campaign and plan how they will wage the "air war" and "ground war" in the run-up to voting day (Marland 2014, 309–10). And consider everyday vernacular, which associates "winning" with violence. Contestants who think they offered a particularly successful performance in a televised cooking or singing competition regularly declare that they "killed it" or "slayed it."

The gendered mediation literature views the discursive transfer of the images and intentions associated with combat into the political field as intensely problematic for women politicians because war is typed masculine. According to this argument, battle metaphors frame women's participation in political competition within norms of hegemonic masculinity and patriarchal militarism (Ette 2013, 249–50; Koller 2004, 17–18; Lazar 2009, 210; Parry-Giles 2014, 187). After all, both war and the "masculine role of warrior-hero have been central to the conceptualization of politics for the last 2,500 years" (Harstock 1982, 283). Metaphors of "high politics reverberate with images of hyper-masculine men ready to 'do battle with their enemies'" (Parpart 1998, 202). While men are understood to perform the heroic roles on the battlefield, women provide support on the home front (Ette 2013, 255). Therefore, by consistently drawing on images, norms, and metaphors of warfare to define and describe political reality, the media reinforce gender-based power imbalances (Gidengil and Everitt 1999; Howe 1988; Koller and Semino 2009). The anomalous position of women in elite public roles is highlighted by news reports drawing attention to and even exaggerating their forceful behaviours through the use of war and aggressive sports metaphors (Gidengil and Everitt 1999, 60; Koller 2004, 13). For example, once Hillary Clinton "entered the spaces of electoral politics as a candidate, a rhetoric of violence became all too common in the press coverage" (Parry-Giles 2014, 185). Further, the trope of the "unruly woman" emerges when the spectre of a woman behaving aggressively disrupts normative expectations of female behaviour (Anderson and Sheeler 2005, 28; Gidengil and Everitt 1999, 52). In short, allegories of aggression and warfare shore up the public man/private woman binary when applied to political competition.

My analysis takes the gendered mediation thesis a step further by investigating the counter-hegemonic potential of militaristic language that firmly situates women in the battle frame. For example, when women enter the "political battlefield" and display putatively "masculine" styles of leadership, they challenge understandings of elite competitive politics as a game that only "manly" (i.e., heterosexual) men can play (Gerrits et al. 2017). By performing leadership in this context, women may be shown to exhibit leadership characteristics and skills falsely associated with men and masculinity, qualities such as strength, determination, willpower, tenacity, and resilience. On the other hand, this disruptive potential cannot be realized if gender regulations are reinforced by representations of women leaders as incapable of winning electoral "wars" because of their gendered identities.

For the women prime ministers, and the male leaders Campbell, Clark and Gillard competed with in general elections, I compiled a corpus of all war-related words and phrases, such as "fight," "attack," "battle," "shoot," and "launch salvos," used in newspaper articles to describe their electoral strategies and performances. I then determined whether the women leaders were more or less likely than the equivalent men leaders to be situated in the battle frame for election news coverage by counting, and comparing, the number of combative words or phrases likening their political behaviour to warfare. My focus, however, was on the meanings offered by the battle metaphors, and I structured my analysis based on two questions about the use of combat language to describe and evaluate the electoral performances of Campbell, Clark, Shipley, and Gillard. Do war metaphors write women out of the political "battle" by evoking images of a male-dominated field of contestation and characterizing rhetorical aggression by women leaders as discomfiting and ineffective? Or does positioning women as full participants on the political "battlefield" suggest that women politicians exercise agency, power, and legitimacy?

I found that each of the women prime ministers was presented within a distinct narrative, one that reflected mediated perceptions of their particular political context and career trajectory. In other words, metaphors helped tell a particular story about their performance of leadership. Kim Campbell was likened to Joan of Arc and judged the least effective of all four women prime ministers on the electoral battlefield, reflecting her party's near obliteration in the 1993 election campaign. News coverage of the so-called "clash of the Xenas," as journalists typed the unique contest between two women, Jenny Shipley and Helen Clark, during the 1999 New Zealand election, highlighted their gendered identities. The evolution of combat metaphors in the coverage of Clark's four other electoral "battles," during which she was described as a "black widow," a "dominatrix," and as the legendary female warrior Boadicea, emphasized her competence and effectiveness against electoral opponents. However, the trope of toughness became increasingly negative over time. The battle language used to describe Julia Gillard's 2010 election campaign, typified by the phrase "female political killing machine," similarly cast Australia's first woman prime minister as strong and authoritative, albeit as under siege from the man she had toppled. I conclude by discussing the ways in which war metaphors can work to empower and delegitimize women political leaders.

Joan of Arc

At the inception of her campaign for the leadership of the Progressive Conservative (PC) Party of Canada, Kim Campbell was "seen by the media and others as the saviour, the Joan of Arc"[7] who could rescue the party from electoral oblivion. An article published at the finale of the party leadership contest said that Campbell "came over as a defiant Joan of Arc confronting the microphone lances of the television crews."[8] These characterizations proved prophetic. They implicated the media as the impetus behind Campbell's rise and as one of the instruments of her cruel political demise. Moreover, like the infamous Joan, Campbell suffered an allegorical immolation after leading her party into a battle it was destined to lose.

During the 1993 Canadian election campaign, Campbell was described as relentlessly aggressive. Violent and militaristic verbs and adverbs positioned her as the antagonist sixty-one times. In comparison, Liberal leader Jean Chrétien was described as "attacking" or "firing at" foes only twenty-seven times. These data parallel the conclusions of Gidengil and Everitt (2003a), who compared the actual behaviour of party leaders during the televised leaders' debates with the reporting of these debates by television news during this electoral contest. As these scholars discovered, although Kim Campbell was no more aggressive than the other leaders in the debates, "she was the most likely to be portrayed as a warrior doing battle or as a street fighter" (ibid., 570). Gidengil and Everitt suggest that the media overstate the aggressive rhetoric or behaviours of women leaders because these actions run counter to gendered expectations (2003b, 210–1). This may be the case, but the use of aggressive battle metaphors also reflects the media's expectations about campaign tactics, and party leaders are at the front and centre of these strategies.

Intriguingly, Campbell was determined to challenge the gendered norms of political competition by "doing politics differently" on the campaign trail. As newspapers revealed, "Tory strategists are striving to position Ms. Campbell as a feeling, issue-oriented Prime Minister who is above the sort of crass, guerrilla attacks favoured by old-style politicians."[9] The plan was to feature the party leader "only in positive, non-combative situations"[10] and offering "low-key expositions of her own policies."[11] In a sense, Campbell rejected the usual script for political "combat" by refusing to step directly into the political trenches or to launch rhetorical attacks on her opponents. For a press corps trained to use the language of warfare as a way of reflecting on a party's campaign progress, Campbell's approach was both baffling and difficult to describe within the discursive confines of the battle frame. The newspapers observed that Campbell dispatched her opponent for the leadership, Jean Charest, into the fray to "attack the enemy when need be."[12] With Campbell electing to stay off the "battlefield," early election news stories described the prime minister as beleaguered by opponents, with Chrétien "sensing blood"[13] and making Campbell "the target" of the Liberal campaign.[14] Campbell's strategy was perceived as a sign of weakness by her primary opponent and by the media.

The battle frame demands a performance of toughness by party leaders. Indeed, when her party took a precipitous drop in the polls, Campbell was urged to "get tough."[15] Her campaign team quickly changed course, adopting a new direction labelled "attack mode" by the press.[16] Campbell was also counselled to lead the party's assault, and she complied. As the *Globe and Mail* announced, "Conservative leader Kim Campbell offered her first detailed attack on the Liberals' economic program yesterday," reflecting "a change in strategy for the Conservative campaign, a switch from low-key expositions of her own policies to a direct attack on her principal rival."[17] "Campbell rallies troops for on-air strike," announced another news report replete with battle metaphors, many of them directly quoting the prime minister.[18] "I'm leading the attack against our major competitors," Campbell asserted before discussing her "strategy of attack" – deploying her "troops" in a "full assault" on the Liberal Party's policies.[19]

However, Campbell's combative approach was judged to be unsuccessful, and war metaphors were used to highlight declining support for the PC Party. By saying that Campbell was leading a "beleaguered campaign," "under siege," "stepping into the minefield," "reeling from the crossfire," and suffering a "near fatal blow," journalists emphasized the ineffectiveness of the new approach.[20] She "was reduced to old-style politics, desperately railing against the Liberals," concluded a columnist.[21] Intensifying the desperation theme, news commentators asserted that Campbell had lost her cool, displaying "an almost childlike temper" by "shouting and screaming at opponents,"[22] "hurling attacks in all directions,"[23] and "flailing across the country in a cloud of angry impotence."[24] Instead of being read as toughness, Campbell's "attacks" on her opponent were represented as hysterical and ineffectual. According to one pundit, Campbell "self-destructed."[25] When a loss at the polls seemed inevitable, some party members blamed the

PCs' impending demise on Campbell's "doing politics differently" strategy.[26] According to news commentators, Campbell "speared" herself by embracing "the type of adversarial combat" she had eschewed at the beginning of the campaign.[27]

Trimble and Arscott (2003, 83) argue that Campbell's campaign was doomed to failure. Her predecessor's popularity had dipped into the single digits before his resignation, and the party's approval rating was at a dismal 18 per cent before the leadership contest. Afterwards, there was precious little time for Campbell to win the hearts of an electorate hardened against her party. Forced to call an election a few short months into her mandate, Campbell found herself performing "partisan CPR," attempting to resuscitate "the party's electoral prospects" (ibid.). Perhaps these damning indictments merely reflected the sheer impossibility of the task with which Campbell was charged. Yet mediated representations of Campbell's 1993 campaign "battle" certainly reinforced gendered norms and assumptions by suggesting that the freshly minted prime minister was unwilling, or incapable, of staging an effective campaign. Campbell's desire to "do politics differently" by avoiding the fray was panned as futile, and her sudden decision to embrace traditional assault-style politics judged an act of desperation. Worse, instead of representing her rhetorical salvos as the discursive style of a fierce and formidable fighter, Campbell's words and actions were called "desperate," "childlike," and "angry." Word choices like "flailing" and "loosing her cool" evoked the trope of the hysterical woman. Campbell's gendered identity, especially her declaration of gender-based "difference," highlighted her putative inability to perform political leadership according to the norms ascribed by the battle frame.

A few years later, in New Zealand, the prospect of two women fighting for the prime minister's post captivated the nation. Even more newsworthy than the presence of a woman on the electoral battlefield was the promise of victory by a woman. As leaders of the two major parties, Jenny Shipley and Helen Clark were at the centre of the political spectacle, and one was guaranteed victory. Not surprisingly, news coverage highlighted the gendered dimensions of the competition.

Clash of the Xenas

When Jenny Shipley entered the prime minister's office in 1997, a news report excitedly anticipated her "eye to eye fight" with Helen Clark

in an end-of-year parliamentary adjournment debate, "the first formal clash between New Zealand's two women leaders."[28] Clark and
Shipley brought particular "weapons" to this battle, readers were told.
While "Helen Clark had much more ammunition," Shipley spoke "as
if she had an army behind her and they were simply leaning on their
rifles. Yet she managed to be convincing when she took the fight to
Labour."[29] It was therefore no surprise when newspapers constructed
the long-anticipated electoral contest between Shipley and Clark as a
"battle" between two women. The idea of women competing for the
top job was enticing and held considerable news value. New Zealanders were keenly "interested … in seeing two women battle it out," said
an observer.[30]

The New Zealand press corps embraced war metaphors during the
campaign. Militaristic words such as "fought," "battled," "attacked,"
"lashed out," and "thrashed" represented the contest as a war, and
phrases such as "crossed swords," "launched a strike," and "fired several salvos" situated Clark and Shipley as generals leading their troops
into combat. Electoral competition was likened to a series of military
manoeuvres as one or the other of the major party leaders "launched an
onslaught"[31] and "ventured into enemy territory,"[32] where she encountered a "hail of gunfire" and faced "death or glory."[33] Clark and Shipley
were equally likely to be described with war metaphors in the news
coverage, with Clark "attacking" opponents forty-nine times compared
with forty-eight references to Shipley's verbal assaults.

In contrast to Campbell, who was deemed ineffective, both Shipley
and Clark were portrayed as strong, determined, and fierce. One pundit called them "political assassins."[34] Clark was labelled a "woman of
steely resolve," a "beautifully tempered samurai sword" who "demonstrated coolness under pressure and steely ability to withstand assaults
that would have felled most men."[35] Shipley was referred to as a "perfumed bulldozer" with an "action woman approach" and a "formidable politician in the mold of Margaret Thatcher."[36] These phrasings
celebrated the leaders' agency and fortitude, while subtly foregrounding gender with gender labels ("woman") and symbols of hegemonic
femininity ("beautifully" and "perfumed").

Characterizations of Shipley and Clark as fierce fighters were even
more resolutely gendered, and demeaned, by "catfight" and "Xena"
references. The catfight trope appeared in response to the first parliamentary debate between the two women after Shipley had been
sworn in as prime minister. Anticipating a dramatic confrontation, a

spectacular "Battle of the Boadiceas," "Clash of the Xenas, the House's version of female Gladiators," one columnist was sorely disappointed when the two leaders maintained parliamentary decorum.

> Mrs. Shipley's retort – that it was appropriate Helen Clark was wearing black given what was coming Labour's way next year – was the afternoon's only moment of *cattiness*. But Helen Clark and Mrs. Shipley were *behaving like kittens* yesterday. The *claws will not come out* until later in the week when the pair finally square off in serious fashion in the end-of-year adjournment debate.[37]

As forecast, the "catfight" was mobilized during the 1999 election campaign when a news story said Clark and Shipley *"circled like wary cats* during a televised party leaders' debate."[38] The catfight is a staple of popular culture, appearing in genres as disparate as porn flicks, advertisements, comic books, daytime and night-time soap operas, and reality-TV shows. Presented as a titillating altercation between two women who resort to purportedly "feminine" tactics like hair pulling and scratching to resolve petty jealousies or disputes over a man, the catfight sexualizes and trivializes disagreements between women. As Douglas observes, the American news media employed a catfight frame to caricature the debates between feminists and anti-feminists during the Equal Rights Amendment debate (1995, 222–7). Similarly, reducing Clark and Shipley's partisan competition to a catfight diminished their legitimacy as political leaders.

The "Xena princesses"[39] epithet equated Shipley and Clark to Xena, the fictitious lead character from the hugely popular American television series *Xena: Warrior Princess*. Filmed in New Zealand and starring New Zealand–born actor Lucy Lawless, the series aired from 1995 to 2001, and it had reached cult status by the time Shipley and Clark "faced off."[40] In some ways, the Xena label was empowering. After all, it likened the women party leaders to a ferocious female warrior. Television Xena was the first woman presented "in the role of the archetypal hero on a quest," plus she was portrayed as a courageous and skilled fighter, "dependent on no man" (Morreale 1998, 79). Yet the Xena character was simultaneously depicted as "stereotypically, even excessively feminine" (Morreale 1998, 80). Clad in thigh- and cleavage-revealing leather miniskirt and bronze breastplates, Xena displayed exaggerated femininity, while deftly wielding her sword to slay male enemies. Similarly, while Shipley and Clark "crossed swords,"[41] their hairdos, wardrobe choices, and make-up were emphasized, highlighting their bodies, as documented in chapter 5.

War metaphors certainly positioned Shipley and Clark as strong and capable, and as willing to pursue political goals with fortitude and determination. But characterizing the incumbent prime minister and her challenger as the "Xena princesses" who engaged in a "catfight" trivialized their political goals and questioned their seriousness of purpose. The electoral competition was narrated as a spectacle, the novelty of women battling for political ground previously held only by men signalled by gendered language and imagery. In contrast, with her victory in this election campaign and subsequent election wins, Clark arguably normalized the presence of a woman in the prime minister's office, and battle language positioned and evaluated her highly successful political career in a way that both foregrounded and disrupted the two-sex/gender binary.

Black Widow, Dominatrix, Boadicea

A profile of Helen Clark titled "Woman of Steely Resolve," published during the 1999 election campaign, painted her as a "hardy warrior queen" who was "tough as old boots," thus able to brave her way "through a lot of heat and heavy fire" with aplomb and determination.[42] Evident in Clark's media representations throughout her career, the trope of toughness intensified as she secured and held political power, and it was inflected by gendered understandings of political competition. From her entry into the electoral battlefield in 1996 until her penultimate campaign in 2005, Clark was as likely as her male competitors, if not more likely, to be described with violent metaphors. Only in Clark's final election campaign, in 2008, was her opponent, John Key, painted with a larger number of combative words and phrases, in large part because he received more news coverage overall.[43]

In Clark's first election campaign as Labour leader, in 1996, news articles used twenty-four battle words to depict her electoral strategies, compared to just sixteen for her opponent, incumbent Prime Minister Jim Bolger. Headlines announced, "Clark Draws First Blood" and "Clark Triumphs in TV Joust."[44] Bolger was described as "rattled by the drubbing he took,"[45] "looking weak,"[46] and "fighting desperately for survival"[47] over the course of the campaign. The press judged Clark's "attacks" on Bolger to be highly effective. "Ms. Clark successfully elbowed her Opposition rivals aside in the battle to take on Mr. Bolger," said an article.[48] In fact, journalists praised Clark's performances, declaring her the campaign winner.[49] Notably, pundits introduced the recurring theme of toughness during this election. For instance, one news story quoted a Labour MP's observation that Clark "doesn't mind who gets steam-rolled in her path."[50]

Having won office in 1999 by defeating Shipley and the National Party, Clark entered the electoral arena in 2002 as the nation's prime minister and with a clear lead in the polls. Her primary opponent was Bill English, who had deposed Shipley as National leader in October 2001. Battle language increased dramatically in newspaper accounts of this campaign. Each leader's actions were described with fifty-nine combat words or metaphors, the most predominant of which were variations on the word *attack*. According to news stories, English delivered "personal attacks on Ms. Clark's leadership style" and integrity,[51] a strategy deemed "the politics of personality assassination."[52] The National leader's tactics were described with violent language: as "torrid" and "blistering" attacks, as "ambushes," and as "declaring war" on Clark.[53] Nevertheless, Clark was not described as politically wounded by her opponent's forceful strategy. As just one example, English was "launching furious attacks" on Clark, but he wasn't "able to dent her."[54] Clark, meanwhile, focused on the media and minor parties, and press reports said that she "savaged the Greens co-leader,"[55] directed a "savage attack" on a TV3 journalist,[56] "turned her guns on United Future,"[57] and "launched a fierce attack on New Zealand First leader Winston Peters."[58] In response to Clark's criticisms of minor parties, including his own, Peters called the prime minister a "black widow" who was eating her coalition partners, and this epithet was circulated in several news stories.[59] As discussed in chapter 5, the label sexualized Clark by likening her to a type of spider who mates, then kills her sexual partner, and it characterized her as cold-hearted and merciless.

The toughness theme intensified during the 2005 campaign, with Clark described as showing "steely resolve"[60] and presenting herself as a "tough, hardened political operator."[61] Newspaper articles about the campaign discursively positioned Clark as the "attacker" almost as often as her male opponent, National leader Don Brash, with fifty violent verbs used to describe Clark's actions compared to fifty-three for Brash. Yet these data fail to reflect the extent to which Clark was characterized as utterly ruthless in her quest for power. The "battle-hardened PM"[62] was again cast as a "political dominatrix"[63] who opted to "crack the whip"[64] and "shoot back"[65] against opponents.

Clark "blasted the right,"[66] made "incursions" into "enemy territory,"[67] and "launched "a vicious assault"[68] on the National Party. Even more damning, her leadership style was likened to that of Stalin as her regime was termed "Helengrad."[69] Militaristic metaphors positioned Clark as more merciless than her male opponents. According to news writers, Clark "easily landed more hits" than Brash,[70] perhaps because of the National leader's initial reluctance to directly engage Clark in rhetorical "battle." As discussed in chapter 3, Brash explained a tepid performance in the first televised leaders' debate as gentlemanly behaviour, declaring it inappropriate "for a man to aggressively attack a woman."[71] Journalists expressed scepticism about Brash's explanation. "When a Rottweiler is biting your head off, pondering its gender would seem of rather secondary importance," commented one writer,[72] and another said he did "not think of Helen Clark as a woman but as a tough political candidate."[73]

During the 2005 campaign, Clark's "steeliness" was explained as a necessary characteristic for "a woman determined to win in a man's game."[74] She had waged a "fight to the top against a weight of obstacles and criticism that would have crushed most men," according to a profile of the soon-to-be-third-term prime minister.[75] In fact, Clark was literally called a man. At a Labour rally, participants held signs pronouncing, "Helen Clark is da man," "UR da man Helen," and "Either way, there is going to be a man in charge."[76] Clark was viewed as performing a kind of political drag, presenting herself as a man in order to win a "man's game." Representations of Clark as a "fighting man" could be read as buttressing the public man/private woman binary by characterizing formal politics as the territory of men, or of women who act like men. However, Judith Butler argues for the subversive potential of actual drag performances, which unsettle the seeming irrevocability of sex/gender binaries (Butler 1993, 231). Drag, like other forms of parody, exposes the instability of gender norms by showing how they are culturally and discursively constructed. By calling Clark "da man," observers were recognizing that putatively "manly" displays are within the purview of women. That a woman could indeed be firmly "in charge" challenged the assumption that only men are capable of enacting commanding leadership.

In the 2008 election campaign, which Clark lost, militaristic allegories continued to bring gender to the fore. Notably, Clark was likened to "Boadicea."[77] The headline "Gladiator v. Boadicea" cast National leader John Key as a Roman gladiator, likely referencing the popular film starring Russell Crowe,[78] and Clark as the "warrior queen" of the British Iceni tribe who led a fierce but ultimately unsuccessful uprising against the occupying forces of the Roman Empire (Hingley and Unwin 2006). According to the news story, "Key has now donned his gladiator robes to try and arrest this political Boadicea in her tracks. But for Clark it's open war as she refuses to concede any points."[79] The two leaders were "locked in a fight to the political death in which there can only be one winner."[80] Clark was once again characterized as "ruthless"[81] as she reputedly took a "shot at," "lashed," and "hit out" against, Key.[82] Yet news reports reported more "attacks" waged by Key (seventy) than by Clark (fifty-two) over the course of the campaign, likely because Key earned more media attention. Key was also judged to be a more successful warrior. As one story put it, the Opposition leader "put in a plucky performance that was the measure of Clark."[83] For the first time in her career as Labour leader, Clark was deemed to be the loser of the televised leaders' "bouts," and the theme of ruthlessness underscored negative evaluations of her approach to governing. News reports used words like "authoritarian" and "dictatorial"[84] to describe Clark's leadership style, as illustrated by a revival of the "Helengrad" epithet.[85]

The nation's "mood for change"[86] brought Clark and the Labour Party's nine years of rule to an end. A political obituary printed in the *Telegraph* put it this way. "Miss Clark, New Zealand's first elected woman prime minister, is at 58 a battle-hardened warrior. ... But like Boadicea, her time had eventually run out."[87] The political eulogies printed in New Zealand's leading newspapers reflected the predominantly adulatory tone of Clark's campaign coverage over the years, highlighting her "remarkable career" and calling her "the strongest Prime Minister ... for a generation."[88] Yet even when summing up Clark's political contributions, news writers could not resist the trope of toughness. "Clark was formidable, ruling her caucus with an iron rod," concluded a political commentator. "She'd frighten, or charm, most journalists into submission."[89]

As reporting about Helen Clark's electoral "battles" demonstrated, a woman leader can be presented as authoritative, decisive, and commanding. Media assessments of German Chancellor Angela Merkel's leadership style similarly foreground her "image as a tough leader" (Sheeler and Anderson 2014, 490). In Clark's case, news reporting displayed unease with a woman in a position of political authority, as evidenced by descriptions like "high-handed" and "ruthless."[90] When, two years after Clark's departure from political office, Australia's first woman prime minister competed to hold on to the job, the trope of hard-heartedness drifted over the Tasman Sea into Australian newsrooms. Like Clark, Julia Gillard was constructed as merciless in her quest for power.

Female Political Killing Machine

Battle language appeared throughout Australian newspaper coverage of the 2010 election, with headlines like "Abbott rolls through western battleground"[91] and "Gillard's policy fightback."[92] Gillard was positioned as a warrior throughout the election coverage, described as attacking opponents and their ideas. Sixty-one combative verbs were used to describe her campaign style, while sixty-eight cast Abbott's approach as aggressive. For example, "Tony Abbott prepared to *destroy* one of his rival's key attack lines,"[93] and "Ms Gillard *savaged* Tony Abbott's work choices gaffes."[94]

As with Campbell, Shipley, and Clark, I determined what these war metaphors communicated about Gillard's performance of political leadership. Overall, she was characterized as a bold and fierce fighter, willing to challenge opponents and drive home her party's policy goals. "Her positive messages are as strong as her negative attack on Abbott is relentless," is one example of this trend.[95] Journalists chose words like "confront," "skewer," "savage," "assault," "target," "mortally wound," "trounce," and "fire" to summarize Gillard's rhetorical strategy, and most evaluated the Labor leader as strong, aggressive, relentless, and even predatory. A story titled "Julia unplugged has the killer lines on Abbott" said, "Gillard proved she's most alive in *predator mode*."[96] Another called her a "flint-hearted, ruthless political operator."[97] News reports said Gillard effectively deflected or returned "fire" from Tony Abbott, "hitting back," "lashing," and turning "the blowtorch" on her opponent.[98] In short, Australia's first woman prime minister was seen as tough enough to withstand the heat of political battle – "a smart, savvy fighter."[99]

Gillard was certainly not represented as invulnerable. Journalists used words such as "attacked," "bashed," and "fired upon" to highlight the ways in which she was opposed. For instance, she "appeared rattled" after a "forensic, almost hostile, interrogation"[100] and faced an "uphill battle to convince voters of her economic credentials."[101] The most damaging "attacks" on Gillard came from within the ranks of the Labor Party as the leadership "coup" resurfaced as a campaign issue. Gillard was said to have endured a "stabbing pain" from a negative advertisement produced by Abbott's Liberal Party, which told voters that Gillard had "backstabbed" Kevin Rudd when she challenged him for the party leadership.[102] Election news reports represented Gillard as "the architect of Rudd's assassination," alleging she had made the "decision to execute Rudd politically."[103] Other stories featured the words "killing"[104] and "decapitating"[105] to describe the manner in which Gillard had unseated her predecessor. Despite the fact that Rudd was meant to be campaigning for a Labor victory, his presence on the campaign trail was deemed to be a form of "friendly fire." "Gillard beset by friendly fire as Rudd marches into campaign," announced the headline of a story replete with militaristic language.

> Sometimes you need a man with a gun on the campaign trail. A hundred or so tough chaps in camouflage and toting assault rifles are even better if you happen to be Julia Gillard. Burdened by the spectral presence of former Prime Minister Kevin Rudd once again gobbling up an increasingly valuable campaign day, Gillard sought sanctuary yesterday at the vast Lavarack military barracks in Townsville.[106]

Here the columnist suggested that Gillard had surrounded herself with a display of military might, in the form of the Australian army, as a form of protection from Rudd and the damage done to her credibility by ousting him.

Despite many representations of Gillard as an effective and convincing political warrior, a few war metaphors emphasized her gender identity. The title of this section is drawn from a news story labelling Gillard Australia's "first female political killing machine."[107] Gillard was also termed a "perfumed political steamroller."[108] These descriptions reveal a persistent cognitive dissonance when women are discursively associated with acts of military might. Thus, while coverage of Gillard suggested that the novelty of a woman leading her partisan troops into "battle" had largely worn off, the spectacle of a women acting brutally was deployed as a way of undermining her political authority. Moreover, as I relay in chapter 7, the media sternly condemned Gillard for allegedly igniting a fiery and destructive "gender war" against Abbott, a battle of words in which the prime minister was judged to be the loser and shamed for her political outspokenness.

Discussion: Women at War

As I have shown, political competition is ubiquitously described as a form of rhetorical warfare. The battle frame is both empowering and limiting for women leaders. When used to praise a woman leader's fortitude, courage, and persistence, as was the case for Clark and Gillard, and to some extent Shipley, war metaphors communicate the idea that women can successfully engage in electoral competition. As she won and held power, Helen Clark was admired for her toughness, determination, and willingness to effectively dispute opponents' ideas. These examples challenge Van Acker's claim that women who are viewed as resolute and commanding are "often portrayed negatively" (2003, 117). Like men leaders, women who are in contention to win an electoral contest are presented as authoritative and forceful. Such was the case for Clark, Shipley, and Gillard.

However, allegories of warfare frame how we view politics. Battle metaphors limit the nature of the acceptable electoral performance to norms of political competition shaped by understandings of warfare. Kim Campbell was judged as being ineffective because she audaciously challenged these norms. The news media could not understand how her non-confrontational, positive, issue-oriented approach to election campaigning fit within the traditional combative frame for describing and evaluating electoral politics. As a result, her performance was considered to be inadequate for the job. When she changed course by abandoning her strategy of "doing politics differently," and less confrontationally, she was deemed to be inauthentic in her performance of heroic warrior leadership. Similarly, when Hillary Clinton's 2008 campaign for the White House shifted from "softening" Clinton's image to portraying the candidate as strong and experienced, the mainstream media assessed her as unlikeable and as a loser, leading Lawrence and Rose to conclude that "even the politically viable female candidate will be treated to the media's relentless game-framing, which male candidates also face, and the negativity that framing entails" (2010, 228).

I argue that war metaphors, however restrictive, are not unrelentingly negative or delegitimizing to women leaders. Helen Clark was frequently praised for her tenacity, for instance. Moreover, representations of women leaders as metaphorically fighting other party leaders to the death on the electoral battlefield can discursively destabilize the public man/private woman binary. While combative metaphors equate politics with warfare, long seen as the domain of men, situating women within these narratives disrupts the association of characteristics like strength, determination, fortitude, and persistence with men and tropes of heroic warrior masculinity. Depictions of women leaders as effective and authoritative actors on the political "battlefield" communicate the understanding that women politicians can exercise both power and agency. Even when trivializing reminders of their gender identities, such as "female political killing machine," "Boadicea," and "clash of the Xenas," are brought into the metaphorical mix, the messages challenge gendered assumptions about who can perform political leadership.

The gendered mediation literature argues that women leaders are seen as capable only when they embrace masculine norms and rhetorical styles (Sheeler and Anderson 2014, 491). But by characterizing election campaigns as fervent battles waged by unwavering enemies, allegories of war highlight the intense and emotionally fraught relationships among political parties. During elections, party leaders are quite literally fighting for the hearts and minds of voters. Passion and emotion, long associated with the private realm of domestic life, are rendered political, and politically salient, during election campaigns. Similarly, as I argue in the next section, by describing party leaders as engaging in political love affairs, political news can politicize romance and highlight the ways in which love resonates in political relationships.

Love Stories

Despite their intimacy, intensity, and longevity, political relationships are rarely narrated using the lexicon of romance. Exceptions punctuate how the language of love deftly captures certain political affiliations. The turbulent relationship between the province of Quebec and the Canadian nation has been represented as an "unhappy marriage," headed for a "painful separation" (Warren and Ronis 2011, 15). Similarly, after the 2007 Serbian election, journalists referred to negotiations among the political parties as "courtships," the coalition agreement as a "marriage," and the dissolved coalition as a "divorce" (Đurović and Silaški 2010, 244–8). For the media, the language of love is both familiar and emotionally evocative. A marriage metaphor is certainly more beguiling than a straightforward account of intra-state differences or coalition pacts, and the romance-gone-sour narrative is instantly recognizable and deeply resonant in Western societies.

All metaphors present partial truths and emphasize particular values (O'Malley and Tynan 1999, 591), and romance metaphors display the ideological boundaries set by social and political constructions of love and marriage. Since popular culture presents an idealized version of romantic love that is both heterosexual and monogamous, some forms of love are accepted, while others are deemed to be out of place (Johnson 2005; Morrison, Johnston, and Longhurst 2013). As a result, relationship metaphors perform ideological work when used to describe political ideas or events. For example, although a unity rally staged by English Canadians in 1995 to sway Quebec voters towards the No side in the sovereignty referendum was depicted as a love-in, scholars who analysed discourses associated with the rally argue that the messages reflected self-love and love of Canada, not true love for Quebec (Warren and Ronis 2011, 23). Similarly, a series of "Israel Loves Iran" and "Iran Loves Israel" Facebook campaigns employed the language of love as a way of eliding inequalities and "brushing away conflicts" (Kuntsman and Raji 2012, 149). In both cases, lexical choices invoking intimacy and affection endorsed the possibility of a happy ending, obscuring the obstinacy of political disputes. Love metaphors can help tell a feel-good story when relationships are conflict-ridden: after all, "love has the power to flatten conflicts, to heal historical wounds, and to transcend ideological differences" (Warren and Ronis 2011, 12).

Relationship metaphors can also reproduce gendered power relationships. For example, love and romance metaphors evoke passion, longing, and sexual intimacy. While these concepts apply to both women and men, men are stereotypically situated as the aggressors in sexual relationships, while women are assumed to be seduced or conquered, thus as acted upon by men (Anderson 2011, 358; Borisoff and Hahn 1993, 254). Underpinning descriptions of "suitors" flirting with, wooing, courting, and marrying is a culturally inscribed view of the suitor as a man who pursues, and ultimately possesses, the object of his affections (Koller 2002, 194). Đurović and Silaški show how marriage metaphors, when used to describe party coalition-building in Serbia, reinforced gendered hierarchies of power by situating smaller, weaker parties as the metaphorical woman in the relationship (e.g., as "a good marriageable girl") and larger, more powerful parties as the metaphorical man ("eligible young man" or "bridegroom") (2010, 241–50). Further, representations of coalitions as marriages of convenience or forced nuptials "rest on an underlying idea of the marriage of un-equals" (Đurović and Silaški 2010, 249). Rape metaphors dramatize and accentuate the power imbalances underpinning sexual violence (Đurović and Silaški 2010, 253; Warren and Ronis 2011, 15). Sexualizing the language of love tends to identify some actors as dominant and authoritative and others as submissive and subjugated.

Anderson argues that love metaphors "pornify" politics, and her research shows how the romance frame has trivialized the process of electioneering by transforming US election campaigns into "cultural peep shows" (2011, 331, 333). Sexualized language became increasingly misogynistic during the 2008 presidential campaign, disciplining women candidates and constituents by instantiating them as "vixens, sex objects, and/or nymphomaniacs" (Anderson 2011, 333, 336). According to Anderson, romance metaphors offer an enticing slippery slope for journalists, sliding from "gendered romance to sexist compliment to dirty joke, from dirty joke to hard-core exploitation" (2011, 354). However, it is important to avoid conflating romance and pornography. The lexicon of love is not always, or necessarily, pornographic, sexist, or hateful towards women. Idealized, heterosexist versions of romantic love are not the only relationships that may be invoked using the language of love. While love is frequently assumed to be romantic (Morrison, Johnston, and Longhurst 2013, 517), there are other forms of love, including love for friends, family, co-workers, and compatriots and love of humanity. Non-sexual relationship metaphors tap into values such as cooperation, caring, trust, and mutuality, values that can empower participants in political relationships and, perhaps, even out power imbalances (O'Malley and Tynan 1999, 593). Relationship metaphors, therefore, can serve as a "site of resistance and subversion" (Morrison, Johnston, and Longhurst 2013, 507).

When analysing the gendered meanings conveyed by relationship metaphors, I carefully considered the cautionary notes sounded by the gendered mediation literature. By casting the period of adulation following the election of a new leader as a "honeymoon," describing a leader's attempt to win votes as a "seduction" of the electorate, and characterizing government coalition-building processes as "romances" featuring "flirtations," "jilted lovers," or "fully consummated marriages," it would seem that certain aspects of electoral politics are branded as feminine and heavily sexualized. For instance, as Anderson notes, the romance frame positions candidates for political office as "suitors" who "woo" voters with their sexual allure rather than as interlocutors who persuade citizens to support their policy ideas (2011, 354). Moreover, sexual metaphors typically locate men as aggressors, lusting after and ultimately subjugating women (Borisoff and Hahn 1993, 264). So I asked whether the metaphorical language of romance reinforced norms of heterosexual love, suggesting that men are active, powerful, and in control, while women are passive objects of men's lust and affection. However, because romance metaphors offer another subversive mechanism in reporting about election campaigns, I also determined whether relationship metaphors worked to subvert gender binaries by emphasizing the importance of emotions and intimacy in the workings of formal political relationships.

As with the war metaphors, I analysed how the lexicon of love and romance was employed to describe the four prime ministers and the men leaders who contested elections in opposition to them. I found that reporters and columnists used the metaphorical language of romance to portray three distinct types of relationships: associations within political parties, links between politicians and supporters, and affiliations among leaders of different political parties seeking to build formal or informal governing coalitions. However, political context mattered as romance metaphors appeared significantly more frequently in New Zealand than in Canadian and Australian newspaper coverage. The emotional connection forged between party leaders and voters was the only type of political relationship presented as a love affair in Canada and Australia; in New Zealand, romance metaphors captured intra-party relationships and coalition-building processes.

In 1993, New Zealand adopted a mixed-member proportional (MMP) electoral system, first used in the 1996 election, whereby minor parties win seats and no one party has the numbers to govern without support from one or more smaller parties. As a consequence, formal or informal coalitions among political parties must be fashioned (Miller 2005, 211–2; Rudd and Hayward 2006, 332–3). The emergence of coalition politics prompted the New Zealand media to adopt the allegorical lexicon of courting, dating, marriage, and divorce when describing possible alliances among parties during election campaigns and to capture the nuances of the post-vote bargaining process as it unfolded. In Canada and Australia, love entered into mediated political discourses only when party leaders were "wooing" voters or enjoying a post-victory political "honeymoon."

The Political Honeymoon

In Western popular culture, the honeymoon is heavily romanticized, understood as an opportunity for the newly bound couple to cement their physical and emotional relationship by spending time together both inside and out of the bedroom. In political discourses, the honeymoon refers to "an initial period of enthusiasm or goodwill" for a newly selected party or government leader.[109] While the features of this political vacation are rarely explicated in news reports, the admiration of supporters, respect of citizens, and perhaps a hiatus from harsh media evaluation are commonly assumed.

The honeymoon metaphor was used in all three countries and abounded in Australian newspaper coverage of Gillard's rise to the prime minister's office. New Zealand's women prime ministers, Helen Clark and Jenny Shipley, were said to luxuriate in lengthy honeymoons,[110] although the metaphor was rarely invoked in their cases and even then only in retrospect, at the denouement of their political careers. In contrast, Kim Campbell's and Julia Gillard's periods of respite from critique were cut short by the vagaries of electioneering and political opposition. Campbell's "brief honeymoon with Canadians," which she enjoyed during the fleeting interval between her leadership victory and the early phase of the election campaign, was "shattered" after the election began in earnest and support for her party evaporated.[111] Then, during the campaign, Campbell announced that she had been "left at the altar" by reporters,[112] thereby accusing the media of denying her the political marriage necessary for a continued relationship with the electorate. In Gillard's case, political opponents interrupted the idyll. Journalists warned that her honeymoon would not last until the election because her predecessor, Kevin Rudd, and the opposition parties were equally determined to wreck her dream vacation with voters.[113]

Honeymoon seems to be a highly sexualized word choice. But in my view, honeymoon metaphors do not unduly sexualize the rapport between prime ministers and the people they serve. Instead, they recognize the act of governing as an intense, often emotional, and even fragile relationship between leaders and citizens. The honeymoon allegory neatly captures an important moment in the relationship between government leaders and citizens. As mentioned in chapter 2, ascents to the prime minister's post may be celebrated as coronations, during which a newly selected leader is admired, exalted, and even viewed as an exemplar of the nation's norms and achievements. This form of adoration is essential to cementing the bonds between leaders and citizens. It allows the new leader time to communicate goals, articulate messages of hope, and express a profound desire to serve the nation, thereby inspiring respect and affection from the people she represents.

A Love Affair with Voters

Political journalists in Australia, Canada, and New Zealand occasionally used metaphors of love and physical intimacy to symbolize supporters' adulation of their political leaders. For example, after she had won the party leadership and become Canada's prime minister, Kim Campbell was "embraced by many Canadians."[114] During the 2002 New Zealand election, Helen Clark basked "in the adoration of the party faithful,"[115] and pundits drew attention to Labour supporters who waved a sign saying, "We love you, Helen" during the 2005 campaign.[116] Journalists scripted John Key's surge in support during the 2008 election as a veritable love-in, personalizing the phenomenon with stories of "fawning 84-year-old twins [and] young mums rushing to put their babies in his arms"[117] plus a breathless "teen fan" keen to openly declare her love for the soon-to-be-elected prime minister.[118] The language of love is a parsimonious way of highlighting the powerful feelings forged during election campaigns. For party leaders, exaltation from voters is a rich political currency.

The relationship is by no means one-sided. Party leaders from all three countries were routinely described as "wooing" or "courting" voters to gain their support at the polls, a trend especially evident in New Zealand election news coverage, although an Australian columnist wrote about how Tony Abbott's wife, Margie, stood loyally by her husband's side while he "wooed" women voters.[119] During the 1999 New Zealand election, "Jenny Shipley and Helen Clark got down to some serious wooing in Auckland, where Saturday's election could be won or lost."[120] In 2008, an article titled "Final sweep to woo voters" explained, "Mr. Key will spend his final days on the campaign trail wooing voters who haven't yet made up their minds; Miss Clark is wooing voters in the key South Auckland electorates who decided the result in 2005."[121] Anderson suggests that this particular romance narrative "casts voters as bachelors and bachelorettes participating in the campaign season version of a reality dating show" (2011, 353). But in New Zealand, where the language of courtship was most regularly deployed, news stories used the word "wooing" to emphasize how party leaders championed their party platforms in an effort to sway undecided voters or to offer students, workers, pensioners, or electoral districts targeted policy promises.[122] This was, in large part, a love affair of the mind, not a physical seduction.

However, some notable exceptions illustrate how a simple word choice can sexualize the relationship between leaders and followers. A headline announcing Kim Campbell's "summertime seduction of the Canadian electorate"[123] drew on the commonly understood meaning of seduction as the act of enticing someone into sexual activity. A pundit's quip that "bared shoulders and a bared soul first drew Canadians to Prime Minister Kim Campbell"[124] exposes the sexual undertone in these media accounts of Campbell's capacity to attract voters. Similarly, during the 2005 New Zealand election, a Maori leader was quoted as saying, "I can't ever see myself getting into bed with [National Party leader] Don Brash."[125] Journalists also reported on signs waved by Labour supporters directing voters not to "wake up with Brash."[126] By equating leaders' vote-getting behaviours with acts of seduction and sexual intercourse, campaign news reports emphasized the intensity of the bonds between leaders and supporters, while sensationalizing and intimizing their emotional attachments.

All in the Family

Only in New Zealand did the press choose romance metaphors when describing intra-party relationships. Relationship allegories abounded in the wake of Helen Clark's quest for the leadership of the Labour Party in 1993. As described in chapter 2, incumbent leader Mike Moore fought her challenge until the bitter end, and the press likened Labour's emotional fallout to a family enduring a messy divorce. There was no doubt about who instigated the marital break-up. Clark was represented as a home-wrecker who destroyed party unity when she went after the leader's job. According to an article titled "Divorce, Labour style," the change in leadership "was more like a divorce and custody battle than a leadership spill."[127] This story cast Clark and Moore as the allegorical parents to Labour's political family, fighting for control after the break-up. "Ms. Clark would keep the family home, contents and custody, and Mr. Moore might perhaps have visiting rights if he chose."[128] By suggesting that Moore was accorded neither the comforts of home nor an ongoing relationship with his political "children" while Clark enjoyed the spoils of the former leader's travails, the metaphor solidified gendered familial roles by casting Clark as Mom, Moore as Dad. Further, it implied that divorce and custody arrangements were unfair to men. Once the post-"coup" acrimony had passed, news coverage invoked the power of love to effect a "miraculous healing" of the rift between Clark and Moore.[129·] The language of splitting up and making up[130] evoked dating practices, sentimentalizing the relationship. "I came over all misty-eyed at the Great Reconciliation played out for the TV cameras," gushed a columnist. "All that was missing was a soft-focus shot of them wandering hand-in-hand into the sunset."[131] Journalists were disappointed when the political "couple" sealed their renewed relationship with "a handshake instead of a kiss."[132] To their delight, a "squabble" between Clark and another former Labour leader, David Lange, ended in loving rapprochement when the pair "kissed and made up."[133]

I find it telling that the press relied on metaphors of family and intimacy to describe the relationships between New Zealand's first woman party leader and her predecessors in the leader's role. Although relationship allegories allow news commentators to highlight the necessarily close alliances among the party elite, casting a woman leader as the object of affection by male colleagues undermines her political legitimacy by situating her as relatively powerless. A similar trend emerged in reporting about relationships among parties which sought to build governing coalitions.

Marriage, Adultery, and Divorce, Coalition-Style

The advent of MMP and multi-party governments enticed the New Zealand news media to use the language of love and marriage when characterizing parties' attempts to construct formal governing coalitions or informal governing arrangements. Although journalists regularly made use of business metaphors, writing about "coalition partners" and parties "working" or "joining" with each other to strike "deals," they also waded into the more intimate waters of romance metaphors, narrating the first three MMP elections as veritable soap operas. News accounts spun tales of overtures from party leaders, hasty and unhappy marriages, attempted adultery, and sordid divorces. As applied to coalition politics, love and marriage metaphors tended to appropriate and reinforce the values associated with traditional patriarchal and heteronormative romantic relationships.

Stories likening relationships among parties to dating and marriage first appeared during the 1996 campaign, when journalists and politicians alike styled pre-election negotiations between Labour and other parties as courtship rituals, anticipating some sort of political marriage. National Party leader Jim Bolger accused Labour leader Helen Clark of "courting the Alliance," for example.[134] But journalists imposed a different script, saying that Labour was "courted" on the right by National and pursued on the left by the Alliance.[135] Clark was "rejecting" the "advances" of her political competitors,[136] newspaper articles claimed, thereby positioning the lone woman leader as the reluctant object of other party leaders' affections. As one author insisted, "Labour found itself the subject of unwelcome attentions by coalition suitors, the Alliance and New Zealand First."[137] Courtship metaphors mirrored traditional dating rituals, with Clark's power resting solely in her ability to accept or reject other leaders' attempts to hook up. In contrast, Jim Bolger and his National Party pursued "coalition partners" who negotiated, bargained, and engaged in "power talks" to form "coalition deals."[138]

Only one romance metaphor was used in reference to National's possible coalition arrangements, offered after the vote produced a close outcome, with neither National nor Labour winning enough seats to govern without support from another party. Because New Zealand First won the third-largest number of seats, leader Winston Peters had the power to declare a winner simply by choosing a coalition partner. According to the press, both Bolger and Clark had to "woo Mr. Peters in an effort to form the next government."[139] One party would be chosen for this first coalition "marriage," leaving the other at the metaphorical coalition altar. "NZ First MPs need to understand that this coalition courting will produce at least one spurned, nasty, vindictive, hell-hath-no-fury ex suitor. It will be a political Fatal Attraction, and the damage will not be limited to domestic pets."[140] New Zealand First opted for a coalition arrangement with National, and no pets were harmed in the process, but characterizations of Clark as a woman who might irrationally seek vengeance if rejected by a potential coalition partner echoed the damaging judgments produced during her leadership "coup," as detailed in chapter 2.

New Zealand's first coalition government featured a chummy relationship between Prime Minister Jim Bolger and NZ First leader Winston Peters.[141] But when Jenny Shipley wrested the National Party's leadership from Bolger a year later, the coalition was characterized as an "uneasy marriage [that] could be headed for the rocks" because its "reluctant groom" threatened a divorce.[142] Marriage and divorce metaphors abounded in news coverage of the Shipley-Peters coalition government, reflecting and reinforcing gender role stereotypes. Shipley, as the coalition's political "wife," was forced to perform a "courtship dance"[143] and "entice" Peters to stay in the relationship.[144] Moreover,

Shipley was compelled to act the part of the good wife, overlooking or forgiving her political husband's indiscretions. Peters was called "the marriage partner from hell"[145] as he demonstrated "dishonorable" intentions by engaging in an "inept secret courtship of Labour leader Helen Clark."[146] In the end, Peters decided to stay in the "marriage," but news commentators did not believe it would last.

> New Zealand First leader Winston Peters has simply postponed his *split* from the Coalition government until he can negotiate a *bitter divorce* settlement. His grudging yes to Coalition life with prime minister-in-waiting Jenny Shipley smacked of a *shotgun marriage* that can only *end in tears*. Mr. Peters gave Mrs. Shipley no advance notice of his decision yesterday not to *jilt her at the Coalition altar*.[147]

Indeed, a split ensued, and the end of the coalition arrangement was once again personalized in news accounts. "The Shipley-Peters relationship ended in tears less than a year later when Mr. Peters stormed out of cabinet."[148] The marriage-headed-for-divorce metaphor cast Peters as the unhappy husband pursuing a mistress and contemplating a divorce and Shipley as the dutiful wife agreeing to overlook her husband's wandering eye for the sake of appearances.[149] This rendition accorded power to Peters, as did another article, which declared, "New Zealand First is still in the marital bed and hogging the covers."[150]

During the 1999 election campaign, romance metaphors continued to personalize and intimize relationships among parties and leaders negotiating possible coalition arrangements. A surge in support for New Zealand First prompted this highly sexualized rendition of the marriage allegory: "With Mr. Peters on the comeback, politics dictates that the Labour and National leaders [Clark and Shipley] must simply lie back and think of New Zealand when it comes to possible partnerships with the wily NZ First leader."[151] According to this text, Shipley and Clark were forced by electoral circumstances to accept Peters as a political "husband" and to fully consummate the marriage by offering him a Cabinet post. In fact, Clark adamantly refused to entertain a political partnership with New Zealand First. A long-standing agreement between Labour and the Alliance party was represented as a courtship and marriage between Clark and Alliance leader Jim Anderton. Tensions between these potential coalition partners, called "the first spat on the left,"[152] were resolved with a "symbolic embrace for the cameras."[153] After the election, as Clark was crafting a governing coalition, news pundits called her relationship with Anderton "positively romantic,"[154] describing the two leaders as "smiling and hugging" when the deal was made.[155] Further, a former Labour minister insisted that Clark was capable of keeping her potentially wayward "marriage partner" in line. "One thinks of the marriage vows – for better or worse, for richer or poorer – and I think that probably if anyone can handle Jim, she can."[156]

The 2002 election was narrated as yet another dating game for Clark, who was in a position to firmly reject unwelcome suitors because Labour was in sight of a majority government. Clark "spurned the advances of New Zealand First leader Winston Peters, declaring him persona non grata at her cabinet table,"[157] but the Peters soap opera did not end there, to the delight of the news media. When it became evident that Labour would need to broker some sort of support agreement with the minor parties, love and relationship metaphors entered news reports about inter-party dealings. For instance, despite being "jilted" by Clark, Peters reportedly "refused to shut the door on coalition possibilities late into election night, clearly still clinging to a belief he had expressed last week that Ms. Clark 'secretly' liked him."[158] Other potential coalition partners "came a-courting" too.[159] First, the "Greens were playing hard to get,"[160] and later, Labour and the Greens were "making up ... after weeks of bitter fighting."[161] A columnist looked for romance in another direction, suggesting that Labour could win the heart of United Future leader Peter Dunne with a "whirlwind romance." "Not, of course, that Dunne would simply roll over," this commentator opined, because this particular bride would have a "price."[162] Here we have the only example of a male party leader being discursively positioned as the political bride. Even so, Clark and her Labour government had to pay a dowry of sorts by offering policies appealing to United Future. In the end, Labour decided to govern with the two-member Progressive Party, an offshoot of the Alliance, relying on the support of supply and confidence votes from United Future.

Significantly fewer romance metaphors appeared in the coverage of Clark's final two election campaigns, in 2005 and 2008. She won a very small plurality in the 2005 election and formed a minority government with support from several parties. Business and bargaining metaphors replaced allegories of romance, with a few exceptions. Marriage was invoked when the Greens became "disappointed bridesmaids at the Cabinet table for the third time running."[163] Appointing the leaders of United Future and New Zealand First to ministerial positions outside of Cabinet was represented as "Clark's decision to embrace Peters and

Dunne."[164] During the 2008 campaign, when it became clear that a man was destined to win the election, love metaphors virtually disappeared from newspaper accounts of inter-party relationships. Clark "courted" the Maori[165] and Key made "goo-goo eyes" at this party,[166] but otherwise, the lexicon of business prevailed in reporting about how the new government would work. New Zealanders were told that their new prime minister "had already cut deals, before the election, to form a coalition with Act and United Future."[167] Intriguingly, a man who had made millions in business before entering politics was not described as entering a political marriage, but rather as making a "deal with his allies,"[168] including a "shrewd deal with the Maori Party."[169]

As a final note, the following dating metaphors challenged heteronormative relationship codes. In 2002, a possible coalition featuring Bill English and the National Party as the main player, supported by three smaller parties, all led by men, was described as a "ménage a quatre."[170] Less pornographically, reporters spoke of "the Maori Party's flirtation with National"[171] during the 2005 campaign, and National leader Don Brash's appeals to the Maori party were called "overtures" and "cosying up" to the party's (male) co-leader.[172] Similarly, in 2008, the ACT New Zealand party leader was called a "right-wing bedfellow" for National leader John Key.[173] By sexualizing the relationships between potential coalition partners, these metaphors unsettled heterosexist conventions of romantic love.

Discussion: Political Love Affairs

Romance metaphors performed three types of gender work in news discourses about political leadership. First, as predicted by the gendered mediation thesis, allegories of love and romance reflected gendered power relationships and shored up the two-sex/gender binary. In New Zealand, where coalitions among parties were likened to courtships, marriages, and divorces, Jenny Shipley and Helen Clark were frequently cast as the metaphorical woman in the relationship, pursued by men leaders of other parties and forced to rebuff their appeals or infidelities. Helen Clark was never described as actively in pursuit of coalition partners. Instead, she was placed in the object position, acted upon by men leaders and protecting her (political) virtue by rejecting their "advances." Her power was discursively limited by metaphorical constructions of her as a virtuous "good girl," saying no to the men seeking her affections. Both Clark and Shipley were positioned as the allegorical wife in political relationships. When she successfully challenged Mike Moore for the Labour Party leadership, Clark was a cruel wife who spitefully ended Moore's relationship with his party, booting him out of the family home. When Jenny Shipley entered the prime minister's office and inherited a governing coalition with New Zealand First, led by Winston Peters, the pact was characterized as a marriage in peril. Press reports read like a daily instalment of a soap opera, with Shipley struggling to keep her wayward husband in check as Peters secretly "courted" another woman (Helen Clark). Although New Zealand's women prime ministers' coalition partnerships were portrayed as romances by the press, the governing relationships forged by the men who preceded or succeeded Shipley and Clark in political office were more typically described with business metaphors, replete with the language of bargaining and deal-making. With a few exceptions, men leaders were presented as active subjects, pursuing deals (or brides), while women leaders were scripted as passive objects of men's advances.

Second, and more subversively, love metaphors affirmed the emotional bonds between leaders and followers, voters and citizens. "Falling in love" metaphors evoke affection, pride, friendship, kindness, reciprocity, and devotion. By saying that newly elected prime ministers enjoyed a honeymoon period, and casting the bonds between party leaders and voters as a reciprocal love affair, news stories reflected the values associated with non-romantic love, such as trust, admiration, and even adulation. In my view, the representative relationship between rulers and ruled is a loosely woven ideational fabric of confidence and reciprocity, easily snagged and torn. As with a post-marital honeymoon, where a respite from the material realities and demands of "real life" helps foster the intimate bonding integral to the success and longevity of the marriage, a political leader's idyll with voters benefits from a hiatus from the forms of evaluation and condemnation that can easily destroy these bonds of political affection. These attachments need to be renewed as party leaders seek support from voters during election campaigns. Media accounts of party leaders "wooing" voters, and voters expressing love and admiration for political authority figures, help cement crucial political friendships. And the language of love underscores the importance of emotion to the performance of political leadership. To be successful, party and government leaders must mobilize the public's feelings.

Third, love metaphors can disrupt the public/private binary by rendering politics a soap opera, a genre associated with women and the private domain of home, family, and intimacy (van Zoonen 2005, 22) The public/private dualism strictly separates the traits and virtues of public and private spheres, placing them in opposition to one another. Emotion and passion, allegedly the jurisdiction of intimate, familial, domestic relationships, are thus seen as being antithetical to reason and logic, putatively the domain of public, corporate, and political relationships. By using the lexicon of love in news narrations of political relationships, the private world of romance and intimacy is discursively imported into the public world of partisan politics, exposing the artificial boundaries between these spheres as an illusion. When love is made political, the political becomes a realm of intimacy and feeling. Scripting politics as a love affair emphasizes the importance of relationships to political success. Tales of courtship and romance situate the ability to cultivate trust and adulation, and to build bonds of affection with both admirers and opponents alike, as a crucial leadership skill.

Conclusions

According to the gendered mediation thesis, the metaphors used by the media to describe political life perform gendered ideological work. Specifically, they shore up the public man/private woman binary and associate political leadership with the performance of hegemonic masculinity. By likening politics to the military, war metaphors present politics as a similarly male-dominated field of activity. In contrast, the literature maintains, love metaphors write women out of official politics by casting them into the private realm of personal relationships. This argument is both supported and contested by the evidence presented in this chapter, which systematically analysed the meanings conveyed by the metaphorical language journalists used to describe political competition. I found that when allegories of love and war were inflected with gendered understandings of political power and romantic relationships, they tended to demean women leaders and challenge the legitimacy of their leadership. Epithets like "catfight" and "Xena princesses," and constructions of women as political wives and objects of male leaders' affections, highlighted stereotypes of femininity such as submission, sexual attractiveness, and even hysteria.

On the other hand, love and war metaphors do not invariably penalize women leaders. When battle language describes them as fierce, determined, and successful agents in political competitions, women are represented as capable, commanding, and authoritative in their exercise of political power. Such was the case for Helen Clark as she led her party into "battle" over the course of five election campaigns. Read cumulatively, much of the coverage of Clark was admiring in tone and celebrated her strength and fortitude. Similarly, while love metaphors were occasionally sexualizing and trivializing, drawing on hetero-normative, monogamous marital-relationship codes, they certainly emphasized the importance of intimacy and passion in formal political associations. For example, allegories about jilted lovers and unhappy marriages highlighted the emotional tensions and injuries caused by ill-fated political relationships. In fact, as described at the beginning of this chapter, the language of warfare was occasionally mobilized when rifts among coalition partners widened or political unions failed. The dramatic juxtaposition of love and conflict underscored the role of emotions in political life.

While there seems to be a discursive contradiction between the "masculine" world of warfare and combative sports and the "feminine" domain of love and romance, what allows these seemingly discordant interpretations of electoral performance to coexist is their insistence that politics is a series of intense and deeply emotional relationships. Electoral "battles" are not won without forming relationships, which can be combative or collaborative, brutal or tender, disastrous or productive. The relationships among political leaders and campaign staff, supporters, and the electorate may be as profound and poignant as a love affair, while interactions with electoral opponents are more aptly characterized as fierce competitions for a prize only one side can win. That women and men leaders can, at one and the same time, be positioned as fighters and lovers reflects the volatile and complicated nature of political relationships. More importantly, perhaps, these characterizations destabilize the idea of formal politics as unflinchingly competitive, a fight to the death by lone combatants. The leader's role in an election campaign may seem like a lonely and exposed march across a dangerous political battlefield, but it is in fact a communal quest reliant on love and adulation for its ultimate success.

Bonds of political affection are easily shredded when a leader's approach to political speech is condemned and she is thus rendered unlovable. As chapter 7 details, Campbell and Gillard were shamed for their public speeches – Campbell for how she spoke politically and Gillard for what she said in Parliament. As demonstrated earlier in this chapter, Campbell's capacity for tough talk was questioned during the 1993 Canadian election, and chapter 7 shows how much of the criticism focused on her manner of speech. In Australia, the press accused Gillard of waging an unjust war against her political opponent by choosing the terrain of gender politics as the discursive battleground. Acceptance of a leader's right to speak, and to speak out about difficult topics, is key to mediated legitimacy. Because women's right to engage public, political speech was once denied by laws and then rendered troublesome by gender regulations, media representations of their political speech acts reflect levels of public acceptance, or discomfort, with women in power.

Chapter Seven

Speech and Shame[1]

Introduction

> [Kim Campbell] regressed into some of her main weaknesses, like dull policy discussions and an almost *childish temper*. "You're the laughing stock!," she *shouted* at Chretien after the Liberal leader made the same accusation regarding Tory deficit projection. Later, she virtually *screamed*: "You don't even care about the deficit!" at Chretien. And when the moderator cut her off at that point, she *whined like a child*.[2]

> [Tony Abbott] was pictured at an anti-carbon tax demonstration in front of sexist placards [about Julia Gillard] that screamed "JULIAR ... BOB BROWNS BITCH" and "DITCH THE WITCH."[3]

Prime ministers and presidents receive a great deal of attention from mainstream and social media. Cited and quoted because of their authoritative roles, they are continuously given voice in the news, especially during highly contested moments (Langer 2007, 2010). Studies confirm that women who achieve positions of political power are accorded substantial media coverage (Goodyear-Grant 2013, 27–8; Vos 2013, 392). Every public utterance is scrutinized, evaluated, and reported. Media interpretations are central to achieving mediated legitimacy because news reports about debate performances, election rallies, and everyday policy pronouncements communicate the extent to which a prime minister's public speeches are comprehended, regarded as authentic, deemed appropriate to the circumstances, and judged to be effective. But public speech is interpreted through a gender lens. The legacy of "real and symbolic silencing of women" (Luke 1994, 211) continues to be reflected in news discourses about women leaders. In the first quotation, above, we see Kim Campbell's election debate tactics being touted as unduly loud, shrill, childish, and whiny, inferring that she lacked crucial leadership qualities. Descriptions such as "witch" and "bitch" once served to mark women as heretics and whores, and they now serve as a strategy of control, as shown by the second quotation, capturing critiques directed at Julia Gillard. The epithet "bitch" renders a woman's speech illegitimate by positing aggressiveness as an unnatural deviation from her "proper role" and by evoking fear of "women's political power" (Anderson 1999, 617). Clearly, media representations of women's speech acts circumscribe or condemn the speaker in ways that discourage such performances.

I make two arguments in this chapter. First, women come under scrutiny when they are judged to transgress speaking rules for political discourse. Second, elite women politicians are chastened when they speak in certain ways or raise certain topics. Kim Campbell and Julia Gillard were censured for aspects of their public speech, Campbell for her unreserved and candid utterances and Gillard for speaking out about the sexism she had experienced while serving as prime minister. Campbell was pilloried for her manner of speech from the moment she entered the Progressive Conservative (PC) Party's leadership race. The Canadian press corps peppered its descriptions of Campbell's interviews, press conferences, and stump speeches with a wide range of adjectives, including "shrill," "strident," "terse," "hectoring," "glib," "whiny," "huffy," "angry," and "arrogant." In fact, many journalists opined that Campbell's "loose lips"[4] robbed her of a first-ballot victory in the leadership vote and sank her party's ship during the 1993 Canadian election campaign. Campbell was mocked and shamed for oratorical mannerisms historically associated with a "womanly"/private mode of speech and judged inauthentic when she emulated the patterns of "manly"/public speech.

Twenty years after Campbell had been censured for how she spoke on the campaign trail, Gillard was condemned for what she said in Parliament. The Australian press used the metaphor of the gender war to characterize her speech on sexism and misogyny, delivered in the House of Representatives on October 9, 2012, as well as subsequent speeches. The trope of the gender wars cast Gillard's rhetorical tactics as a violation of deeply held cultural norms about appropriate topics for political speech. Invoking this metaphor worked both to discipline Gillard for raising issues such as sexism and gender inequality in politics and to subtract gendered power relations from everyday understandings of political competition.

After reviewing the literature on the silence/shame double bind, I explore these two examples of mediated shaming of the women prime ministers. The section titled "Kim-Speak" describes how Campbell was disciplined for her putative inability to mirror the patterns of political speech set down by her male predecessors. In "Julia Gillard and the Gender Wars," I demonstrate the ways in which Gillard was censured for speaking out about sexism in politics. The conclusion highlights the discursive norms and practices governing political communication and identifies the constraints and pitfalls that future women leaders may encounter when transgressing, or confronting, these norms.

Women, Power, and Public Speech

A latent sense of disquiet about powerful women is reflected in persistent cultural anxiety about, and resistance to, the female voice in public contexts. After all, women and the performance of femininity have long been associated with silence and reticence (Cameron 2006, 5), resulting in a double bind that Kathleen Hall Jamieson (1995) calls "silence/shame." Historically, the choice was clear: women could remain voiceless and powerless, or they could speak out and be punished, often quite brutally. Gender-specific forms of shaming included characterizing women who speak too much, too loudly, or too presciently as whores, heretics, witches, and hysterics – or as unduly manly (ibid., 85–98). Public speech by women was regarded for centuries as defiance of male authority, the work of the devil, a symptom of a "distressed mind," or an unnatural outpouring of emotion and illogic (Jamieson 1995, 85–93). Women's speech was seen as a profound disruption to the social order, a threat to the family, the Church, and the state. Silence, on the other hand, represented "outward submission to appropriate authority" (Jamieson 1995, 80). The civic consequences were profound, as Luke (1994, 213–14) observes.

> Women's historical location in the private sphere of muted domesticity and servitude has excluded them from education, from reading, writing and speaking the public tongue of politics. That is, women have been written out of the public civic sphere where allegedly impartial laws, judgements, and "universally human" (albeit distinctively male) political interests are articulated.

While most women are no longer excluded from engaging in and speaking about politics, their speech acts are still closely watched and interrogated. Women's public speech is more likely than men's to be described and characterized (Jamieson 1995, 172; Shaw 2011, 277). And a rich vocabulary is mobilized to "condemn female speech" (Jamieson 1995, 82) or to cast it as inappropriate, ineffective, or offensive. Characterizations of women's speech as "shrill" or "strident" and of the women who speak as "bitches" mark the speaker as both inept and bothersome. Anderson argues that the "fear of outspoken, politically active women has informed much of popular culture and political discourse," as evidenced by the use of the epithet "bitch" as a "contemporary rhetoric of containment disciplining women with power" (1999, 601–2). Many examples could be given to illustrate this point, but perhaps the most vivid feature Hillary Clinton. Clinton was labelled a "bitch" when she, as First Lady of the United States, dared to step out of the boundaries of the private sphere to lead a health care reform task force. When she sought the Democratic nomination for president, she was called a "cunt" (Anderson 1999, 2011). Epithets like "Shrillery" censure the speaker and act as a discursive form of silencing.

Less condemnatory but no less demeaning terms are used to trivialize, doubt the authenticity of, or question the effectiveness of women's political speech. "For women who sound unusually high-pitched, soft, or otherwise not baritone stentorian, the voice generally becomes the story" (Bashevkin 2009, 78). That observers may be more attentive to the style, pitch, and tone of a woman's voice than the words she is speaking is illustrated by criticism of Canadian New Democratic Party leader Audrey McLaughlin. Because she eschewed a combative style in favour of "a soft-spoken, consultative approach to public speaking," McLaughlin was seen to lack direction and authority (Bashevkin 2009, 79). In contrast, Canadian Liberal MP and leadership contender Sheila Copps "employed a feisty, conflictual, no-holds-barred approach" and was called "strident," "pushy," "shrill," and "abrasive" (ibid.). As McLaughlin's experience confirms, women politicians may be judged harshly for speaking in ways thought to be stereotypically "feminine." But adopting an approach to speech stereotyped as "masculine" because of its adversarial style may also put the speaker at a disadvantage, as shown by the negative reactions to Copps.

Describing women politicians as unable to speak for themselves or as merely echoing the words of others constitutes another powerful form of disparagement. A clear example of this trend is provided by mediated reactions to the campaign speeches of Conservative Party of Canada leadership candidate Belinda Stronach. By calling her "highly scripted," reporters insinuated that she was simply parroting the thoughts, words, and desires of the men seeking to put her into power (Trimble and Everitt 2010, 66). Worse, depictions of Stronach as little more than an attractive "front" for the ambitions of party "back room boys" reinforced the assumption that she could not, or would not, speak for herself. Describing women politicians' political utterances as weak, strident, or scripted undermines their authority and authenticity.

As these examples illustrate, gender regulations are evident in mediated representations of women's public speech, especially when women disrupt the socially constructed edifice of separate spheres. "Powerful speech has long been associated with masculinity and powerless speech with femininity" (Baxter 2006, xvi). Gaining access to discursive space is a way of claiming power as territory. So when women enter the public square from a position of power, and must by virtue of their leadership roles be heard, the public man/private woman binary is unsettled. As Bashevkin (2009, 77–8) observes, a "women plus power equals discomfort" syndrome is evident in unease with women politicians' voices and language use. The media reflect the disquieting reactions to women's speech circulating in society, especially in political circles. Experimental research has found that male audiences rank men's speech as more knowledgeable, trustworthy, and convincing than women's speech, even when the content is identical (Aalberg and Jenssen 2007). As a result, women political leaders may be subjected to more interpretation and judgment by the press than their male counterparts (Gidengil and Everitt 2003b, 210; Trimble and Everitt 2010, 66). Political women are censured for speaking too softly, too diplomatically, too much, too pointedly, too passionately, or in a manner critical of patriarchy and other hegemonic power structures. At particular risk of disapproval are women who attempt to change the speaking rules governing political institutions (Litosseliti 2006, 45). Speaking rules are particularly important to heavily mediated "high performance" events such as leadership and election debates, parliamentary debates, and prime ministerial speeches (Shaw 2011, 279). As a result, news coverage of politicians' public speeches can reveal the largely unspoken regulations guiding political discourse and expectations of political leadership.

The mediated condemnations of Campbell's and Gillard's speaking styles and statements disclose important norms governing political speech. First, political speech by women is evaluated based on the styles and patterns established by men in elite positions. Historically, "womanly speech was thought to be personal, excessive, disorganized, and unduly ornamental," while the "manly style" was thought to be driven by reason, thus "factual, analytic, organized, and impersonal" (Jamieson 1995, 91–2). To be regarded as prime ministerial, a leader's speech must be "manly" in the sense that it is appropriately confident and commanding, yet controlled and judicious. Campbell's speech mannerisms were often judged to be too revealing, frank, intimate, or loquacious – too "womanly." Yet Campbell was soundly criticized when she attempted a more measured and contained approach to speaking to the press and public, thereby disrupting entrenched news values. Second, as demonstrated by the virulently negative reaction by the Australian media to Gillard's "sexism and misogyny" speech, a woman leader cannot, without risking censure, mobilize gender as a political strategy or identify gender disadvantage as a problem in the political sphere. Gillard was accused of enacting an unfair and unjustifiably violent form of speech that threatened the political order. Campbell's case shows how the presence of a pioneer woman in an elite political position challenges the public man/private woman binary policing public speech. Gillard's experience illustrates how patriarchal assumptions and practices rest upon and maintain women's silence.

"Kim-Speak"[5]

Kim Campbell's "verbosity is her Achilles Heel."[6]

"She will fall back into the strident voice ... or even into the shrill, scolding voice."[7]

"She has a way of tripping over her tongue in ad-lib situations."[8]

The title of this section is drawn from a lengthy analysis of Kim Campbell's speaking style published in the *Globe and Mail*. In addition to coining the phrase "Kim-speak" ("the way she says things, the language she uses") to capture Campbell's alleged linguistic missteps, the columnist opined that Campbell had lost credibility with the media because of her "orotund" and "intensely bureaucratic" manner of speaking.[9] Other journalists and observers thought she was too quick to speak, spoke too quickly, said too much, and was far too candid.

Yet some of Campbell's speeches were described as stilted and boring. Members of the press corps reacted negatively to them, their criticisms emerging early in the leadership contest and reaching a crescendo during the 1993 election. In fact, Campbell's speaking style was cited as a crucial factor in her political downfall.

I was surprised by the number of derisory comments about Canada's first woman prime minister's speaking style as they stood in stark contrast to the largely positive assessments of Clark's, Shipley's, and Gillard's manner of speaking. I wondered whether my reading was reactively partial and overly attuned to the negative evaluations, so I decided to systematically analyse news representations of Campbell's mode of speech in three different ways. First, I compared the amount of attention paid to Campbell's speaking style with that of a comparable male leader, Jean Chrétien. Chrétien won the leadership of the Liberal Party in 1990, prevailed against Campbell in the 1993 Canadian federal election, and served as prime minister for ten years. While more successful than Campbell with respect to his longevity as government leader, Chrétien is a useful comparator because he competed against Campbell during the 1993 election campaign and succeeded her in office.[10] For each leader, I examined newspaper stories published at four key points in their political careers: the leadership contest, the 1993 election campaign, a governance phase immediately after their ascent to the prime minister's post, and resigning or retiring from the party leader's role. After conducting quantitative analysis of the amount of attention given to the speaking styles of these two leaders, I compiled an inventory of descriptions and/or evaluations of each leader's speech performances. Each discrete comment or assessment was classified as an individual case and categorized as positive, negative, or neutral. This inventory of comments about their speech was used to compare the ways in which journalists interpreted Campbell's and Chrétien's campaign utterances. Finally, I took a closer look at the characterizations of Campbell's public speech at all four career phases, identifying patterns of containment and condemnation.

Media Coverage of Campbell's and Chrétien's Speaking Styles

The observation that women's speech is more likely than men's to be noticed and appraised is supported by my analysis of the amount of attention that Campbell's and Chrétien's speaking mannerisms received in their news coverage. Content analysis determined whether a leader's speaking style was mentioned in each article, and it revealed a dramatic difference in the levels of attention to their public speech. Kim Campbell's speaking style was more than twice as likely as Chrétien's to be discussed as it was raised in almost half (45 per cent) of the news stories about her, compared with only 21 per cent of the news stories about Chrétien. However, as with other quantitative measures, these data tell only part of the story. A leader's speech may be mentioned once in a news item, or it may be elaborated with a number of depictions. So I turned to the qualitative database of assessments of these two leaders' speech, counting the number of discrete comments (descriptions or evaluations) about their speech acts or style of speaking. These data confirmed that Campbell's rhetorical mannerisms were significantly more likely to be noticed and assessed as she received almost four times as many comments as did Chrétien. There were 146 remarks about Campbell, compared with only 38 for Chrétien.

I carefully examined each comment, determining whether it communicated a positive or negative assessment or was neutral or balanced in tone.[11] To be counted as positive or negative, statements had to unequivocally convey approval or disapproval. For example, saying that Chrétien "mangles his syntax in both official languages"[12] conveys a criticism, as does the observation that Campbell was "disappointing in tone and substance."[13] Praise for Chrétien's "plain speech and passionate tone,"[14] and for Campbell's ability to talk "instinctively and from the heart,"[15] were classified as positive. As table 7.1 illustrates, Campbell's speech was evaluated more harshly than was Chrétien's. More of the comments about Chrétien were positive than negative, although by a slim margin; in contrast, Campbell received more than twice as many negative judgments as positive remarks. Overall, the evaluations of Chrétien's speech were largely admiring or neutral in tone, but for Campbell, the vast majority of the appraisals were critical, even condemnatory.

The more intense level of scrutiny accorded Campbell is illustrated by the coverage of the 1993 Canadian federal election, which the Campbell-led PC Party lost to Chrétien's Liberal Party. While Campbell's political oratory prompted fifty-nine descriptions, Chrétien's speeches and linguistic abilities attracted only thirteen comments. There were some critical views of Chrétien's public speech, a few of which questioned his capacity to deliver a sophisticated style of argumentation. For example, the Liberal leader was "mocked by the intellectuals for his

Table 7.1 Tone of Evaluations of Kim Campbell's and Jean Chrétien's Speaking Styles (All Career Phases)

Leader	Evaluations, N (%)		
	Positive	Negative	Neutral or balanced
Kim Campbell	38 (26)	88 (60)	20 (14)
Jean Chrétien	18 (47)	16 (42)	4 (11)

populist style of speech and his unsubtle arguments."[16] He "hesitated and then began rambling" in a question-and-answer session, said one article, and another asserted that "he barks" when responding to tough questions.[17] As well, a columnist referred to Chrétien's speech as "fractured," and another indicated that "his heavy accent in English and his unpolished French have been the butt of jokes."[18] Yet most descriptions of Chrétien's speech performances were positive and applauded his capacity to charm audiences across the country. He was the "serene, warm and frequently funny Mr. Chretien," who "has an extremely sensitive feel for comic timing" and could "have a standing-room only crowd of skeptical university students roaring with laughter."[19] News commentators lauded Chrétien's ability to connect with the public "on a visceral level," "speak to Canadians' emotions," and pull "on people's heartstrings" with his speeches.[20] A few weeks into the campaign, the Liberal leader's campaign communication was described as "confident" and delivered with a "statesmanlike" tone or a "prime ministerial demeanour."[21]

In contrast, Campbell's speaking style was rarely praised during the election campaign, and it was never characterized as prime ministerial or statesmanlike. In fact, a commentator said, "I don't think she came across as very prime ministerial" during a televised party leaders' debate.[22] Campbell's public speech was put under a microscope, examined from every angle, and appraisals were abundant, diverse, and often harshly unsympathetic. They ranged from descriptions of her literal incapacity to speak ("hoarse from a cold") to criticisms of her tone ("snapped," "mocked," "raised her voice") to evaluations of her speaking style ("articulate," "lecturing," "preaching," "outspoken," "wooden," "glib," "hesitant"). The author of an opinion piece even deployed stereotypical representations of women's speech by predicting that Campbell "will fall back into the *strident* voice ... or even into the *shrill*, scolding voice."[23] Moreover, in contrast to depictions of Chrétien as able to talk "to Canadians on a visceral level," journalists accused Campbell of speaking in a way that distanced herself from the people she sought to represent. By saying that she lectured and hectored her audiences, they questioned her capacity to connect with regular people.[24] Indeed, journalists took pains to report lacklustre reactions to the prime minister's major campaign events – for instance, "The crowds were small and generally unenthusiastic,"[25] and her speech was "read in a plodding fashion to a bored half-filled hall" and received only "perfunctory applause."[26]

Journalists explained that these unforgiving evaluations of Campbell's speeches were justified by what she said. However, the newspaper coverage did not merely report the words she chose. Reporters and columnists evaluated how she said them, and most of the negative assessments were of her manner of communication. Moreover, evaluations of her speech as "shrill," "strident," "preaching," and "hectoring" revealed gender-specific ideas about, and unease with, women's political speech. These judgments reflected the unspoken, and gendered, norms of electoral debate and served as strategies of containment. To understand how the critique of Campbell's speech acts developed over time, I used feminist critical discourse analysis to identify patterns of critique and condemnation in the coverage of her leadership campaign and brief career as prime minister.

"Tripping on Her Lip"[27]

In the very early "Campbellmania" stages of the PC Party's leadership contest, a few media reports were complimentary, with journalists portraying the leading contender as "warm, inclusive and funny," "unusually articulate ... confident and comfortable," and presenting herself and her ideas "like a star."[28] But Campbell's performances in the first two of five televised all-candidates' debates were judged to be "wooden," "rocky," "disappointing in tone and substance," "weak," "uninspiring," and lacking in "spontaneity," "humor," or "fire."[29] According to the *Vancouver Sun*, by sticking "mostly to a prepared text [Campbell] left eyes glazed."[30] A *Globe and Mail* columnist said her "tactic was to show strength, but quiet strength."[31] But Campbell's non-adversarial approach to debating was regarded as inappropriate for a televised campaign "battle" among the leadership candidates.

In the third candidates' debate, Campbell went off script, using the phrase "enemies of Canadians" to characterize those who refused to see the burgeoning federal government deficit as a serious problem.

Opponents, pundits, and journalists alike immediately condemned her choice of words. Characterized as a "mistake" and "obvious blunder,"[32] and as evidence that Campbell was "rapidly developing a case of foot-in-mouth disease,"[33] the comment opened the floodgates to criticism, with members of the press dredging up examples of maladroit or intemperate public speech, some of them from her distant past. A lengthy magazine article was mined for trenchant "Campbellisms" thought to reveal conceit and overconfidence. For instance, an article titled "Campbell tripping on her lip" diagnosed the problem as "a tongue too directly connected to a mind that tends towards arrogance."[34] Other excerpts from the article were cited as evidence of excessive emotion and immoderate speech, with descriptions of Campbell having "screamed at anti-free trade protesters" and "engaged in shouting matches during her 1980–84 period on the Vancouver school board."[35] Even though most of the contentious statements were made years, even decades, before the leadership contest, they circulated through the campaign coverage and were regularly cited as evidence of Campbell's alarming and politically dangerous candour. From this point on, assessments of her speech acts were overwhelmingly negative. While a few pundits applauded Campbell's outspoken style, calling it "candid and humorous"[36] and "a refreshing change from clichés and platitudes,"[37] others cast her manner of speech as "disquieting" and "controversial."[38] Campbell's ad-libs were represented as "verbal slips" and "bombshells."[39]

Gendered evaluations were evident in assessments of Campbell's articulations. Indeed, a *Montreal Gazette* opinion writer went so far as to say that she "sounded like a woman."[40] Evaluations of Campbell's speech as excessive, disorganized, and lacking in substance reflect the historically and culturally inscribed features of "womanly" speech outlined by Jamieson (1995, 91). For example, although "her mind runs fast," opined a columnist, "her tongue sometimes outpaces it, causing political trouble and occasionally personal offence."[41] Incontinent, unrestrained speech has long been associated with women, who have been thought to be governed by emotion rather than logic. By opining that Campbell's "ability to say silly things cannot be overlooked"[42] and she "talks too much without thinking,"[43] columnists trivialized and denigrated her attempts to occupy the discursive territory of elite political competition. Even worse, Campbell was said to "kill" her career by opening her mouth. A column dissecting her campaign featured a section titled "The mouth," which asserted, "Her verbosity is her Achilles

` Heel. A handler's worst nightmare, she'll always be one sentence away from political suicide."[44]

As argued in chapter 2, the first impressions of leaders communicated by the media are instrumental in shaping their public image. Mediated representations of Campbell's speech acts during the election campaign echoed many of the judgments offered in news reports of her quest for the leadership of the PC Party. Initially, the Campbell election team attempted to model a new style of political communication, avoiding direct confrontation of opponents' views[45] to focus on policy and "thoughtful dialogue" (Campbell 1996, 359). But this strategy was condemned for being insufficiently spontaneous and engaging. Campbell was described as embracing a "wooden, sessional-lecturer style"[46] and being "flat and uninspiring"[47] – for instance, "She could not deliver a political speech without sounding like she was reading from poli-sci lecture notes."[48] Factual, analytical, impersonal speech of this sort is associated with men (Jamieson 1995, 91). Characterizing Campbell's attempts to emulate this mode of speaking as ineffective and uninspiring reveals discomfort with women performing in a putatively "masculine" oratorical style. Moreover, the approach disrupted reporters' routines because it was difficult to integrate these speeches into the game frame used to describe election events. In fact, Campbell's approach to interacting with Canadians on the campaign trail, described in one report as "her lecturing, analytical 'new politics,'" was panned by journalists, who found it tedious, long-winded, and "devoid of passion, poetry or partisan fire."[49]

During the leadership race, the media typecast Campbell as overly verbose (for instance, one news story said she suffered from "foot in mouth disease"),[50] and news writers relied heavily on this script during the 1993 election campaign. Friction between the prime minister and the press developed when the news media pounced on ad-libbed comments, one of which was made right at the start of the election campaign. In response to a reporter's question about unemployment rates, Campbell offered a "sobering" prediction that the rates would remain high for some time to come.[51] Then, a few weeks into the campaign, her observation that "you can't have a debate on such a key issue as the modernization of social programs in forty-seven days" was represented as "Prime Minister Kim Campbell says the future of Canada's social programs is too important to discuss during an election campaign."[52] These remarks were called verbal "stumbles,"[53] the second deemed a "disastrous statement,"[54] and both were identified as central to the "unravelling" of the Tory campaign and the party's eventual electoral downfall.[55] Campbell was represented as the author of her own, and her party's, electoral demise because of her approach to public speaking. "From the moment she stepped up to the microphones [to announce the election] her campaign has gone downhill – her quick tongue and candid naiveté a synopsis of her recent political career."[56]

Newspaper stories conveyed the impression of a leader out of control because of her vocal *faux pas* and indeed as uncontrollable by her handlers. A lengthy article whose title referred to Campbell as a "loose cannon" said her party had to "endure" its leader regularly straying off script and remaining "frank, outspoken, inattentive to political advice."[57] In addition to calling Campbell unruly and ungovernable, print journalists described her as throwing the rhetorical equivalent of a hissy fit when polls began to show that the PC campaign was in serious trouble. According to news reports, Campbell started "scolding,"[58] "lecturing," and "snapping" at reporters[59] and "lashing out"[60] at the news media. One report said she "whined like a child" in a televised party leaders' debate.[61] The gendered lexical choices of "shrill" and "strident" were also mobilized in critique of her reaction to the media coverage.[62] These representations of Campbell's reactions to reporting about her party's impeding electoral downfall cast her as petulant, unduly emotional, and inappropriately angry.

Expressive, inconstant speech by women was once associated with hysteria, the cure for which was "confinement, seclusion and silence" (Jamieson 1995, 89). In Campbell's case, confinement came in the form of restricting opportunities to engage with the press. "Unable to control their candidate, the campaign planners have decided to control media access to her and the unstructured news scrums where most of Ms. Campbell's controversial remarks have been made," announced one report.[63] Another said that the PC leader chose this tactic, opting to seal herself away "in a media-proof bubble" because she is "impulsive" and "prone to prickliness."[64] But preventing opportunities for ad-libs, a form of silencing in itself, proved problematic for the campaign. Rather than focusing on what Campbell was saying, the media critiqued her delivery.

As Campbell recorded in her memoir, *Time and Chance*, by the third week of the campaign, it had become clear that the town-hall-meeting approach to interacting with the public was not resonating with the media, so she agreed to go "on the offensive against the Liberal platform" (1996, 365). The campaign team's decision to abandon the "doing politics differently" strategy in favour of a traditional approach featuring direct and fiery criticisms of opponents' policy positions was perceived as a direct reversal of Campbell's determination to model a different, less combative style of political discourse. Journalists saw it as phoney, purely strategic, and desperate. Campbell was accused of "hurling attacks in all directions," "desperately railing against the Liberals," and "flailing across the country in a cloud of angry impotence."[65] Assessed by one columnist as "obviously bright, articulate and impressive with people in small groups," Campbell was judged to be constantly "faltering" and "stumbling" in speeches to large audiences and in conversations with the press.[66] In short, when her attempts to change the discursive rules of the game failed, Campbell's decision to revert to the traditional script for electoral competition was seen as counterfeit and treated with disdain.

Discussion: Gender, Speech, and Authenticity

A clear pattern of critique emerged during the PC leadership contest and intensified during the 1993 election campaign. Attempting to model a "new style" of political engagement, Campbell avoided the barn-burner style of campaign speech replete with attacks on political opponents, opting for more measured articulations of her views on a number of issues. This rhetorical style fell flat. Campbell was chastised for "carefully reading a prepared text" in an "uninspiring" and "wooden" manner that at best was characterized as "too rehearsed"[67] and at worst as "preaching," "lecturing," or "scolding."[68] Her attempts at "manly" speech (detached, analytical, rational, organized) were judged to be boring and unconvincing. Yet Campbell was equally criticized for unrehearsed speech, described as "tripping over her tongue in ad-lib situations," taking a "shot from the lip," and making "disastrous statements."[69] When Campbell spoke spontaneously and extemporaneously, she was considered too candid and outspoken, and her words and mannerisms were described as unrestrained, impolitic, and extremely harmful to her political ambitions and the success of her political party. Moreover, her off-the-cuff comments and ad-libs were interpreted as evidence of an impulsive and irrational rhetorical style, one that could not be contained by (male) handlers. Based on Jamieson's (1995) account of the silence/shame double bind, Campbell's "ad-lib" speech acts were read and described as "womanly" (personal, excessive, unrestrained, disorganized) and improper because they did not accord with the (unspoken) rules of political speech. As Campbell's experience demonstrates, "Women's public rhetoric is likely to be fractured by competing, often contradictory, norms and expectations" (Shaw 2011, 277).

Kim Campbell's alleged inability to speak effectively in public was reinforced over and over by news coverage of the leadership and election campaigns. To some extent, the criticism reflected news values and the dominance of the game frame, which demand conflict, controversy, and bombast. Detailed narrations of facts and figures are anathema to a press corps searching for drama and excitement. As a result, Campbell's ad-libs became the spectacle, and reporters turned their laser focus on "candid Kim time"[70] – moments when the candidate went off script or off message. As one newspaper writer observed during the election campaign, the media would "sift reams of tape and notes to pick out the 'potentially controversial' … quote of the day."[71] Even when Campbell responded to media critiques by dropping the interactive, town-hall style of campaigning in favour of a more traditional, scripted approach featuring adversarial stump speeches attacking the Liberals, who were leading in the polls, her speaking style was panned by the press. Despite complying with the game frame for election coverage, these attempts to respond to media criticism were seen as mere tactics and not as an authentic mode of communication.

Ostensibly, the sensational story of "how Campbell self-destructed," as one headline phrased it, was a tale of ill-timed and maladroit comments. While journalists pounced on Campbell's statements, their criticism was more attuned to how she spoke than to what she actually said. Campbell's public speech acts were judged to be inappropriately personal,[72] excessively loquacious,[73] "long-winded,"[74] and even ill tempered and rude.[75] Lexical choices such as "sharp-tongued," "lecturing," "hectoring," "strident," and "volatile"[76] focused attention on the manner of speech and expressed unease and anxiety about the speaker. Characterizations of Campbell's utterances as "silly," "glib," and "impulsive"[77] trivialized her performance of leadership through public speech. These assessments suggested that she lacked oratorical power. On the other hand, the PC leader's words were described as both powerful and profoundly destructive "verbal bombshells"[78] that exploded her party's chances of electoral success. This pattern of condemnation reveals the scepticism with which Campbell's rise to the prime minister's post was greeted. Narrations of her public speech illustrate how a woman's quest for power may be challenged and contained through mediated discourses about political leadership.

Julia Gillard and the Gender Wars

"The PM's parliamentary speech may have moved the political battleground on to the turf of the gender wars."[79]

"Gillard started a gender war and has used her sex to belittle Tony Abbott and other critics."[80]

Gillard's "government is reduced to a soap opera with a Prime Minister invoking a gender war sure to diminish Labor and cast more doubt on her judgment."[81]

On October 9, 2012, Prime Minister Julia Gillard delivered a powerful, fifteen-minute speech to the Australian House of Representatives, castigating Opposition leader Tony Abbott for sexist and misogynist statements and behaviours, several of which had been directed at Gillard herself. The Misogyny Speech, as it has been labelled, went viral. "Even as it was being delivered, Twitter lit up. Soon the blogosphere was aglow."[82] Indeed, a YouTube clip of the prime minister's presentation in its entirety quickly gained over a million hits.[83] While her performance won praise from commentators in other parts of the world (Joseph 2015, 256; Lester 2012; Wright and Holland 2014, 455),[84] the Australian press gallery widely and vociferously condemned Gillard for "playing the gender card" and inciting "a gender war."[85] Subsequent public speech acts were similarly characterized.

As shown in chapter 6, war metaphors are ubiquitous in mediated political discourses; however, the metaphor of the gender war rarely appears in news coverage of politics. Legal restrictions on women's reproductive rights have been said to constitute a "war on women" (Faludi 1991; Melich 1996), but gender itself is not typically represented as a field of engagement. The "war on women" metaphor casts women's bodies as the terrain on which strategic policy or partisan battles are fought. In this formulation, women are objects whose bodies are governed by politics, not the agents of political decision-making. In contrast, the Australian "gender wars" presented gender as the site of contestation and cast a powerful woman politician as the instrument of political "warfare." Julia Gillard's case represents a singular example of a government leader accused by pundits and opponents of deliberately initiating a series of destructive debates on the discursive battlefield of gender politics.

Because the gender card and gender war metaphors appeared outside of the data collection points for this study, I drew the sample of texts used in this particular analysis by using the terms *gender card* and *gender wars* and *Gillard* or *prime minister* to search three Australian newspapers throughout Gillard's term as prime minister, from June 23, 2010, when she assumed office, until June 26, 2013, when she was defeated in a leadership vote.[86] The gender war metaphor appeared almost twice as frequently (ninety-two times) as the playing-the-gender-card metaphor (fifty-two uses). The "gender war" and "gender wars"[87] phrases were used in fifty-nine news articles printed over an eight-and-a-half-month period (September 15, 2012, to June 25, 2013) and featured in twelve headlines. All but four of the articles containing the gender war metaphor were published after Gillard had delivered her so-called sexism and misogyny speech in Parliament on October 9, 2012. The trope of the gender wars continued to circulate well after the speech, appearing in news stories until Gillard's removal from office.

The Political Context of the Australian "Gender Wars"

My goal in this section is not to dissect the accuracy or validity of the media coverage, or to "damask the 'untruth' of political metaphors" (Mottier 2008, 191), but rather to analyse the meanings revealed by the allegorical constructions of Gillard's speeches as a series of destructive gender wars. Challenges to Gillard's leadership formed a crucial backdrop to the mobilization of the gender war(s) metaphor as critics from the ideological right, including the Coalition parties comprising the Official Opposition and Coalition-friendly media outlets, derided her character in ways that often directly referenced her gender. Gillard's political ambition was characterized as unseemly, and unduly brutal, for a woman (Hall and Donaghue 2013, 638). The new prime minister's approach to governing was disparaged, with popular radio commentator Alan Jones accusing Gillard and other powerful Australian women of "destroying the joint" (Sawer 2013, 113). Most disturbingly, Gillard was confronted with sexist and hateful attacks from anonymous critics, as a plethora of pornographic and degrading images of her appeared on websites, email, and social media (see Johnson 2015, 304–5; Summers 2012, 2013).

Initially, Gillard chose to say nothing about these attacks, nor did she discuss sexist comments by Opposition leader Tony Abbott.[88] Despite her silence, the public shaming continued unabated, especially online and on talk radio. As Gillard relayed in her memoir, it "actually worsened" (Gillard 2014, 113). While the Australian feminist movement protested these characterizations of Gillard (Joseph 2015; McLean and Maalsen 2013; Sawer 2013), the news media were largely silent about the sexism directed at her, even when Opposition leader Tony Abbott was directly implicated. For instance, while delivering a speech to carbon-tax protesters, Abbott stood in front of a banner reading "JULIAR[89] ... BOB BROWNS bitch." A newspaper account of this incident reported that protest signs also likened Gillard to a witch by exclaiming, "Ditch the witch."[90] Both labels are hostile to women, and they strongly evoke "the myth of women's power as unnatural and threatening" (Anderson and Sheeler 2005, 29). As these examples illustrate, gender had become integral to public discourses about Gillard well before she delivered her sexism and misogyny speech.[91] The gender war metaphor emerged before her parliamentary speech, but the majority of its usages were published in reaction to it. As one article put it, the sexism and misogyny speech "did not launch the gender war but rather signaled its zenith."[92] So it was clearly a pivotal event, key to understanding the discursive context in which the gender war(s) metaphor was produced, framed, and consumed by news audiences.

In a formal sense, Gillard's speech served as a rebuttal to Opposition leader Tony Abbott's motion to censure the Speaker of the House, Peter Slipper.[93] After the media leaked controversial text messages written by Slipper, one of which made crude references to female genitalia,[94] Abbott rose in the House to demand Slipper's resignation from the Speaker's position. He argued that by refusing to call for Slipper's removal, Gillard was acting hypocritically because she was quick to decry sexism and misogyny except when it came to the actions of one of her own supporters (McLean and Maalsen 2013, 250). In reply, Gillard accused Abbott of hypocrisy for decrying sexist and misogynist attitudes in Parliament, while himself regularly expressing such attitudes in public.[95] Opening with the words "I will not be lectured about sexism and misogyny by this man. I will not," she gave several examples of statements by Abbott indicating that he held essentialist views about gender roles and viewed women's lack of power as socially appropriate.[96] Gillard's address also referenced Abbott's admonition that the prime minister should "make an honest woman of herself," and it drew attention to his implied endorsement of those who called her a "witch" or "bitch" in public protests.[97]

The Press, the PM, and the Gender Wars

The gender war metaphor first appeared in newspaper coverage almost a month before Gillard's speech, in response to the Labor Party's critiques of opposition leader Tony Abbott's views on women. Four articles published in the *Australian* described Labor's strategy as a "concerted, inflammatory and calculated gender war campaign" in the form of a "frontal assault" on Abbott's character.[98] This "battle" was said to target him by "encouraging the view that Abbott is a misogynist."[99] As one headline put it, "Demonization of Abbott is Labor's new game plan."[100] The *Australian*'s political commentators alleged that the "attacks" were being carried out by Labor's senior cabinet ministers, mostly women, and trivialized them with the label "handbag hit-squad."[101] Labor's strategy was characterized as "offensive and false,"[102] "farcical," and "inflammatory."[103] One columnist maintained that the "war" on Abbott defied the common sense of the Australian public.[104] In short, Labor was charged with launching an unprovoked and unwarranted attack on Abbott to provide a diversion from the Labor government's inability to gain traction in the polls. By deriding Gillard and Labor for using gender as an instrument of political "warfare," newspaper columnists began the process of positioning gender inequality issues as an inappropriate subject of political contestation.

Gillard's October 9, 2012, parliamentary speech on sexism and misogyny was widely characterized by the press as a deliberate and calculated move designed to persist with, and indeed to intensify, Labor's rhetorical "strike" on Abbott. According to the *Australian*, the "Prime Minister continued her gender war against Tony Abbott."[105] The emotive and intense lexicon of warfare worked to frame Gillard's words as an extreme and unusual form of aggression against a political opponent. Newspaper coverage was replete with violent words and phrases, as Gillard's speech was labelled "vicious," "virulent," an "explosive attack," a "tirade," a "vitriolic" and "shrill attack," a "sexism crusade," a "gender salvo," and a "war on misogyny."[106] With few exceptions, reporters and columnists alike expressed indignation that the prime minister would persecute her political opponent in this manner. The speech was termed an "attempt to destroy Abbott instead of concentrating on governing."[107] Once again, allegations of disingenuousness and hypocrisy came into play. As one article claimed, the "nation's first female Prime Minister deliberately escalated the so-called gender war in order to defend a discredited Speaker."[108]

The trope of the unjust war dominated the coverage. Gillard's criticisms of Abbott for his sexist statements and views were judged "unfounded,"[109] "implausible," and "farcical,"[110] a "barrage of confected outrage"[111] designed to stoke a dangerous and "artificial gender war."[112] In these characterizations of Gillard's speech as an unwarranted declaration of war against Abbott, gender was constituted as a weapon of combat and as a form of defensive armour. Deputy Opposition leader Julie Bishop was quoted as saying, "The PM uses gender as a *shield* against criticism and she's using these vile claims of sexism and misogyny as a *sword* against her critics."[113] Comments such as "Girls, girls, girls. Put down your gender guns,"[114] "a female PM recklessly and ruthlessly uses gender as a weapon,"[115] and "Gillard started a gender war and has used her sex to belittle Tony Abbott and other critics"[116] cast gender as an instrument of political aggression. Raising the issue of gender was itself deemed to be a cynical and desperate defensive manoeuvre designed to protect the prime minister from what news commentators saw as appropriate censure from political opponents.[117]

In the speech, Gillard drew attention to some of the sexist and negative evaluations of her integrity and character. Yet only one column suggested that Gillard's words were a reaction not merely to Abbott's charge that she was condoning sexism by defending Slipper but also to the hurtful and often pornographic representations she herself had endured in silence over the years. In the *Age*'s Katharine Murphy's view, the prime minister's speech was spontaneous, "a blow-up of pure frustration: volcanic and howling in intensity because *the prelude to the explosion is a long period of not saying*. What woman can't relate to that? We've all been there, not saying, broiling about *the injustice of not saying*."[118] But this interpretation was anomalous. That Gillard had been the subject of sexist commentary from political opponents, including Abbott, was rarely acknowledged in the articles invoking the gender war metaphor.[119] Moreover, when the sexism directed at Gillard was mentioned, she herself was censured for raising the issue. The perpetrators of sexist and sexually explicit commentary against Gillard were, according to one columnist, merely "'misogynists and cranks' who anonymously libeled and reviled the Prime Minister online."[120] In other words, this sort of sexism could not be taken seriously because it was taking place in the marginal and anonymous spaces of unofficial political discourses. Another news commentator conceded that "some of the ire directed at Gillard has been sexist, even offensively so. Yet it has been *her choice* to shift this unseemly fringe of political life to centre stage."[121] According to this narrative, by refusing to remain silent about sexism, Gillard chose to move an unpalatable subject from places where it was allegedly private and/or harmless into public sites of mainstream political discourse, where it did not belong.

The prime minister's willingness to invoke her own gendered social location was also read as being profoundly damaging to women, the feminist cause, and political dialogue more generally.[122] Gillard's speech was characterized as "an affront to women who *have* suffered harm from sexism and misogyny."[123] Also, it was seen to be anti-feminist: by "making deliberately empty allegations of misogyny against Tony Abbott, the gender-card-waving PM rates poorly as a feminist role model."[124] The press asserted that Gillard's words and actions demeaned political debate and deflected attention from more important topics. For instance, the "gender wars have poisoned the political discourse and polarized debate," thus "must be set aside if Julia Gillard is to govern in the national interest."[125] As another wrote, the "quality of the political debate has become risible. Instead of discussing the government's priority areas or debating a serious economic reform agenda, we are reduced to gender wars."[126] These assessments characterized discussions about gender inequality and sexism as inherently polarizing and destructive, as opposed to arguments about other contentious political issues, which, by implication, made valid contributions to public debates.

The metaphor continued to circulate in press coverage for eight months after Gillard's parliamentary speech, and it was reinvigorated in June 2013 in response to two events. The first was the prime minister's presentation to a Labor Party fundraising group called Women for Gillard. According to media accounts, Gillard said that a government dominated by "men in blue ties" would banish women from the centre of political decision-making and make abortion "the political plaything of men who think they know better."[127] The day after this speech was delivered, the government released information about a satirical menu created for a Coalition fundraiser, which "included a dish described as 'Julia Gillard Kentucky Fried Quail – Small Breasts, Huge Thighs & a Big Red Box.'"[128] Labor argued that the menu illustrated the pattern of sexism directed at Gillard by political opponents.[129] These two events were linked in media commentary and described as "Julia Gillard's return to the gender trenches."[130] She was alleged to have "reignited the gender wars."[131] Dramatic headlines such as "PM fires abortion salvo in gender war" illustrated the extent to which the metaphor had structured the press coverage of Gillard's statements in the waning days of her political career.[132]

With the notable exception of Anne Summers's column, titled "It's Gillard's right to fight back,"[133] news reports once again strongly rebuked the prime minister for discussing sexism in public life. Gillard's "men in blue ties" speech was deemed a "cynical ploy"[134] and an "unfounded attack on blue ties as symbolic of institutionalized sexism."[135] An editorial titled "Julia Gillard's clumsy and manipulative gender wars" cast the speech to Parliament as "an act of desperation that ill-judged its intended audience."[136] Invocations of the metaphor once again positioned gender as a site of political struggle, with Gillard attacking men and sexism in an effort to win support, especially from women, in a last-ditch effort to salvage her political career in the face of a mounting leadership challenge from Kevin Rudd, the man she had deposed just three years earlier. Journalists quickly and unequivocally pronounced the campaign an abject failure, with headlines like "Gender war misfires for PM"[137] and assertions that "Julia Gillard's retreat to the gender trenches backfired savagely."[138] The trope of the failed war percolated through these texts, prefiguring the events to come. Less than two weeks later, Rudd and his supporters toppled Gillard from the Labor Party leadership and the prime minister's post.

Discussion: Metaphor as a Strategy of Containment

By associating the source domain of the metaphor with a plethora of battle words and violent images, the gender wars metaphor positioned gender as a weapon of war and Gillard as the aggressor. Words such as "battles," "fights," "campaigns," "crusades," "strikes," "offensives," "bunkers," "trenches," and "front lines" peppered the news coverage, and Gillard and members of her government were said to "take up arms," "attack," "launch salvos," "erupt firestorms," "deploy hit-teams," and even "slay opponents." When used in concert with the gender war construct, adjectives such as "artificial," "phony," "farcical," "ridiculous," "inappropriate," "desperate," "clumsy," "manipulative," and "disastrous" represented gender as an inauthentic and fundamentally inappropriate site of political struggle. The widespread, indeed ubiquitous, use of combat metaphors to describe political behaviour conveys approval for certain political tactics and performances. Underlying these metaphors is the understanding that there are norms guiding "just" political warfare. Gillard's speeches drawing attention to sexism were metaphorically constructed as *unjust* – a bizarre twist of logic.

These lexical choices are not, in and of themselves, surprising. After all, war metaphors are so prevalent in mediated representations of politics that the literal meaning of the metaphor – politics is conflict – has become completely conventionalized (Charteris-Black 2011, 3). War metaphors are regularly used to characterize a wide range of "civilian social practices as militarized spaces," signalling "the entry of war mentality into the realm of the general 'commonsense'" (Lazar 2009, 209). Because the language of combat and belligerence is regularized in media discourses about politics, political actors are not blamed for planning, strategizing, or enacting rhetorical violence. The news media simply take for granted that political leaders will figuratively fight each other to the death on the political battlefield, as described in chapter 6. This form of verbal aggression is typically lauded as evidence of power, strength, and the will to succeed (Charteris-Black 2011, 3).

Despite the fact that mediated military metaphors are regularly used to celebrate ruthlessness and fearlessness in political competitions, Gillard's rhetorical "warfare" was denounced. The Australian press corps vociferously and almost universally disparaged her reproach to Abbott for his sexist attitudes, and it derided her attempt to discuss the gender bias she had experienced in her role as the most powerful political actor in Australia. In fact, the gender war metaphor was used to characterize Gillard and her party as the aggressors and Abbott and other critics of the government as the innocent victims of Labor's ongoing and increasingly virulent "attacks." Moreover, Gillard's intentions were represented as deceptive, cynical, and hypocritical, her actions judged to be dangerous, ruthless, vicious, and vitriolic. Hyperbolic terms such as "inflammatory," "destructive," "offensive," "poisonous," and "polarizing" punctuated the deleterious impact of the so-called gender wars. Gillard's "wars" were said to directly and unfairly wound political opponents and cause collateral damage to political discourse and to society as a whole. By labelling her and her party's actions as a series of injurious gender wars, the media rendered contestations of sexism and gender inequality a destructive and dishonourable approach to political engagement.

In addition to delegitimizing Gillard by invoking the trope of the unruly woman (Anderson and Sheeler 2005, the allegory of the gender war both revealed and reinforced inequitable power relations. Metaphors "hide relations of power and dominance" (Falk 2013, 204) by asserting particular positions and arguments, while masking or delegitimizing others. By scripting the narrative of "Julia, the Feminist Warrior, slaying misogynists whenever they cross her path"[139] and saying that she was "exploiting her gender as a political weapon,[140] news reports maintained that Gillard's position as prime minister, coupled with her gender, allowed her to wage an unfair war against her opponent. Obscured in this interpretation was the gender-based unfairness that she had experienced as prime minister. Also elided was Abbott's role in the "battle" over sexism and misogyny (Johnson 2015, 299–300). Most of the coverage ignored his complicity, and the few articles acknowledging his sexist characterizations of Gillard declared the prime minister out of line for charging her opponent with sexism and especially for using the word "misogynist." The chauvinistic and at times overtly hostile comments that Abbott directed towards Gillard were thus occluded by the outrage directed at Gillard for raising the issue.

The gender war metaphor performed a similar kind of ideological work by containing and constraining any discussion of sexism and gender inequality in Australian political life. As Falk (2013, 194) observes, metaphors "can help society to highlight what it wants to believe and avoid what it does not wish to face." That Gillard was rebuked for refusing to stay silent about sexism, and blamed for bringing the issue to the attention of the public, illustrates this point. As one commentator came right out and said, society will condemn those who raise issues of sexism. "On race and gender – we are aware of injustice but the accusatory finger is unwelcome."[141] News accounts represented Gillard's challenge to the gender order as an unjust form of political contestation, thus precluding the opportunity to examine gendered power relations and political inequality as real problems in the political environment.

Metaphors are powerful instruments of discourse because they tap into commonly held understandings about society and politics. In fact, "One of the main rhetorical purposes of metaphor is to contribute to developing political myths" (Charteris-Black 2011, 38). Gillard's decision to speak out about the sexism she had encountered as prime minister violated deeply held and highly valued myths about Australian society – in particular, the myth of the "fair go." In Australian culture, the perception that everyone who works hard enough will have an equal chance to succeed is widely held and frequently invoked in political party and government documents (see Berry 2017). This value was publicly challenged when Gillard, speaking from her own experience, exposed unfair treatment and inequality. Very simply, Australia's top politician pointed out that she was not having a "fair go." As Johnson (2015, 310) observes, "It is an immensely powerful moment to have a prime minister stand up and say she had been discriminated against." The gender war metaphor worked to undermine this critique and re-establish the myths of equal opportunity and fair play. In fact, one columnist expressed incredulity in response to the prime minister's examples of sexism. "Gillard's career has not suffered because of her sex and it's demeaning to pretend it has."[142] The fact that a woman had risen to the premiership was, in and of itself, seen as supporting the myth that gender equality guaranteed every Australian's chance at a fair go.

Conclusions

This chapter has shown how powerful speakers at "high performance" events such as election campaigns and parliamentary speeches are evaluated for their "real and metaphorical identities ... strategies and goals" (Coupland 2007, 157). These evaluations reflect the speaking rules of the institution, organization, or process within which speech takes place (Baxter 2010, 10; Shaw 2006, 82). When performed by women, certain topics and speaking mannerisms are judged to violate the norms governing political speech. Ostensibly, Kim Campbell was rebuked for ill-advised and intemperate comments, but the most virulent forms of denunciation focused on *how* she spoke. Julia Gillard, on the other hand, was reprimanded for what she said. By speaking from her position as prime minister and drawing attention to the sexism she had endured while serving in that office, she challenged socially agreed-upon topics of discursive silence. Both examples reflect gendered norms of political discourse.

In Canada, at a time when women political leaders were rare and the press and public were used to men speaking in a certain way, Campbell prompted consternation the moment she opened her mouth. She could not "seem to talk right" (Bashevkin 2009, 77). Scripted speech and off-the-cuff remarks alike were met with criticism and, sometimes, outright condemnation, reflecting unease with Campbell's quest for power. Extemporaneous comments were deemed to be controversial and damaging, while prepared remarks were judged as inauthentic and insufficiently bombastic to enliven the electorate. Certainly, campaign strategies and news values shaped the media's reaction to Campbell, and some of the criticism was sparked by inopportune comments, but gender played a role. As Sheeler and Anderson (2014, 482) note, female pioneers are "regarded with skepticism – they are new, untested, and can easily be marginalized." I have argued that Canada's first woman prime minister's insistence on speaking politics "differently" challenged the discursive rules of the political game. As a result, Campbell's speech acts were interpreted as gendered performances and judged accordingly.

Twenty years later, the Australian press, particularly the pro-Coalition newspaper, the *Australian*, used the gender war metaphor to condemn that nation's first woman prime minister for employing gender as both a subject and an apparatus of political contestation. The metaphor suggested that Gillard's parliamentary and public speeches on the subject of sexism violated deeply held cultural norms about appropriate behaviour on the so-called political battlefield. Through the invocation of the metaphor, Gillard was represented as aggressively and irrationally attacking a political opponent, in the process inflicting collateral damage on women, the feminist cause, and the national interest. By fashioning speeches about gender inequality and sexism as acts of extreme political violence, and locating Gillard's speech acts outside the boundaries of legitimate political discourses, the gender war(s) metaphor fostered a particular narrative about political strategies and the appropriate rules of engagement for political debate.

In both instances, the media reaction to a woman prime minister's public speeches served to silence and contain certain forms of speech. In Australia, the metaphorical construct of the gender-based war rendered Gillard discursively powerless. The gender war metaphor subtracted gendered power relations from normative understandings of the political. By disciplining Gillard for challenging important national myths and violating the unspoken norms of "just" political combat, the gender war narrative precluded discussions about gender bias and discrimination against women. Campbell's experience shows that candid, frank, passionate, seemingly unrestrained modes of speaking by women were regarded as inappropriate in the formal political sphere. Campbell was, in effect, silenced for being herself. Her "unusual style"[143] was continuously scrutinized and found wanting. Yet when she adopted the usual strategies, of restrained and analytical speech, or played to the game frame for election coverage with speeches attacking her opponent, she was criticized for *not* being herself. By the mid-way point of the election campaign, there seemed to be no approach to political speech that Campbell could adopt without being shamed or judged inauthentic. As Bourdieu (1991, 82) observes, "silence or hyper-controlled language" is required for some speakers, while others are granted the "liberties of a language that is securely established."

It is possible that a woman political leader could, more than twenty years after Kim Campbell was castigated for her forms of speech, address the media and the public in a forthright, emotionally honest, and animated fashion without being shamed. Campbell's form of candour is certainly more welcomed today than it was in 1993. The former prime minister's twenty thousand enthusiastic Twitter followers "appreciate her unrestrained, straight-talking style" and rather ribald wit (McKnight 2017). After all, humour and frankness are regarded as evidence of emotional accessibility. Further, the intimization of politics invites deeply personal disclosures, so a politician willing to share details of her love life may no longer disconcert the press. Women leaders still tread carefully on this rhetorical territory, for good reason, as revealed in chapter 4 (Sheeler and Anderson 2014, 485–6). More case studies are needed to determine whether an equally unrestrained and loquacious woman, speaking from a position of power and relative privilege, would be so sternly censured today.

Chapter Eight

Conclusion: Dealing (with) the Gender Card

In her final speech as Australia's prime minister, Julia Gillard sounded a note of optimism for the women who will, one day, follow in her footsteps. "What I am absolutely confident of is it will be easier for the next woman, and the woman after that, and the woman after that."[1] Having read this book, you might well be sceptical. Gillard's memoir, *My Story*, recognizes an intense media focus on her gender throughout her tenure as leader (Gillard 2014). And, as I have shown, Gillard's intimate relationship with partner Tim Mathieson was put under the media microscope, her body profiled in an invasive and at times pornographic manner, and her gender identity mobilized against her as a form of demonization. When Gillard finally spoke out about the gender discrimination she had encountered during her term as prime minister, she was discursively silenced and condemned for launching a destructive "gender war."

Is there any evidence to support Australia's first woman prime minister's bold assertion that the nation's next woman prime minister would face less daunting challenges? I think so, for two reasons. First, as Gillard acknowledged in her resignation speech, gender does not explain everything about the reactions to her leadership by the press, opponents, and the public. Her situation was extraordinary in many respects and unlikely to be repeated. Timing was not on her side as her widely anticipated rise to the top job required toppling a first-term prime minister, Kevin Rudd, who had been popular in the electorate and with the press. Worse, Rudd refused to back down, mounting numerous subterranean attempts to undermine Gillard's leadership, aided and abetted by journalists who so delighted in the spectacle created by internal party dissent they reported over 150 claims that a challenge was imminent before Rudd finally made his move (Curtin 2015, 194). Leading a minority government presented enough difficulties without the constant sniping from the Rudd camp and anti-woman rhetoric from Opposition leader Tony Abbott (Johnson 2015). Finally, many critics thought that the prime minister was unable to effectively articulate the reasons why she had challenged Rudd in the first place, persuade voters of the efficacy of her government's reform agenda, or win much media traction (or praise) for its legislative successes (Aulich 2014, 6). That Gillard survived for three years despite being "stalked" by her predecessor, labelled a liar, assessed as the worst prime minister in history, and accused of corruption is remarkable (Walsh 2013). That she was so resilient, and departed from office with such dignity, is equally noteworthy. Although she and the nation were scarred by the spectacle of the "gender wars," these news-mediated contestations rendered gender a point of conversation and reflection (see Curtin 2015; Goldsworthy 2013; Rogers-Healey 2013; Summers 2013). It will no doubt be easier for the next woman because many of the gendered discursive landmines have been unearthed and some of them exploded during Gillard's tenure as the nation's first woman prime minister.

Second, the findings of this study provide some basis for optimism. *Ms. Prime Minister* has expanded the gendered mediation thesis by acknowledging and observing the disruptive potential of news reporting about political leaders. As I have shown, women who perform the role of party and government leader unsettle the established gender order simply by occupying elite political spaces and enacting governmental authority. Their very presence and performances transgress gender binaries and expose putatively "masculine" and "feminine" identities as social constructs. Gendered mediation can work to celebrate the sight of woman as leader, highlight women's persistent under-representation in political office, challenge sexist assumptions, and disrupt the public man/private woman binary. However, overstating the prevalence and subversive potential of these discursive impositions is both inaccurate and unwise. After all, I offer abundant evidence that women leaders are viewed through the lens of their gendered identities, evaluated as ineffective and inauthentic *because* they are women. For women seeking top political leadership roles, news-mediated normalization remains elusive, as was evident in reporting about Hillary Clinton's 2016 presidential campaign.[2]

This concluding chapter builds on the evidence presented in chapters 2 to 7, which revealed how culturally and politically constructed understandings about gender and political leadership were applied to Campbell, Shipley, Clark, and Gillard. Here I employ the concept of *mediated legitimacy* as a framework for analysing media depictions and evaluations of each of the four women prime ministers. Political actors enjoy mediated legitimacy when, regardless of their identities, news coverage accepts the validity of their participation in the political realm. After assessing the extent to which news representations conveyed political legitimacy for Campbell, Shipley, Clark, and Gillard, I turn to the practical implications of their experiences, offering a gendered mediation primer designed to inform the gender strategies of aspiring women prime ministers and the techniques used by journalists to reflect on the "gender factor." The final section of this concluding chapter highlights my theoretical and empirical contributions to the gendered mediation literature and offers a number of suggestions for further research.

Women Prime Ministers and Mediated Legitimacy

Enli (2015) coined the term "mediated authenticity" to capture the desire among those who perform, produce, and consume media products to achieve, or experience, an authentic representation – one that seems real. For politicians, authenticity is crucial to electoral success. Their identities and appeals cannot be perceived as fake, the product of mere gloss and spin; instead, communication must be accepted as a projection of the "real self" of the political actor who is trying to win support from the public. Clinton's bid for the US presidency in 2016 offers a vivid example of mediated inauthenticity. "She knows what it's like to be the subject of the stereotype that a powerful woman cannot be likeable," wrote Julia Gillard in a column for the *New York Times*.[3] Indeed, the spectre of unlikeability plagued Clinton throughout her campaign, typified by a *Washington Post* article declaring her "more wooden, distant and disconnected than ever before."[4] But authenticity is not enough for political leadership. Candidates need to project both authenticity *and* legitimacy – a performance of leadership that is considered by observers to be convincing, appropriate, authoritative, competent, trustworthy, and reliable.

The validity of a politician's claim to power should not be questioned on the basis of gender, race, class, physical ability, or sexual orientation. However, as I have shown throughout this volume, mediated legitimacy is more likely to be conferred upon politicians who conform to the rules of the political game, embody the dominant cultural values of the nation, and mirror the demographics of the archetypal politician. News content reflects these norms by applying the socially and discursively constituted gender regulations policing the boundaries between the public and the private spheres. Accordingly, it is difficult for women to achieve mediated legitimacy in political roles, especially when their performance is interpreted through the lens of their gender. Most men are assumed to be rightful players of the political game, seen as possessing the qualities and attributes essential to effective political leadership. It is a greater challenge for women leaders to be accepted as credible and convincing occupants of elite political roles, as demonstrated by the experiences of Campbell, Shipley, Clark, and Gillard. Yet women who govern for extended periods of time command respect and commendation. News and entertainment media coverage of Angela Merkel regularly portrays the long-serving German chancellor as an "active, competent and powerful individual," for example (Lünenborg and Maier 2015, 188). Below, I explore the extent to which media representations of the four women prime ministers of Australia, Canada, and New Zealand evaluated them as rightfully and persuasively exercised political leadership. Based on my observation that greater electoral success is associated with a higher level of mediated legitimacy, I order the prime ministers based on their longevity in the role, beginning with Campbell, who had the shortest term in office, before turning to Shipley, Gillard, and Clark.

Kim Campbell

Kim Campbell should have gained a legitimacy boost from her successful party leadership campaign as she was the clear front-runner in a hotly contested race, with the winner destined to become Canada's new prime minister. Moreover, Campbell was politically experienced, having served in important Cabinet positions; she enjoyed widespread support from party and caucus members; and her well-financed campaign so inspired both party and public that the phenomenon was dubbed "Campbellmania." However, by adopting the fable of the tortoise and the hare as a narrative frame, news storytelling cast doubt on Campbell's capacity to enact party and government leadership roles. Drawing on the moral of the story – the hare's arrogance and overconfidence cost it the race, while the turtle's plodding determination won the day – reporting questioned Campbell's character, motivations, and authenticity. She was assessed as being too ambitious for a woman, too eager for power, too quick to brag, too arrogant and calculating to deserve the job.

Research on public perceptions of political leadership highlights the importance of humbleness and reliability (Miller, Wattenberg, and Malanchuk 1986, 528), so scripting Campbell as the boastful and flighty hare challenged her credibility. By presenting her two divorces and childlessness as evidence of emotional instability, opponents and reporters pitted Campbell's alleged unreliability against the presumed fidelity and steadfastness of her primary opponent, Jean Charest, who pitched himself as a stable, devoted family man, the determined turtle fighting to overcome the capricious hare. However, a few columnists identified the tactic as sexist, and others pointed out the gender-based double standard underpinning the critiques of Campbell. While some of the early coverage praised the lone female contender for her intelligence, fortitude, and frankness, the overall scripting of the leadership story suggested that she did not deserve to win, prevailing only because the Progressive Conservatives thought it was time for a woman as leader.

Campbell did enjoy a brief period of mediated legitimacy thanks largely to the gravitas, power, and authority of the prime minister's role. When she was sworn in, her victory was celebrated as a remarkable achievement and a breakthrough for women. Canada's first woman prime minister enjoyed a brief "honeymoon" phase with the press and public before calling an election that she and her party were destined to lose. That said, from the moment her candidacy was announced until the end of her party's ill-fated election campaign, Campbell's ability to lead was viewed through the prism of her body, her capacity to embody political authority questioned by references to her diminutive stature, "fluffy" blonde hair, and sexual allure. News accounts drew attention to Campbell's body as a visual departure from the culturally inscribed standard of the physically imposing, buttoned-up, conservatively attired political leader. She was depicted as performing a role rather than authentically and legitimately embodying that role, as evidenced by assessments that she did not look the part of a prime minister.

The most damaging form of gendered news coverage, however, was the intense scrutiny, and outright censure, of Campbell's speaking style. Evaluations of her speech as shrill, strident, and hectoring revealed unease with women speaking from a position of power. By judging her campaign speeches and interactions with reporters to be inept, lacking in spontaneity, uninspiring, weak, desperate, unrestrained, excessive, childlike, and angry, the reporting communicated misgivings about Campbell's competence and her capacity to articulate the hopes and dreams of Canadians. Indeed, she was represented as a "loose cannon," constantly "tripping on her lip," and ultimately causing the party's downfall because of her "quick tongue" and unwillingness to follow the advice of handlers. Excessive and ungovernable speech is associated with women, who have historically been condemned for such performances. When Campbell challenged the dominant speaking rules for electoral politics, which demand unswerving loyalty to a heroic and warlike performance, she was cast as being ineffective because of her impulsive rhetorical style. At a time when women journalists were rare,[5] women party leaders were even rarer, and press and public alike were used to men politicians looking, speaking, and acting in a certain way, Campbell prompted consternation and critique. Gendered mediation of her persona and performance contributed to a perceived crisis of legitimacy.

Jenny Shipley

Of the four prime ministers, Jenny Shipley enjoyed the highest level of mediated legitimacy when she entered the party leadership role. Although she deposed a sitting government leader, her move to unseat Jim Bolger was supported by the National Party caucus. Even better for Shipley's reputation, reporters did not cast her as traitorous or villainous, as they did when describing Helen Clark's overthrow of Labour leader Mike Moore four years earlier. Because Shipley's "coup" was called "bloodless" by virtue of its consideration for the feelings and reputation of the man she had overturned, the new prime minister was seen to have integrity, a valued characteristic of political leadership (Miller, Wattenberg, and Malanchuk 1986, 528). Reporting of the swearing-in ceremony was celebratory, heralding Shipley's rise as a historic occasion for women and the nation, and highlighting her political experience and acumen. However, subtle visual gendering was evident in televised accounts, with lingering shots of her husband and children situating New Zealand's first woman prime minister within the traditional, patriarchal family form. Further, gendered mediation of Shipley's tenure in the prime minister's office highlighted the fact that her primary parliamentary opponent was a woman, Helen Clark. Both before and during the 1999 election campaign, "catfight" and "Xena princesses" tropes delegitimized both Shipley and Clark, as did trivializing gender markers ("First Ladies") and lavish attention to hairstyles, wardrobes, and make-up. Yet war metaphors positioned Shipley as strong, determined, and decisive, capable of "crossing swords" with the formidable Labour leader.

Shipley's archetypal family proved both an asset and a liability. On the one hand, it lent a veneer of respectability, which shielded her from the intense and invasive sexualization experienced by Campbell, Clark, and Gillard. On the other hand, because she chose to characterize herself as "Mrs. Shipley" and to foreground her stable nuclear family, the "wife of" motif prevailed. For instance, a television news report about her rise warned that some party members did not "want to be led by a farmer's wife."[6] Then, when Winston Peters, leader of the governing National Party's coalition partner, expressed unhappiness with Shipley taking the reins, tensions were likened to a marital squabble. By recounting the story as a marriage headed for divorce, news coverage cast her as the wronged but dutiful wife, ruled by the whims of her wayward political husband. But Shipley's attempt to strategically contrast her status as a mother with Clark's childlessness during the 1999 election was identified as spin and decried as disingenuous by Clark and a few journalists. Having been deemed the "Iron Lady" of New Zealand politics, praised for her political toughness, and identified as "the only man in Cabinet," Shipley was pronounced inauthentic when she wanted to project the image of a caring, smiling "mother of the nation." As phrases such as "*perfumed* bulldozer" and "*female* gladiator" illustrated, depictions of her character and political style were ripe with discursive contradictions, both reinforcing and questioning the artificial separation of family and political life, and the association of aggression, independence, and toughness with men and masculinity.

Julia Gillard

News coverage of Julia Gillard's rise both verified and undermined her claim to the prime minister's post. Gillard challenged a first-term prime minister, unseating Kevin Rudd just months before an election was due to be called because of concerns within the party that Labor would not be re-elected under his leadership. Called the "Gillard revolution" by the press and a "political execution" by the Opposition leader, the "coup" stunned the nation. Gillard escaped initial condemnation because she was seen as the "puppet" of factions within the Labor

Party who wanted Rudd gone, and Rudd was pronounced the author of his political misfortune. Australians celebrated the swearing-in of their first woman prime minister with considerable fanfare, and the national broadcaster presented Gillard as a heroic figure who "marched to glory." Although the coronation motif lent a veneer of legitimacy to the "coup," it quickly wore off as events unfolded and party members expressed concerns about the power of internal factions and the circumstances of Gillard's rise. The spectre of Rudd haunted Gillard throughout her tenure in the prime minister's office, injuring her election campaign with damaging leaks, exposing dissent within the party, and casting a looming shadow over her leadership.

Gillard's gender was often central to the story, underscoring a lack of confidence in her abilities. Of the four women, she was the most intensely gendered in reporting about her leadership ascendance, with the highest level of gender marking and attention to physical appearance, marital situation, and childlessness. Deemed the "first unmarried PM," described as "deliberately barren," questioned about her intimate partner's sexual identity, mocked and maligned for this relationship, called a "bitch" and a "liar" by opponents, and intensely sexualized and vilified in online and social media, Gillard did in fact experience sexism and misogyny. Political opponents, some of whom were operating within her own party, constantly questioned her character and integrity, undermining her legitimacy. At the same time, Gillard was praised in news stories for her strength, intelligence, and competence, qualities considered essential for a persuasive enactment of political leadership (Miller, Wattenberg, and Malanchuk 1986, 528). Represented as convincingly combative during the election campaign, called a "smart, savvy fighter," Gillard's capacity to do electoral battle was sporadically overtly gendered with phrases such as "female political killing machine" and "perfumed political steamroller." Romance metaphors were rare in media renditions of electoral politics in Australia, so Gillard's ability to cultivate inter-party relationships, forge alliances, and inspire emotional allegiance from voters was not affirmed with the language of love.

Finally, the invocation of the gender card and gender war(s) metaphors in the last eight months of her tenure as prime minister severely damaged Gillard's reputation. The allegory of the gender wars worked to condemn and silence her for speaking in Parliament about the sexism and misogyny that had been directed at her by her political opponents. Political opponents and media commentators mobilized the "gender card" label to characterize her speech as a desperate political move designed to deflect attention from her government's shortcomings. By so publicly and passionately challenging the deeply held cultural myth of the "fair go," Gillard exposed hidden relations of power and dominance. That media coverage worked so hard to recuperate the myth of equal opportunity and contain the perceived damage caused to the nation's reputation reveals how dangerous it was for a woman to break the speaking rules for political discourse. There is no more profoundly damaging form of mediated illegitimacy than to be charged, as Gillard was, with dishonourable and destructive conduct. When accused of unfairly mobilizing her gender as a weapon of political warfare, Gillard was delegitimized for being a woman.

Helen Clark

At the end of her tenure as prime minister, Helen Clark was praised fulsomely in news accounts, described as New Zealand's "most popular Prime Minister, ever,"[7] a "leader of the highest intellect and international credentials," and "the strongest Prime Minister with the most disciplined team for a generation."[8] Amid the praise, however, were reminders of the gendered forms of mediation that Clark had encountered throughout her fifteen years as Labour leader. For instance, one writer singled out her childlessness with this observation: "Having spent nine years at the top of a political career she had single-mindedly chosen for herself at the expense of other pursuits, including raising children."[9] Another juxtaposed the sight of a male colleague's eyes welling with tears while Clark "straightened her back, maintained her poise and walked briskly" towards her political exit.[10]

Clark challenged incumbent Labour leader Mike Moore in 1993, after he had led the party to its second successive electoral defeat. Despite the validity of the process used to unseat him, Moore's refusal to "go down without a fight," plus violent and sensationalized depictions of the "coup" by television news, implied that Clark's challenge was inappropriate. Characterizations of her as calculating, heartless, and conspiratorial formulated her quest for the leadership role as treachery, not heroism. Melodramatic storytelling rendered Clark the villain of the piece, brutally and single-mindedly pursuing her (unruly) political aspirations by metaphorically knifing Moore in the back. Melodrama's emphasis on emotion and pathos threw the gender regulations associated with the public man/private woman binary into stark relief, as reflected in a newspaper column presenting the "coup" as a marital break-up, with Clark as the home-wrecker and Moore as the wronged (and innocent) dad who had been booted out of the Labour family home. Doubts about Clark's ability to lead the party reflected gender regulations underpinning the public man/private woman binary. How could a party led by a cold and merciless woman appeal to the electorate, a television interviewer asked? Moore's supporters spread rumours about Clark's sexual orientation and maligned her character during and after the leadership transition, further diminishing her reputation (Edwards 2001, 235–9). Trustworthiness is essential to political legitimacy, and news accounts of Clark's leadership challenge presented her as a "double-crosser," thereby undermining her integrity and likeability.

Despite a very shaky start in the leadership race, and a tough road to the prime minister's office, Clark emerged as a highly popular and successful politician, and ultimately, she was treated to a considerably higher level of mediated legitimacy than were Campbell, Shipley, and Gillard. Clark told her biographer that the period from 1993 to 1996 was "unbelievably difficult" (Edwards 2001, 246). After being "written off" by the news media, with one television reporter predicting, "Helen Clark won't last the year as Leader of the Labour Party," and suffering persistently low approval ratings, Clark engineered an impressive political comeback by addressing disunity within the party and undertaking an image makeover (Edwards 2001, 248–50). Efforts to polish her media communication skills and personal styling cultivated approbation from reporters, who warmed to the Labour leader and began representing her performances as polished, compelling, and commanding. Indeed, during her first election as leader, in 1996, reporters were full of praise for Clark, declaring her the campaign winner. Adulatory words appeared in newspaper accounts about each of her five election campaigns, emphasizing her intelligence, toughness, and exemplary debating skills. Key features of legitimacy, especially competence, strength, decisiveness, and persistence, were increasingly highlighted by the news mediation of Clark.

Yet in many respects, reporting about Clark was a mess of gendered contradictions. News stories drew attention to her body, assessing her make-up, clothing choices, and hairstyles, while at the same time depicting her campaign style as uncompromising, fearless, and effective. Simultaneously portrayed as the agent of political success for her party and as the object of pursuit by party leaders seeking a place in her government, Clark was sexualized by love metaphors and continual invocations of her sexual identity as ruthless and dangerous. Her family life was profiled as a symbol of her "unusual" ambition and cited as evidence that a childless woman could not relate to the needs of "ordinary" families, but she was able to deftly contest some of these representations. Called a "man" during election campaign rallies, Clark's political acumen and campaign prowess indicated that a woman could, in fact, be in charge of the country. Successful women politicians cannot easily be slotted into binary understandings of gender identities and power relationships, as shown by the discursive incongruities evident in this reportage.

Clark's case demonstrates how political longevity may attenuate certain forms of gendered mediation. Gender markers, references to family life, and depictions of her physical appearance became less prevalent over time, indicting media and public acceptance of a woman prime minister or the waning novelty value of these news tropes. Yet the numerical data do not capture the ways in which gender regulations wove through mediated political discourses about Clark in trivializing and delegitimizing ways. Despite the many characterizations of her as exhibiting strength, tenacity, agency, and authority, the questioning of her performance of femininity (and sexuality) undercut confidence in her body as an appropriate site of political leadership. In the waning years of her premiership, unease was expressed with Clark's governing style as she was called "arrogant," "authoritarian," and "dictatorial," her regime termed "Helengrad." The news-mediated transformation from "Cinderella Clark" in 1996 to "political dominatrix" in 2005 illustrates how the trope of toughness can serve as both a laudatory and a destructive discursive manoeuvre. Negotiating gender regulations is extraordinarily difficult, even for the most successful woman leader. Yet Clark triumphed nonetheless. When she resigned, a *Dominion Post* writer said that she had run the government "masterfully and for three terms. ... What is not in doubt is that she has been by far the best prime minister since Holyoake trod the political stage in the 1960s."[11] Clark departed from the prime minister's office a respected political figure, widely acclaimed for her accomplishments.

Lessons Learned: How to Deal (with) the "Gender Card"

Clear patterns emerge from the experiences of Campbell, Shipley, Clark, and Gillard, offering valuable insights for the women prime ministers to come as well as helpful tips for the journalists who will tell their stories. Below I offer six lessons, drawn from each of the substantive chapters of this book. The take-away message is that any woman seeking the highest political office needs a gender strategy. Her legitimacy is never assumed and may be acknowledged only after years of dedicated service as party or government leader. It must be cultivated through carefully crafted campaign tactics and nuanced approaches to political communications. My top tip for journalists and news editors is to exercise greater awareness of the impact of "gender grammar,"[12] the words used to describe a woman's quest for power. It is possible to relay a woman's leadership story in a dramatic and compelling manner without minimizing her accomplishments or questioning her capacity for political leadership because of her gender identity.

Lesson 1: Control Timing and First Impressions

As described in chapter 2, "Ascension Stories," the fictional storytelling techniques reporters use to script morality tales about women's political ascents create powerful first impressions. The tropes and judgments introduced through these "real fictions" are echoed throughout a woman's tenure in office, so journalists should be aware of the impact of storylines borrowed from fables, science fiction, or melodrama. There are few historical models of women as heroes, fighters, revolutionaries, or saviours, so when a woman overturns a man to claim the party leadership role, dominant archetypes of political power and authoritative leadership are invoked. Reporters should consider telling a different type of story, bucking the trend. If a particular angle (such as the dramatic spectacle of a "coup" or a certain plot) is firmly locked in, creating a bandwagon effect, try exposing any overt or implicit sexism evident in the moral of the story being told. After all, a man who aggressively pursues a political leadership position is not usually considered traitorous, overly ambitious, cold-hearted, or mean-spirited. Characterizing women in these ways is both damaging and unfair.

For women who want to lead political parties, timing is key. Ideally, the quest for the top job should be perceived as heroic and honourable, but unseating a popular sitting prime minister may well be scripted as duplicitous and cruel. It is not always possible to wait for an incumbent to retire (as did Campbell) or be considered past his prime, as was the case for Shipley, so opportunities must be seized, as Clark and Gillard concluded. If timing is beyond an aspiring leader's control, she should be prepared to manage the narrative. Her campaign team must find the language to present the candidate as the saviour of the party and/ or the nation and explain why her quest should be championed by the press and accepted by the public as heroic. The rules of the leadership game in Australia and New Zealand make it difficult for women to emerge from these transitions unscathed, but it may be possible for supporters and party spokespersons to challenge the debilitating lexicon of the "coup." It is not a conspiracy – it is a legitimate way for a party to decide whether it wants to replace a sitting leader. Unseating a leader in this manner is an accepted political decision-making process, not a bloody execution.

Lesson 2: Challenge and Change the Gender Grammar for Political Leadership

Chapter 3, "First Women and the X Factor," explained how gender markers – words and phrases that explicitly identify the gender identity of a political actor – are both helpful and harmful to women's political ambitions. The media deal the gender card every time a performance is plainly labelled the act of a *female* leader or *woman* prime minister. Journalists should press the Delete key every time they find themselves gendering political nouns like *candidate, leader, minister*, and *prime minister*. After all, they rarely if ever refer to the *man* prime minister or *male* leader. Doing so for women suggests that their gender is the focal point of the story, more important than their political ideas, acumen, or accomplishments. On the other hand, "first woman" labelling can be helpful as it draws attention to women's historic under-representation in political life. But reporters should not embrace the novelty value of the "first" if the label is inaccurate. And news writers should not assume that because a second or third woman has won the role, gender equality has magically been achieved. Use the opportunity to highlight histories of exclusion and expose the gendered power structures impeding women's political representation.

High-profile political women will invariably be described with gender labels. The same is true of men. I found that the men against whom Campbell, Clark, and Gillard competed during federal elections were as likely, or almost as likely, to have their gender identities explicitly marked in news accounts of their campaigns. Reporters use gender labels to tell readers something about the type of woman or man a leader is perceived to be. Since these labels tend to normalize and laud men's leadership ("action man," "family man," "honest man"), the most effective gender strategy for women pursuing a top political job is to subtly cultivate acceptance of their performance of leadership by celebrating "alternative myths, icons and character traits" (Parry-Giles and Parry-Giles 1996, 350). Articulate and demonstrate, using words, deeds, and images, as many positive qualities as possible, with the goal of prompting the media's use of acclamatory adjectives like *intelligent, knowledgeable, qualified, capable, resilient, resolute, eloquent*, and *inspiring*. As an example, an advertisement titled "Never Stop," broadcast in the lead-up to her successful election campaign, projected Ontario Premier Kathleen Wynne's strength and determination by filming her running.[13] That Wynne runs every day lent credence to her declaration, in the ad, that she was unwavering in the pursuit of her goals, be they personal or political.

As for the X factor – the misguided assertion that women will vote for women because of some sort of innate gender solidarity – members of any campaign team charged with crafting a gender strategy need to anticipate and counter the presumption that women politicians have an unfair advantage with women voters. In chapter 3, I presented evidence that some reporters embrace and others dismiss the "gender affinity" proposition. Reporters who question this form of gendering offer a handy rebuttal: she won because of her skills and political effectiveness, not because she is a woman. Invocations of the "gender factor" by opponents need to be contested as simply ridiculous, as did Hillary Clinton when Republican candidate Donald Trump accused her of "playing the woman card" to gain support in the 2016 Democratic primary. In reaction to Trump's assertion that "the only thing she's got is the woman card," Clinton said, "Well, if fighting for women's health care and paid family leave and equal pay is playing the woman card, then deal me in."[14] By pointing out that the cards she was playing represented her ideas and policies, not her gender identity, Clinton's responsive was affirmative and action-oriented.

Lesson 3: Craft a New Type of Family Strategy

Chapter 4, "First Men and the Family Strategy," established that the four women's family lives were placed in the media spotlight when they competed for party leadership roles. After a flurry of attention to the "first man" (or lack thereof, in Campbell's case) and children or childlessness, intimate relationships were not as frequently mentioned unless the leader chose to introduce the topic, as did Shipley during the 1999 New Zealand election campaign. Intriguingly, journalists gave as much, if not more, consideration to the spouses and children of the men in my sample because these leaders deliberately profiled their wives and children as a campaign tactic I call the family strategy. But this approach is simply not available to most women. As Shipley's experience reveals, a woman leader who foregrounds her traditional family risks being typecast as "the wife," with all the culturally inscribed values and duties of the role. Women who are single and/or childless are at a disadvantage, too, as doubts are raised about their devotion to family life and ability to represent the policy needs of "ordinary families."

Given the personalization of politics and growing public interest in every aspect of a prime minister's life, women seeking this job must expect attention to their family situations. But it is unwise for women leaders to invite the media to peer into every nook and cranny of their personal lives. No doubt Helen Clark regretted agreeing to an invasive "at home with" television interview, during which the host probed her and husband, Peter Davis, about the intimate details of their physical relationship. Women leaders are advised to refuse requests for these sorts of intrusions, while remaining open about and willing to discuss the importance of family relationships. A different approach to talking about family from a position of political leadership is needed, ideally one that destabilizes the association of women with caregiving and nurturing roles and rebuts the primacy of the hetero-normative nuclear family. Politicians should acknowledge and celebrate the rich diversity of family forms, the importance of the extended family, and the value of personal and political friendships. Also, continue to explain, as did Clark and Gillard, that the policy needs of families can indeed be understood by listening empathetically to citizens.

I found that some columnists were willing to expose sexism by showing how the family strategy can be used as an underhanded way of maligning a woman's credibility or character. Also, journalists occasionally confronted this double standard by asking whether a man leader's childlessness would ever be interrogated or cited as an impediment to effectively legislating in the interests of "ordinary" families. Campaign spin that works to reify the hetero-normative, traditional nuclear family or critique opponents' not-so-nuclear family forms *should* be questioned by the media. This is a productive way of exposing damaging tactics directed at divorced or childless women (or men, for that matter). Discursive silence on the subject of the family is not necessarily better for women leaders. Journalists should write about families, not least as a way of showing that politicians' public and private lives, like those of ordinary folk, are integrated and inseparable.

Lesson 4: Perform Embodied Leadership

The physical appearance of any high-profile politician is routinely scrutinized for the political messages it conveys, as discussed in chapter 5, "Body Politics." Entire news stories were devoted to offering advice on the hairstyles and wardrobe choices of the four women prime ministers, and Campbell, Clark, and Gillard were sexualized by press coverage of their physical allure and sexual identities. With the partial exception of Clark, for whom descriptions of make-up and styling conveyed an image of strength and determination, the aesthetic element of the media gaze tended to situate these women leaders as novelties and objects of male desire rather than as active subjects capable of embodying political legitimacy. That journalists are just as consumed with appearance now as they were in 1993, when Kim Campbell became Canada's prime minister, was evident in commentary about Gillard's hair and "hotness" in 2010.

It seems politicians must accept that the shape, size, demeanour, and styling of their bodies (although *not* their whiteness) will be described by reporters and pundits as a way of interpreting authenticity and legitimacy in the performance of leadership roles. Grooming is simply part of the performance (Gundle and Castelli 2006). As approval of Helen Clark's "makeovers" indicates, wardrobe and make-up are as essential for political theatre as they are for actual theatrical roles. Unfortunately, there is no set uniform for women politicians, but choices identified with codes of exaggerated femininity (e.g., wearing a loose, flowing dress, knitting in hand) should be strictly avoided, as Gillard discovered. The most significant problem is that women are rarely described as looking prime ministerial. Hopefully, when enough women win elite political roles, ideas about what a leader looks like will broaden. It would help a great deal if journalists would stop obsessing about women politicians' shoes, hair, or jewellery and refrain from making gratuitous references to the ways in which certain bodies differ from the leadership prototype of the robust, physically imposing, suit-and-tie-wearing, white heterosexual man.

"Pornification" – defined by Anderson (2011, 335) as the act of highlighting "sexuality in contexts that are not normally sexualized" or disciplining those who "do not conform to traditional gender norms" – is unacceptable. Emphasizing a prime minister's sexual desirability demeans both the role and its inhabitant, as does questioning a leader's sexual orientation. Those who are subjected to these forms of denigration could quietly orchestrate a reaction, with the aim of shaming perpetrators and drawing attention to gender-based inequalities and power imbalances. As for the news media, should online obscenities directed at a sitting prime minister be discussed in mainstream media accounts? This is a difficult question to answer, but it is shocking that much of the sexist and, yes, misogynistic treatment of Julia Gillard on social and web-based media went unchallenged by opinion-leading, respectable news outlets. A virtue of the "unlovable press" is its willingness to expose unfair treatment.

Lesson 5: Act Allegorically

Allegorical language is ubiquitous, as illustrated by the prevalence of sport and war metaphors in news about politics, especially the words *fight* and *attack*. The battle frame serves as a master script for reporting political competitions, as described in chapter 6, "Love and War." Women and men leaders alike are so routinely described and evaluated using the lexicon of bloody combat that we now understand politics as a form of rhetorical warfare. The media are unlikely to adopt a new narrative for political competition any time soon, so the lesson for politicians is to accept the allegorical language of electoral "combat" and act accordingly. After all, leaders are expected to act with confidence and determination during election campaigns by firmly challenging the ideas presented by opposing forces, speaking and acting forcefully, and pursuing the ultimate prize with fortitude and determination. None of these skills are intrinsically "masculine," although they are assumed to be a natural part of a man leader's repertoire, while women leaders must enact them. It is crucial to perform in an authentic manner. If vicious verbal ripostes are not a woman leader's style, she should communicate strength and determination in other ways.

The problem is not the war metaphors, per se, but how the "battle" itself is gendered in news accounts. I showed how tropes of the angry, shrill, or hysterical woman and the spectacle of the "catfight" demeaned women's performances. Descriptors like "perfumed political bulldozer," "clash of the Xenas," and "political dominatrix" present trivializing reminders of gender norms and assumptions. Journalists should consider the impact of their assessments when positioning women within the battle frame. Again, the practice of gendering nouns (e.g., *"female* political killing machine") unfairly situates the performance within the body, thereby questioning its authority and authenticity. Women politicians' electoral performance can be empowered and legitimized by war allegories if news writers are careful to watch their gender grammar. Also, why not break the mould by occasionally employing gender-neutral metaphors, perhaps drawn from theatre, nature, travel, or education?

Chapter 6 reveals another side to the metaphorical lexicon of politics: the language of love. Romance metaphors can easily reproduce unequal gendered relations of power by positioning women leaders as the subservient "wife" in political relationships. Journalists should take care not to inflect love allegories with gendered understandings of power and intimacy. When employed carefully, love metaphors can help erode the artificial boundaries constituting public spaces as spheres of rationality, detachment, and independence and private spaces as realms of emotionality, personal connections, and nurturing roles. Through metaphors of romance and affection, politics is rendered a realm of intimacy and feeling. Politicians can act allegorically by highlighting the importance of political relationships, especially the bonds of affection cultivated between prime ministers and the people they represent.

Lesson 6: Deal with (but Do Not Deal) the "Gender Card"

As I argued in chapter 7, "Speech and Shame," it seems unimaginable that a contemporary woman government leader could be so thoroughly ridiculed and censured for her manner of public speech, as was Kim Campbell in 1993. One commentator said that Campbell "sounded like a woman." In other words, she did not "sound right" for politics. Yet women politicians continue to be shamed for speaking politically – for instance, with the "bitch" epithet. "Bitch" has become a "synonym for an 'uppity,' 'vocal,' or 'pushy' woman" (Anderson and Sheeler 2005, 28). Consider the vicious forms of silencing directed at Hillary Clinton during the 2016 US presidential campaign. Chants of "Lock her up" were a constant refrain at Republican rallies, and campaign paraphernalia featured slogans like "Trump that bitch" and "Don't be a pussy, vote for Trump in 2016."[15] But women politicians cannot stop making demands and expecting action. They do not have the option of remaining silent, or letting others speak for them, to avoid derision (Wilz 2016). After all, authoritative, persuasive, and forceful speech is the hallmark of the successful leader.

So what can an aspiring leader do (or say) without risking denunciation by opponents and pundits? Cultivate measured, confident, and sincere forms of speech. Avoid intemperate, impulsive, overly intimate, and seemingly unrestrained speech mannerisms and topics. Yes, this is grossly unfair as men are not similarly restrained. It may be possible to subtly challenge the discursive rules of the political game by offering a less combative rhetorical demeanour, but politicians should keep this strategy to themselves and their campaign teams. Do not tell the media. As Campbell found, "doing politics differently" was interpreted as "doing politics like a woman," and the strategy was read as an affront to the long-standing rules of the (political) game. I believe it is possible for leaders to embrace a diversity of oratorical styles, but explicitly constructing these modes of speech as a gendered performance invites scorn.

Turning to Julia Gillard and the "gender wars," clearly even the most hyper-controlled speech cannot salvage the perceived challenge to unspoken norms and understandings that is the "gender card." Although this is a card every woman is dealt and opponents certainly do not hesitate to use it, a woman leader risks censure when seen to play the card herself by drawing attention, in public speeches, to the gender bias she endures every day by participating in political life. The media should be questioning these norms; after all, challenging authority is one of the key virtues of a recalcitrant, "unlovable" press. Given the virulent and spectacularly hostile reaction to Gillard's "misogyny" speech by the press, it is unwise for women political leaders to highlight the sexist, biased, and hateful treatment directed at them. As I argued in chapter 7, the myth of social equality has so permeated Western industrialized democracies that exposing gendered power relations from a position of power violates unspoken norms of political discourse. It is incumbent upon all of us to identify and decry attempts to silence those who speak out about subjugation and powerlessness, be it experienced as gender, racial, sexual, or class-based inequality.

Where to Go from Here? Expanding Gendered Mediation Research

Research on gendered mediation tends to look for the ways in which news reporting reflects gender stereotypes and upholds dualistic constructions of gender. This is important work, and *Ms. Prime Minister* makes useful contributions to it, not least by showing how commonly used metaphors and modes of news storytelling reinforce long-standing gender regulations. In an effort to stretch the concept of gendered mediation in theoretically and empirically productive ways, I argue that research in this area should consider the possibility of resistance and change through the enactment of political leadership and in news accounts of its performance. I define "gendered news" as news content that explicitly or implicitly reflects gender norms and binaries. Because these customs and dualisms are socially and discursively constructed, they are both artificial and unstable, thus open to contestation. So while gendered news is evident – indeed, often abundant – it does not always or necessarily reinforce the hegemonic gender order. News mediation of political leaders can reify *or* subvert taken-for-granted gender schemas by supporting *or* unsettling the lines of demarcation between woman/man, public/private, and feminine/masculine.

I explored these possibilities by observing gendered mediation in and across four case studies and by blending complementary quantitative and qualitative methods. Some questions were answered with content analysis, which was used to compare the amount of attention given to the gender identities, bodies, and family lives of four women prime ministers and six comparable men leaders. The comprehensive approach I took to operationalizing these variables makes a significant contribution to gendered mediation scholarship, as does analysis of the (often surprising) findings. Why are men leaders as likely as women leaders, if not more likely, to see their gender marked and their families discussed in reporting about their campaign strategies and activities? What does it mean when news reports fixate on the bodies of women leaders? Answering these questions with careful qualitative analysis proved fruitful. Perhaps the most important methodological lesson to be learned is the value of seeing news as a complex and nuanced form of storytelling, one that embraces the myths and plot lines of fiction and constructs dramatic confrontations around resonant metaphors of power and emotion. As I demonstrated, news narratives evolve, echoing ideas introduced at the inception of a leader's career and reconstructing others to reflect changes in political context. Disaggregating certain themes or topics, such as references to looks or families, from overarching patterns of gendering risks overlooking the complex and intriguing ways in which political legitimacy is mediated.

Ms. Prime Minister makes several important contributions to the study of gender, media, and leadership, but there is much more work to be done. As argued in chapter 1 and discussed throughout this volume, every political actor is a gendered subject, viewed through the lenses of gendered identities. Yet there is insufficient research on gendered mediation of men, sexual minority, and gender non-conforming politicians. Work on the gendering of men politicians in news discourses tends to focus on the ways in which reporting exalts hegemonic forms of masculinity and "feminizes" men politicians as a strategy of critique and containment (Anderson 2002; Duerst-Lahti 2007; Fahey 2007; Lünenborg and Maier 2015). My admittedly limited examination of newspaper reporting about men leaders tends to support this argument by documenting adulatory "manly men" and "family men" tropes plus overt criticisms of the lone male leader who appeared insufficiently burly and commanding to reporters accustomed to an overtly pugilistic political style. We cannot overlook the possibility that representations of men who perform non-normative versions of masculinity might destabilize dualistic gender categories or challenge the association of leadership with heroic warrior masculinity. Canada's current prime minister, Justin Trudeau, distinguished himself from tough guy competitors during the 2015 election campaign by presenting a nuanced version of masculinity. Muscular displays of boxing prowess and athleticism were juxtaposed against poignant images of the leader rocking babies to sleep, happily embracing members of the public, and taking endless smiling selfies. How are these sorts of emotive, sensitive versions of masculinity received by the press (and the public)? Would they be interpreted differently if displayed by a non-hetero-normative male politician?

Trudeau's campaign style highlights the importance of candidate self-presentation, another valuable site of scholarly investigation into gendered mediation, as Tolley (2016) and Goodyear-Grant (2013) have shown. Elite politicians have considerable control over their political communications strategies because they employ large coteries of media handlers, whose job it is to manipulate the messages conveyed by mainstream and social media (Enli 2015, 128). That said, as I argued in chapter 1 and demonstrated to be the case for Campbell, Shipley, Clark, and Gillard, political actors can help craft the media message, but they certainly cannot control it. Are gender-binary-compliant performances, those reflecting "culturally established lines of coherence" (Butler 2006, 33), more likely to find purchase with reporters? Probably. Political actors who reproduce dominant discourses and myths are at a distinct advantage (Pusnik and Bulc 2001, 409). For instance, in an effort to render his gender performance normative and comprehensible to the public, Justin Trudeau employed a recuperative gender strategy before seeking the leadership of the Liberal Party (Maiolino 2015). Mediated perceptions of the aspiring party leader as "precariously masculine" were effectively disrupted when he took part in, and won, a highly publicized boxing match (ibid., 116). The tactic reconfigured Trudeau as sufficiently tough and tenacious to assume the role of Liberal leader and, eventually, prime minister. While this is clearly an example of candidate self-presentation, the news media played a central role in documenting and interpreting the event and in reifying dualistic understandings of gender and politics. Analysis of the mutually constitutive nature of candidate self-presentation and gendered, sexual, or racial mediation will help unveil additional gender strategies and develop egalitarian journalistic practices.

Sexual mediation is a concept that should be introduced, theorized, and operationalized, as Tolley (2016) has done so successfully with racial mediation. Despite evidence that hetero-normativity informs public perceptions of gay and lesbian candidates for political office (Doan and Haider-Markel 2010), there is insufficient research on the ways in which news represents LGBTQ politicians (however, see Everitt and Camp 2009a, 2009b; Smith 2013; Trimble et al. 2015). The performances of queer or non-binary politicians have the potential to disrupt the two-sex/gender schema by exposing the politically and discursively constructed nature of sexual difference (Butler 2004, 176). But as Butler emphasizes, the body itself is "shaped by political forces with strategic interests in keeping that body bounded and constituted by the markers of sex" (2006, 175). For example, when cultural responses to gender fluidity and nonconformity reflect "fixing strategies" such as "wrong body discourses," they reinforce rather than erode gender binaries (Barker-Plummer 2013, 711–12).

Much more exploration of intersectionality is needed. Mediation of complexly intertwined identities cannot be gauged by looking at media coverage of exclusively white, cisgender, heterosexual politicians such as the four women and six men included in my study. Understandings of gender are entangled in narratives about sexuality and race (Hancock 2007; Trimble et al. 2015). In her analysis of newspaper reporting about twenty-three racial-minority women who had served as members of Canada's Parliament, Erin Tolley identified three distinct frames, or lenses, through which the identities of these women were constructed. First, by focusing on socio-demographics, news accounts communicated difference by highlighting culturally inscribed views of exoticized bodies and traditional family relationships, or elided issues of race by ascribing sameness to visible-minority women's bodies and actions (Tolley 2016, 108–12). Second, viability framing emphasized novelty, positioning some women as "famous firsts" and others as token representatives of their ethnicity. Either way, women's credentials were minimized or overlooked entirely (Tolley 2016, 113–14). Third, the immigrant narrative was central to the framing of visible-minority politicians, as were portrayals of women politicians acting parochially by representing "their own" communities (Tolley 2016, 121). "That visible minority women are often presented as racialized and gendered subjects first and political actors second" damages voter perceptions of their legitimacy by questioning the validity of their presence in formal political spaces (Tolley 2016, 123). The complex ways in which mediated legitimacy reflects a myriad of identities can be investigated only by examining news portrayals of a demographically diverse sample.

Finally, although my study of four women prime ministers from three countries offered a comparative, longitudinal, and deeply contextualized account of gendered mediation, one of its primary limitations is the small sample size. While aspects of their political contexts and levels of political success differed, Campbell, Shipley, Clark, and Gillard were similar in their early career trajectories and demographic characteristics. Adding news mediation of Prime Ministers Theresa May and Jacinda Ardern to the analysis would certainly be illuminating, but would not afford an intersectional lens as they share the identity characteristics of the four women I studied. Since women prime ministers of Westminster democracies are in short supply, a fruitful avenue for further research is media coverage of sub-national leaders, where women are becoming more plentiful. Canada has had eleven women premiers, eight at the provincial level, and three leaders of territorial governments. In Australia, seven women have occupied the state-level premier's office, and four have served as chief minister in the nation's territories. These leaders have no doubt experienced different career opportunities and obstacles, and are more diverse than most federal government leaders. For example, two Indigenous women have led territorial governments in Canada, and Ontario's current premier, Kathleen Wynne, is openly gay. Have recently elected women premiers been subjected to less delegitimizing or politically harmful forms of gendered (and/or sexual or racial) mediation than were the four women prime ministers profiled in this book?

When conducting new research on the topic of gendered mediation, scholars ought to explore both social and mainstream media content and consider the interactions between them. In their book about Hillary Clinton's quest for the US presidency in 2008, Lawrence and Rose (2010, 198–200) describe the virulently sexist and often misogynistic treatment of Clinton in online commentary, the worst of which incited her metaphorical murder. If anything, Clinton's 2016 presidential campaign spawned even worse abuse, with "Trump that bitch" shouted at Republican rallies, reproduced on banners and T-shirts, and widely reported in news accounts of the campaign.[16] How extensively do the tropes circulating on social media platforms bleed into mainstream news coverage? For example, Alberta Premier Rachel Notley has been subjected to the sorts of online misogyny that "far exceed those aimed at male politicians" as she has been called a "bitch" and a "cunt" and threatened with violence and death.[17] When she and her New Democratic Party swept to power in May 2015, overturning forty-three years of Progressive Conservative rule and expanding a four-member caucus into a majority government, this profound electoral upset unleashed a series of online diatribes, many of which were profoundly sexist and odious. "Someone's gotta man up and kill her," said just one of the dozens of hateful comments circulating on Facebook and other social media sites.[18] A year and a half later, the cyber attacks continue, with social media posts saying that Notley should be "shot, stabbed, or even thrown into a tree grinder."[19] Mainstream news organizations have responded appropriately, reporting the threats as serious criminal behaviour and highlighting the misogynistic language employed by anonymous online assailants. The news media are calling out sexism, as coverage of the vicious body shaming, death threats, and other forms of sexist cyber-abuse directed at women premiers and Cabinet ministers in Canada indicates.[20] But are news stories about these online hate and death threats merely serving as "click bait," or do they offer an educative function? And how do social media commentaries affect women leaders' perceived political legitimacy?

Other intervening variables to be explored include partisanship and longevity in office. My study did not find any overt differences in gendered mediation of the four women prime ministers based on their party affiliation, but Murray (2010b, 19–20) suggests that women leaders on the left of the ideological spectrum suffer from stereotypes associating their parties' policies with the communal traits and qualities branded "feminine" (thus, weak). Canada's women premiers represent different political parties, from social democratic to centrist to fiscally conservative, thus offering a fruitful basis for comparison. As for investigating the impact of political success, scholars do not have an abundance of cases to explore. Few women government leaders have enjoyed the longevity of Helen Clark, the only one of the four women prime ministers in my study who held office long enough for the "gender factor" to grow stale and the sight of woman as leader to become conventionalized, at least to a certain degree. A comparison of Clark's media coverage with that of Angela Merkel, elected to a fourth term as German chancellor in 2017, would offer a useful test of the conventionalization thesis.

Clark is, in many respects, the quintessential political success story (Trimble and Treiberg 2010, 115). After her departure from New Zealand politics in 2009, the former prime minister's international expertise and experience were recognized with an appointment as head of the United Nations Development Programme, a post she held until 2017. Clark aspired to be the first woman to be chosen as secretary-general of the United Nations, and an article in the *Guardian* argued that her "reputation as a fighter who survived nine years as [prime minister] amid the rough-and-tumble of New Zealand politics" placed her "as a serious contender" for the job.[21] Unfortunately, Clark was not chosen, but the fact that she was considered to be one of the front-runners for this prestigious and influential position underscores the esteem in which she is held, in New Zealand and around the word. The presence of a woman in the prime minister's office, regardless of how long she serves in the role, has a powerful socio-cultural impact. As Canadian news columnist Elizabeth Renzetti reasons, the "presence of women in the highest echelons of power normalizes the idea that the proper place for women is in the higher echelons of power."[22] When citizens see women winning elections, enacting governmental authority, and cultivating approval, conventional understandings of politics as the domain of men are disrupted. The courage, resilience, and determination displayed by Campbell, Shipley, Clark, and Gillard offer inspirational examples for the women who will, one day, follow in their footsteps. Their legacies will, as Gillard confidently asserted, make it "easier for the next woman, and the woman after that, and the woman after that."[23]

Appendix: Methodological Details

News Sources and Sampling

I chose domestic news sources because my focus was on the ways in which party leaders were mediated by news reporting in their own countries.

Newspaper Coverage

Canada had one national newspaper when Kim Campbell's political star rose and fell, the *Globe and Mail*, which was, and remains, the largest-circulation national newspaper and an opinion leader among governmental and political elites (Taras 1999, 18). Dozens of local newspapers were published in Canada's ten provinces and two territories at this time, so I gathered news stories from the highest-circulation English-language newspaper published in the home province of each of the leaders included in this study: the *Vancouver Sun* in the case of Campbell and the *Montreal Gazette* for Liberal leader Jean Chrétien. Because New Zealand does not have a national newspaper, news stories published by widely read daily newspapers in major cities on the North and South Islands were selected for analysis: the capital city (Wellington) papers, the *Dominion* and the *Evening Post*, which merged in 2002 to become the *Dominion Post*; Auckland's *New Zealand Herald*, which had the largest circulation of any daily in the country; and the main South Island paper, Christchurch's the *Press* (Cross and Henderson 2004, 143–4; Ross and Comrie 2012, 973). Three leading Australian broadsheets – the *Australian*, the *Sydney Morning Herald*, and the *Age* – were chosen for analysis because of their wide circulation in the most populated markets, Sydney and Melbourne, and across the country (Young 2011, 115).

The research team accessed Canadian newspaper articles from the Factiva and Canadian Newsstand databases. Factiva was also used to search the Australian newspapers and the New Zealand news articles published after 1999. For pre-1999 New Zealand newspaper coverage, a LexisNexis search was supplemented with archival research and searches of microfilm sources.[1] Some of the coverage, notably Clark's 1993 leadership challenge, was available only on microfilm at the National Library of New Zealand.

Television Coverage

For each of the three leadership "coups" in New Zealand and Australia, I analysed a census of television news stories, including "regular" news stories, updates and news specials, and interviews with Clark, Shipley, and Gillard. In the case of New Zealand, television news programs from the two networks operating at the time – state-owned TV New Zealand's One Network News and private broadcaster TV3's Three National News – were retrieved from the Chapman Archives at the University of Auckland. For the Australian case study, I focused on all coverage televised by the state-owned broadcaster, the Australian Broadcasting Corporation (ABC) because of its public service mandate and continued audience appeal. Coverage was accessed through the ABC's website[2] as the story unfolded.

Sampling Criteria and Time Frames

Newspaper articles meeting specific sampling criteria were gathered for each of the four stages of the women leaders' careers (leadership win, governance, election[s], and departure from the party leadership role) and for the men leaders during the election campaigns. The criteria were designed to capture in-depth coverage of the leaders. To ensure that the focus of each article selected was on the leader in question, at least half the text of the story had to reflect on that leader's campaign or persona. All news articles over 250 words in length, including regular news, columns, opinion pieces, features, and editorials, offering substantive and detailed coverage of each of the leaders were included in the study. Letters to the editor were excluded because they were written by readers rather than by a news organization. There were significant differences in word length among the newspapers in the three countries: Canadian news stories published during the 1993 leadership contest and federal election were often well over 1,000 words in length, while equivalent articles published in New Zealand newspapers were typically between 300 and 600 words long. Australian newspaper articles were generally between 300 and 800 words long.

Search dates were established by the events themselves. For the women who became prime minister as a result of their leadership challenges (Campbell, Shipley, and Gillard), I gathered coverage of the party leadership contests from the day a woman politician announced her candidacy, or news of a "coup" was leaked to the press, to the point when she was sworn in as prime minister. For Helen Clark, who became leader of the Official Opposition rather than prime minister after she successfully challenged the Labour Party leadership, I included all stories published between the day the story broke until the newspapers had exhausted discussion of the impact on the party and electoral politics in New Zealand. The governance phase captured each woman's first month in office. For Campbell and Gillard, who called elections a few weeks after they had been sworn in as prime minister, this phase took place immediately after their leadership ascensions. Although Shipley did not call an election until 1999, I examined the news coverage of her first four weeks in office. Helen Clark won three elections, and her governance phases thus included the month after each election victory, in 1999, 2002, and 2005.

Search dates for the election news stories were adapted to the features of the electoral system in each country, although in each case, sampling began the day the election was called. Canada's 1993 election results were announced on the day of the vote because a majority government was elected. The search began the day the writ was dropped and extended until a week after the vote to include post-mortems on Campbell's leadership. For the New Zealand and Australian elections, the story search began the day the writ was dropped and ended the day after a government was established. This end point was chosen because, in each of these elections, a government was not immediately formed after the votes had been counted, and I wanted the analysis to include the crucial post-vote coalition-building phase of the electoral contests. In Australia, the 2010 election resulted in a tie, and the two major party leaders had to seek support from the Independents and other parties to try and form a government. Finally, the resignation or retirement phases included all news stories meeting the search criteria published the day of, until three days immediately after, the leaders stepped down.

Coding Scheme for Content Analysis

The following variables were included for analysis in this volume. The unit of analysis was the news story.

Structural Variables

- Case ID (leader's initials, followed by a number)
- Nation (Australia, Canada, New Zealand)
- Newspaper in which the article appeared
- Leader discussed in the article
- Career phase of the leader discussed in the article
- Length of article, in words

Substantive Variables

Coders were asked to determine whether a particular aspect of a leader's identity was mentioned. To count as a "yes," these notations had to be both explicit and direct, as indicated by the coding notes.

- Is the leader's gender identity mentioned?
  o Gender must be explicitly marked with words such as *woman, female, lady, girl, mother, sister, daughter, queen,* or *empress*; or *man, male, guy, boy, father, brother, son,* or *king.*
- Is the leader's physical appearance mentioned?
  o Any aspect of physical appearance that is described or evaluated counts as a "yes," including literal mentions of looks, descriptions, or evaluations of any aspect of the body and its adornment, and discussion of the leader's physical persona or attractiveness.
- Is the leader's racial identity mentioned?
  o Reference to the leader as Caucasian or white. (Note: All party leaders in the sample were white. None had their racial identity mentioned in any of the articles included in this study.)
- Is the leader's marital status mentioned?
  o Count as mentioned any references to the leader's spouse or intimate partner, previous spouses, divorce(s), or common-law status.

- Are the leader's children (or his/her childlessness) mentioned?
  o This can include mention of the leader's biological children, step-children, or grandchildren or the fact that the leader does not have children.

Intercoder Reliability

Coding of the newspaper stories was conducted by five research assistants,[3] all masters and doctoral students in the Department of Political Science at the University of Alberta in Edmonton. Each coder was trained using an extensive coding instrument, complete with detailed coding notes, which were elaborated when necessary to ensure consistency. Intercoder reliability tests were based on 20 per cent of the articles analysed for each leader included in the study. These tests confirmed near-perfect levels of agreement for all structural variables except for career phase (Landis and Koch 1977; Perreault and Leigh 1989). In these cases, minor inconsistencies were discussed and resolved.

While agreement was very strong on the substantive variables, with an average of 96 per cent pairwise agreement and a range of 92.8 to 100 per cent, my goal was to achieve an error-free data set. Two processes caught and corrected errors. First, whenever a coder was unsure about the appropriate response, I discussed the issue with the original coder and another coder, and the three of us reached agreement. Also, to ensure that coders did not draw inferences from latent meanings, or read in meanings based on knowledge gained from reading other news items in the sample, I read through each of the qualitative databases of all references to that particular variable, noting any areas of disagreement. These were discussed with the original coder and one additional member of the team until we reached consensus on the appropriate response category. Finally, a review of my own detailed discourse notes captured any omissions. When necessary, the Statistical Package for the Social Sciences (SPSS) database was changed to reflect these decisions. All quantitative data analysis was conducted using SPSS.

Qualitative Databases

Databases comprising all references to gender, physical appearance, marital status, children or childlessness, and sexualization (discussion of a leader's sexual identity/orientation, sex life, or sexual allure) documented the following information:

- Leader
- Case ID
- What was said: direct quotation
- Who said it: the leader, a reporter or columnist, an opponent, a supporter, or other
- Context: where relevant, the context in which the comment was made

We also compiled a list of all aggressive metaphors (e.g., words like *fight, attack, blast*) and allegories of love or romance (e.g., *wooing, honeymoon, marriage,* and *divorce*) used to describe each party leader's behaviours and/or strategies during the election campaigns. The love and war metaphors discussed in chapter 6 were drawn from these lists.

Discourse Analysis Notes

As described in chapter 1, I took detailed notes about how leadership was represented in the articles written about each prime minister over the course of her term as party leader and about how the men leaders were represented during the election campaigns. This method identified subtle and complex forms of gendered mediation not captured by the content coding, such as representations of the politicians' speaking styles and the authenticity of their public speech acts.

Notes

Chapter 1

1 Excerpt from Julia Gillard's resignation speech, which was broadcast on www.abc.net.au, June 26, 2013; emphasis mine.
2 According to Skard (2014), there have been twelve women prime ministers of Westminster democracies, including Campbell, Shipley, Clark, and Gillard. Theresa May's rise in 2016 and Jacinda Ardern's election in 2017 bump the number to 14.
3 UN Women, "Facts and Figures: Leadership and Political Participation," accessed November 28, 2016, http://www.unwomen.org/en/what-we-do/leadership-and-political-participation/facts-and-figures.
4 *Economist*, "Gender Inequality Goes Right to the Top," November 2, 2016, accessed November 3, 2016, http://www.economist.com/blogs/graphicdetail/2016/11/daily-chart?fsrc=scn/tw/te/bl/ed/.
5 As of April 2016; see http://www.ipu.org/wmn-e/classif.htm, accessed April 20, 2016.
6 Clare Foran, "Will Hillary Clinton's Defeat Set Back Women in Politics?," *Atlantic*, November 27, 2016, accessed November 29, 2016, www.theatlantic.com.
7 Emma Gray, "Clinton's loss has motivated thousands of women to consider running for office," *Huffington Post*, December 12, 2016, accessed December 16, 2016, www.huffingtonpost.com.
8 During her lone election campaign as New Zealand's prime minister, Shipley competed against and lost to Helen Clark.
9 Jason Groves, "Theresa shows her steel," *Daily Mail Online*, December 8, 2016, accessed December 8, 2016, www.dailymail.co.uk.

10 Elizabeth Renzetti, "Feminists should get over Theresa May's politics," *Globe and Mail*, July 13, 2016, accessed July 25, 2016, www.theglobeandmail.com.

11 Hadley Freeman, "Theresa May, Margaret Thatcher: Spot the difference – and the sexism," *Guardian*, July 23, 2016, accessed December 8, 2016, www.theguardian.com.

12 New Zealand presently has a population of four and a half million people, while Australia has just over twenty-four million and Canada just over thirty-six million human inhabitants.

13 The PC Party was ruptured in the late 1980s, producing two parties that split the conservative vote. In 2004, the parties united to create the Conservative Party of Canada.

14 However, after the Gillard and Rudd "coups," which undermined the party's electoral fortunes in 2010 and 2013, the Australian Labor Party changed its leadership selection rules to include voting by party members.

15 *Cisgender* is defined, in the *Oxford English Dictionary*, as an adjective "denoting or relating to a person whose sense of personal identity and gender corresponds with their birth sex"; see https://en.oxforddictionaries.com/definition/cisgender.

16 Dan Bilefsky, "With 'Trousergate,' politics and pants collide in Britain," *New York Times*, December 13, 2016, accessed December 15, 2015, www.nytimes.com.

Chapter 2

1 The section of this chapter titled "Prime Time Melodramas" is adapted from my article "Melodrama and Gendered Mediation: Television Coverage of Women's Leadership 'Coups' in New Zealand and Australia," *Feminist Media Studies* 14, no. 4 (2014): 663–87.

2 Patricia Herbert, "Moore pledges to fight coup without cease," *New Zealand Herald*, November 27, 1993.

3 New Zealand television news about Clark's and Shipley's leadership challenges was available from the Chapman Archives at the University of Auckland, and I was able to access television coverage of Gillard's ascension in Australia online as the event unfolded.

4 Joan Bryden, "Campbell finds herself in rerun of 1984 Liberal leadership race," *Vancouver Sun*, June 14, 1993, A4.

5 Hugh Winsor, "Warm, funny side of Campbell being served up," *Globe and Mail*, March 26, 1993, A4.

6 Hugh Winsor, "Tortoise chases the hare," *Globe and Mail*, April 3, 1993, A1.
7 Ross Howard, "The turtle picks up momentum," *Globe and Mail*, May 10, 1993, A5.
8 Hugh Winsor, "Numbers favour a Campbell win: Charest's late momentum not enough to carry the tortoise past the hare," *Globe and Mail*, May 8, 1993, A1.
9 Hugh Winsor and Ross Howard, "Tortoise runs out of time and luck," *Globe and Mail*, June 14, 1993, A1.
10 Clyde H. Farnsworth, "In Canada's race for premier, front-runner falters," *New York Times*, June 13, 1993, downloaded August 17, 2013, from www.nytimes.com.
11 Warren Caragata, "Five who would be PM: Promises and profiles – Jean Charest," *Vancouver Sun*, June 19, 1993, A4.
12 Jeffrey Simpson, "Before uttering a word, Ms. Campbell is the prisoner of expectations," *Globe and Mail*, March 25, 1993, A24.
13 For instance, Pauline Couture, "Charting the course of Campbellmania," *Globe and Mail*, April 1, 1993, A23.
14 Hugh Winsor, "Is Kim Campbell's star beginning to dim?," *Globe and Mail*, April 17, 1993, A1.
15 Doug Ward, "The girl most likely: Doug Ward takes a look at Kim Campbell's ascendancy," *Vancouver Sun*, March 25, 1993, A4.
16 Ross Howard, "Front-runner taking the risk-free approach," *Globe and Mail*, April 8, 1993, A4.
17 Winsor, "Warm, funny side of Campbell being served up."
18 Hugh Winsor, "Campbell vows to tell it like it is: Controversy over remarks doesn't faze Tory front-runner," *Globe and Mail*, May 19, 1993, A1.
19 Ward, "The girl most likely."
20 *Vancouver Sun*, "Campbell's touch-feely image is going down the drain fast," May 20, 1993, A4.
21 Peter O'Neil, "Is media focus on Campbell sexist?," *Vancouver Sun*, May 28, 1993, A5.
22 Michael Valpy, "Misrepresenting Kim Campbell," *Globe and Mail*, May 19, 1993, A2.
23 Jeffrey Simpson, "Does Kim Campbell's nature allow for the 'politics of inclusiveness?'" *Globe and Mail*, May 20, 1993, A24.
24 O'Neil, "Is media focus on Campbell sexist?"
25 Hugh Winsor, "Is Kim Campbell's star beginning to dim?"
26 Hugh Winsor, "Campbellmania fizzles: Kim Campbell generated little excitement in her Atlantic tour," *Globe and Mail*, May 25, 1993, A1.

27 David Roberts, "Campbell wins delegates in West but support wobbly," *Globe and Mail*, April 24, 1993, A7; Peter O'Neil, "Suddenly, Queen Kim starts looking shaky on Tory throne," *Vancouver Sun*, April 17, 1993, A5.

28 Jeffrey Simpson, "The Campbell image glows but the performances need polishing," *Globe and Mail*, June 9, 1993, A20.

29 Howard, "The turtle picks up momentum." Howard wrote, "The Charest bus tour of Eastern Ontario draws a large contingent of the national media."

30 Hugh Winsor, "Tortoise chases the hare."

31 André Picard, "Turtlemania: Tory contender has sights on storybook ending," *Globe and Mail*, June 5, 1993, A1.

32 Hugh Winsor, "Numbers favour a Campbell win."

33 Jeff Sallot and Ross Howard, "Tories brace for contest past first ballot: Campbell, Charest organizers court uncommitted delegates," *Globe and Mail*, June 12, 1993, A1.

34 Picard, "Turtlemania."

35 Julian Beltrame, "'Turtle' inches along on Ontario leg of Tory race," *Vancouver Sun*, May 19, 1993, A5.

36 Hugh Winsor, "Numbers favour a Campbell win"; Daniel Drolet, "The delegates party as Charest and Campbell struggle," *Vancouver Sun*, June 11, 1993, A1.

37 Jeffrey Simpson, "When the tortoise starts to gain, it's time to ask some questions," *Globe and Mail*, June 4, 1993, A30.

38 Trevor Lautens, "Man who would be kingmaker," *Vancouver Sun*, June 12, 1993, A11.

39 Peter MacQueen, "Campbell tripping on her lip," *Vancouver Sun*, May 21, 1993, A17.

40 For example, Peter O'Neil, "Embattled Campbell set to come out swinging at Charest," *Vancouver Sun*, June 3, 1993, A4.

41 Mark Kennedy, "The challenges ahead: The leadership race was the first hurdle, but does Kim Campbell have what it takes to clear them all?," *Vancouver Sun*, June 14, 1993, A11.

42 For example, Peter O'Neil, "Campbell's camp claims first ballot win still there," *Vancouver Sun*, June 1, 1993, A1.

43 Julian Beltrame and Joan Bryden, "Tories would face disaster under Campbell, poll says," *Vancouver Sun*, June 12, 1993, A1.

44 *Globe and Mail*, "Just the beginning for Kim Campbell," June 14, 1993, A14.

45 Winsor and Howard, "Tortoise runs out of time and luck."

46 Ross Howard and Jeff Sallot, "Campbell calls for unity as Tories elect her leader," *Globe and Mail*, June 14, 1993, A1.

47 André Picard, "Charest works hard to come out of his shell," *Globe and Mail*, June 5, 1993, A1.
48 Winsor and Howard, "Tortoise runs out of time and luck"; emphasis mine.
49 Ibid.; emphasis mine.
50 Lysiane Gagnon, "Why isn't Campbell judged by the same yardstick as male politicians?," *Globe and Mail*, June 5, 1993, D3.
51 Peter O'Neill, "Is media focus on Campbell sexist?"; Francine Pelletier, "The media factor: Kim Campbell has gone from darling to target of the press," *Vancouver Sun*, June 1, 1993, A13.
52 Gagnon, "Why isn't Campbell judged by the same yardstick as male politicians?"; Jeffrey Simpson, "Ripples of sexism still make waves in political waters," *Globe and Mail*, June 11, 1993, A22.
53 Simpson, "Ripples of sexism still make waves in political waters."
54 Gagnon, "Why isn't Campbell judged by the same yardstick as male politicians?"
55 Susan Delacourt, "Tories strain to keep battles within bounds," *Globe and Mail*, June 11, 1993, A4.
56 Margaret Wente, "She's the pioneer, but is she good at governing?," *Globe and Mail*, June 15, 1993, A21.
57 Ross Howard, "A big step – down a dimly lit road," *Globe and Mail*, June 15, 1993, A5.
58 Pelletier, "The media factor."
59 Simpson, "When the tortoise starts to gain."
60 Gagnon, "Why isn't Campbell judged by the same yardstick as male politicians?"; emphasis mine.
61 Because the House of Representatives is a component of the New Zealand Parliament, those who are elected to serve in the House are known as members of Parliament.
62 TV New Zealand (hereafter TVNZ), National News, Auckland, November 27, 1993.
63 TVNZ, November 28, 1993; and December 1, 1993.
64 Three Network (hereafter TV3), National News, Auckland, November 29, 1993.
65 TVNZ, November 26, 1993; TVNZ, November 28, 1993.
66 TVNZ, November 26, 1993; TVNZ, November 28, 1993.
67 TVNZ, November 29, 1993.
68 TVNZ, December 1, 1993.
69 TVNZ, November 30, 1993.
70 TV3, December 1, 1993; emphasis mine.
71 Ibid.

72 Ibid.
73 Ibid.
74 TVNZ, December 1, 1993.
75 Ibid.
76 Ibid.
77 TV3, December 1, 1993.
78 Ibid; emphasis mine.
79 TV3, November 30, 1993.
80 TVNZ, December 1, 1993.
81 Ibid.
82 The quotation describing Shipley's ascension is from a caller to a talk radio program.
83 Christine Cessford, "No-nonsense Jenny fulfills early promise," *Evening Post*, November 4, 1997.
84 *Evening Post*, "A textbook coup, swift and clean," November 4, 1997.
85 TV3, November 3, 1997.
86 TV3, November 4, 1997.
87 TV3, November 3, 1997.
88 TV3, November 4, 1997.
89 TVNZ, November 4, 1997; emphasis mine.
90 TVNZ, November 3, 1997.
91 TV3, November 4, 1997.
92 Ibid.; emphasis mine.
93 TVNZ, November 4, 1997; TVNZ, December 8, 1997.
94 TVNZ, December 8, 1997.
95 TV3, November 4, 1997.
96 TV3, December 8, 1997; emphasis mine.
97 TV3, November 4, 1997.
98 John Kincade, "Dreams Are Ten a Penny," accessed October 15, 2010, http://www.lyricsmode.com/.
99 Mark Davis, "Building ambition from the sandpit of politics," *Sydney Morning Herald*, June 24, 2010, 3.
100 Australian Broadcasting Corporation (hereafter ABC), National News, Sydney, June 23, 2010.
101 ABC, June 23, 2010.
102 ABC, June 24, 2010.
103 Ibid.
104 Ibid.
105 Ibid.
106 ABC, June 25, 2010.

107 Ibid.
108 ABC, June 24, 2010.
109 ABC, June 26, 2010.
110 Ibid.
111 ABC, June 24, 2010.
112 Ibid.; ABC, June 25, 2010.
113 ABC, June 24, 2010.
114 ABC, June 25, 2010.
115 Ibid.
116 ABC, June 24, 2010.
117 Ibid.
118 ABC, June 25, 2010.
119 ABC, June 26, 2010.
120 ABC, June 24, 2010.
121 Ibid.
122 ABC, June 25, 2010.
123 Ibid.
124 ABC, June 24, 2010.
125 Ibid.
126 Ibid.
127 ABC, June 25, 2010.
128 Ibid.
129 ABC, June 24, 2010; emphasis mine.

Chapter 3

1 Edward Greenspon, "Tories ready – finally – to accept a woman leader," *Globe and Mail*, June 14, 1993, A9.
2 Brian Rudman, "Woman of steely resolve in good times and bad," *New Zealand Herald*, November 9, 1999.
3 Helen Bain, "Mixed reaction to first woman PM," *Dominion*, November 5, 1997.
4 Nicolas Perpitch, "She's right on tax, and a woman, too," *Australian*, June 25, 2010, 6.
5 Warren Gamble, "Jenny joins the winners," *New Zealand Herald*, November 5, 1997.
6 David A. Graham, "Why Trump Might Regret Playing 'the Woman Card' against Clinton," *Atlantic*, April 27, 2015, accessed May 1, 2016, www.theatlantic.com.

7   Elizabeth Wasserman Bloomberg, "Hillary Clinton wouldn't be in presidential race if she were a man, Trump says," *Toronto Star,* May 1, 2016, accessed May 1, 2016, www.thestar.com.

8   *New York Times Live,* "Women play the #womancard on Twitter in response to Trump," April 27, 2016, accessed May 1, 2016, www.nytlive.nytimes.com. For example, "Historically the #womancard is the most effective way to win the Presidency so I get the frustration."

9   Patricia Herbert, "Parties' stand-off masks common goal on coalition," *New Zealand Herald,* November 5, 1997.

10 Helen Bain, "Trying to look the part," *Dominion,* November 9, 1999.

11 For example, see Robert Mason, "My decision to quit, resigned Campbell says," *Vancouver Sun,* December 14, 1993, A1.

12 The *"petit gar de Shawinigan"* phrase was designed to rebrand Chrétien's political persona. A corporate lawyer and experienced politician who had served for many years as a Cabinet minister before winning the Liberal Party leadership, Chrétien referenced his humble roots in the small Quebec town of Shawinigan as a way of situating himself as a regular guy and man of the people.

13 Susan Delacourt, "Chretien eager to get to work," *Globe and Mail,* October 26, 1993, D1.

14 Ruth Berry and Julie Middleton, "Credibility the theme for big day," *New Zealand Herald,* September 16, 2005.

15 Ben Bawkes, "Leader's wife likes quiet life," *Dominion Post,* October 18, 2008.

16 Patricia Karvelas, "Abbott treads heavily on marginal ground," *Australian,* August 19, 2010, 9.

17 *New Zealand Herald,* "Writing was on the wall for leader two years ago," November 10, 2008.

18 Of Key's gender markers, 29 per cent used the word *boy.*

19 Ross Howard, "Liberal leader has had it easy," *Globe and Mail,* September 30, 1993, A1; Susan Delacourt, "Relying on instinct paid off for Jean Chretien," *Globe and Mail,* October 25, 1993, A1; Robert Sheppard, "A PM with few strings attached," *Globe and Mail,* October 26, 1993, A25.

20 Ruth Laugesen, "Bolger changes image from great helmsman to coalition man," *Dominion,* November 18, 1996.

21 Christine Langdon, "Clark has more to fear from the worm than from English," *Dominion,* July 1, 2002.

22 Tracy Watkins, "Sharp yes, but ruthless enough?," *Dominion Post,* July 9, 2002.

23 Geoff Collett, "Southern MPs back English," *Christchurch Press*, July 29, 2002.

24 Dan Eaton, "ACT will back a Nat government," *Christchurch Press*, October 17, 2008.

25 *New Zealand Herald*, "Let the show begin," November 16, 2008.

26 Tony Wright, "Rugby man Abbott puts himself in Melbourne's forty picture," *Age*, July 30, 2010, 5.

27 Katharine Murphy, "Abbott's message to independents is clear – deal with me," *Age*, August 23, 2010, 3.

28 Tony Wright, "Action Man Abbott eats raw fish, operates very big machines," *Age*, July 28, 2010, 7.

29 Tom Dusevic, "Abbott's put the Coalition back in the game," *Australian*, July 19, 2010, 6.

30 Ainsley Thomson and Ruth Berry, "Gentleman Don affronted by sexist tag," *New Zealand Herald*, August 24, 2005.

31 Colin Espiner, "Clark scorns Brash's claim to have 'gone easy' on her," *Christchurch Press*, August 24, 2005.

32 Thomson and Berry, "Gentleman Don affronted by sexist tag."

33 Ibid.

34 Adele Ferguson, "Gillard gets cautious nod of approval from investors as preferred Labor leader," *Age*, July 1, 2010, 6.

35 Patricia Herbert, "Clark moves to heal battle scars," *New Zealand Herald*, December 2, 1993, 1.

36 Rayan Tabbaa, Lauren Gale, and Matilda Gillis, "You go, girls: Gillard's rise to top hailed as an inspiration," *Sydney Morning Herald*, June 28, 2010, 6.

37 Kenneth Whyte, "Campbell has not demonstrated a western consciousness," *Globe and Mail*, June 12, 1993, D2.

38 Jeff Sallot, "Message not going out clearly, Campbell declares," *Globe and Mail*, October 20, 1993, A4.

39 Audrey Young, "Relief as weeks of waiting end and leadership role begins," *New Zealand Herald*, December 9, 1997.

40 *Dominion Post*, "Of Miss Helen Clark," November 15, 2008; Keri Welham, "The prime of Miss Helen Clark," *Dominion Post*, November 15, 2008.

41 Mike Munro, "Lange wades in behind Clark," *Dominion*, December 1, 1993, 6.

42 Paul Kelly, "Gillard leans to the left," *Australian*, August 14, 2010, 11.

43 *Dominion*, "Shipley likened to Thatcher," November 6, 1997; Paul Koring, "Flabbergasted by support, Campbell says," *Globe and Mail*, March 31, 1993, A3.

44 Paul Koring, "Flabbergasted by support, Campbell says."

45 Joel Gibson, "Money's on the filly with a fast finish but a rough track," *Sydney Morning Herald*, June 25, 2010, 7.

46 *Evening Post*, "Peters opts to bluff in coalition talks," November 10, 1997.

47 *Evening Post*, "A cautious first initiative," December 6, 1997.

48 Margaret Wente, "She's the pioneer, but is she good at governing?," *Globe and Mail*, June 15, 1993, A21.

49 Ellie Harvey, "Job seen as poisoned chalice for Gillard," *Sydney Morning Herald*, June 24, 2010, 2.

50 Christine Cessford, "No-nonsense Jenny fulfills early promise," *Evening Post*, November 4, 1997.

51 *Dominion Post*, "Time to bring out the big guns," October 18, 2008.

52 Liane Faulder, "How much does Kim Campbell's gender affect how we perceive her?," *Vancouver Sun*, April 2, 1993, C12.

53 *Australian*, "Giggles galore as Gillard goes back to school," August 11, 2010, 9.

54 Hugh Winsor, "Warm, funny side of Campbell being served up," *Globe and Mail*, March 26, 1993, A4.

55 Doug Ward, "The girl most likely: Doug Ward takes a look at Kim Campbell's ascendancy," *Vancouver Sun*, March 25, 1993, A4.

56 Thomson and Berry, "Gentleman Don affronted by sexist tag."

57 Samantha Maiden, "Gillard treads warily on *Women's Weekly*," *Australian*, July 27, 2010, 5.

58 Colin Espiner, "Remember where you came from," *Christchurch Press*, August 24, 2005.

59 *New Zealand Herald*, "Labour's shame won't be Clark's," November 9, 2008.

60 Roger Wakefield, "No sign of a coup cuppa," *New Zealand Herald*, November 7, 1997; Andrew Laxon, "Strength propels Shipley to top," *New Zealand Herald*, November 4, 1997; Lisa Fitterman, "Making book on Kim Campbell," *Vancouver Sun*, July 31, 1993, B3.

61 Michelle Grattan, "Gillard a fraud on population: Latham," *Age*, July 22, 2010, 7.

62 John Wanna, "Gillard gambles on her political capabilities," *Australian*, July 19, 2010, 16.

63 Fran O'Sullivan, "Shipley displays strength in difficult situations," *New Zealand Herald*, September 25, 1997.

64 Tracy Watkins, "'Da man' strikes friendly crowd," *Dominion Post*, August 27, 2005.

65 *Dominion*, "The prime of Ms Helen Clark," December 2, 1993, 12.

66 See https://en.wikipedia.org/wiki/The_X_Factor.

67 For instance, Jeff Sallot, "Campbell hews to line: Jokes but no hokum,"
    Globe and Mail, September 11, 1993, A6; and Jeff Sallot, "Campbell shrinks
    the gender gap," *Globe and Mail*, September 17, 1993, A5.
68 Simon Kilroy, "Clark attacks 'cruel stereotyping' to win women's votes,"
    Dominion, September 28, 1996.
69 Simon Kilroy, "Battle of female contrast looms," *Dominion*, November 5,
    1997.
70 Julian Lee, "Performance, not personality, key to how Labor will sell
    Gillard to voters," *Sydney Morning* Herald, July 2, 2010, 10.
71 Peter Hartcher, "Gillard can count on the XX factor," *Sydney Morning
    Herald*, July 24, 2010, 6.
72 Janet Albrechtson, "Mea culpa time? Not so fast," *Australian*, July 21, 2010, 14.
73 Nick O'Malley, "Gillard has more on her mind than gender," *Sydney
    Morning Herald*, June 26, 2010, 5.
74 *New Zealand Herald*, "New hand at the helm," December 8, 1997.
75 Stephen Lunn, "Partner faces life in the limelight – First Man," *Sydney
    Morning Herald*, June 26, 2010, 5.
76 *Globe and Mail*, "Kim Campbell, for all we know," March 26, 1993, A22.
77 Ross Howard, "Tortoise, hare labels switch near finish," *Globe and Mail*,
    June 8, 1993, A4. Brian Mulroney was the highly unpopular outgoing
    leader.
78 Colin James, "Is it time for a change of women at the top?," *New Zealand
    Herald*, November 24, 1999.
79 I used the search terms *Gillard* and *gender card* to identify articles in
    the three newspapers included in this study: the *Australian*, the *Sydney
    Morning Herald*, and the *Age*.
80 Sid Maher, "Slipper defence failed, Abbott attack escalates," *Australian*,
    October 11, 2012, 1.
81 Christopher Pearson, "Gender card hides failures," *Australian*, October 13,
    2012, 22.
82 Mark Kenny, "PM's chamber of horrors," *Sydney Morning Herald*, March
    20, 2013, 1.
83 Janet Albrechtsen, "Gender wars can't help the Labor cause any more than
    a quota PM," *Australian*, June 5, 2013, 10.
84 Janet Albrechtson, "PM's fake feminism is man made," *Australian*, January
    23, 2013, 10.
85 Niki Savaa, "Odds shorten on Bill as Brutus," *Australian*, June 13, 2013, 12.
86 Julia Baird, "Words that millions of women have rehearsed, yet never
    spoken," *Sydney Morning Herald*, October 13, 2012, 12.

87 Anna Goldsworthy, "Missing messiah: 'Getting stuff done' helped Gillard dodge the Golden Girl trap but became her un-doing," *Age*, June 22, 2013, 16.
88 George Megalogenis, "Online sensation exposes Abbott's gender card play to millions," *Australian*, October 20, 2012, 24.

Chapter 4

1 Margaret Wente, "Pierre Trudeau and his (many) women," *Globe and Mail*, October 28, 2009, accessed April 24, 2014, http://www.theglobeandmail.com/globe-debate/pierre-trudeau-and-his-many-women/article791993/.
2 See, for instance, "Photos: The Trudeau family past and present," *Vancouver Sun*, accessed March 26, 2013. http://www.vancouversun.com/news/photos+trudeau+family+past+present/11453609/story.html.
3 Tristan Hopper, "The Trudeau manipulation: Behind the most image-conscious campaign in Canadian history," *National Post*, October 12, 2015, accessed October 13, 2015, www.nationalpost.com.
4 Tim Murphy and Adelia Ferguson, "Opera lover, linguist, leader," *New Zealand Herald*, December 2, 1999, 9.
5 Doug Ward, "The girl most likely: Doug Ward takes a look at Kim Campbell's ascendancy," *Vancouver Sun*, March 25, 1993, A4; Robert Russo, "Five who would be PM: Promises and profiles – Kim Campbell," *Vancouver Sun*, June 10, 1993, A4.
6 Robert Mason Lee, "Sex and the single leaders," *Vancouver Sun*, September 30, 1993, A17.
7 Susan Delacourt, "These women are not two of a kind," *Globe and Mail*, April 6, 1993, A1.
8 Ibid.
9 Debbie Guest and Sallie Don, "Latham's views offside with soccer moms," *Australian*, June 26, 2010, 7.
10 Stephen Lunn, "Let's wait and see on marriage, says her partner," *Australian*, June 24, 2010, 3.
11 Farah Farouque and Nick Butterly, "Politics built into her genetic code, says new leader's father," *Sydney Morning Herald*, June 25, 2010, 5.
12 Phillip Coorey, "Odds-on Gillard clears decks," *Sydney Morning Herald*, June 29, 2010, 1.
13 Bettina Arndt, "Shacking up is hard to do: Why Gillard may be leery of the Lodge," *Sydney Morning Herald*, June 29, 2010, 11.
14 Lunn, "Let's wait and see on marriage."

15 Matthew Franklin, "Religious right's attack on Gillard," *Australian*, July 13, 2010, 5.
16 Tony Wright, "'First dude' watches on," *Age*, June 25, 2010, 4.
17 Farouque and Butterly, "Politics built into her genetic code."
18 Christine Cessford, "No-nonsense Jenny fulfills early promise," *Evening Post*, November 4, 1997.
19 Victoria Main, "Stakes high for Shipley," *Dominion*, November 5, 1999.
20 Val Aldridge, "Burton's up to the job," *Dominion*, December 13, 1999.
21 Ibid.
22 Murphy and Ferguson, "Opera lover, linguist, leader"; *Dominion*, "Relationship withstands pressures," December 2, 1993, 2.
23 *Dominion*, "The prime of Ms. Helen Clark," December 2, 1993, 12.
24 *Dominion*, "Parents confident of daughter's ability," December 2, 1993, 2.
25 Mike Munro and Ruth Laugesen, "Maoris may quit: Clark win sparks faction fears," *Dominion*, December 2, 1993, 1.
26 Patricia Herbert, "Clark moves to heal battle scars," *New Zealand Herald*, December 2, 1993, 1.
27 Jane Bowron, "Telling chat with spouses," *Dominion Post*, September 1, 2005.
28 Colin Espiner, "A woman of substance," *Christchurch Press*, November 1, 2008.
29 Murphy and Ferguson, "Opera lover, linguist, leader."
30 Helen Bain, "Slow ride to the ninth floor," *Dominion*, November 29, 1999.
31 Christine Langdon, "Clark has more to fear from the worm than from English," *Dominion*, July 1, 2002.
32 Tracy Watkins, "'Da man' strikes friendly crowd," *Dominion Post*, August 27, 2005.
33 *Dominion*, "The prime of Ms. Helen Clark"; Jon Morgan, "Clark too busy for kids – husband," *Dominion Post*, July 12, 2002.
34 Stephen Lunn, "Partner faces life in the limelight – first man," *Sydney Morning Herald*, June 26, 2010, 5.
35 Lunn, "Let's wait and see on marriage."
36 Farouque and Butterly, "Politics built into her genetic code."
37 Carol Nader and Dylan Welch, "Someone else can fill the fruit bowl …," *Age*, June 25, 2010, 9.
38 Lunn, "Let's wait and see on marriage."
39 Lunn, "Partner faces life in the limelight."
40 Julia Baird, "Lessons from sisters who fell on the way," *Sydney Morning Herald*, June 25, 2010, 2.

41 For example, Lunn, "Partner faces life in the limelight."
42 Rafael Epstein and Royce Millar, "Mathieson's property job likely casualty of Gillard election win," *Sydney Morning Herald*, August 19, 2010, 7; Dennis Shanahan and Paul Kelly, "I'll do it my way, declares Gillard," *Australian*, August 20, 2010, 4.
43 Lunn, "Let's wait and see on marriage."
44 Samantha Maiden, "Queen Julia's got the right touch," *Australian*, June 29, 2010, 5; Lanai Vasek, "Cover to cover, glossy mags swoop on Julia and Tim," *Australian*, June 29, 2010, 5.
45 Lunn, "Let's wait and see on marriage."
46 Rania Spooner, "Shock jock suspended for 'gay' question to PM." *Sydney Morning Herald*, June 13, 2013, accessed from www.smh.com.au.
47 Cathy Newman, "Political spouses could learn from Denis Thatcher," *Telegraph Online*, January 30, 2013.
48 For example, Audrey Young, "Relief as weeks of waiting end and leadership role begins," *New Zealand Herald*, December 9, 1997.
49 Bain, "Slow ride to the ninth floor."
50 Julie Szego, "Revolution is worth a shout," *Age*, June 25, 2010, 5.
51 Chris Johnston, "Alison, the quiet Gillard: I was more of a problem child," *Sydney Morning Herald*, July 24, 2010, 9.
52 Peter O'Neil, "Campbell sees double standard in media spin on her campaign," *Vancouver Sun*, May 12, 1993, A7.
53 Matthew Dearnaley, "Characteristic exit for pragmatic Clark," *New Zealand Herald*, November 10, 2008.
54 Colin James, "Is it time for a change of woman at the top?," *New Zealand Herald*, November 24, 1999.
55 Morgan, "Clark too busy for kids."
56 John Roughan, "Clark a clear winner on points," *New Zealand Herald*, November 24, 1999.
57 Espiner, "A woman of substance."
58 Josephine Tovey, "Being a first will not get Gillard off the hook," *Sydney Morning Herald*, June 25, 2010, 23.
59 Baird, "Lessons from sisters who fell on the way"; Michael Smith, "First-name basis with PM a sexist throwback," *Age*, June 26, 2010, 11.
60 Anne Summers, "Historic moment, but barriers remain for half the population," *Sydney Morning Herald*, June 24, 2010, 23.
61 Anne Summers, "Insight: Gillard," *Age*, June 26, 2010, 3.
62 Arndt, "Shacking up is hard to do: Why Gillard may be leery of the Lodge."
63 Tovey, "Being a first will not get Gillard off the hook."

64 Farah Farouque, "Brought up on hard work and hot issues," *Age*, June 25, 2010, 8.

65 Mary-Anne Toy, "Never one of the boys," *Age*, June 26, 2010, 9.

66 Smith, "First-name basis with PM a sexist throwback."

67 Guest and Sallie Don, "Latham's views offside with soccer moms."

68 Ibid.

69 Roughan, "Clark a clear winner on points."

70 Phillip Coorey, "Gillard: I understand your family sacrifices," *Sydney Morning Herald*, July 13, 2010, 5.

71 Tony Wright, "Kid stuff: Gillard cuddles the past," *Age*, July 19, 2010, 1; Jon Pierik, Samantha Lane, and Ari Sharp, "It's a perfect day for Gillard as her other team wins big," *Sydney Morning Herald*, August 2, 2010, 6.

72 *Vancouver Sun*, "Campbell wants to be the down-to-earth den mother of us all," May 14, 1993, A4.

73 Jeff Sallot and Ross Howard, "Tories brace for contest past first ballot: Campbell, Charest organizers court uncommitted delegates," *Globe and Mail*, June 12, 1993, A1.

74 Hugh Winsor, "Campbellmania fizzles: Kim Campbell generated little excitement in her Atlantic tour," *Globe and Mail*, May 25, 1993, A1.

75 Ross Howard, "Campbell reassesses support," *Globe and Mail*, June 4, 1993, A9.

76 Jeff Sallot, "Jabs require subtlety in Tory race: Politically correct critics won't note Campbell divorces, Charest's roots," *Globe and Mail*, June 5, 1993, A1.

77 Ibid.

78 Lysianne Gagnon, "Why isn't Campbell judged by the same yardstick as male politicians?," *Globe and Mail*, June 5, 1993, D3; Sallot and Howard, "Tories brace for contest past first ballot"; Liane Faulder, "How much does Kim Campbell's gender affect how we perceive her?," *Vancouver Sun*, April 2, 1993, C12; O'Neil, "Campbell sees double standard in media spin on her campaign."

79 Ross Howard and Jeff Sallot, "Campbell calls for unity as Tories elect her leader," *Globe and Mail*, June 14, 1993, A1; Daphne Bramham, "Canada's first female PM will put gender issue to rest," *Vancouver Sun*, June 14, 1993, A11.

80 See, in particular, Ward, "The girl most likely"; and Russo, "Five who would be PM."

81 Sallot, "Jabs require subtlety in Tory race."

82 Peter O'Neil, "Embattled Campbell set to come out swinging at Charest," *Vancouver Sun*, June 3, 1993, A4; see also the editorial, "In matters of conscience: Campbell it is," *Vancouver Sun*, June 12, 1993, A10.

83 Edward Greenspon, "Tories ready – finally – to accept a woman leader," *Globe and Mail*, June 14, 1993, A9.

84 Charlotte Grey, "The speech: Damned if she does, damned if she doesn't," *Globe and Mail*, June 19, 1993, D5.

85 Ibid.

86 Ibid.

87 Sallot, "Jabs require subtlety in Tory race."

88 Gagnon, "Why isn't Campbell judged by the same yardstick as male politicians?"; Peter O'Neil, "Is media focus on Campbell sexist?," *Vancouver Sun*, May 28, 1993, A5.

89 Faulder, "How much does Kim Campbell's gender affect how we perceive her?"

90 Greenspon, "Tories ready – finally – to accept a woman leader."

91 Ron Graham, "The Campbell Gamble," *Globe and Mail Report on Business Magazine*, August 27, 1993, 30.

92 Sallot and Howard, "Tories brace for contest past first ballot."

93 Bramham, "Canada's first female PM will put the gender issue to rest."

94 Jeff Sallot, "PM blitzes nation's parties: Canada Day trip shows Campbell's pre-election advantage," *Globe and Mail*, July 2, 1993, A1.

95 Susan Delacourt, "BC vents anger at Campbell on the air," *Globe and Mail*, September 28, 1993, A4.

96 See Peggy Curran, "Chretien wins Liberal leadership," *Montreal Gazette*, June 24, 1990, A1; and Hubert Bauch, "Chretien promises to make employment key election issue," *Montreal Gazette*, September 9, 1993, A4.

97 Tom Arup and Kirsty Needham, "Family ties or in a bind? Abbott welcomes his wife as Gillard goes it alone," *Age*, July 27, 2010, 1.

98 Ibid.

99 Ibid.

100 Phillip Coorey, "Margie stands by her man as Abbott woos women," *Sydney Morning Herald*, July 27, 2010, 5.

101 Ibid.

102 Arup and Needham, "Family ties or in a bind?"

103 Dan Harrison, "Gillard's top end token: $2m sports aid," *Age*, August 9, 2010, 7.

104 For example, Sid Maher, "On a roll, Abbott chews 'n chats," *Australian*, August 16, 2010, 6; Katharine Murphy, "Abbott team barnstorms Queensland," *Age*, August 19, 2010, 7; Kirsty Needham, "Abbott gaffe mars baby policy launch," *Age*, August 4, 2010, 4; Michelle Grattan, "Abbott sets plan of attack," *Age*, August 9, 2010, 1; Rhys Muldoon,

"All aboard the Abbott express!," *Sydney Morning Herald*, August 13, 2010, 6.

105 Arup and Needham, "Family ties or in a bind?"

106 Matthew Franklin, "Abbott to stall childcare reforms." *Australian*, July 27, 2010, 5.

107 Coorey, "Margie stands by her man as Abbott woos women."

108 Tony Wright, "Action Man Abbott eats raw fish, operates very big machines," *Age*, July 28, 2010, 7.

109 Simon Kilroy, "Battle of female contrasts looms," *Dominion*, November 5, 1997.

110 *New Zealand Herald*, "Shipley lacking common touch," October 30, 1999; *Dominion*, "Shipley's 'Mum' angle misjudged, says Clark," October 30, 1999.

111 James, "Is it time for a change of woman at the top?"; Roughan, "Clark a clear winner on points."

112 Colin James, "Soft sell with mistaken spin (honestly)," *New Zealand Herald*, November 8, 1999.

113 *Dominion*, "Shipley's 'Mum' angle misjudged."

114 Ibid.

115 Tracy Watkins, "Sharp yes, but ruthless enough?," *Dominion Post*, July 9, 2002; *Dominion Post*, "Bill woos elderly 'just like Keith,'" July 16, 2002.

116 Langdon, "Clark has more to fear from the worm than from English."

117 Morgan, "Clark too busy for kids."

118 *New Zealand Herald*, "Brash candid on his adultery," August 31, 2005.

119 Ibid.

120 Tracy Watkins, "The selling of Helen Clark," August 26, 2005.

121 Mike Crean, "Is Don Brash racist?," *Christchurch Press*, September 10, 2005.

122 Tracy Watkins, "I'm no feminist, says Brash," *Dominion Post*, August 25, 2005.

123 Errol Kiong, "Clark hits back over abuse during debate," *New Zealand Herald*, September 5, 2005.

124 Eugene Bingham, "Key's flip-flop on puppy for the kids," *New Zealand Herald*, November 10, 2008.

125 Ben Bawkes, "Leader's wife likes quiet life," *Dominion Post*, October 18, 2008.

126 *Christchurch Press*, "Key and family to stay in Auckland," November 10, 2008.

127 Tracy Watkins, "PM won't need a mansion in capital," *Dominion Post*, November 10, 2008.
128 Colin Espiner, "Key faces campaign blowtorch," *Christchurch Press*, October 25, 2008.

Chapter 5

1 Mark MacKinnon and Omar El Akkad, "The world welcomes Justin Trudeau, Canada's 'superhot new leader,'" *Globe and Mail*, October 20, 2015, accessed October 25, 2015, www.theglobeandmail.com.
2 The terms *appearance* and *looks* are used interchangeably in this section.
3 Terrance Wills, "Chretien seems sure winner," *Montreal Gazette*, October 16, 1993, A8.
4 Audrey Young and Vernon Small, "Chips, oysters – all for votes," *New Zealand Herald*, July 2, 2002.
5 Katharine Murphy, "Abbott's campaign rides rough, but it sure can be fun," *Age*, July 22, 2012, 7.
6 *Evening Post*, "Mr. Unflappable blows his cool," September 30, 1996.
7 Steve Rendle, "National family rallies around Southern Man," *Dominion Post*, July 29, 2002.
8 Colin Espiner, "Brash shows poor judgment over denials," *Christchurch Press*, September 9, 2005; *Christchurch Press*, "What trivia reveals," September 9, 2005; Matt Conway, "Political sideshows," *Christchurch Press*, September 10, 2005; Mike Crean, "Is Don Brash racist?" *Christchurch Press*, September 10, 2005; Haydon Dewes, "Red-faced Brash stuck in Powhiri at Wanaga," *Christchurch Press*, September 14, 2005; Haydon Dewes, "Brash heckled on race plans," *Dominion Post*, August 30, 2005; Vernon Small, "Brash wearing thin as the absent-minded professor," *Dominion Post*, September 8, 2005; and Haydon Dewes, "Wananga ambushes critical Brash," *Dominion Post*, September 14, 2005.
9 William Johnson, "With Liberal leader Chretien, what you see is what you get," *Montreal Gazette*, September 25, 1993, B5.
10 Edward Greenspon, Ross Howard, and Susan Delacourt, "Tories try to recover from goof: Campbell pulls ads emphasizing paralysis of Chretien's face," *Globe and Mail*, October 16, 1993, A6.
11 Norman Webster, "Making waves: 30 years in politics taught Chretien a thing or two," *Montreal Gazette*, October 16, 1993, B6.
12 *New Zealand Herald*, "Taxing times on the factory floor," August 27, 2005.
13 Francesca Mold, "Campaign foes ready to haggle," *New Zealand Herald*, July 20, 2002.

14 Warren Caragata, "Boss at last: Second fiddle for years, Liberal leader now leads the whole orchestra," *Montreal Gazette*, October 23, 1993, A8. As Delacourt (2013, 151) notes, the wardrobe choice was key to the Liberal leader's "everyman" brand.

15 Tracy Watkins, "Debate lost amid the din," *Dominion Post*, August 23, 2005.

16 Claire Trevett, "Key takes in the nation by air for some last-minute rallying," *New Zealand Herald*, November 7, 2008.

17 Katharine Murphy, "All aboard the Abbott straight spin express," *Age*, July 19, 2010, 5.

18 Michael Smith, "First name basis with PM a sexist throwback," *Age*, June 26, 2010, 11.

19 Gabriella Coslovich, "Why style has a substantial place in the volatile world of politics," *Age*, June 26, 2010, 8.

20 Melissa Singer, "Gillard hopes to avoid history as fifth-shortest-serving PM," *Sydney Morning Herald*, July 19, 2010, 4; Paul Metherell, "Plenty of time for a coffee when Gillard gads about," *Sydney Morning Herald*, July 20, 2010, 4; Patricia Karvelas, "Gillard defends tax stumble," *Australian*, July 28, 2010, 5.

21 Mark Davis, "Building ambition from the sandpit of politics," *Sydney Morning Herald*, June 24, 2010, 3.

22 Barbara Yaffe, "Kim of Green Gables? Books look at PM," *Vancouver Sun*, July 10, 1993, A7.

23 Doug Ward, "The girl most likely: Doug Ward takes a look at Kim Campbell's ascendancy," *Vancouver Sun*, March 25, 1993, A4.

24 Christina McCall, "The PM is looking like one of the boys: Is the real Kim Campbell still in the package?," *Globe and Mail*, June 25, 1993, A1.

25 Catherine Masters, "Image gurus say it won't take a lot to get Shipley shipshape," *New Zealand Herald*, November 6, 1997; Helen Bain, "Odd couple gel in coalition," *Dominion*, September 20, 1997.

26 Masters, "Image gurus say it won't take a lot to get Shipley shipshape."

27 *New Zealand Herald*, "Savage response in Christchurch," December 2, 1993.

28 *Dominion Post*, "Diary," October 28, 2008.

29 *New Zealand Herald*, "Gangster chic gets our vote," July 20, 2002.

30 Helen Bain, "Trying to look the part," *Dominion*, November 9, 1999; emphasis mine.

31 Bain, "Odd couple gel in coalition."

32 Peter Luke, "Gloves off as PM targets 'lies,'" *Christchurch Press*, November 12, 1999.

33 Tracy Watkins, "Debate lost amid the din," *Dominion Post*, August 23, 2005.

34 *Dominion Post*, "Diary"; Alice Hudson, "War paint aids the campaign," *New Zealand Herald*, October 19, 2008.

35 Tess Livingstone, "Sisterhood a reminder of its irrelevance," *Australian*, June 26, 2010, 5.

36 Tony Wright, "'First dude' watches on," *Age*, June 25, 2010, 4; Samantha Maiden, "Gillard treads warily on *Women's Weekly*," *Australian*, July 27, 2010, 5.

37 Sid Maher and Dennis Shanahan, "Defiant PM to force plotters into the open," *Australian*, June 26, 2013, 1.

38 *Australian*, "PM author of her own demise," June 29, 2013, 23.

39 Peter O'Neil, "Suddenly, Queen Kim starts looking shaky on Tory throne," *Vancouver Sun*, April 17, 1993, A5.

40 Bain, "Trying to look the part."

41 *New Zealand Herald*, "Shipley lacking common touch," October 30, 1999.

42 *New Zealand Herald*, "Showdown – how to be a winner," July 25, 2002.

43 Nick Venter, "Political heavyweights hit prime time," *Dominion*, June 29, 2002.

44 Colin Espiner, "Labour's new start," *Christchurch Press*, July 29, 2002.

45 Jean Fraser, "A few fashion pointers for the neophyte prime minister," *Vancouver Sun*, August 3, 1993, C1.

46 Masters, "Image gurus say it won't take a lot to get Shipley shipshape."

47 For example, see Carroll du Chateau, "The final straight," *New Zealand Herald*, November 1, 2008.

48 *Dominion*, "Clark's mouth 'really is hers,'" November 6, 1999.

49 Gabriella Coslovich, "Why style has a substantial place," *Age*, June 26, 2010, 8.

50 Fraser, "A few fashion pointers for the neophyte prime minister."

51 Dennis Shanahan, "Gillard got the cover but Abbott is looking better," *Australian*, July 30, 2010, 14.

52 Terrence Wills, "Chopper deal dies as soon as I'm sworn in: Chretien," *Montreal Gazette*, October 28, 1933, A1.

53 *New Zealand Herald*, "Let the show begin," November 16, 2008.

54 Colin Espiner, "Warm welcome for Key on the coast," *Christchurch Press*, October 25, 2008.

55 Jacqueline Maley, "She held us up to the mirror – do you like what you saw?," *Sydney Morning Herald*, June 29, 2013, 11.

56 Peter O'Neil, "Kimmanie fuels Campbell's campaign bandwagon in Quebec," *Globe and Mail*, April 21, 1993, A5; emphasis mine.

57 Jennifer Hewett, "A confused nation asks, will the real Julia Gillard stand up?," *Australian*, July 31, 2010, 11; emphasis mine.

58 Julie Szego, "Revolution is worth a shout: Julia Gillard – a feminist hero," *Age*, June 25, 2010, 5.
59 Niki Savva, "Abbott's campaign flatlines as Gillard captures the momentum," *Australian*, August 14, 2010, 11.
60 Masters, "Image gurus say it won't take a lot to get Shipley shipshape."
61 Colin James, "Third term-it is makes for hard Labour," *New Zealand Herald*, November 7, 2008.
62 *New Zealand Herald*, "Labour's shame won't be Clark's," November 9, 2008.
63 *Dominion*, "PM waits her turn," December 10, 1997.
64 Matt Conway, "Political sideshows," *Christchurch Press*, September 10, 2005; Dewes, "Red-faced Brash stuck in Powhiri at Wanaga."
65 For example, *New Zealand Herald*, "Taxing times on the factory floor"; Colin Espiner, "What you see is what you get," *Christchurch Press*, August 24, 2005; Mike Crean, "Is Don Brash racist?"; and Dewes, "Wananga ambushes critical Brash."
66 Claire Harvey, "Ritual humiliation and other tests of leadership," *New Zealand Herald*, September 10, 2005.
67 Colin Espiner, "What you see is what you get."
68 *New Zealand Herald*, "Jeremy Wapp, a 22 year-old car parts salesman," August 26, 2005.
69 Ron Graham, "The Campbell Gamble," *Globe and Mail*, August 27, 1993, A30.
70 See, for instance, Hugh Winsor, "Campbelmania fizzles," *Globe and Mail*, May 25, 1993, A1; and Hugh Winsor and Ross Howard, "Tortoise runs out of time and luck," *Globe and Mail*, June 14, 1993, A1.
71 Christina McCall, "The PM is looking like one of the boys."
72 Ward, "The girl most likely."
73 Peter O'Neil, "Kimmanie fuels Campbell's campaign bandwagon in Quebec," A5.
74 Francine Pelletier, "The media factor: Kim Campbell has gone from darling to target of the press," *Vancouver Sun*, June 1, 1993, A13.
75 Lianne Faulder, "How much does Kim Campbell's gender affect how we perceive her?," *Vancouver Sun*, April 2, 1993, C12.
76 See Hugh Winsor, "Is Campbell's star beginning to dim?," *Globe and Mail*, April 17, 1993, A1; and Peter O'Neil, "Tory leader doffs gloves, but fails to fashion boost in her campaign," *Vancouver Sun*, October 4, 1993, A4.
77 Graham, "The Campbell gamble."
78 Ibid.

79 Peter O'Neil, "Put on a happy face: PM works on her image, with success," *Vancouver Sun*, August 7, 1993, B1.

80 Frank Davey, "Kim Campbell and the endless summer," *Globe and Mail*, September 16, 1993, A27.

81 According to the program's website (http://www.tv.com/shows/ extreme-makeover/, accessed August 13, 2013), *"Extreme Makeover* follows the stories of the lucky individuals who are chosen for a once-in-a-lifetime chance to be given a truly 'Cinderella-like' experience: a real life fairy tale in which their wishes come true, not just by changing their looks, but their lives and destinies. This magic is conjured through the skills of an 'Extreme Team,' including the nation's top plastic surgeons, eye surgeons and cosmetic dentists, along with a talented team of hair and makeup artists, stylists, and personal trainers, led by an on-camera Extreme Makeover expert."

82 Eileen O'Leary, "Ice-Breaker decides time is right," *Evening Press*, December 1, 1993.

83 *New Zealand Herald*, "Savage response in Christchurch."

84 TV3, November 30, 1993.

85 *Dominion*, "Attacks 'spurred by Clark's strong showing,'" September 28, 1996.

86 Anna Kominik, "'Cinderella' Clark can thank media trainers," *Dominion*, October 10, 1996.

87 *Dominion*, "Nats seek new angle for attack on Clark," October 4, 1995.

88 Kominik, "'Cinderella' Clark can thank media trainers."

89 Sarah Boyd, "Personal note as Clark gains confidence," *Evening Post*, September 28, 1996.

90 Ruth Laugesen, "Clark draws first blood," *Dominion*, September 27, 1996.

91 Brent Edwards, "The election campaign is just the beginning," *Evening Post*, October 11, 1996.

92 Nick Venter, "The political prime of Miss Helen Clark," *Dominion Post*, July 8, 2002.

93 Jonathan Milne, "Clark paints picture of integrity," *Dominion Post*, July 9, 2002.

94 *New Zealand Herald*, "Showdown – how to be a winner."

95 Helen Bain, "Slow ride to the ninth floor," *Dominion*, November 29, 1999.

96 Bain, "Trying to look the part."

97 Ibid.

98 *Dominion*, "Clark's mouth 'really is hers.'"

99 Ibid.

100 Ibid.

101 Ibid.

102 Bain, "Trying to look the part."

103 Christine Langdon, "Clark has more to fear from the worm than from English," *Dominion,* July 1, 2002; Venter, "The political prime of Miss Helen Clark."

104 *New Zealand Herald,* "Showdown – how to be a winner."

105 Manufacturers cashed in on the phenomenon, marketing a blow-up Palin doll "complete with bursting cleavage and sexy business suit" and a Clinton nutcracker featuring "stainless steel thighs that, well, bust nuts" (Carlin and Winfrey 2009, 330, 337).

106 *New Zealand Herald,* "Brash candid on his adultery," August 31, 2005; Jane Bowron, "Telling chat with spouses," *Dominion Post,* September 1, 2005.

107 Claire Trevett, "Key winning the free parsley vote," *New Zealand Herald,* October 21, 2008.

108 Paul Austin, "Stupid, funny or a dirty trick? Abbott laughs off Speedos stunt," *Age,* July 21, 2010, 6.

109 Peter O'Neil, "PM adopts Little Orphan Annie self-image, biographer says," *Vancouver Sun,* July 30, 1993, A4.

110 Peter O'Neil, "Kimmanie fuels Campbell's campaign bandwagon in Quebec."

111 Warren Caragata, "Kim Campbell ignites book publishing boon," *Globe and Mail,* July 7, 1993, C5.

112 Ross Howard, "Far from a Campbell Accord: The politics of Kim Campbell," *Globe and Mail,* August 7, 1993, C18.

113 Hugh Winsor and Ross Howard, "Campbell, Mulroney woo Charest Conservatives," *Globe and Mail,* June 16, 1993, A1.

114 Christina McCall, "This PM is looking like one of the boys."

115 Jeff Sallot, "Campbell hews to line: Jokes but no hokum," *Globe and Mail,* September 11, 1993, A6.

116 Hugh Winsor and Ross Howard, "Tortoise runs out of time and luck."

117 Peter O'Neil, "Kimmanie fuels Campbell's campaign bandwagon in Quebec."

118 *Vancouver Sun,* "Campbell wants to be the down-to-earth den mother of us all," May 14, 1993, A4.

119 For example, "The other day, Campbell asked reporters, 'Is that a Crayola in your pocket, or are you just glad to see me?'" Robert Mason, "Sex and the single leader," *Vancouver Sun,* September 30, 1993, A17.

120 Hugh Winsor, "Mugging the media: Kim factor triumphs in the battle of the barbeques," *Globe and Mail,* August 21, 1993, D1.

121 André Picard, "Campbell expels Quebec MPs," *Globe and Mail,* August 3, 1993, A1.

122 Lee, "Sex and the single leader."
123 Ross Howard, "Campbell's popularity may speed election call," *Globe and Mail*, August 21, 1993, A1.
124 Doug Ward, "PM takes summertime seduction of Canadian electorate to airwaves," *Vancouver Sun*, August 11, 1993, A3.
125 Julie Szego, "Revolution is worth a shout."
126 Ibid.
127 Matt Buchanan and Tim Elliott, "Red alert for Gillard fans," *Sydney Morning Herald*, July 5, 2010, 18.
128 Mike Carlton, "The heat's turned up but Tony Abbott has shivers up his spine," *Sydney Morning Herald*, June 25, 2010, 14. .
129 Nick Savva, "Red Maggie's rise raises great expectations," *Australian*, June 25, 2010, 16.
130 *Australian*, "Julia Gillard recycles a second-hand idea," July 26, 2010, 15.
131 Julie Szego, "Revolution is worth a shout."
132 The series can be viewed on YouTube: http://www.youtube.com/watch?v=0du9PrI95oc.
133 Marilyn Lake, "How the PM's gender took over the agenda," *Age*, June 24, 2013, 20.
134 This was demonstrably the case for Hillary Clinton during the 2008 Democratic primaries; see Lawrence and Rose 2010, 180–204.
135 Lake, "How the PM's gender took over the agenda."
136 See Anne Summer's 2012 Human Rights and Social Justice lecture, titled "Her Rights at Work," at http://annesummers.com.au/speeches/her-rights-at-work-r-rated/.
137 Rania Spooner, "Shock jock suspended for 'gay' question to PM," *Sydney Morning Herald*, June 13, 2013, accessed August 4, 2013, www.syh.com.au.
138 Paul Osborne, "Lewd menu 'pattern of behaviour': Gillard," *Sydney Morning Herald*, June 12, 2013, accessed August 4, 2013, smh.com.au. The "other offensive remark" was "a Big Red Box."
139 Lake, "How the PM's gender took over the agenda."
140 Michael Rentoul, "Clark challenge looks likely to leave Labour Party in pieces," *Christchurch Press*, December 1, 1993; *Evening Post*, "It's Clark: Moore loses, Caygill wins deputy job," December 1, 1993.
141 O'Leary, "Ice-Breaker decides time is right."
142 *Dominion*, "The prime of Ms. Helen Clark," December 2, 1993.
143 Tracy Watkins, "Clark lost her rag – Nats," *Dominion Post*, July 12, 2002.
144 *New Zealand Herald*, "It's going down to the wire," September 6, 2005.
145 Jane Bowron, "Telling chat with spouses," *Dominion Post*, September 1, 2005.

146 Nick Venter, "More suits vie for hand of 'black widow,'" *Dominion Post*, July 23, 2002.
147 Ibid.; Jonathan Milne, "'Black Widow' steers clear of Peters' web," *Dominion Post*, July 24, 2002; David McLoughlin, "Leaders get on with 'little creep,'" *Dominion Post*, July 26, 2002.
148 Tagline accessed June 16, 2014, www.imdb.com.
149 *New Zealand Herald*, "Helen Clark demonstrated superior debating skills in her final face-off with Don," September 16, 2005.
150 Tabatha Southey, "Note to world: Please stop ogling our new prime minister," *Globe and Mail*, October 23, 2015. As Southey details, the words and phrases used by British, Australian, and American newspapers to describe Trudeau included "smoking-hot syrupy fox," "the sexiest politician in the world," and "Canada's new, incredibly good-looking prime minister."

Chapter 6

1 Excerpts from Trimble (2014) are featured in the sections titled "Metaphors and Gendered Mediation" and "Electoral Battlefields."
2 Fran O'Sullivan, "Gladiator v. Boadicea: No Contest?," *New Zealand Herald*, October 30, 2008.
3 Tracy Watkins, "Sugar and spice – and Clark wins at being nice," *Dominion Post*, November 6, 2008.
4 Vernon Small, "Clark plays her winning card," *New Zealand Herald*, July 1, 2002.
5 Colin Espiner, "Labs, Greens make up," *Christchurch Press*, July 25, 2002.
6 Peter Luke, "Party at Helen's?," *Christchurch Press*, July 20, 2002.
7 Robert Matas, "Campbell to offer policy 'tidbits': Defence minister entering Tory leadership race with television address today," *Globe and Mail*, March 25, 1993, A3.
8 Hugh Winsor and Ross Howard, "Tortoise runs out of time and luck," *Globe and Mail*, June 14, 1993, A1.
9 Kirk Makin, "Chretien questions Campbell ability after PC shifting," *Globe and Mail*, September 14, 1993, A4.
10 Ross Howard, "Campbell belittles Liberal policies," *Globe and Mail*, September 16, 1993, A6.
11 Kenneth Whyte, "Campbell has not demonstrated a Western consciousness," *Globe and Mail*, June 12, 1993, D2.
12 Makin, "Chretien questions Campbell ability after PC shifting."
13 Ibid.

14 Geoffrey York, "Campbell grilled on deficit plan," *Globe and Mail*, September 18, 1993, A1.
15 Ross Howard, "Political memo: Get tough, Campbell urged," *Globe and Mail*, September 23 2003, A8.
16 Jeff Sallot, "Campbell rallies troops for on-air strike," *Globe and Mail*, October 2, 1993, A6.
17 Hugh Winsor, "Campbell slams Chretien's plan as inflationary," *Globe and Mail*, September 23, 1993, A6.
18 Sallot, "Campbell rallies troops for on-air strike."
19 Ibid.
20 Hugh Winsor, "Beleaguered, game Campbell manages to land a few blows," *Globe and Mail*, October 4, 1993, A10; Robert Mason, "Sex and the single leader," *Vancouver Sun*, September 30, 1993, A17; Robert Mason, "Campbell remaining coy on deficit cuts," *Vancouver Sun*, September 27, 1993, A1; Ross Howard, "'Weekend from hell' stuns Tories," *Globe and Mail*, October 18, 1993, A1; Peter O'Neil, "McLaughlin picks up steam as Campbell loses her cool," *Vancouver Sun*, October 5, 1993, A4; Jamie Lamb, "PM's letter undermines her own mining minister," *Vancouver Sun*, September 22, 1993, A3.
21 Ross Howard, "Campbell calm in defeat: Conservative leader consoles her fallen Cabinet ministers," *Globe and Mail*, October 26, 1993, D1.
22 O'Neil, "McLaughlin picks up steam as Campbell loses her cool."
23 Ross Howard, "The strategists: Nervous Tories consider survival, not success," *Globe and Mail*, October 7, 1993, A4.
24 Hugh Winsor, "Liberals teach a lesson: Pick one message and stick to it," *Globe and Mail*, October 23, 1993, A6.
25 Edward Greenspon and Jeff Sallot, "How Campbell self-destructed," *Globe and Mail*, October 27, 1993, A1.
26 Howard, "'Weekend from hell' stuns Tories."
27 Mason, "Sex and the single leader."
28 *New Zealand Herald*, "Eye-to-eye fight for the hearts of the 'real' New Zealanders," December 13, 1997.
29 Ibid.
30 Helen Bain, "Trying to look the part," *Dominion*, November 9, 1999.
31 Graeme Peters, "ACT-Nat tax policy rift widens," *Evening Post*, November 6, 1999.
32 *Evening Post*, "Into enemy territory," November 10, 1999.
33 Brian Rudman, "Woman of steely resolve in good times and bad," *New Zealand Herald*, November 29, 1999.
34 *Evening Post*, "An untrodden path ahead," January 3, 1998.

35 Rudman, "Woman of steely resolve in good times and bad"; Colin James, "Is it time for a change of woman at the top?," *New Zealand Herald*, November 24, 1999.

36 Victoria Main, "Stakes high for Shipley," *Dominion*, November 5, 1999.

37 John Armstrong, "Leaders' confrontation a mere damp squib," *New Zealand Herald*, December 10, 1997; emphasis mine.

38 Helen Bain, "Action woman," *Dominion*, November 29, 1999.

39 Bain, "Trying to look the part."

40 Michael Rentoul, "Shipley pushes welfare reforms," *Christchurch Press*, December 9, 1999.

41 *Evening Post*, "Shipley, Nats up, Labour down in polls," November 25, 1997.

42 Rudman, "Woman of steely resolve in good times and bad."

43 A total of 127 news articles about Clark met the sampling criteria (leader named in the headline or lead paragraph and discussed in at least 50 per cent of the article), while 198 articles about Key met these criteria.

44 John Roughan, "Clark triumphs in TV joust with rival political leaders," *New Zealand Herald*, September 27, 1996; Ruth Laugesen, "Clark draws first blood," *Dominion*, September 27, 1996.

45 Patricia Herbert, "Bolger may boycott next leader's joust," *New Zealand Herald*, September 28, 1996.

46 *Christchurch Press*, "Prebble urges National to rule out deals with the left," September 30, 1996.

47 Bevan Rapson, "Slugger Bolger fighting desperately for survival," *New Zealand Herald*, October 5, 1996.

48 Laugesen, "Clark draws first blood."

49 *New Zealand Herald*, "Prize to Clark before a vote cast," October 11, 1996.

50 Graeme Speden, "Clark, Lange working together again," *Dominion*, October 7, 1996.

51 Ibid.

52 Peter Luke, "Bill English – New Zealand needs a strong National Party," *Christchurch Press*, July 15, 2002, 6.

53 Tracy Watkins, "Blistering words over 'Paintergate,'" *Dominion Post*, July 8, 2002; Audrey Young, "PM threatens to sue over 'Paintergate,'" *New Zealand Herald*, July 8, 2002.

54 Tracy Watkins, "Lawyer joins in Paintergate saga," *Dominion Post*, July 8, 2002; Tracy Watkins, "English fails to land body blows," *Dominion Post*, July 23, 2002.

55 Vernon Small and Helen Tunnah, "Clark in fury at GM ambush," *New Zealand Herald*, July 11, 2002.

56 Peter Luke, "PM lightens mood after 'Corngate,'" *Christchurch Press*, July 12, 2002.
57 Ruth Berry, "Be very wary of those behind Dunne – Clark," *Dominion Post*, July 26, 2002.
58 Ruth Berry, "Peters declares war on gov't," *Christchurch Press*, July 29, 2002.
59 Nick Venter, "More suitors vie for hand of 'black widow,'" *Dominion Post*, July 23, 2002; Watkins, "English fails to land body blows"; Jonathan Milne, "Clark – I have ruled out a coalition with NZ First," *Christchurch Press*, July 24, 2002.
60 Colin James, "Clark's challenge is to be bold and make big changes," *New Zealand Herald*, October 11, 2005.
61 Ainsley Thomson and Ruth Berry, "Gentleman Don affronted by sexist tag," *New Zealand Herald*, August 24, 2005.
62 *Dominion Post*, "Debates blood sport," August 24, 2005.
63 *New Zealand Herald*, "Helen Clark demonstrated superior debating skills in her final face-off with Don," September 16, 2005.
64 *New Zealand Herald*, "Clark in action faster than you can say motorcade," September 20, 2005.
65 Colin Espiner, "Clark wins final debate," *Christchurch Press*, September 16, 2005.
66 Kevin Taylor, "Helen Clark: Stability or division voters' stark choice," *New Zealand Herald*, September 15, 2005.
67 *New Zealand Herald*, "National's resurgence on tax promises rings wake-up call for Clark," September 19, 2005.
68 Haydon Dewes, "Buxom blondes, 'weird sex,'" *Dominion Post*, September 12, 2005.
69 *New Zealand Herald*, "Helen Clark demonstrated superior debating skills in her final face-off with Don."
70 Audrey Young, "PM lets a little mongrel off the leash," *New Zealand Herald*, August 23, 2005.
71 Thomson and Berry, "Gentleman Don affronted by sexist tag."
72 *New Zealand Herald*, "It's going down to the wire: Leadership battle," September 6, 2005.
73 Thomson and Berry, "Gentleman Don affronted by sexist tag."
74 James, "Clark's challenge is to be bold and make big changes."
75 Colin Espiner, "Remember where you came from," *Christchurch Press*, August 24, 2005.

76 Tracy Watkins, "'Da man' strikes friendly crowd," *Dominion Post*, August 27, 2005.

77 O'Sullivan, "Gladiator v. Boadicea: No contest?" This woman warrior is also known as Boudica and Boudicca.

78 See the description of *Gladiator* on the Internet Movie Database: http://www.imdb.com/title/tt0172495/.

79 O'Sullivan, "Gladiator v. Boadicea?"

80 Ibid.

81 *New Zealand Herald*, "Writing was on the wall for leader two years ago," November 10, 2008.

82 *Dominion Post*, "Campaign diary," October 14, 2008; *Christchurch Press*, "Clark hits out at Key, TVNZ," October 16, 2008; Emily Watt, "PM slams contract directors' 'greed,'" *Christchurch Press*, October 23, 2008.

83 Colin Espiner, "Key matches Clark in fiery debate," *Christchurch Press*, October 15, 2008.

84 *New Zealand Herald*, "Clark fixes the small shower to avoid a bath," October 15, 2008.

85 *New Zealand Herald*, "Where to now?," November 9, 2008.

86 *New Zealand Herald*, "Mood for change got a lot tougher," November 9, 2008.

87 Paul Chapman, "New Zealand election: The vanquished Helen Clark," *Telegraph*, November 8, 2008, downloaded November 8, 2008, www.telegraph.co.uk.

88 *New Zealand Herald*, "Out: It's only right Clark goes after Labour loss," November 10, 2008.

89 *New Zealand Herald*, "Helen Clark's nine years as prime minister come near to Peter Fraser's record," November 15, 2008.

90 *New Zealand Herald*, "Where to now?"

91 Sid Maher, "Abbott rolls through western battleground," *Australian*, August 17, 2010, 7.

92 Michelle Grattan, Ari Sharp, and Tom Arup, "Gillard's policy fightback," *Age*, August 11, 2010, 1.

93 Lenore Taylor and Phillip Coorey, "Gillard's moment of truth," *Sydney Morning Herald*, July 17, 2010, 1.

94 Cameron Stewart, "Rock star reception for Gillard," *Australian*, July 21, 2010, 4.

95 Paul Kelly, "Gillard fights for second chance," *Australian*, August 17, 2010, 1.

96 Samantha Maiden, "Julia unplugged has the killer lines on Abbott," *Australian*, August 17, 2010, 5; emphasis mine.

97 Peter Hartcher, "Ghost of Rudd turns Gillard honeymoon into worst nightmare," *Sydney Morning Herald*, July 31, 2010, 9.

98 Matthew Franklin and Patricia Karvelas, "Underdog Abbott defies doubters," *Australian*, July 26, 2010, 1; Christian Kerr, "Labor digs up Abbott's words," *Australian*, August 4, 2010, 5; Sid Maher, "Gillard prepares to turn the blowtorch on Abbott," *Australian*, August 9, 2010, 7.

99 Jennifer Hewett, "A confused nation asks, will the real Julia Gillard stand up?," *Australian*, July 31, 2010, 11.

100 Michael Gordon, "Gillard gets a head start," *Age*, July 19, 2010, 15.

101 Jessica Mahar, "Gillard throws a bone to battling budget balancers," *Sydney Morning Herald*, August 3, 2010, 5.

102 Jennifer Hewett, "The Liberal ad that created a stabbing pain for Gillard," *Australian*, August 23, 2010, 2.

103 Kelly, "Gillard fights for second chance."

104 Samantha Maiden, "Gillard treads warily on *Women's Weekly*," *Australian*, July 27, 2010, 5.

105 Hewett, "The Liberal ad that created a stabbing pain for Gillard."

106 Tony Wright, "Gillard beset by friendly fire as Rudd marches into campaign," *Age*, August 6, 2010, 6.

107 Maiden, "Gillard treads warily on *Women's Weekly*."

108 Sid Maher, "On a roll, Abbott chews 'n chats," *Australian*, August 16, 2010, 6.

109 Oxford Dictionaries online, s.v. "honeymoon," https://en.oxforddictionaries.com/definition/honeymoon.

110 Colin Espiner, "Key grins as political dynasties crumble," *Christchurch Press*, November 10, 2008; Main, "Stakes high for Shipley."

111 *Vancouver Sun*, "PM-elect assigned Mountie protection," June 14, 1993, A4.

112 Ross Howard, "'Left at altar' by reporter, Campbell vows feistier campaign," *Globe and Mail*, June 3, 1993, A4.

113 Christopher Pearson, "Same old Labor under Gillard," *Australian*, July 17, 2010, 14; Hartcher, "Ghost of Rudd turns Gillard honeymoon into worst nightmare"; Jacob Saulwick, "Rudd tears still rain on Gillard's parade," *Age*, August 16, 2010, 8.

114 Peter O'Neil, "Campbell covers up that shoulder, and soul, for the campaign," *Vancouver Sun*, September 17, 1993, A1.

115 Nick Venter, "National stumbles on home straight," *Dominion Post*, July 22, 2002.

116 Ruth Berry and Julie Middleton, "Credibility the theme for big day," *New Zealand Herald*, September 14, 2005.

117 Marty Sharpe, "Wooing young and old," *Dominion Post*, October 24, 2008.

118 Martin Kay, "Key gets teen fan breathless," *Dominion Post*, November 3, 2008. Her exact words were, "He's just awesome. I love him. He's a fun guy."

119 Phillip Coorey, "Margie stands by her man as Abbott woos women," *Sydney Morning Herald*, July 27, 2010, 5.

120 Audrey Young, "Queen city target of first ladies," *New Zealand Herald*, November 23, 1999.

121 Vernon Small, "Final sweep to woo voters," *Dominion* Post, November 3, 2008.

122 *Evening Post*, "Clark, English target marginal," July 3, 2002; Tracy Watkins, "Labour's turn to woo voters," *Dominion Post*, November 3, 2008; Anna Kominik, "Bolger pays court to the ordinary people," *Dominion*, September 27, 1996.

123 Doug Ward, "PM takes summertime seduction of Canadian electorate to airwaves," *Vancouver Sun*, August 11, 1993, A3.

124 O'Neil, "Campbell covers up that shoulder, and soul, for the campaign."

125 Colin Espiner, "Strong Brash line on treaty upsets Maori," *Christchurch Press*, August 30, 2005, 5.

126 Berry and Middleton, "Credibility the theme for big day."

127 Jane Clifton, "Divorce, Labour-style," *Dominion*, December 2, 1993, 1.

128 Ibid.

129 Kari Du Fresne, "Helen and Mike in miraculous healing," *Evening Post*, October 4, 1996.

130 Simon Kilroy, "No kissing as Moore and Clark appear in reconciliation scene," *Dominion*, October 4, 1996.

131 Du Fresne, "Helen and Mike in miraculous healing."

132 Kilroy, "No kissing as Moore and Clark appear in reconciliation scene."

133 Toney Stickley, "Lange, Clark cool their squabbling," *New Zealand Herald*, October 7, 1996.

134 Andrew Laxton, Patricia Herbert, and Audrey Young, "Party leaders joust in last-gasp power plays," *New Zealand Herald*, October 11, 1996.

135 Patricia Herbert, "Labour jumps back from the brink," *New Zealand Herald*, September 21, 1996.

136 Anna Kominik, "Clark rejects Anderton's new coalition advances," *Dominion*, September 18, 1996.

137 Michael Rentoul, "Parties show MMP tactics little different from other elections," *Christchurch Press*, September 21, 1996.

138 Ruth Laughesen, "Bolger changes image from great helmsman to coalition man," *Dominion*, November 18, 1996; Graeme Speden, "Nats, NZ First

begin power talks," *Dominion*, October 22, 1996; Brent Edwards, "Damned if they do, damned if they don't," *Evening Post*, December 7, 1996.

139 *Evening Post*, "Middle man Peters," October 14, 1996.

140 The reporter was referring to the "bunny boiling" episode in the 1987 film *Fatal Attraction*. For a capsule description of the film, see http://www.imdb.com/title/tt0093010/.

141 *Dominion*, "Shipley must collar Peters," November 5, 1997.

142 Victoria Main, "Peters plays the reluctant groom," *Dominion*, November 5, 1997; Victoria Main, "Coalition split closer as leadership changes," *Dominion*, November 4, 1997.

143 *Dominion*, "Shipley yet to prove she can ride out her own tempest," November 10, 1997.

144 Victoria Main, "Shipley uses Birch to entice Peters," *Dominion*, November 6, 1997.

145 *Dominion*, "Shipley yet to prove she can ride out her own tempest."

146 *Dominion*, "Peters wants to get out – but not before he has got even," November 17, 1997.

147 Helen Bain, "Peters plays true to form again," *Dominion*, November 5, 1999; emphasis mine.

148 Ibid.

149 *Dominion*, "Peters wants to get out."

150 Michael Laws, "Dilemmas facing Shipley in high office," *Evening Post*, December 2, 1997.

151 Bain, "Peters plays true to form again."

152 Victoria Main, "Clark hurries to silence bickering," *Dominion*, November 11, 1999.

153 John Armstrong, "Now down to business," *New Zealand Herald*, November 29, 1999.

154 Rudman, "Woman of steely resolve in good times and bad."

155 Peter Luke, "Labour sweeps to power," *Christchurch Press*, November 29, 1999.

156 Rudman, "Woman of steely resolve in good times and bad."

157 Luke, "Party at Helen's?"

158 Ruth Berry, "Peters declares war on Clark," *Dominion Post*, July 29, 2002.

159 "A Bob each way with Helen the horse whisperer," *Christchurch Press*, July 30, 2002.

160 Colin Espiner, "Greens playing hard to get," *Christchurch Press*, July 29, 2002.

161 Espiner, "Labs, Greens make up."

162 Luke, "Party at Helen's?"

163 Audrey Young, "Prime Minister Helen Clark will try to avoid formal coalitions," *New Zealand Herald,* September 19, 2005.

164 *Christchurch Press,* "Triumph of expediency," October 18, 2005.

165 *Dominion Post,* "Clark courts Maori with seats offer," October 29, 2008.

166 *New Zealand Herald,* "Clark's the circus ringleader," October 19, 2008.

167 Jonathan Milne, "New Zealand takes," *New Zealand Herald,* November 9, 2008.

168 Paula Oliver, "Flying start: Key puts talks into top gear," *New Zealand Herald,* November 11, 2008.

169 *New Zealand Herald,* "Shrewd deal with Maori Party good start for National leader," November 16, 2008.

170 *Christchurch Press,* "Grand coalition," July 25, 2002, 8.

171 Audrey Young and Ruth Berry, "Helen Clark appears poised to seal a deal with Winston Peters' party," *New Zealand Herald,* October 13, 2005.

172 Haydon Dewes, "Suitors court Maori Party," *Dominion Post,* September 20, 2005, 2; Tracy Watkins, "Seating arrangements at Mad Hatter's Tea Party," *Dominion Post,* October 17, 2005, 7.

173 *New Zealand Herald,* "Tough talk won't solve jails issue," October 8, 2008.

Chapter 7

1 The section of this chapter titled "Julia Gillard and the Gender Wars" is adapted from Trimble (2016), and the analysis of Kim Campbell's speaking style is inspired by Trimble, Treiberg, and Girard (2010).

2 Peter O'Neil, "McLaughlin picks up steam as Campbell loses her cool," *Vancouver Sun,* October 5, 1993, A4; emphasis mine.

3 Michelle Grattan, "Election game plan 101: How to be a hit with the opposite sex," *Sydney Morning Herald,* December 22, 2012, 6.

4 Hugh Winsor, "Liberals teach a lesson: Pick one message and stick to it," *Globe and Mail,* October 23, 1993, A6.

5 Robert Sheppard, "The provinces: Keeping track of Campbell's voices," *Globe and Mail,* September 30, 1993, A27.

6 Mark Kennedy, "The challenges ahead: The leadership race was the first hurdle, but does Kim Campbell have what it takes to clear them all?," *Vancouver Sun,* June 14, 1993, A11.

7 Frank Davey, "Kim Campbell and the endless summer," *Globe and Mail,* September 16, 1993, A27.

8 Jeff Sallot, "The fading of Kim," *Globe and Mail,* October 23, 1993, D1.

9 Sheppard, "The provinces."

10 As discussed in chapter 1, the sampling method was designed to capture news stories focusing on that particular leader, as evidenced by naming them in the headline and devoting at least half the text to a description or evaluation of that leader's performance.

11 Neutral comments did not communicate judgment. For example, "She replied with the standard answer" (Campbell): "Mr. Chretien is talking to his crowds differently."

12 Hugh Winsor, "The two faces of Jean Chretien," *Globe and Mail*, September 20, 1993, A1.

13 Ross Howard, "Campbell under gun in Calgary: Handlers look for edge in candidates' debates," *Globe and Mail*, April 26, 1993, A3.

14 Ross Howard, "Liberals poised to select Chretien," *Globe and Mail*, June 23, 1990, A1.

15 *Vancouver Sun*, "Campbell's touchy-feely image is going down the drain fast," May 20, 1993, A4.

16 Peter O'Neil, "Campbell feels she's sharp judge of judgment," *Vancouver Sun*, May 21, 1993, A4.

17 Edward Greenspon, "Chretien brandishes program, says Tories have none," *Globe and Mail*, September 23, 1993, A6; Ross Howard, "Liberal leader has had it easy," *Globe and Mail*, September 30, 1993, A1.

18 Warren Caragata, "Boss at last: Second fiddle for years, Liberal leader now leads the whole orchestra," *Montreal Gazette*, October 23, 1993, A8.

19 Winsor, "The two faces of Jean Chretien"; Howard, "Liberal leader has had it easy"; Susan Delacourt, "Liberals go after 'protest' vote," *Globe and Mail*, October 9, 1993, A6.

20 Susan Delacourt, "Relying on instinct paid off for Jean Chretien," *Globe and Mail*, October 25, 1993, A1.

21 Delacourt, "Liberals go after 'protest' vote"; Tu Thanh Ha, "The 'unpackaging' of Jean Chretien: Top Liberals have spent 2 years remaking party leader's image," *Montreal Gazette*, October 19, 1993, A7; Edward Greenspon, "Chretien sets out his priority list," *Globe and Mail*, October 13, 1993, A1.

22 O'Neil, "McLaughlin picks up steam as Campbell loses her cool."

23 Davey, "Kim Campbell and the endless summer"; emphasis mine.

24 Jeff Sallot, "Campbell can't fill arenas on eastern tour," *Globe and Mail*, October 7, 1993, A4.

25 Jeff Sallot, "Major western Tories steer clear of Campbell," *Globe and Mail*, October 14, 1993, A6.

26 Dave Todd, "We're retreating, Campbell signals the world," *Vancouver Sun*, October 2, 1993, A15; Jeff Sallot, "PM avoids aid issue in UN speech," *Globe and Mail*, September 30, 1993, A1.

27 Ken MacQueen, "Campbell tripping on her lip," *Vancouver Sun*, May 21, 1993, A17.

28 Hugh Winsor, "Warm, funny side of Campbell being served up," *Globe and Mail*, March 26, 1993, A4; Julian Beltrame and Patrick Nagle, "Campbell scores points as Tory candidates face off for the third time," *Vancouver Sun*, May 1, 1993, A4; Pauline Couture, "Quebecois voices: Charting the course of Campbellmania," *Globe and Mail*, April 1, 1993, A23.

29 Colin Vaughan, "Toronto: Campbell no longer has Metro locked up," *Globe and Mail*, April 26, 1993, A10; Ross Howard, "Early lead in race ceded to Campbell: Charest foresees Quebec victory," *Globe and Mail*, April 30, 1993, A6; Ross Howard, "Campbell under the gun in Calgary," *Globe and Mail*, April 6, 1993, A3; Ross Howard, "Campbell team shuffles management: New advisers to add toughness, sharpen focus in flat campaign," *Globe and Mail*, April 23, 1993, A1; Peter O'Neil, "Kimmanie fuels Campbell's campaign bandwagon in Quebec," *Vancouver Sun*, April 21, 1993, A5.

30 O'Neil, "Kimmanie fuels Campbell's campaign bandwagon in Quebec."

31 Susan Delacourt, "Campbell turns feisty debate to advantage," *Globe and Mail*, May 1, 1993, A1.

32 Geoffrey York, "Campbell tried to eat her words, it was too late," *Globe and Mail*, May 15, 1993, A6.

33 Hugh Winsor, "Campbell vows to tell it like it is: Controversy over remarks doesn't faze Tory front-runner," *Globe and Mail*, May 19, 1993, A1.

34 MacQueen, "Campbell tripping on her lip."

35 Peter O'Neil, "Campbell sees double standard in media spin on her campaign," *Vancouver Sun*, May 12, 1993, A7.

36 Rhéal Séguin and Ross Howard, "Law not broken, Campbell says: Tory leadership candidate sees no crime in experimenting with marijuana," *Globe and Mail*, May 22, 1993, A3.

37 *Vancouver Sun*, "Campbell's touchy-feely image is going down the drain fast."

38 Alan Freeman, "Undecideds crucial to winner: Campbell's conventional speech just fine by some," *Globe and Mail*, June 14, 1993, A7.

39 Peter O'Neil, "Campbell's gloves-off campaign a softie," *Vancouver Sun*, June 4, 1993, A1.

40 See Liane Faulder, "How much does Kim Campbell's gender affect how we perceive her?," *Vancouver Sun*, April 2, 1993, C12.

41 Jeffrey Simpson, "The gnawing question: Just who is she?," *Globe and Mail*, June 14, 1993, A15.

42 *Vancouver Sun*, "In matters of conscience: Campbell it is," June 12, 1993, A10.

43 Jeff Sallot and Ross Howard, "Tories brace for contest past first ballot: Campbell, Charest organizers court uncommitted delegates," *Globe and Mail*, June 12, 1993, A1.

44 Kennedy, "The challenges ahead."

45 Jeff Sallot, "Message not going out clearly, Campbell declares," *Globe and Mail*, October 20, 1993, A4.

46 Edward Greenspon and Jeff Sallot, "How Campbell self-destructed," *Globe and Mail*, October 27, 1993, A1.

47 Sallot, "Major western Tories steer clear of Campbell."

48 Sallot, "The fading of Kim."

49 Peter O'Neil, "Campbell covers up that shoulder, and soul, for the campaign," *Vancouver Sun*, September 17, 1993, A1.

50 Colin Vaughan, "Toronto gets cold shoulder from Campbell," *Globe and Mail*, May 31, 1993, A10.

51 Jeff Sallot, "Jobless rate won't drop soon, Campbell warns," *Globe and Mail*, September 9, 1993, A6.

52 Jeff Sallot and Hugh Winsor, "PM won't touch key issue: Social programs called too vital for campaign trail," *Globe and Mail*, September 24, 1993, A1.

53 Ross Howard, "'Weekend from hell' stuns Tories," *Globe and Mail*, October 18, 1993, A1.

54 Greenspon and Sallot, "How Campbell self-destructed."

55 Robert Mason, "If Campbell sinned with the truth, her riding sounds forgiving," *Vancouver Sun*, September 17, 1993, A5; Sallot, "Message not going out clearly, Campbell declares"; Winsor, "Liberals teach a lesson"; Sallot, "The fading of Kim"; Ross Howard, "The quick unraveling of a campaign," *Globe and Mail*, October 26, 1993, D2.

56 Winsor, "Liberals teach a lesson."

57 Edward Greenspon and Ross Howard, "Tories endure loose cannon: Liberals making hay with gaffes, but Campbell just being herself," *Globe and Mail*, September 25, 1993, A1.

58 Mark Hume, "A Campbellian gaffe, and 'The Plan' is revealed," *Vancouver Sun*, September 18, 1993, B4.

59 Mark Hume, "Campbell's second week off to a rocky start," *Vancouver Sun*, September 21, 1993, A5.

60 Robert Mason, "The uphill struggle of my campaign: Kim Campbell," *Vancouver Sun*, October 25, 1993, A1.

61 O'Neil, "McLaughlin picks up steam as Campbell loses her cool."

62 Davey, "Kim Campbell and the endless summer"; Carol Goar, "She's no Mulroney ...," *Vancouver Sun*, September 28, 1993, A15.

63 Hugh Winsor, "Staying the course with Campbell," *Globe and Mail,* September 14, 1993, A1.

64 Kirk Makin, "Chretien questions Campbell ability after PC shifting," *Globe and Mail,* September 14, 1993, A4.

65 Ross Howard, "Nervous Tories consider survival, not success," *Globe and Mail,* October 7, 1993, A4; Ross Howard, "Campbell calm in defeat," *Globe and Mail,* October 26, 1993, D1; Winsor, "Liberals teach a lesson."

66 Sallot, "The fading of Kim."

67 Peter O'Neil, "Tory leader doffs gloves, but fails to fashion boost in her campaign," *Vancouver Sun,* October 4, 1993, A4.

68 Greenspon and Howard, "Tories endure loose cannon"; Sallot, "Major western Tories steer clear of Campbell"; Sallot, "The fading of Kim"; Greenspon and Sallot, "How Campbell self-destructed."

69 Greenspon and Howard, "Tories endure loose cannon"; Winsor, "Liberals teach a lesson."

70 Greenspon and Sallot, "How Campbell self-destructed."

71 Frances Bula, "Was PM wearing a Freudian slip?," *Vancouver Sun,* September 11, 1993, A6.

72 Jeff Sallot, "Campbell hews to line: Jokes but no hokum," *Globe and Mail,* September 11, 1993, A6.

73 Jeff Sallot, "Campbell rallies troops for on-air strike," *Globe and Mail,* October 2, 1993, A6.

74 O'Neil, "Campbell covers up that shoulder, and soul, for the campaign."

75 Susan Delacourt and Jeff Sallot, "Reform grill Campbell over deficit," *Globe and Mail,* October 5, 1993, A4.

76 Winsor, "Warm, funny side of Campbell being served up"; Bula, "Was PM wearing a Freudian slip?"; Simpson, "The gnawing question?"; Doug Ward, "The girl most likely: Doug Ward takes a look at Kim Campbell's ascendancy," *Vancouver Sun,* March 25, 1993, A4; Freeman, "Undecideds crucial to winner."

77 *Vancouver Sun,* "In matters of conscience"; Winsor, "Staying the course with Campbell."

78 Stephen Hume, "Campbell's verbal bombshells aren't loaded with ideas," *Vancouver Sun,* May 28, 1993, A19.

79 Peter Van Onselen, "Is this the turning point?," *Australian,* October 30, 2012, 11.

80 Dennis Shanahan, "For Labor's sake, PM must drop the words that divide," *Australian,* March 23, 2012, 13.

81 Paul Kelly, "Misogyny tactic will backfire," *Australian,* October 13, 2012, 15.

82 Australian Broadcasting Corporation, "The speech that burst the press gallery's bubble," *ABC Watch*, episode 27, October 15, 2012, retrieved February 19, 2014, www.abc.net.au.

83 As of February 19, 2014, the clip had been viewed over two and a half million times.

84 For example, see Amelia Lester, "Ladylike: Julia Gillard's misogyny speech," *New Yorker* online, October 9, 2012, retrieved February 19, 2014, www.newyorker.com.

85 Australian Broadcasting Corporation, "The speech that burst the press gallery's bubble."

86 See the Appendix for a discussion of how these papers were chosen.

87 The singular and the plural forms of the metaphor appeared equally frequently, so I use them interchangeably here.

88 For example, "Are you suggesting to me that when it comes from Julia, no doesn't mean no?" Or "I think if the Prime Minister wants to make, politically speaking, an honest woman of herself ..." (Gillard 2014, 106).

89 "Juliar" was a widely used slur on Gillard's character. By adding the letter *r* to the end of Gillard's first name, critics, notably radio "shock jock" Alan Jones, cast the PM as a liar.

90 Grattan, "Election game plan 101."

91 The full text of Gillard's speech can be accessed from the *Sydney Morning Herald* (www.smh.com.au), which published it on October 10, 2012.

92 Chris Kenny, "Abbott's big fight back," *Australian*, January 8, 2013, 9.

93 Although the Opposition's motion was narrowly defeated in the House, Slipper was convinced to resign from the Speaker's position.

94 The text message at the heart of the controversy said, "Look at a bottle of mussel meat! Salty cunts in brine" (Goldsworthy 2013, 1).

95 *Sydney Morning Herald*, "Transcript of Julia Gillard's speech," October 10, 2012, retrieved February 19, 2014, www.smh.com.au.

96 Ibid. For instance, Abbott said, "If it's true ... that men have more power generally speaking than women, is that a bad thing?" and "What if men are by physiology or temperament, more adapted to exercise authority or to issue command?"

97 This was a reference to Gillard's marital status as she was not legally married to her partner.

98 Paul Kelly, "Hypocrisy rules but both sides of politics are courting danger," *Australian*, October 3, 2012, 12.

99 Ibid.

100 Paul Kelly, "Demonisation of Abbott is Labor's new game plan," *Australian*, September 14, 2012, 15.

101 Kelly, "Hypocrisy rules but both sides of politics are courting danger."
102 Chris Kenny, "Labor's British import brought the 'problem with women' spin in his baggage," *Australian*, October 6, 2012, 24.
103 Kelly, "Hypocrisy rules but both sides of politics are courting danger."
104 Kelly, "Demonisation of Abbott is Labor's new game plan."
105 John Ferguson and Patricia Karvelas, "PM 'lets women down on pay,'" *Australian*, June 14, 2012, 1.
106 The quotations are from, respectively, *Australian*, "Labor now moves forward from gender wars mistake," October 15, 2012, 13; Grattan, "Election game plan 101"; Gabrielle Chan, "Shades of outrage in Parliament's sordid story," *Australian*, October 10, 2012, 1; Chris Kenny, "Gillard's hypocrisy stripped bare by her defence of demonstrable misogyny," *Australian*, October 13, 2012, 24; Joe Kelly, "Warning to PM on sexism crusade," *Australian*, October 15, 2012, 2; Rick Morton and Mark Schliebs, "Men retreat to bunker over PM's gender salvo," *Australian*, June 18, 2013, 4; Kelly, "Hypocrisy rules but both sides of politics are courting danger."
107 Dennis Shanahan, "Labor continues with strategy of delusion," *Australian*, October 11, 2012, 6.
108 *Australian*, "The PM, the Speaker, his texts and their misogyny," October 10, 2012, 13.
109 Christopher Pearson, "Labor living on borrowed time," *Australian*, December 15, 2012, 20.
110 Kelly, "Misogyny tactic will backfire."
111 Janet Albrechtson, "PM's fake feminism is man made," *Australian*, January 23, 2013, 10.
112 Christine Jackman, "Dangers of an artificial gender war," *Australian*, January 12, 2013, 13.
113 Stephanie Peatling and Farrah Tomazin, "Wong calls for truce in gender war," *Sunday Age*, October 14, 2012, 5; emphasis mine.
114 Janet Albrechtsen, "Gender wars can't help the Labor cause any more than a quota PM," *Australian*, June 5, 2013, 10.
115 Albrechtsen, "PM's fake feminism is man made."
116 Shanahan, "For Labor's sake, PM must drop the words that divide."
117 For example, see *Australian*, "The PM, the Speaker, his texts and their misogyny"; and Kelly, "Warning to PM on sexism crusade."
118 Katharine Murphy, "Life moments in the kitchen of the great House," *Age*, October 14, 2012, 11; emphasis mine.
119 Grattan, "Election game plan 101"; Kelly, "Warning to PM on sexism crusade."

120 Dennis Shanahan, "PM's gender war ends in spectacular self-wedge," *Australian*, October 12, 2012, 14.
121 Kenny, "Gillard's hypocrisy stripped bare by her defence of demonstrable misogyny"; emphasis mine.
122 By characterizing the so-called gender wars in this manner, the press reinforced radio personality Alan Jones's admonition that Gillard and other powerful women were "destroying" Australia.
123 Niki Sava, "Gillard could learn from Obama that it's about winning not whining," *Australian*, November 8, 2012, 12.
124 Albrechtsen, "PM's fake feminism is man made."
125 Shanahan, "For Labor's sake, PM must drop the words that divide."
126 Chris Kenny, "Early poll is Labor's best hope of saving the brand," *Australian*, October 27, 2012, 22.
127 Mark Kenny, "PM targets 'men in blue ties,'" *Sydney Morning Herald*, June 12, 2013, accessed October 19, 2016, www.smh.com.au.
128 Andrew Fraser and Sid Maher, "Menu offensive is still only half-baked," *Australian*, June 14, 2013, 1.
129 Rick Morton, "ABC slow to digest story's course," *Australian*, June 14, 2013, 4.
130 Morton and Schliebs, "Men retreat to bunker after PM's gender salvo."
131 Fraser and Maher, "Menu offensive is still only half-baked."
132 Sid Maher, "PM fires abortion salvo in gender war," *Australian*, June 12, 2013, 1.
133 Anne Summers, "It's Gillard's right to fight back," *Sydney Morning Herald*, June 14, 2013, 12.
134 Peter Hartcher, "PM's cynical ploy fails to win voters," *Sydney Morning Herald*, June 17, 2013, 4.
135 Michael Laziol, "Big issues ignored in *papier maché* policy showdown," *Sydney Morning Herald*, June 14, 2013, 33.
136 *Australian*, "Julia Gillard's clumsy and manipulative gender war," June 13, 2013, 1.
137 Dennis Shanahan, "Gender war misfires for PM," *Australian*, June 25, 2013, 1.
138 Morton and Schliebs, "Men retreat to bunker after PM's gender salvo."
139 Janet Albrechtson, "The perils of the prime minister's feminist fantasies," *Australian*, November 7, 2012, 12.
140 Grattan, "Election game plan 101."
141 Kenny, "Early poll is Labor's best hope of saving the brand."
142 Savva, "Gillard could learn from Obama that it's about winning not whining."
143 Peter O'Neil, "Campbell covers up that shoulder, and soul, for the campaign."

Chapter 8

1 Julia Gillard's resignation speech, broadcast June 26, 2013, on www.abc.net.au.

2 Peter Beinart, "Fear of a Female President," *Atlantic*, October 2016, accessed November 20, 2015, www.theatlantic.com.

3 Julia Gillard, "First woman to first woman," *New York Times*, July 26, 2016, accessed July 31, 2016, www.scribd.com.

4 Marc Fisher, "Is she 'likeable enough?'" *Washington Post*, September 23, 2015, accessed December 15, 2016, www.washingtonpost.com.

5 The vast majority – 80 per cent – of the news stories about Campbell's rise and fall included in this study were written solely by male journalists.

6 TV3, December 8, 1997.

7 *New Zealand Herald*, "Labour's shame won't be Clark's," November 9, 2008.

8 *New Zealand Herald*, "Out: It's only right Clark goes after Labour loss," November 10, 2008.

9 Matthew Dearnaley, "Characteristic exit for pragmatic Clark," *New Zealand Herald*, November 10, 2008.

10 Paula Oliver and Claire Trevett, "Tearful goodbye turns to smiles for new leader," *New Zealand Herald*, November 20, 2008.

11 Keri Welham, "The prime of Miss Helen Clark," *Dominion Post*, November 15, 2008.

12 I would like to thank University of Alberta PhD candidate Daisy Raphael for coining this phrase.

13 Robert Benzie, "Slick new pre-election ad showcases Kathleen Wynne," *Toronto Star*, November 13, 2013, accessed May 18, 2016, www.thestar.com.

14 David A. Graham, "Why Trump Might Regret Playing 'the Woman Card' against Clinton," *Atlantic*, April 27, 2015, accessed May 1, 2016, www.theatlantic.com.

15 Beinart, "Fear of a Female President."

16 Tamara Keith, "Sexism is out in the open in the 2016 campaign," *Morning Edition*, National Public Radio, October 23, 2016, accessed December 18, 2016, www.npr.org.

17 Kate Adach, "Notley online threats far exceed those aimed at male politicians, professor says," *CBC News*, December 14, 2015, accessed May 20, 2016, www.cbc.ca.

18 Mariam Ibrahim, "Alberta premier won't be deterred in wake of online threats," *Edmonton Journal*, December 12, 2014, accessed May 20, 2016, www.edmontonjournal.com.

19 Adach, "Notley online threats far exceed those aimed at male politicians, professor says."

20 Drew Anderson, "Alberta MLA Sandra Jansen latest in long string of
    female politicians to face abuse," *CBC News*, November 23, 2016, accessed
    December 13, 2016, www.cbc.ca.
21 Ed Pilkington, "Helen Clark, former New Zealand PM, enters race for UN
    Secretary General," *Guardian*, April 4, 2016, accessed May 23, 2016, www.
    theguardian.com.
22 Elizabeth Renzetti, "Feminists should get over Theresa May's
    politics," *Globe and Mail*, July 13, 2016, accessed July 25, 2016, www.
    theglobeandmail.com.
23 The quotation is from Julia Gillard's resignation speech, broadcast June 26,
    2013, on www.abc.net.au.

Appendix

1 I am very grateful for the research assistance of Natasja Treiberg, Gabrielle
   Betts, and Liz Moore, who patiently and diligently conducted news
   database and microfilm searches to complete the New Zealand sample.
2 Available at http://www.abc.net.au/news/video.
3 Sue Girard coded the Canadian news articles. Natasja Treiberg coded all
   New Zealand news stories with the exception of the 2008 general election;
   for that campaign, she and I trained Elizabeth Macve to carry out the
   coding. Finally, Bailey Gerrits and I coded the Australian news content.

Works Cited

Aalberg, Toril, and Anders Todal Jenssen. 2007. "Gender Stereotyping of Political Candidates: An Experimental Study of Political Communication." *Nordicom Review* 28 (1): 17–32. https://doi.org/10.1515/nor-2017-0198.

Aalberg, Toril, Jesper Strömbäck, and Claes H. de Vreese. 2012. "The Framing of Politics as Strategy and Game: A Review of Concepts, Operationalizations and Key Findings." *Journalism* 13 (2): 162–78. https://doi.org/10.1177/1464884911427799.

Adams, Michele. 2011. "Is Family a Moral Capital Resource for Female Politicians? The Case of ABC's Commander in Chief." *Media, Culture & Society* 33 (2): 223–41. https://doi.org/10.1177/0163443710393383.

Ahrens, Kathleen. 2009. "Analysing Conceptual Metaphors in Political Language." In *Politics, Gender and Conceptual Metaphors*, edited by Kathleen Ahrens, 1–5. Basingstoke, UK: Palgrave Macmillan. https://doi.org/10.1057/9780230245235_1.

Alexander-Floyd, Nicol G. 2008. "Framing Condi(licious): Condoleezza Rice and the Storyline of 'Closeness' in U.S. National Community Formation." *Politics & Gender* 4 (3): 427–49. https://doi.org/10.1017/S1743923X08000354.

Allen, Stuart. 2004. *News Culture.* 2nd ed. Berkshire, UK: Open University Press.

Anderson, Karrin Vasby. 1999. "'Rhymes with Rich': 'Bitch' as a Tool of Containment in Contemporary American Politics." *Rhetoric & Public Affairs* 2 (4): 599–623. https://doi.org/10.1353/rap.2010.0082.

– 2002. "From Spouses to Candidates: Hillary Rodham Clinton, Elizabeth Dole, and the Gendered Office of U.S. President." *Rhetoric & Public Affairs* 5 (1): 105–32. https://doi.org/10.1353/rap.2002.0001.

– 2011. "'Rhymes with Blunt': Pornification and U.S. Political Culture." *Rhetoric & Public Affairs* 14 (2): 327–68. https://doi.org/10.1353/rap.2010.0228.

Anderson, Karrin Vasby, and Kristina Horn Sheeler. 2005. *Governing Codes: Gender, Metaphor, and Political Identity*. Lanham, MD: Lexington Books.

Anker, Elisabeth. 2005. "Villains, Victims and Heroes: Melodrama, Media, and September 11." *Journal of Communication* 55 (1): 22–37. https://doi.org/10.1111/j.1460-2466.2005.tb02656.x.

Aulich, Chris, ed. 2014. *The Gillard Governments*. Carlton: Melbourne University Press.

Bahry, Donna L. 1991. "Crossing Borders: The Practice of Comparative Research." In *Empirical Political Analysis: Research Methods in Political Science*, 3rd ed., edited by Jarol B. Manheim and Richard C. Rich, 203–26. Englewood Cliffs, NJ: Prentice-Hall.

Barker-Plummer, Bernadette. 2013. "Fixing Gwen: News and the Mediation of (Trans)gender Challenges." *Feminist Media Studies* 13 (4): 710–24. https://doi.org/10.1080/14680777.2012.679289.

Barr, Marleen S. 2012. "Science Fiction Language/Political Reporting: Communicating News via Words from Nowhere Real." *Etc: A Review of General Semantics* 69 (1): 21–31.

Bashevkin, Sylvia. 2009. *Women, Power, Politics: The Hidden Story of Canada's Unfinished Democracy*. Don Mills, ON: Oxford University Press.

Baxter, Judith, ed. 2006. *Speaking Out: The Female Voice in Public Contexts*. Hampshire, NY: Palgrave. https://doi.org/10.1057/9780230522435.

Baxter, Judith. 2010. *The Language of Female Leadership*. Basingstoke, UK: Palgrave. https://doi.org/10.1057/9780230277915.

Beail, Linda, and Rhonda Kinney Longworth. 2013. *Framing Sarah Palin: Pit Bulls, Puritans and Politics*. New York: Routledge.

Beckwith, Karen. 2005. "A Common Language of Gender?" *Politics & Gender* 1 (1): 128–37. https://doi.org/10.1017/S1743923X05211017.

– 2015. "Before Prime Minister: Margaret Thatcher, Angela Merkel, and Gendered Party Leadership Contests." *Politics & Gender* 11 (4): 718–45. https://doi.org/10.1017/S1743923X15000409.

Bennett, Lance. 1998. *News: The Politics of Illusion*. 2nd ed. White Plains, NY: Longman.

Berry, Nicholas. 2017. "In Australia, Land of the 'Fair Go,' Not Everyone Gets an Equal Slice of the Pie." *The Conversation* (blog). https://theconversation.com/in-australia-land-of-the-fair-go-not-everyone-gets-an-equal-slice-of-the-pie-70480.

Blankenship, Jane. 1996. "The Search for the 1972 Democratic Party Nomination: A Metaphorical Perspective." In *Rhetoric and Communication*, edited by Jane Blankenship and Hermann Stelzner, 236–60. Urbana: University of Illinois Press.

Blankenship, Jane, and Jong Guen Kang. 1991. "The 1984 Presidential and Vice Presidential Debates: The Printed Press and 'Construction' by Metaphor." *Presidential Studies Quarterly* 41 (2): 307–18.

Borisoff, Deborah, and Dan F. Hahn. 1993. "Thinking with the Body: Sexual Metaphors." *Communication Quarterly* 41 (3): 253–60. https://doi.org/10.1080/01463379309369886.

Bourdieu, Pierre. 1991. *Language and Symbolic Power*. Cambridge: Polity and Blackwell.

Braden, Maria. 1996. *Women Politicians and the Media*. Lexington: University Press of Kentucky.

Brescoll, Victoria L. 2016. "Leading with Their Hearts? How Gender Stereotypes of Emotion Lead to Biased Evaluations of Female Leaders." *Leadership Quarterly* 27 (3): 415–28. https://doi.org/10.1016/j.leaqua.2016.02.005.

Bryman, Alan, James J. Teevan, and Edward Bell. 2009. *Social Research Methods*. 2nd Canadian ed. Don Mills, ON: Oxford University Press.

Budd, Richard W., Robert K. Thorp, and Lewis Donohew. 1967. *Content Analysis of Communications*. New York: Macmillan.

Burke, Cindy, and Sharon R. Mazzarella. 2008. "'A Slightly New Shade of Lipstick': Gendered Mediation in Internet News Stories." *Women's Studies in Communication* 31 (3): 395–418. https://doi.org/10.1080/07491409.2008.10162548.

Burnette, Ann E., and Rebekah L. Fox. 2012. "My Three Dads: The Rhetorical Construction of Fatherhood in the 2012 Republican Presidential Primary." *Journal of Contemporary Rhetoric* 2 (3/4): 80–91.

Burr, Vivien. 1995. *An Introduction to Social Constructionism*. London: Routledge. https://doi.org/10.4324/9780203299968.

Burrell, Barbara, Laurel Elder, and Brian Frederick. 2011. "From Hillary to Michelle: Public Opinion and the Spouses of Presidential Candidates." *Presidential Studies Quarterly* 41 (1): 156–76. https://doi.org/10.1111/j.1741-5705.2010.03835.x.

Butler, Judith. 1993. *Bodies That Matter*. New York: Routledge.

– 2004. *Undoing Gender*. New York: Routledge.

– 2006. *Gender Trouble*. New York: Routledge.

Byerly, Carolyn, and Karen Ross. 2006. *Women and Media: A Critical Introduction*. Malden, MA: Blackwell. https://doi.org/10.1002/9780470774908.

Bystrom, Dianne G., Mary Christine Banwart, Lynda Lee Kaid, and Terry A. Robertson. 2004. *Gender and Candidate Communication*. New York: Routledge.

Bystrom, Dianne G., Narren J. Brown, and Megan Fiddelke. 2013. "'Barriers Bent but Not Broken: Newspaper Coverage of Local and State Elections."

In *Women and Executive Office: Pathways and Performance*, edited by Melody Rose, 159–79. Boulder, CO: Lynne Rienner.

Bystrom, Dianne, and Daniela V. Dimitrova. 2014. "Migraines, Marriage, and Mascara: Media Coverage of Michelle Bachmann in the 2012 Republican Presidential Campaign." *American Behavioral Scientist* 58 (9): 1169–82. https://doi.org/10.1177/0002764213506221.

Bystrom, Dianne, Terry A. Robertson, and Mary Christine Banwart. 2001. "Framing the Fight: An Analysis of Media Coverage of Female and Male Candidates in Primary Races for Governor and U.S. Senate in 2000." *American Behavioral Scientist* 44 (12): 1999–2013. https://doi.org/10.1177/00027640121958456.

Cameron, Deborah. 2006. "Theorizing the Female Voice in Public Contexts." In *Speaking Out: The Female Voice in Public Contexts*, edited by Judith Baxter, 3–20. Hampshire, NY: Palgrave. https://doi.org/10.1057/9780230522435_1.

Cammaerts, Bart. 2012. "The Strategic Use of Metaphors by Political and Media Elites: The 2007–11 Belgian Constitutional Crisis." *International Journal of Media & Cultural Politics* 8 (2 & 3): 229–49. https://doi.org/10.1386/macp.8.2-3.229_1.

Campbell, Beatrix. 2015. "Margaret Thatcher: To Be or Not to Be a Woman." *British Politics* 10 (1): 41–51. https://doi.org/10.1057/bp.2014.27.

Campbell, Kim. 1996. *Time and Chance: The Political Memoirs of Canada's First Woman Prime Minister*. Toronto: Doubleday Canada.

Campus, Donatella. 2010. "Mediatization and Personalization of Politics in Italy and France: The Cases of Berlusconi and Sarkozy." *International Journal of Press/Politics* 15 (2): 219–35. https://doi.org/10.1177/1940161209358762.

– 2013. *Women Political Leaders and the Media*. Houndmills, UK: Palgrave Macmillan. https://doi.org/10.1057/9781137295545.

Cantrell, Tania H., and Ingrid Bachmann. 2008. "Who Is the Lady in the Window? A Comparison of International and National Press Coverage of First Female Government Heads." *Journalism Studies* 9 (3): 429–46. https://doi.org/10.1080/14616700801999253.

Cappella, Joseph N., and Kathleen Hall Jamieson. 1997. *Spiral of Cynicism: The Press and the Public Good*. New York: Oxford University Press.

Carlin, Diana B., and Kelly L. Winfrey. 2009. "Have You Come a Long Way, Baby? Hillary Clinton, Sarah Palin, and Sexism in 2008 Campaign Coverage." *Communication Studies* 60 (4): 326–43. https://doi.org/10.1080/10510970903109904.

Carver, Terrell, and Jernij Pikalo. 2008. "Editor's Introduction." In *Political Language and Metaphor*, edited by Terrell Carver and Jernej Pikalo, 1–11. London: Routledge.

Castells, Manuel. 1996. *The Rise of the Network Society.* Oxford: Basil Blackwell.

Charteris-Black, Jonathan. 2009. "Metaphor and Gender in British Parliamentary Debates." In *Politics, Gender and Conceptual Metaphors,* edited by Kathleen Ahrens, 139–65. Basingstoke, UK: Palgrave Macmillan. https://doi.org/10.1057/9780230245235_7.

– 2011. *Politicians and Rhetoric: The Persuasive Power of Metaphor.* 2nd ed. Basingstoke, UK: Palgrave Macmillan. https://doi.org/10.1057/9780230319899.

Cirksena, Kathryn, and Lisa Cuklanz. 1992. "Male Is to Female as ___ is to ___: A Guided Tour of Five Feminist Frameworks for Communication Studies." In *Women Making Meaning: New Feminist Directions in Communication,* edited by Lana Rakow, 18–44. New York: Routledge.

Clare, Jillian. 2002. "Making Spectacles of Ourselves: The Site/Sight of Woman as Leader." *Communication: Reconstructed for the 21st Century – Refereed Proceedings of the Australia and New Zealand Communication Association International Conference, Gold Coast, Queensland, July 10–12, 2002 (ANZCA On-line Journal),* edited by Mary Power. Accessed March 12, 2003. www.anzca.net/documents/2002-conf-papers/377-making-spectacles-of-ourselves-the-site-sight-of-woman-as-leader-1.html.

Clayton, Edward W. 2005. "The Political Philosophy of Aesop's Fables." Paper presented at the 2005 Midwest Political Science Association Annual Meeting.

Connell, R.W., and J.W. Messerschmidt. 2005. "Hegemonic Masculinity: Rethinking the Concept." *Gender & Society* 19 (6): 829–59. https://doi.org/10.1177/0891243205278639.

Connor, J.D. 1997. Review of *Disappearing, Inc.: Hollywood Melodrama and the Perils of Criticism. MLN* (Modern Language Notes) 112 (5): 958–70. https://doi.org/10.1353/mln.1997.0071.

Costar, Brian. 2012. "Seventeen Days to Power: Making a Minority Government." In *Julia 2010: The Caretaker Election,* edited by Marian Simms and John Wanna, 357–70. Canberra: ANU E-Press.

Coulomb-Gully, Marlène. 2009. "Beauty and the Beast: Bodies Politic and Political Representation in the 2007 French Presidential Election Campaign." *European Journal of Communication* 24 (2): 203–18. https://doi.org/10.1177/0267323108101832.

Coupland, Nikolas. 2007. *Style: Language Variation and Identity.* Cambridge: Cambridge University Press. https://doi.org/10.1017/CBO9780511755064.

Courtney, John C. 1995. *Do Conventions Matter? Choosing National Party Leaders in Canada.* Montreal and Kingston: McGill-Queen's University Press.

Cross, Simon, and John Henderson. 2004. "Public Images and Private Lives: The Media and Politics in New Zealand." *Parliamentary Affairs* 57 (1): 142–56.

Cross, William, and André Blais. 2012a. *Politics at the Centre: The Selection and Removal of Party Leaders in the Anglo Parliamentary Democracies*. New York: Oxford University Press.

– 2012b. "Who Selects the Party Leader?" *Party Politics* 18 (2): 127–50. https://doi.org/10.1177/1354068810382935.

Curtin, Jennifer. 2008. "Women, Political Leadership and Substantive Representation: The Case of New Zealand." *Parliamentary Affairs* 61 (3): 490–504. https://doi.org/10.1093/pa/gsn014.

– 2015. "Review Essay: The Prime Ministership of Julia Gillard." *Australian Journal of Political Science* 50 (1): 190–204. https://doi.org/10.1080/10361146.2015.1010481.

Dayan, Daniel, and Elihu Katz. 1992. *Media Events: The Live Broadcasting of History*. Cambridge: Harvard University Press.

Delacourt, Susan. 2013. *Shopping for Votes*. Madeira Park, BC: Douglas & McIntyre.

Devere, Heather, and Sharyn Graham Davies. 2006. "The Don and Helen New Zealand Election 2005: A Media A-Gender?" *Pacific Journalism Review* 12 (1): 65–85.

Devitt, James. 1999. *Framing Gender on the Campaign Trail: Women's Executive Leadership and the Press*. Washington, DC: Women's Leadership Fund.

Doan, Alesha, and Donald P. Haider-Markel. 2010. "The Role of Intersectional Stereotypes on Evaluations of Gay and Lesbian Political Candidates." *Politics & Gender* 6 (1): 63–91. https://doi.org/10.1017/S1743923X09990511.

Dolan, Kathleen. 2014. "Gender Stereotypes, Candidate Evaluations and Voting for Women Candidates: What Really Matters." *Political Research Quarterly* 67 (1): 96–107. https://doi.org/10.1177/1065912913487949.

Douglas, Susan J. 1995. *Where the Girls Are: Growing Up Female with the Mass Media*. New York: Three Rivers Press.

Duerst-Lahti, Georgia. 2006. "Presidential Elections: Gendered Space and the Case of 2004." In *Gender and Elections: Shaping the Future of American Politics*, edited by Susan J. Carroll and Richard L. Fox, 12–42. Cambridge: Cambridge University Press.

– 2007. "Masculinity on the Campaign Trail." In *Rethinking Madam President: Are We Ready for a Woman in the White House?*, edited by Lori Cox Han and Caroline Heldman, 87–112. Boulder, CO: Lynne Rienner.

Duerst-Lahti, Georgia, and Rita Mae Kelly. 1995. "On Governance, Leadership, and Gender." In *Gender Power, Leadership and Governance*, edited by Georgia Duerst-Lahti and Rita Mae Kelly, 1–7. Ann Arbor: University of Michigan Press.

Đurović, Tatjana, and Nadežda Silaški. 2010. "Metaphors We Vote By: The Case of 'Marriage' in Contemporary Serbian Political Discourse." *Journal of Language and Politics* 9 (2): 237–59. https://doi.org/10.1075/jlp.9.2.04dur.

Edwards, Brian. 2001. *Helen: Portrait of a Prime Minister*. Auckland: Exisle Publishing.

Engdahl, Ulrica. 2014. "Wrong Body." *Transgender Studies Quarterly* 1 (1–2): 267–9. https://doi.org/10.1215/23289252-2400226.

Enli, Gunn. 2015. *Mediated Authenticity: How the Media Constructs Reality*. New York: Peter Lang. https://doi.org/10.3726/978-1-4539-1458-8.

Entman, Robert M. 1993. "Framing: Toward Clarification of a Fractured Paradigm." *Journal of Communication* 43 (34): 41–58.

Ette, Mercy. 2013. "Gendered Frontlines: British Press Coverage of Women Soldiers Killed in Iraq." *Media, War & Conflict* 6 (3): 249–62. https://doi.org/10.1177/1750635213487276.

Everitt, Joanna, and Michael Camp. 2009a. "Changing the Game Changes the Frame: The Media's Use of Lesbian Stereotypes in Leadership versus Election Campaigns." *Canadian Political Science Review* 3 (3): 24–39.

– 2009b. "One Is Not Like the Others: Allison Brewer's Leadership of the New Brunswick NDP." In *Opening Doors Wider: Women's Political Engagement in Canada*, edited by Sylvia Bashevkin, 127–44. Vancouver: UBC Press.

Fahey, Anna Cornelia. 2007. "French and Feminine: Hegemonic Masculinity and the Emasculation of John Kerry in the 2004 Presidential Race." *Critical Studies in Media Communication* 24 (2): 132–50. https://doi.org/10.1080/07393180701262743.

Fairclough, Norman. 2001. *Language and Power*. 2nd ed. Harlow, UK: Longman.

Falk, Erika. 2010. *Women for President: Media Bias in Nine Campaigns*. Urbana: University of Illinois Press.

– 2013. "Clinton and the Playing-the-Gender Card Metaphor in Campaign News." *Feminist Media Studies* 13 (2): 192–207. https://doi.org/10.1080/14680777.2012.678074.

Faludi, Susan. 1991. *Backlash: The Undeclared War against American Women*. New York: Crown.

Farnsworth, Stephen J., Blake Andrew, Stuart Soroka, and Antonia Maioni. 2007. "The Media: All Horse Race, All the Time." *Policy Options* 28 (4): 62–8.

Flicker, Eva. 2013. "Fashionable (Dis-)order in Politics: Gender, Power and the Dilemma of the Suit." *International Journal of Media and Cultural Politics* 9 (2): 201–19. https://doi.org/10.1386/macp.9.2.201_3.

Fountaine, Susan. 2002. *Women Players: The Game Frame in the 1999 General Election*. Palmerston North, NZ: New Zealand Centre for Women and Leadership, Massey University. Working Paper Series 02/2, September.

Fountaine, Susan, and Judy McGregor. 2003. "Reconstructing Gender for the 21st Century: News Media Framing of Political Women in New Zealand."

Accessed February 6, 2003. http://www.massey.ac.nz/massey/fms/Colleges/
College%20of%20Business/NZCWL/pdfs/JMcGregorSFountainePaper.pdf.

Gamson, William A. 1989. "News as Framing." *American Behavioral Scientist*
33 (2): 157–61. https://doi.org/10.1177/0002764289033002006.

Garcia-Blanco, Inaki, and Karin Wahl-Jorgenson. 2012. "The Discursive
Construction of Women Politicians in the European Press." *Feminist Media
Studies* 12 (3): 422–41.

George, Alexander L., and Andrew Bennett. 2006. *Case Studies and Theory
Development in the Social Sciences.* Cambridge, MA: MIT Press.

Gerrits, Bailey, Linda Trimble, Angelia Wagner, Daisy Raphael, and
Shannon Sampert. 2017. "Political Battlefield: Aggressive Metaphors,
Gender and Power in News Coverage of Canadian Party Leadership
Contests." *Feminist Media Studies* online. http://dx.doi.org/10.1080/
14680777.2017.1315734.

Gibson, Katie L. 2009. "Undermining Katie Couric: The Discipline Function of
the Press." *Women & Language* 32 (1): 51–8.

Gidengil, Elisabeth, and Joanna Everitt. 1999. "Metaphors and Misrepresentation:
Gendered Mediation in News Coverage of the 1993 Canadian Leaders'
Debates." *International Journal of Press/Politics* 4 (1): 48–65. https://doi.org/
10.1177/1081180X99004001005.

– 2000. "Filtering the Female: Television News Coverage of the 1993 Canadian
Leaders' Debates." *Women & Politics* 21 (4): 105–31. https://doi.org/10.1300/
J014v21n04_04.

– 2003a. "Conventional Coverage/Unconventional Politicians: Gender
and Media Coverage of Canadian Leaders' Debates, 1993, 1997, 2000."
Canadian Journal of Political Science 36 (3): 559–77. https://doi.org/10.1017/
S0008423903778767.

– 2003b. "Talking Tough: Gender and Reported Speech in Campaign News
Coverage." *Political Communication* 20 (3): 209–32. https://doi.org/10.1080/
10584600390218869.

Gillard, Julia. 2014. *My Story.* London: Bantam Press.

Gilmartin, Patricia. 2001. "Still the Angel in the Household: Political Cartoons
of Elizabeth Dole's Presidential Campaign." *Women & Politics* 22 (4): 51–67.
https://doi.org/10.1300/J014v22n04_03.

Goldsworthy, Anna. 2013. "Unfinished Business: Sex, Freedom and Misogyny."
Quarterly Essay 50: 1–79.

Goodyear-Grant, Elizabeth. 2009. "Crafting a Public Image: Women MPs
and the Dynamics of Media Coverage." In *Opening Doors Wider: Women's
Political Engagement in Canada,* edited by Sylvia Bashevkin, 147–66.
Vancouver: UBC Press.

– 2013. *Gendered News: Media Coverage and Electoral Politics in Canada.* Vancouver: UBC Press.

Gundle, Stephen, and Clino T. Castelli. 2006. *The Glamour System.* Hampshire, NY: Palgrave Macmillan. https://doi.org/10.1057/9780230510456.

Halevi, Sharon. 2012. "Damned If You Do, Damned If You Don't?" *Feminist Media Studies* 12 (2): 195–213. https://doi.org/10.1080/14680777.2011.597100.

Hall, Lauren J., and Ngaire Donaghue. 2013. "'Nice Girls Don't Carry Knives': Constructions of Ambition in Media Coverage of Australia's First Female Prime Minister." *British Journal of Social Psychology* 52 (4): 631–47.

Hall, Stuart. 1980. "Encoding/Decoding." In *Culture, Media, Language: Working Papers in Cultural Studies, 1972–79*, edited by Stuart Hall, Dorothy Hobson, Andrew Lowe, and Paul Willis, 117–27. London: Routledge.

Hanauer, David I., and Shoshi Waksman. 2000. "The Role of Explicit Moral Points in Fable Reading." *Discourse Processes* 30 (2): 107–32. https://doi.org/10.1207/S15326950DP3002_02.

Hancock, Ange-Marie. 2007. "Intersectionality as a Normative and Empirical Paradigm." *Politics & Gender* 3 (2): 248–54. https://doi.org/10.1017/S1743923X07000062.

Harp, Dustin, Jaime Loke, and Ingrid Bachmann. 2010. "First Impressions of Sarah Palin: Pit Bulls, Politics, Gender Performance, and a Discursive Media (Re)contextualization." *Communication, Culture & Critique* 3 (3): 291–309. https://doi.org/10.1111/j.1753-9137.2010.01072.x.

– 2017. "The Spectacle of Politics: Wendy Davis, Abortion, and Pink Shoes in the Texas 'Fillybuster.'" *Journal of Gender Studies* 26 (2): 227–39. https://doi.org/10.1080/09589236.2016.1175924.

Harstock, Nancy. 1982. "The Barracks Community in Western Political Thought: Prolegomena to a Feminist Critique of War and Politics." *Women's Studies International Forum* 5 (3/4): 283–6. https://doi.org/10.1016/0277-5395(82)90037-1.

Heith, Diane J. 2003. "The Lipstick Watch: Media Coverage, Gender and Presidential Campaigns." In *Anticipating Madam President*, edited by Robert P. Watson and Ann Gordon, 123–30. Boulder, CO: Lynne Rienner.

Heldman, Caroline, Susan J. Carroll, and Stephanie Olson. 2005. "'She Brought Only a Skirt': Print Media Coverage of Elizabeth Dole's Bid for the Republican Presidential Nomination." *Political Communication* 22 (3): 315–35. https://doi.org/10.1080/10584600591006564.

Higgins, Michael, and Angela Smith. 2013. "'My Husband, My Hero': Selling the Political Spouses in the 2010 General Election." *Journal of Political Marketing* 12 (2–3): 197–210. https://doi.org/10.1080/15377857.2013.781473.

Hingley, Richard, and Christina Unwin. 2006. *Boudica: Iron Age Warrior Queen.* London: Bloomsbury Academic.

Hirdman, Anja, Madeleine Kleberg, and Kristina Widestedt. 2005. "The Intimization of Journalism: Transformations of Mediatized Public Spheres from the 1880s to Current Times." *Nordicom Review* 26 (2): 109–17.

Hole, Anne. 2003. "Performing Identity: Dawn French and the Funny Fat Female Body." *Feminist Media Studies* 3 (3): 315–28. https://doi.org/10.1080/1468077032000166540.

Holland, Shannon L. 2006. "The Dangers of Playing Dress-Up: Popular Representations of Jessica Lynch and the Controversy Regarding Women in Combat." *Quarterly Journal of Speech* 92 (1): 27–50. https://doi.org/10.1080/00335630600687123.

Holmes, Mary. 2000. "When Is the Personal Political? The President's Penis and Other Stories." *Sociology* 34 (2): 305–21.

Hooghe, Marc, Laura Jacobs, and Ellen Claes. 2015. "Enduring Gender Bias in Reporting on Political Elite Positions: Media Coverage of Female MPs in Belgian News Broadcasts (2003–2011)." *International Journal of Press/Politics* 20 (4): 395–414. https://doi.org/10.1177/1940161215596730.

Howe, Nicholas. 1988. "Metaphor in Contemporary American Political Discourse." *Metaphor and Symbolic Activity* 3 (2): 87–104. https://doi.org/10.1207/s15327868ms0302_2.

Hoyt, Crystal L., and Susan E. Murphy. 2016. "Managing to Clear the Air: Stereotype Threat, Women, and Leadership." *Leadership Quarterly* 27 (3): 387–99. doi:10.1016/j.leaqua.2015.11.002.

Hurst, John. 1993. "Kirner and the Media." *Australian Journalism Review* 15 (1): 126–34.

Hvenegard-Lassen, Kirsten. 2013. "Disturbing Femininity." *Culture Unbound* 5 (2): 153–73. https://doi.org/10.3384/cu.2000.1525.135153.

Ibroscheva, Elza, and Maria Raicheva-Stover. 2009. "Engendering Transitions: Portrayals of Female Politicians in the Bulgarian Press." *Howard Journal of Communications* 20 (2): 111–28. https://doi.org/10.1080/10646170902869429.

Jalalzai, Farida. 2006. "Women Candidates and the Media: 1992–2000 Elections." *Politics & Policy* 34 (3): 606–33. https://doi.org/10.1111/j.1747-1346.2006.00030.x.

– 2010. "Madam President: Gender, Power and the Comparative Presidency." *Journal of Women, Politics & Policy* 31 (2): 132–65. https://doi.org/10.1080/15544771003697643.

Jamieson, Kathleen Hall. 1995. *Beyond the Double Bind: Women and Leadership.* New York: Oxford University Press.

Jenkins, Cathy. 1999. "Media Treatment of Women in Politics in Australia." In *Journalism Theory and Practice: Proceedings of the 1998 Journalism Education Association Conference*, edited by Jacqui Ewart.

– 2006. "Women in Australian Politics: Mothers Only Need Apply." *Pacific Journalism Review* 12 (1): 54–63.

Johnson, Carol. 2013. "From Obama to Abbott: Gender Identity and the Politics of Emotion." *Australian Feminist Studies* 28 (75): 14–29. https://doi.org/ 10.1080/08164649.2012.759311.

Johnson, Carol. 2015. "Playing the Gender Card: The Uses and Abuses of Gender in Australian Politics." *Politics & Gender* 11 (2): 291–319. https:// doi.org/10.1017/S1743923X15000045.

Johnson, Paul. 2005. *Love, Heterosexuality and Society*. Abingdon, UK: Routledge.

Johnson-Cartee, Karen. 2005. *News Narratives and News Framing*. Lanham, MD: Rowman & Littlefield.

Joseph, Sue. 2015. "Australia's First Female Prime Minister and Gender Politics: Long-Form Counterpoints." *Journalism Practice* 9 (2): 250–64. https://doi.org/10.1080/17512786.2014.924732.

Joyrich, Lynne. 1988. "All That Television Allows: TV Melodrama, Postmodernism and Consumer Culture." *Camera Obscura* 6 (1 16): 128–53. http://cameraobscura.dukejournals.org/content/6/1_16/ 128.citation.

Kahn, Kim Fridkin. 1992. "Does Being Male Help? An Investigation of the Effects of Candidate Gender and Campaign Coverage on Evaluations of U.S. Senate Candidates." *Journal of Politics* 54 (2): 497–517. https://doi.org/ 10.2307/2132036.

– 1996. *The Political Consequences of Being a Woman*. New York: Columbia University Press.

Kahn, Kim Fridkin, and Edie N. Goldenberg. 1991. "Women Candidates in the News: An Examination of Gender Differences in U.S. Senate Campaign Coverage." *Public Opinion Quarterly* 55 (2): 180–99. https://doi.org/ 10.1086/269251.

Kaneva, Nadia, and Elza Ibroscheva. 2015. "Pin-Ups, Strippers and Centrefolds: Gendered Mediation and Post-Socialist Political Culture." *European Journal of Cultural Studies* 18 (2): 224–41. https://doi.org/10.1177/ 1367549414563296.

Karvonen, Lauri. 2009. *The Personalisation of Politics: A Study of Parliamentary Democracies*. Colchester, UK: ECPR Press.

Koller, Veronika. 2002. "'A Shotgun Wedding': Co-occurrence of War and Marriage Metaphors in Mergers and Acquisitions Discourse." *Metaphor and Symbol* 17 (3): 179–203. https://doi.org/10.1207/S15327868MS1703_2.

– 2004. "Businesswomen and War Metaphors: 'Possessive, Jealous and Pugnacious'?" *Journal of Sociolinguistics* 8 (1): 3–22. https://doi.org/10.1111/ j.1467-9841.2004.00249.x.

Koller, Veronika, and Elena Semino. 2009. "Metaphor, Politics and Gender: A Case Study from Germany." In *Politics, Gender and Conceptual Metaphors*, edited by Kathleen Ahrens, 9–35. Basingstoke, UK: Palgrave Macmillan. https://doi.org/10.1057/9780230245235_2.

Kuntsman, Adi, and Sanaz Raji. 2012. "'Israelis and Iranians, Get a Room!' Love, Hate and Transnational Politics from the 'Israel Loves Iran' and 'Iran Loves Israel' Facebook campaigns." *Journal of Middle East Women's Studies* 8 (3): 143–54. https://doi.org/10.2979/jmiddeastwomstud.8.3.143.

Laher, Yumna. 2014. "Pageant Politics: Framing Gendered Images of Women in Leadership." *Politicon* 41 (1): 103–20.

Lakoff, George, and Mark Johnson. 1980. *Metaphors We Live By*. Chicago: University of Chicago Press. https://doi.org/10.7208/chicago/9780226470993.001.0001.

Landis, J. Richard, and Gary G. Koch. 1977. "The Measurement of Observer Agreement for Categorical Data." *Biometrics* 33 (1): 159–74. https://doi.org/10.2307/2529310.

Langer, Ana Ines. 2007. "A Historical Exploration of the Personalisation of Politics in the Print Media: The British Prime Ministers 1945–1999." *Parliamentary Affairs* 60 (3): 371–87. https://doi.org/10.1093/pa/gsm028.

– 2010. "The Politicization of Private Persona: Exceptional Leaders or the New Rule?" *International Journal of Press/Politics* 15 (1): 60–76. https://doi.org/10.1177/1940161209351003.

Lawrence, Regina G., and Melody Rose. 2010. *Hillary Clinton's Race for the White House: Gender Politics and the Media on the Campaign Trail*. Boulder, CO: Lynne Rienner.

Lazar, Michelle M. 2005. "Politicizing Gender in Discourse: Feminist Critical Discourse Analysis as Political Perspective and Praxis." In *Feminist Critical Discourse Analysis: Gender, Power and Ideology in Discourse*, edited by Michelle M. Lazar, 1–28. New York: Palgrave Macmillan. https://doi.org/10.1057/9780230599901_1.

– 2007. "Feminist Critical Discourse Analysis: Articulating a Feminist Discourse Praxis." *Critical Discourse Studies* 4 (2): 141–64. https://doi.org/10.1080/17405900701464816.

– 2009. "Gender, War and Body Politics: A Critical Multimodal Analysis of Metaphor in Advertising." In *Politics, Gender and Conceptual Metaphors*, edited by Kathleen Ahrens, 209–34. Basingstoke, UK: Palgrave Macmillan. https://doi.org/10.1057/9780230245235_10.

Leder, Drew. 1990. *The Absent Body*. Chicago: University of Chicago Press.

Lester, Amelia. 2012. "Ladylike: Julia Gillard's Misogyny Speech." *New Yorker*, October 9. Accessed September 10, 2012. http://www.newyorker.com

Lim, Elvin T. 2009. "Gendered Metaphors of Women in Power: The Case of Hillary Clinton as Madonna, Unruly Woman, Bitch and Witch." In *Politics, Gender and Conceptual Metaphors*, edited by Kathleen Ahrens, 254–69. Basingstoke, UK: Palgrave Macmillan. https://doi.org/10.1057/9780230245235_12.

Lipari, Lisbeth. 1994. "As the World Turns: Drama, Rhetoric, and Press Coverage of the Hill-Thomas Hearings." *Political Communication* 11 (3): 299–308. https://doi.org/10.1080/10584609.1994.9963034.

Litosseliti, Lia. 2006. "Constructing Gender in Public Arguments: The Female Voice as Emotional Voice." In *Speaking Out: The Female Voice in Public Contexts*, edited by Judith Baxter, 40–58. Hampshire, NY: Palgrave. https://doi.org/10.1057/9780230522435_3.

Lloyd, Justine, and Lesley Johnson. 2003. "The Three Faces of Eve: The Post-War Housewife, Melodrama, and Home." *Feminist Media Studies* 3 (1): 7–25. https://doi.org/10.1080/1468077032000080103.

Loke, Jaime, Dustin Harp, and Ingrid Bachmann. 2011. "Mothering and Governing: How News Articulated Gender Roles in the Cases of Governors Jane Swift and Sarah Palin." *Journalism Studies* 12 (2): 205–20. https://doi.org/10.1080/1461670X.2010.488418.

Luke, Carmen. 1994. "Women in the Academy: The Politics of Speech and Silence." *British Journal of Sociology of Education* 15 (2): 211–30. https://doi.org/10.1080/0142569940150204.

Lünenborg, Margreth, and Tanja Maier. 2015. "'Power Politician' or 'Fighting Bureaucrat': Gender and Power in German Political Coverage." *Media Culture & Society* 37 (2): 180–96. https://doi.org/10.1177/0163443714557979.

Maiolino, Elise. 2015. "Political Pugilists: Recuperative Gender Strategies in Canadian Electoral Politics." *Canadian Review of Sociology* 52 (2): 115–33. https://doi.org/10.1111/cars.12067.

Mandziuk, Roseann M. 2008. "Dressing Down Hillary." *Communication and Critical/Cultural Studies* 5 (3): 312–6. https://doi.org/10.1080/14791420802239685.

Marland, Alex. 2012. "Political Photography, Journalism, and Framing in the Digital Age: The Management of Visual Media by the Prime Minister of Canada." *International Journal of Press/Politics* 17 (2): 214–33. https://doi.org/10.1177/1940161211433838.

– 2014. "Political Communication in Canada." In *Canadian Politics*, 6th ed., edited by James Bickerton and Alain-G. Gagnon, 309–26. Toronto: University of Toronto Press.

McCartney, Hunter P. 1987. "Applying Fiction Conflict Situations to Analysis of News Stories." *Journalism Quarterly* 64 (1): 163–70.

McGregor, Judy. 1996. "Gender Politics and the News: The Search for a Beehive Bimbo-Boadicea." In *Dangerous Democracy? News Media Politics in New Zealand*, edited by Judy McGregor, 181–96. Palmerston North, NZ: Dunmore Press.

McKnight, Zoe. 2017. "Canada's Coolest PM. (It's Not Justin Trudeau)." *Maclean's*, July 20, 2017. Accessed July 25, 2017. http://www.macleans.ca.

McLean, Jessica, and Sophia Maalsen. 2013. "Destroying the Joint and Dying of Shame? A Geography of Revitalised Feminism in Social Media and Beyond." *Geographical Research* 51 (3): 243–56.

McLeay, Elizabeth. 2006a. "Climbing On: Rules, Values and Women's Representation in the New Zealand Parliament." In *Representing Women in Parliament: A Comparative Study*, edited by Marian Sawer, Manon Tremblay, and Linda Trimble, 67–82. London: Routledge.

– 2006b. "Leadership in Cabinet under MMP." In *Political Leadership in New Zealand*, edited by Raymond Miller and Michael Mintrom, 92–112. Auckland: Auckland University Press.

Meeks, Lindsey. 2012. "Is She 'Man Enough?' Women Candidates, Executive Political Offices, and News Coverage." *Journal of Communication* 62 (1): 175–93. https://doi.org/10.1111/j.1460-2466.2011.01621.x.

Melich, Tanya. 1996. *The Republican War against Women*. New York: Bantam.

Messner, Michael A., Margaret Carlisle Duncan, and Kerry Jensen. 1993. "Separating the Men from the Girls: The Gendered Language of Televised Sports." *Gender & Society* 7 (1): 121–37. https://doi.org/10.1177/089124393007001007.

Milburn, Michael A., and Anne B. McGrail. 1992. "The Dramatic Presentation of News and Its Effects on Cognitive Complexity." *Political Psychology* 13 (4): 613–32. https://doi.org/10.2307/3791493.

Miller, Arthur H., Martin P. Wattenberg, and Oksana Malanchuk. 1986. "Schematic Assessments of Presidential Candidates." *American Political Science Review* 80 (2): 521–40. https://doi.org/10.2307/1958272.

Miller, Melissa K., Jeffrey S. Peake, and Brittany Anne Boulton. 2010. "Testing the *Saturday Night Live* Hypothesis: Fairness and Bias in Newspaper Coverage of Hillary Clinton's Presidential Campaign." *Politics & Gender* 6 (2): 169–98. https://doi.org/10.1017/S1743923X10000036.

Miller, Raymond. 2005. *Party Politics in New Zealand*. South Melbourne: Oxford University Press.

Monro, Surya. 2005. *Gender Politics: Citizenship, Activism and Sexual Diversity*. London: Pluto Press.

Morreale, Joanne. 1998. "Xena: Warrior Princess as Feminist Camp." *Journal of Popular Culture* 32 (2): 79–86. https://doi.org/10.1111/j.0022-3840.1998.00079.x.

Morrison, Carey-Ann, Lynda Johnston, and Robyn Longhurst. 2013. "Critical Geographies of Love as Spatial, Relational and Political." *Progress in Human Geography* 37 (4): 505–21. https://doi.org/10.1177/0309132512462513.

Motion, Judy. 1999. "Politics as Destiny, Duty, and Devotion." *Political Communication* 16 (1): 61–76. https://doi.org/10.1080/105846099198776.

Mottier, Véronique. 2008. "Metaphors, Mini-narratives and Foucauldian Discourse Theory." In *Political Language and Metaphor*, edited by Terrell Carver and Jernej Pikalo, 182–94. London: Routledge.

Muir, Kathie. 2005a. "Media Darlings and Falling Stars: Celebrity and the Reporting of Political Leaders." *Westminster Papers in Communication and Culture* 2 (2): 54–71.

– 2005b. "Political Cares: Gendered Reporting of Work and Family Issues in Relation to Australian Politicians." *Australian Feminist Studies* 20 (46): 77–90. https://doi.org/10.1080/0816464042000334555.

Mukda-anan, Rattima, Kyoko Kusakabe, and Rosechongporn Komolsevin. 2006. "The Thai Vernacular Press and the Woman Politician: Stereotypical Reporting and Innovative Response." *Asian Journal of Communication* 16 (2): 152–68. https://doi.org/10.1080/01292980600638637.

Murray, Rainbow. 2010a. "Conclusion: A New Comparative Framework." In *Cracking the Highest Glass Ceiling*, edited by Rainbow Murray, 223–47. Santa Barbara, CA: Praeger.

– 2010b. "Introduction: Gender Stereotypes and Media Coverage of Women Candidates." In *Cracking the Highest Glass Ceiling*, edited by Rainbow Murray, 3–27. Santa Barbara, CA: Praeger. https://doi.org/10.1057/9780230275294_1.

Neuendorf, Kimberly A. 2002. *The Content Analysis Guidebook*. Thousand Oaks, CA: Sage.

Neuman, W. Lawrence. 2000. *Social Research Methods: Qualitative and Quantitative Approaches*. 4th ed. Toronto: Allyn and Bacon.

– 2007. *Basics of Social Research: Qualitative and Quantitative Approaches*. Boston: Pearson Education.

Nicholson, Linda. 1994. "Interpreting Gender." *Signs: Journal of Women in Culture and Society* 20 (1): 79–105. https://doi.org/10.1086/494955.

Nielsen, Rasmus Kleis, and Kim Chritina Schroder. 2014. "The Relative Importance of Social Media for Accessing, Finding, and Engaging with News." *Digital Journalism* 2 (4): 472–89. https://doi.org/10.1080/21670811.2013.872420.

Nimmo, Dan, and James E. Combs. 1982. "Fantasies and Melodramas in Television Network News: The Case of Three Mile Island." *Western Journal of Speech Communication* 46 (1): 45–55. https://doi.org/10.1080/10570318209374064.

Norris, Pippa. 1997a. "Introduction: Women, Media and Politics." In *Women, Media and Politics*, edited by Pippa Norris, 1–40. New York: Oxford University Press.

– 1997b. "Women Leaders Worldwide: A Splash of Color in the Photo Op." In *Women, Media and Politics*, edited by Pippa Norris, 149–65. New York: Oxford University Press.

Nunn, Heather. 2002. *Thatcher, Politics and Fantasy: The Political Culture of Gender and Nation*. London: Lawrence & Wishart.

O'Brien, Diana Z. 2015. "Rising to the Top: Gender, Political Performance, and Party Leadership in Parliamentary Democracies." *American Journal of Political Science* 59 (4): 1022–39. https://doi.org/10.1111/ajps.12173.

O'Malley, Lisa, and Caroline Tynan. 1999. "The Utility of the Relationship Metaphor in Consumer Markets: A Critical Evaluation." *Journal of Marketing Management* 15 (7): 587–602. https://doi.org/10.1362/026725799785037067.

Pan, Zhongdang, and Gerald M. Kosicki. 1993. "Framing Analysis: An Approach to News Discourse." *Political Communication* 10 (1): 55–75. https://doi.org/10.1080/10584609.1993.9962963.

Parpart, Jane. 1998. "Conclusion: New Thoughts and New Directions for the 'Man' Question in International Relations." In *The "Man" Question in International Relations*, edited by Marysia Zalewski and Jane Parpart, 199–208. Boulder, CO: Westview Press.

Parry-Giles, Shawn J. 2014. *Hillary Clinton in the News: Gender and Authenticity in American Politics*. Urbana: University of Illinois Press.

Parry-Giles, Shawn J., and Trevor Parry-Giles. 1996. "Gendered Politics and Presidential Image Construction: A Reassessment of the 'Feminine Style.'" *Communication Monographs* 63 (4): 337–53. https://doi.org/10.1080/03637759609376398.

Patterson, Thomas E. 1994. *Out of Order*. New York: Vintage.

Perks, Lisa Glebatis, and Kevin A. Johnson. 2014. "Electile Dysfunction: The Burlesque Binds of the Sarah Palin MILF Frame." *Feminist Media Studies* 14 (5): 775–90. https://doi.org/10.1080/14680777.2013.829860.

Perreault, William D., Jr., and Laurence E. Leigh. 1989. "Reliability of Nominal Data Based on Qualitative Judgments." *JMR, Journal of Marketing Research* 26 (2): 135–48. https://doi.org/10.2307/3172601.

Pond Eyley, Claudia, and Dan Salmon. 2015. *Helen Clark: Inside Stories*. Auckland: Auckland University Press.

Purvis, June. 2013. "What Was Margaret Thatcher's Legacy for Women?" *Women's History Review* 22 (6): 1014–8. https://doi.org/10.1080/09612025.2013.801136.

Pusnik, Marusa, and Gregor Bulc. 2001. "Women in Their Own Reflection: Self-Representation of Women Politicians in the Slovenian Press."

Journal of Communication Inquiry 25 (4): 396–413. https://doi.org/10.1177/0196859901025004005.

Rakow, Lana F., and Kimberlie Kranich. 1991. "Women as Sign in Television News." *Journal of Communication* 41 (1): 8–23. https://doi.org/10.1111/j.1460-2466.1991.tb02289.x.

Rogers-Healey, Diann. 2013. *Considerations for Australia's Next Woman Prime Minister.* Minnamurra, NSW: Australian Centre for Leadership for Women.

Ross, Karen. 1995. "Gender and Party Politics: How the Press Reported the Labour Leadership Campaign, 1994." *Media Culture & Society* 17 (3): 499–509. https://doi.org/10.1177/016344395017003009.

– 2002. *Women, Politics, Media.* Cresskill, NJ: Hampton Press.

– 2010. *Gendered Media: Women, Men, and Identity Politics.* Plymouth, UK: Rowman & Littlefield.

Ross, Karen, and Margie Comrie. 2012. "The Rules of the (Leadership) Game: Gender, Politics and News." *Journalism* 13 (8): 969–84. https://doi.org/10.1177/1464884911433255.

Ross, Karen, and Annabelle Sreberny-Mohammadi. 1997. "Playing House – Gender, Politics and the News Media in Britain." *Media Culture & Society* 19 (1): 101–9. https://doi.org/10.1177/016344397019001007.

Roth, Elaine. 2004. "'I Just Want to Be a Decent Citizen': Melodrama as Political Appeal in *Erin Brockovich.*" *Feminist Media Studies* 4 (1): 51–66. https://doi.org/10.1080/14680770410001674644.

Rudd, Chris, and Janine Hayward. 2006. "Campaigning." In *New Zealand Government and Politics,* 4th ed., edited by Raymond Miller, 327–37. Melbourne: Oxford University Press.

Sampert, Shannon, and Linda Trimble. 2010. *Mediating Canadian Politics.* Toronto: Pearson Canada.

Sanghvi, Minita, and Nancy Hodges. 2015. "Marketing the Female Politician: An Exploration of Gender and Appearance." *Journal of Marketing Management* 31 (15–16): 1676–94. https://doi.org/10.1080/0267257X.2015.1074093.

Sawer, Marian. 2012. "Managing Gender: The 2010 Federal Election." In *Julia 2010: The Caretaker Election,* edited by Marian Simms and John Wanna, 251–66. Canberra: ANU E Press.

– 2013. "Misogyny and Misrepresentation: Women in Australian Parliaments." *Political Science (Wellington, N.Z.)* 65 (1): 105–17. https://doi.org/10.1177/0032318713488316.

Sawer, Marian, Manon Tremblay, and Linda Trimble. 2006. *Representing Women in Parliament: A Comparative Study.* Abingdon, NY: Routledge.

Scheufele, Dietram A., and David Tewksbury. 2007. "Framing, Agenda Setting and Priming: The Evolution of Three Media Effects Models." *Journal of Communication* 57 (1): 9–20.

Schudson, Michael. 2005. "The Virtues of an Unlovable Press." Supplement, *Political Quarterly* 76 (S1): 23–32. https://doi.org/10.1111/j.1467-923X.2006.00745.x.

Semetko, Holli A., and Hajo G. Boomgaarden. 2007. "Reporting Germany's 2005 Bundestag Election Campaign: Was Gender an Issue?" *Harvard International Journal of Press/Politics* 12 (4): 154–71. https://doi.org/10.1177/1081180X07307383.

Shaw, Sylvia. 2006. "Governed by the Rules? The Female Voice in Parliamentary Debates." In *Speaking Out: The Female Voice in Public Contexts*, edited by Judith Baxter, 81–102. Hampshire, NY: Palgrave. https://doi.org/10.1057/9780230522435_5.

– 2011. "'I Am Not an Honourable Lady': Gender and Language in the National Assembly for Wales." *Journal of Applied Linguistics and Professional Practice* 8 (3): 275–94.

Sheeler, Kristina Horn, and Karrin Vasby Anderson. 2014. "Gender, Rhetoric, and International Political Systems: Angela Merkel's Rhetorical Negotiation of Proportional Representation and Party Politics." *Communication Quarterly* 62 (4): 474–95. https://doi.org/10.1080/01463373.2014.922484.

Siltanen, Janet, and Michelle Stanworth. 1984. "The Politics of Private Woman and Public Man." *Theory and Society* 13 (1): 91–118. https://doi.org/10.1007/BF00159258.

Singer, Ben. 2001. *Melodrama and Modernity*. New York: Columbia University Press.

Skard, Torild. 2014. *Women of Power: Half a Century of Female Presidents and Prime Ministers Worldwide*. Bristol: Policy Press.

Smith, Donna. 2013. *Sex, Lies & Politics: Gay Politicians in the Press*. Eastbourne, UK: Sussex Academic Press.

Sreberny, Annabelle, and Liesbet van Zoonen. 2000. *Gender, Politics and Communication*. Cresskill, NJ: Hampton Press.

Sreberny-Mohammadi, Annabelle, and Karen Ross. 1996. "Women MPs and the Media: Representing the Body Politic." *Parliamentary Affairs* 49 (1): 103–15. https://doi.org/10.1093/oxfordjournals.pa.a028661.

Stanyer, James. 2013. *Intimate Politics*. Cambridge: Polity Press.

Stanyer, James, and Dominic Wring. 2004. "Public Images, Private Lives: An Introduction." *Parliamentary Affairs* 57 (1): 1–8. https://doi.org/10.1093/pa/gsh001.

Stevenson, Ana. 2013. "Making Gender Divisive: 'Post-Feminism,' Sexism and Media Representations of Julia Gillard." *Bergmann Journal* 2: 53–63.

Street, John. 2004. "Celebrity Politicians: Popular Culture and Political Representation." *British Journal of Politics and International Relations* 6 (4): 435–52. https://doi.org/10.1111/j.1467-856X.2004.00149.x.

Strömbäck, Jesper. 2008. "Four Phases of Mediatization: An Analysis of the Mediatization of Politics." *International Journal of Press/Politics* 13 (3): 228–46. https://doi.org/10.1177/1940161208319097.

Summers, Anne. 2012. "Her Rights at Work: The Political Persecution of Australia's First Female Prime Minister." Human Rights and Social Justice Lecture, University of Newcastle, August 31. Available at http:// annesummers.com.au. https://doi.org/10.1177/103530461202300409.

– 2013. "Her Rights at Work: The Political Persecution of Australia's First Female Prime Minister." *Economic and Labour Relations Review* 23 (4): 116–26.

Taras, David. 1990. *The Newsmakers: The Media's Influence on Canadian Politics.* Scarborough, ON: Nelson.

– 1999. *Power and Betrayal in the Canadian Media.* Peterborough, ON: Broadview Press.

– 2015. *Digital Mosaic: Media, Power, and Identity in Canada.* Toronto: University of Toronto Press.

Tolley, Erin. 2016. *Framed: Media and the Coverage of Race in Canadian Politics.* Vancouver: UBC Press.

Trimble, Linda. 2007. "Gender, Political Leadership and Media Visibility: *Globe and Mail* Coverage of Conservative Party of Canada Leadership Contests." *Canadian Journal of Political Science* 40 (4): 969–93. https://doi.org/10.1017/ S0008423907071120.

– 2014. "Melodrama and Gendered Mediation: Television Coverage of Women's Leadership 'Coups' in New Zealand and Australia." *Feminist Media Studies* 14 (4): 663–78. https://doi.org/10.1080/14680777.2013.826268.

– 2016. "Julia Gillard and the Gender Wars." *Politics & Gender* 12 (2): 296–316. https://doi.org/10.1017/S1743923X16000155.

Trimble, Linda, and Jane Arscott. 2003. *Still Counting: Women in Politics across Canada.* Peterborough, ON: Broadview Press.

Trimble, Linda, and Joanna Everitt. 2010. "Belinda Stronach and the Gender Politics of Celebrity." In *Mediating Canadian Politics*, edited by Shannon Sampert and Linda Trimble, 50–74. Toronto: Pearson Canada.

Trimble, Linda, Daisy Raphael, Shannon Sampert, Angelia Wagner, and Bailey Gerrits. 2015. "Politicizing Bodies: Hegemonic Masculinity, Heteronormativity, and Racism in News Representations of Canadian Political Party Leadership Candidates." *Women's Studies in Communication* 38 (3): 314–30. https://doi.org/10.1080/07491409.2015.1062836.

Trimble, Linda, and Shannon Sampert. 2004. "Who's in the Game? The Framing of Election 2000 by the *Globe and Mail* and the *National Post.*" *Canadian Journal of Political Science* 37 (1): 51–71. https://doi.org/10.1017/ S0008423904040028.

Trimble, Linda, and Natasja Treiberg. 2010. "'Either Way, There's Going to Be a Man in Charge': Media Representations of New Zealand Prime Minister Helen Clark." In *Cracking the Highest Glass Ceiling: A Global Comparison of Women's Campaigns for Executive Office*, edited by Rainbow Murray, 115–36. Santa Barbara, CA: Praeger.

– 2015. "Textual Analysis." In *Explorations: Conducting Empirical Research in Canadian Political Science*, 3rd ed., edited by Loleen Berdahl and Keith Archer, 227–44. Don Mills, ON: Oxford University Press.

Trimble, Linda, Natasja Treiberg, and Sue Girard. 2010. "'Kim-Speak': l'effet du genre dans la médiatisation de Kim Campbell durant la campagne pour l'élection nationale canadienne de 1993" ["'Kim-Speak': Gendered Mediation of Kim Campbell during the 1993 Canadian National Election"]. *Recherches féministes* 23 (1): 29–52. https://doi.org/10.7202/044421ar.

Trimble, Linda, Angelia Wagner, Shannon Sampert, Daisy Raphael, and Bailey Gerrits. 2013. "Is It Personal? Gendered Mediation in Newspaper Coverage of Canadian National Party Leadership Contests, 1975–2012." *International Journal of Press/Politics* 18 (4): 462–81. https://doi.org/10.1177/1940161213495455.

Van Acker, Elizabeth. 1999. *Different Voices: Gender and Politics in Australia.* S. Yarra: Macmillan Education.

– 2003. "Media Representations of Women Politicians in Australia and New Zealand: High Expectations, Hostility or Stardom." *Policy and Society* 22 (1): 116–36. https://doi.org/10.1016/S1449-4035(03)70016-2.

Van Aelst, Peter, Tamir Sheafer, and James Stanyer. 2012. "The Personalization of Mediated Political Communication: A Review of Concepts, Operationalizations and Key Findings." *Journalism* 13 (2): 203–20. https://doi.org/10.1177/1464884911427802.

van Dijk, Teun. 1991. *Racism and the Press.* London: Routledge.

– 1993. "Principles of Critical Discourse Analysis." *Discourse & Society* 4 (2): 249–83. https://doi.org/10.1177/0957926593004002006.

– 2008. *Discourse and Power.* Hampshire, NY: Palgrave Macmillan.

van Zoonen, Liesbet. 1991. "A Tyranny of Intimacy? Women, Femininity and Television News." In *Communication and Citizenship: Journalism and the Public Sphere in the New Media Age*, edited by P. Dahlgren and C. Sparks, 217–35. London: Routledge.

– 2005. *Entertaining the Citizen: When Politics and Popular Culture Converge.* Oxford: Rowman & Littlefield.

– 2006. "The Personal, the Political and the Popular: A Woman's Guide to Celebrity Politics." *European Journal of Cultural Studies* 9 (3): 287–301. https://doi.org/10.1177/1367549406066074.

van Zoonen, Liesbet, Floris Muller, Donya Alinead, Martijn Dekker, Linda Duits, Pauline van Romondt Vis, and Wendy Wittenberg. 2007. "Dr. Phil Meets the Candidates: How Family Life and Personal Experience Produce Political Discussions." *Critical Studies in Media Communication* 24 (4): 322–38. https://doi.org/10.1080/07393180701560849.

Vos, Debby. 2013. "The Vertical Glass Ceiling: Explaining Female Politicians' Underrepresentation in Television News." *Communications* 38 (4): 389–410. https://doi.org/10.1515/commun-2013-0023.

Walsh, Clare. 2015. "Media Capital or Media Deficit?" *Feminist Media Studies* 15 (6): 1025–34. https://doi.org/10.1080/14680777.2015.1087415.

Walsh, Kerry-Anne. 2013. *The Stalking of Julia Gillard*. Crows Nest, NSW: Allen & Unwin.

Warren, Jean-Philippe, and Eric Ronis. 2011. "The Politics of Love: The 1995 Montreal Unity Rally and Canadian Affection." *Journal of Canadian Studies* 45 (1): 5–32. https://doi.org/10.3138/jcs.45.1.5.

Wasburn, Philo C., and Mara H. Wasburn. 2011. "Media Coverage of Women in Politics: The Curious Case of Sarah Palin." *Media Culture & Society* 33 (7): 1027–41. https://doi.org/10.1177/0163443711415744.

Weldon, Michelle. 2008. *Everyman News: The Changing American Front Page*. Columbia: University of Missouri Press.

White, Hayden V. 1987. *The Content of the Form: Narrative Discourse and Historical Representations*. Baltimore, MD: Johns Hopkins University Press.

Wiliarty, Sarah Elise. 2010. "How the Iron Curtain Helped Break through the Glass Ceiling: Angela Merkel's Campaigns in 2005 and 2009." In *Cracking the Highest Glass Ceiling: A Global Comparison of Women's Campaigns for Executive Office*, edited by Rainbow Murray, 137–57. Santa Barbara, CA: Praeger.

Wilz, Kelly. 2016. "Bernie Bros and Women Cards: Rhetorics of Sexism, Misogyny, and Constructed Masculinity in the 2016 Election." *Women's Studies in Communication* 39 (4): 357–60. https://doi.org/10.1080/07491409.2016.1227178.

Wright, Katharine A.M., and Jack Holland. 2014. "Leadership and the Media: Gendered Framings of Julia Gillard's 'Sexism and Misogyny' Speech." *Australian Journal of Political Science* 49 (3): 455–68. https://doi.org/10.1080/10361146.2014.929089.

Young, Sally. 2011. *How Australia Decides: Election Reporting & the Media*. Melbourne: Cambridge University Press.

Index